Unless Recalled Earlier
Date Due

BRODART, INC.   Cat. No. 23 233   Printed in U.S.A.

THE YOUNG EARTH

TITLES OF RELATED INTEREST

The dark side of the Earth
R. Muir Wood

The inaccessible Earth
G. Brown & A. Mussett

The interpretation of igneous rocks
K. Cox, D. Bell & R. Pankhurst

Introduction to X-ray spectrometry
K. Williams

Komatiites
N. Arndt & E. Nisbet (eds)

Perspectives on a dynamic Earth
R. Paton

Planetary landscapes
R. Greeley

Rheology of the Earth
G. Ranalli

Simulating the Earth
J. Holloway & B. Wood

Volcanic successions
R. Cas & J. Wright

THE YOUNG EARTH

An introduction to Archaean geology

E. G. NISBET

Department of Geological Sciences,
University of Saskatchewan,
Canada

Boston
ALLEN & UNWIN
London   Sydney   Wellington

Allen & Unwin, Inc.,
8 Winchester Place, Winchester, Mass. 01890, USA

the U.S. company of

Unwin Hyman Ltd

PO Box 18, Park Lane, Hemel Hempstead, Herts HP2 4TE, UK
40 Museum Street, London WC1A 1LU, UK
37/39 Queen Elizabeth Street, London SE1 2QB, UK

Allen & Unwin (Australia) Ltd,
8 Napier Street, North Sydney, NSW 2060, Australia

Allen & Unwin (New Zealand) Ltd in association with the Port Nicholson Press Ltd,
60 Cambridge Terrace, Wellington, New Zealand

First published in 1987

Library of Congress Cataloging in Publication Data

(applied for)

British Library Cataloguing in Publication Data

Nisbet, E. G.
  The young earth : an introduction to
  archaean geology.
  1. Geology, Stratigraphic—Archaean
  2. Geology, Stratigraphic—Pre-
  Cambrian
  1. Title
  551.7′12   QE653
  ISBN 0-04-550045-2

Typeset in 10 on 12 point Times by
Mathematical Composition Setters Ltd, Salisbury, Wiltshire
and printed in Great Britain by
St Edmundsbury Press, Bury St Edmunds, Suffolk

To C.M.R.N.

ἘΝ ἀρχῇ ἦν ὁ λόγος, καὶ ὁ λόγος ἦν πρὸς τὸν Θεὸν, καὶ Θεὸς ἦν ὁ λόγος. ² οὗτος ἦν ἐν ἀρχῇ πρὸς τὸν Θεόν. ³ Πάντα δι' αὐτοῦ ἐγένετο, καὶ χωρὶς αὐτοῦ ἐγένετο οὐδὲ ἕν, ὃ γέγονεν. ⁴ ἐν αὐτῷ ζωὴ ἦν, καὶ ἡ ζωὴ ἦν τὸ φῶς τῶν ἀνθρώπων, ⁵ καὶ τὸ φῶς ἐν τῇ σκοτίᾳ φαίνει, καὶ ἡ σκοτία αὐτὸ οὐ κατέλαβεν.

John 1, 1–5

Preface

'What are we going to do with a parcel of old stones?' wrote the director of an African museum a century and a half ago, when one of my ancestors presented him with a splendid collection of fossils of mammal-like reptiles. Old stones, however intriguing, are difficult to interpret, dusty, and do not fit well in the neatly ordered contents of a house of learning. Archaean geology, which is the study of the Earth's history in the period from after the end of planetary accretion ($4.5-4.4 \times 10^9$ years ago) up to the beginning of the Proterozoic (2.5×10^9 years ago) is much the same – a parcel of old stones seemingly impossible to understand. Yet these stones contain the history of our origins: they can tell us a story that is interesting not just to the geologist (for whom this book is primarily written) but instead addresses the human condition in general.

Archaean rocks are very diverse, and each type of rock demands highly specialised and sophisticated science. The Archaean does not give up its secrets easily, for the most part, except on rare occasions in the field. In this book I have attempted to outline the diversity of the subject and to describe each specialised topic, while yet remaining within the scope of the general reader who is conversant with the basic principles of geology. Perhaps the subject is too vast for any single author – for which I apologise – but I believe that in order to understand the Archaean those who work in one specialised subdiscipline must be aware of the results of the others. What the experimental petrologist finds out about the mantle is relevant to the work of the atmospheric physicist, and the work of both affects the research of the palaeontologist. In studying Archaean rocks, more than in any other geological research, it is necessary to have a world view. It is this global concept of the history of the young Earth that I have attempted to outline. The Archaean includes more than a third of the Earth's history, and within the Archaean geological record is the record of the beginning of our own existence. Archaean geology is a vast, complex and very rewarding topic full of unsolved and unrecognized problems.

This book should perhaps be subtitled 'a personal view'. It is not a compendium of fact. Instead, it is something that has grown out of an advanced undergraduate course in which I attempted to convey something of the excitement and the challenge inherent in the subject. It is a 'personal' view, because it reflects so strongly my own interests and my own research. The book is intended for use in advanced undergraduate and postgraduate courses in geology, but it is my hope that it will also be useful to physicists, biologists, chemists and the like who are interested in the early history of the Earth. Obscure terminology abounds in geology, as in any science; nevertheless I have attempted to make the book at least partially accessible to non-geologists. They may not be able to follow some of the gobble-degook, but I hope they will at least follow the general argument. A glossary of geological terms has been inserted at the end of the book to help them.

Controversy surrounds most Archaean theories: I have not attempted in the text to sidestep controversy, and I have often taken sides. Perhaps this is dangerous, but the book is intended for an audience capable of critical judgement; the reader is encouraged to disbelieve! At the heart of the controversy is the quest for our own origin: it is a subject well worth arguing about, for by argument comes advancement. Perhaps we shall never know quite how the Earth became a suitable home for life, but the problem is like no other problem in geology. It is central to the human condition, and it is worth pursuing.

Acknowledgements

Many people have helped me in this work, ranging from the group of fellow workers in Zimbabwe (M.J. Bickle, A. Martin, J.L. Orpen, J.F. Wilson) to my colleagues in Saskatoon. I should like to thank Roger Jones of George Allen & Unwin, for suggesting and comissioning the book, S. Moorbath, N.T. Arndt, D. Bridgwater, D. Caldwell, W.E. Cameron, R.P. Foster, P.H. Fowler, Sir Charles Frank, S. Goldstein, J.E. Lovelock, E. Hegner, R. Kerrich, T.K. Kyser, L. Margulis, A. Martin, P.A. Nisbet, D. Sagan, W.A.S. Sarjeant, Janet Watson and M.E. Wilks for their very helpful remarks, F.H.C. Crick for his tolerance, P. McNair for his comments on Dante and W.G.E. Caldwell for providing the necessary habitat for research in an active and friendly department. In particular, M.J. Bickle is thanked for his strong and penetrative comments, and for his detailed advice both in the construction of the manuscript and in checking to avoid silly errors. Sharon Ford, Roxanne Hebig, Maryce Reeves and especially Angie Heppner in Saskatoon, Geoff Palmer in Hemel Hempstead, and Connie Wilsack, helped enormously in their patient handling of manuscripts, diagrams and eternal corrections. The University of Saskatchewan and the Natural Sciences and Engineering Research Council of Canada made it possible.

Finally, I wish to acknowledge my debt to those geologists who have worked for the Zimbabwe Geological Survey and its predecessors over the past 90 years. Their work, much of which was of the highest quality, and the work of their associates in Canada, Australia and India, showed that we will, eventually, comprehend the fabric of the Archaean Earth.

The following individuals and organisations have kindly given permission for the reproduction of text illustrations:

Figure 2.1 reproduced from M. Dodson, *Contrib. Mineral. Petrol.* **40**, by permission of Springer-Verlag; Figure 2.2 reprinted by permission from *Nature* **307**, 353, copyright © 1984 Macmillan Journals Limited; Figure 2.3 reproduced from P.J. Hamilton, 'Great Dyke and Bushveld mafic phase', *J. Petrol.* **18**, 1977 by permission of Oxford University Press; Elsevier Science Publishers (2.4, 3.8, 3.11, 3.1c, 3.19, 3.23, 3.33, 3.38, 3.39, 4.11b–h, 4.12, 4.14, 4.15, 4.19, 4.21, 4.22, 5.3, 5.8, 5.9, 5.11, 5.12, 5.14–16, 5.22, 6.14, 6.24, 7.16, 8.1 & 8.12); Figures 2.6 & 6.25 reproduced from B. Dupré, *Geochim. Cosmochim. Acta* **48**, by permission of Pergamon Press; Figures 2.7–2.12 reproduced with permission from D.J. Paolo, *EOS* **62**, no. 14, 1981, copyright © American Geophysical Union.

A. Bisschoff (3.1); Figures 3.2 & 3.3 reproduced with permission from Nicolaysen *et al.*,

ACKNOWLEDGEMENTS

J. Geophys. Res. **86**, 10653–61, 1981, copyright © American Geophysical Union; John A. Percival and the Lunar and Planetary Institute (3.4, 3.5 & 3.6); E. Schweizerbart'sche Verlagsbuchhandlung (3.7, 3.12, 3.21, 3.27 & 3.28); National Research Council of Canada (3.10); Geological Society of Australia (3.22, 3.29, 3.32 & 5.17); John B. Henderson (3.24); M. & R. Viljoen (3.17); Figures 3.25 & 3.26 reproduced from D. Bridgewater *et al.* 1978, in *Evolution of the Earth's crust*, D.H. Tarling (ed.), by permission of Academic Press Inc.; W.M. Schwerdtner (3.27); The Geological Society of America (3.30 & 8.7); Figure 3.31 reproduced from S.M. McLennan and S.R. Taylor in *Geochemical constraints on the growth of the continental crust*, by permission of The University of Chicago Press;. Figure 3.32 reproduced by permission of *J. Geol.* (from vol. 90, 1982), and the Bureau of Mineral Resources, Geology & Geophysics, Australia.

Figures 4.4 & 4.5 reproduced by permission from *Nature*, copyright © 1986 Macmillan Journals Limited; Figures 4.11a & 6.3 reproduced from M.J. Bickle, *Contrib. Mineral. Petrol.* **84**, 1983, by permission of Springer-Verlag; Figure 4.16 reproduced from E. Nisbet, *J. Mol. Evol.* **21**, 1985, by permission of Springer-Verlag; Figures 4.21 & 4.22 reproduced from 'Evolutionary connections of biological kingdoms based on nucleic acid sequence evidence', *Precamb. Res.* **20**, 299–318, 1983 by permission of the National Biomedical Research Foundation; Figure 4.23 copyright © D. Riedel Publishing Company, Dordrecht, Holland, 1983.

Figures 5.4, 5.5, 5.6, 5.7 & 7.4 reproduced from *Gold 82*, Special Publication of the Geological Society of Zimbabwe, R.P. Foster (ed.), by permission of A.A. Balkema, Postbus 1675, NL-3000 BR Rotterdam, Holland; Figure 5.13 reproduced from N. B. Harris *et al.*, 'Geobarometry, geothermometry, and late Archean geotherms from the granulite facies terrain of South India', *J. Geol.* **90**, 1982, by permission of the University of Chicago Press; Figure 5.20 reproduced from P. England and M. Bickle, 'Continental thermal and tectonic regimes during the Archean', *J. Geol.* **92**, 1984, by permission of the University of Chicago Press; Figure 5.24 reproduced from S.A. Drury *et al.*, 'Precambrian tectonics and crustal evolution in South India', *J. Geol.* **92**, 1984, by permission of the University of Chicago Press.

Figure 6.1 reproduced from *Geol Surv. Bull.* No. 67 by permission of the Director, Zimbabwe Geological Survey; Figure 6.3 reproduced from M. Bickle, *Contrib. Mineral. Petrol.* **84**, 198x, by permission of The Editor, *Econ. Geol.*; Figure 6.5 reproduced from E. G. Nisbet *et al.*, 'The mafic and ultramafic rocks of the Belingwe Greenstone Belt, Rhodesia', *J. Petrol.* **18**, 1977 by permission of Oxford University Press; Yale University, *Econ. Geol.* (6.17, 7.17, 7.18, 7.19, 7.20, 7.21, 7.25, 7.26 & 7.27); Figure 6.21 reprinted by permission from *Nature* **315**, copyright © 1985 Macmillan Journals Limited; Figures 6.22 reproduced by permission from *Nature* **279**, 689–92, copyright © 1979 Macmillan Journals Limited; Figure 6.27 reproduced from *The continental crust* by permission of Blackwell Scientific Publications Ltd.

Canadian Institute of Mining and Metallurgy (7.2, 7.3, 7.5 &).11); Figures 7.6 & 7.7 reproduced from Ontario Geological Survey Miscellaneous Paper 118, Ontario Ministry of Natural Resources, by permission of the Queen's Printer for Ontario; Figures 7.8 & 7.9 reproduced from Tenkard *et al.*, in *Crustal evolution of Southern Africa*, 1982, by permission of Springer-Verlag; Figures 7.12, 7.13 & 7.14 reproduced from GAC Special Paper 25, with the permission of the Geological Association of Canada; Mineralogical Association of Canada (7.22 & 7.24); Figure 7.28 reproduced from 'The Great Dyke', *J. Petrol.* **23**, 1982, by permission of Oxford University Press; Figure 7.29 reproduced from *Geol Surv. Bull.* No. 83, by permission of the Director, Zimbabwe Geological Survey.

Figure 8.4 reproduced by permission from *Nature* **315**, 541, copyright © 1985 Macmillan Journals Limited; Figure 8.6 reproduced by permission from *Nature*, News and Views article on 'Experimental petrology, isotopes and the nature of the Archaean Mantle', copyright © Macmillan Journals Limited; Adam Hilger Ltd (8.13); *Tellus* (8.15); Figures 8.16 & 8.17 reproduced from E.G. Nisbet, *J. Mol. Evol.* **21**, 1985, by permission of Springer-Verlag.

Contents

List of tables

PART I

Background concepts and
field evidence

1 Introduction

Ye Powers... And spirits of this nethermost Abyss
Chaos and Ancient Earth, I come no spy
With purpose to explore and to disturb
The secrets of your realm... Here Nature first begins
Her furthest verge, and Chaos to retire

Milton *Paradise Lost, II*

1.1 Purpose and scope

The Archaean, which is the period in the Earth's history after its accretion and prior to 2.5×10^9 years ago, is still almost unknown, the frontier territory of geology, with only fragmentary evidence from the rocks and the guidelines of the basic physical and chemical laws to chart our ignorance. In this is the challenge and the reward of Archaean geology.

The foundations of the Earth were laid in the first part of its history. The purpose of this book is to attempt to demonstrate the importance of Archaean rocks, and to show that the study of the Archaean is perhaps the most interesting and exciting of all branches of geology. Phanerozoic rocks can be interpreted within the uniformitarian framework of modern plate tectonics, but there is as yet no accepted model to explain how the Archaean Earth worked and no understanding of how it came to be inhabited by life.

Two problems dominate Archaean geology: understanding the origin of life, and discovering the tectonic system by which the surface of the Archaean Earth was constructed. These problems are closely interlinked and cannot be studied in isolation. This book is an attempt to outline what is known and what has been speculated about the Archaean Earth, in the hope of stimulating a deeper insight into these two great problems. Aspects of Archaean geology have been described excellently and in detail in a variety of recent volumes (Condie 1981, Hunter 1981, Kröner 1981, Windley 1984, Taylor & McLennan, 1985). This book is not intended to duplicate such detailed and compendious coverage. Instead the intention is to show that the study of the Archaean is a distinctive subdiscipline of geology, with its own characteristic problems, methodology and philosopy. The interpretation of Archaean rocks is very different from the interpretation of Phanerozoic rocks, and the philosophy of the Archaean geologist is correspondingly different from the philosophy of the Phanerozoic worker. Even the assumption of uniformity – the principle that the work-

3

ings of the modern Earth can be used as a guide to the past − so basic to modern geology − is suspect; the fabric of interpretation of Archaean rocks must be built up again from first principles.

The Archaean covers the period from after the catastrophes during the formation of the Earth 4.4 Ga ago (roughly) until approximately 2.5 Ga ago (1 Ga $= 10^9$ years, 1 Ma $= 10^6$ years). This is almost 45% of the total history of the Earth. During the Archaean the surface crust of the Earth formed, the oceans and continents were established, life began. The foundations of the environment were laid, the mantle and core evolved toward their modern states and the intricate interaction between life and its habitat began. The geological record of these events is fragmentary in comparison with the Phanerozoic record but, nevertheless, large areas of exposed Archaean crust (Fig. 1.1) exist, and much information can be deduced from them. Yet with all Archaean investigation there is doubt whether a full explanation will ever be found − would plate tectonics have ever been fully understood had earth scientists been banned from the oceans and furthermore restricted to a small and probably not particularly representative area of land?

The exposed areas of Archaean crust include the ancient nuclei of Southern Africa, parts of the Canadian Shield, Greenland, Australia, India, Brazil and the USSR, as well as other less well-known areas. In many of these areas Archaean rocks have been of great economic and historical importance. The search for gold has perhaps been the most significant factor. Over the millennia Indian and, later, Zimbabwean miners have exploited Archaean greenstone belts. More recently, gold rushes caused waves of settlement in Australia, Canada and in Southern Africa. During this century Archaean rocks have been major sources of Ni, Cr, U, asbestos and many other minerals, as well as retaining their status as a supplier of gold. In this is the economic impetus behind the study of the Archaean.

The scope of this study is geological, limited to what can be deduced from the rock. There are only minor excursions into geophysical and astronomical theory. Within that limitation, Archaean geology as a subdiscipline has a remarkably broad scope. 'Modern' geology is highly specialised into distinct compartments with little intercommunication, such as the study of microfossils, the study of obscure volcanic rocks, the study of porosity. In contrast, the Archaean geologist must be prepared to stumble over a highly magnesian lava on one day and the remains of early life on the next. All of the subdisciplines of 'modern' geology are relevant; the evolution of the mantle and of igneous rocks controlled the evolution of the biosphere, the temperature constraints imposed by the presence of the biosphere controlled the metamorphism of the crust and may have helped to stabilise water. As a result, the investigator can ignore none of these; to overspecialise is to risk becoming generally ignorant.

4

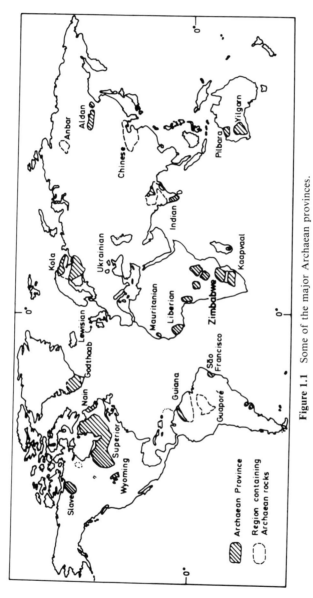

Figure 1.1 Some of the major Archaean provinces.

Aldan
Anbar
Chinese
Pilbara
Yilgarn
Kola
Ukrainian
Indian
Lewisian
Godthaab
Nain
Mauritanian
Liberian
Zimbabwe
Kaapvaal
Superior
Wyoming
Slave
Guiana
São Francisco
Guaporé

Archaean Province
Region containing
Archaean rocks

0°

1.2 Concepts

'In the economy of the world' said Hutton in 1795, 'I can find no traces of a beginning, nor prospect of an end'. On this declaration has been built much of the modern science of geology. In his synthesis which created our discipline, Lyell (1872) has graphically described the sensation when Hutton 'with unhallowed hand erased, from the granitic nucleus of the planet, the sacred characters "Dinanzi a me non fur cose create, se non eterne" (Before me things create were none, save things eternal)'.

It is the business of the Archaean geologist to remain sceptical of the over-rigid application of uniformity, and perhaps to attempt to restore those words to their proper place.

The doctrine of uniformity is most commonly expressed as 'The present is the key to the past'. So it is, but this leads to a very restricted interpretation of Hutton's doctrine, an interpretation of which the Archaean geologist must beware. First, there is the problem of the infrequent event – the meteorite impact, the volcanic explosion or the catastrophic flood. These are actualistic events (they happen 'today'), but they are rare and are poorly understood. In the Archaean their frequency may have been much greater and the geological consequences correspondingly different. Second, even the basic physical environment may have been subtly different in the Archaean, and the chemical, biological and geological consequences of this may have been considerable. To take examples: solar luminosity was almost certainly less – a constraint of major importance in the development of the biosphere; and the heat production of the mantle was certainly much greater – a fact which may be of major tectonic significance.

To a geologist, used to rocks more than to theories, this ground is uncertain. One must advance with caution. Fortunately, the basic 'laws' of geology (Steno's law of superposition, the horizontality of stratification, the concept of lateral continuity) depend only on the existence of gravity. The 'laws' hold, provided due account is taken of deformation. Much of the basic fact-finding of geology depends on simple physical properties or on gravity: sedimentary structures, pillow lavas, deformation patterns in rocks, temperature of equilibration of minerals – all these provide a reliable basis for the investigation of Archaean rocks. Only where biological activity is suspected (e.g. in the formation of specific sedimentary rocks), or where grand theories are relied upon (e.g. plate tectonics), is the uniformitarian approach a dangerous path. Often, Archaean geologists tend to assume that if particular rocks or forms are known to be produced by a particular process today, the same was true in the past: thus, a stromatolite is assumed to be biogenic. This approach is 'common sense', yet it is dangerous. The geologist will grasp the nearest modern analogue and apply it until it is proven unsuitable. Obviously, where the *burden of proof* is very great (such as in the search for early life forms), such common sense may be perilous. What test can be applied to distinguish the reliable from the unreliable? Perhaps the only test available is to examine the basic principles behind the interpretation: if these principles are simple and unquestioned then the interpretation is trustworthy; on the other hand if the principle is complex and dependent on the interpretation of recent analogues, then the interpretation is speculation, not deduction. To illustrate this, consider two examples. In the first case, the assumption that the force of gravity existed is a basic axiom of Archaean geology, although it is possible that the gravitational constant G may have had a very slightly different value. On this simple axiom is based the uniformitarian interpretation of a wide variety of igneous structures in rocks. Few would challenge this interpretation. In contrast, the existence of Archaean andesites has often been thought to be evidence for Archaean subduction. The basic assumption in this case is a complex analogy with modern plate tectonics and the interpretation is thus surely speculation (for which, see Chs. 6 & 8).

1.3 Catastrophes vs. uniformity

The debate between the catastrophists and the uniformitarians in the 18th and 19th centuries laid the foundations of the modern discipline of geology. In that debate the uniformitarians were victorious, yet in the study of the Archaean the debate still continues. *Archaean geology is the study of the Earth's history as revealed by Archaean rocks*: any process external to that system is a catastrophe; any process constrained within the system is uniformitarian, though usually in a modified fashion. The 'system' is that represented by the rocks; in other words it was the crust and higher mantle of the Archaean Earth. To illustrate this, compare the making of a pot of coffee with the process involved in producing a slice of toast (Fig. 1.2). In making coffee (at its simplest and least technological as done by the poorly equipped but desperate field geologist) one adds hot water to grounds, then waits. After the initial catastrophe the mixture evolves within its internal constraints, evolving slowly to coffee (curve b). In the latter part of its history the liquid is drinkable and recognisably coffee, if a little weak and gritty. Earlier, it is not drinkable, yet it evolves smoothly from one state to the other, and is not externally influenced. Eventually, the grounds sink to the bottom of the pot and good coffee results. The behaviour is uniformitarian, although not in the restricted sense usually put on the expression 'the present is the key to the past' (curve a). In contrast, consider curve c, which depicts the processes involved in making a slice of toast in any country west of France. Initially flour, yeast and a variety of peculiar additives are mixed, then baked, then sliced, then wrapped, stored overlong

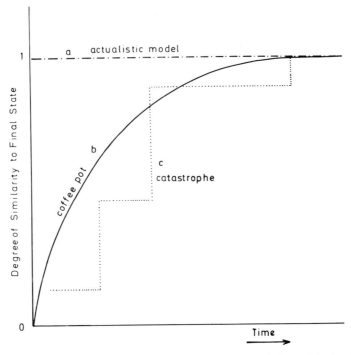

Figure 1.2 Varying models of geological evolution. (a) Actualistic model of uniformity. (b) Evolving, 'coffee-pot' mutability. (c) Catastrophe model (e.g. toast).

on a supermarket shelf, then toasted. The catastrophes are mostly external to the defined system (the bread). The present is not a key to the past; it may not even be a guide.

The distinction between catastrophist and uniformitarian models depends of course on the bounds placed on the system. To the Earth a meteorite impact is a catastrophe; to the solar system it is a normal event whose frequency becomes less as the system ages. Despite the fact that his tools of observation are uniformitarian, the Archaean geologist must not be frightened to invoke a catastrophe if necessary, and his uniformity is of the modified coffee pot variety, not the strict '*aktualismus*' of the Phanerozoic geologist. Nevertheless, a Huttonian bias lingers: Occam's razor surely cuts off any catastrophist argument unless there really is no alternative. The basic framework of Archaean geology *is* uniformitarian, but only if the system is defined very broadly, at least to include the solar system.

1.4 Archaean stratigraphy and mapping

1.4.1 Definition

All geological study depends on some sort of geological mapping or sample collecting, and at the heart of any study is the need to understand the stratigraphy. In Phanerozoic terrains the stratigraphic guidelines are usually well established: in contrast the Archaean stratigrapher is faced with a new and very different set of problems. In some ways the tasks of the Archaean geologist are similar to those faced by Sedgwick and Murchison (1835) in their pioneering studies of the lower Palaeozoic.

First, how does one formally *define* the Archaean or, at least, its end? Various research groups have various traditions, and the definition followed in India or the Soviet Union may not be that followed in Canada or Australia. Rankama (1970), in a survey of the literature, found a range in supposed age of the Proterozoic/Archaean boundary of over 1000 Ma. All depends on the criterion for choosing the boundary. Various authors have placed stress on supposed major biological or tectonic changes that took place around this period, and have suggested that the onset of these changes should be used to define the start of the Proterozoic. For instance, it is possible that the tectonic regime changed around 2500 Ma ago since greenstone belts and komatiites (Ch. 3) are relatively rare after this date, and thick continental sedimentary basins may be more common. It is also possible that life forms became either more abundant or more diverse around 2000 Ma ago (Cloud 1983a); at the same time the chemistry of sea water may have changed. These and other 'events' have been proposed as suitable markers of the end of the Archaean. But to define the end of a stratigraphic aeon in this way is most unsatisfactory. Hypotheses change, new evidence is discovered. Even if the definition were later to be changed to accommodate a change in the hypothesis on which it was based, problems and controversy and residual inconsistency would remain. It is worth remembering that we retain in common stratigraphic usage the words 'Tertiary' and 'Quaternary', but where are the 'Primary' and 'Secondary'?

In the past few years, the definition of the Archaean as 'that period after the accretion of the planet and prior to 2500 Ma' (e.g. Condie 1981, Sims 1980) has gained wide acceptance, especially amongst field geologists. Apart from being a 'nice round number', this definition of the end of the Archaean is very useful in areas such as Canada, Zimbabwe and to some extent in Australia, where it tacitly acknowledges an apparent change in tectonic style at around that time: in other words the apparently arbitrary choice of 2500 Ma satisfies both those who simply need a boundary for nomenclature but do not mind where it is placed, and also those who look to the boundary as a mark of a tectonic or biological event.

9

However, the arbitrary choice of a number is quite as unsatisfactory as the choice of an 'event'. Our knowledge of isotopic decay constants is not particularly accurate, and if an arbitrary age is chosen, wholescale transfer of stratigraphic units from one aeon to another may take place if decay constants are revised. Ideally, under the rules of stratigraphic nomenclature, a stratigraphic boundary should be defined 'in the rock', with reference to a specific chosen rock unit. If this rule is followed, any changes in the generally accepted values of isotopic decay constants do not cause the wholescale reclassification of stratigraphic units. Thus the formal definition of the end of the Archaean adopted here is that: 'The end of the Archaean is defined as the time of cooling of the Hartley Complex of the Great Dyke of Zimbabwe' (Nisbet 1982a).

The best present measurement (Hamilton 1977) is that this took place around 2500 Ma ago (2461 $\pm$ 14 Ma using $\lambda_{Rb} = 1.42 \times 10^{-11} a^{-1}$ or 2514 $\pm$ 14 Ma using $\lambda_{Rb} = 1.39 \times 10^{-11} a^{-1}$). For almost all practical uses this is deliberately synonymous with common usage that the Archaean includes 'anything older than 2500 Ma', but it provides a fixed rock reference point. The reasons for this choice are argued in more detail elsewhere (Nisbet 1982a). A possible alternative choice would be to place the boundary in the Hamersley Group of Western Australia (see Section 7.7.3) in which zircons with an age very close to 2500 Ma have been found (Compston et al. 1981).

1.4.2 Mapping

The basis of geological study is mapping, and mapping in Archaean terrains has its own special problems and peculiarities. First there is the lack of stratigraphically useful fossils. In other words there is no easy way to judge the relative stratigraphic levels of strata not in some way laterally connected. Radiometric dating can be used in a limited way to correlate stratigraphic sequences, but inevitably the difficulty of dating means that such opportunities are few and far between. Many of the problems of Phanerozoic correlation (e.g. whether a particular fossiliferous horizon is a chronological marker or is diachronous) become irrelevant. Within the enormous timescale of the Archaean, whose horizons can only rarely be correlated to better than 5–10 Ma (there are important exceptions to this), the circa 0.5 Ma resolution of Phanerozoic stratigraphic zones can seldom be attained. Typically, Archaean stratigraphers make little distinction between lithological and chronological correlation. Only in a few well studied areas can sufficient precision be attained to identify lithological diachroneity.

Next, the Archaean geologist faces the problem of unfamiliar rock types. Many of the most common Archaean lithologies are subtly different from the Phanerozoic rock types that are their closest equivalents. In Archaean igneous sequences, basalts are abundant; but many of these are komatiitic basalts, which are lavas rich in magnesium. Komatiites, or very magnesian lavas, are widespread in the Archaean, though very rare in younger sequences. Mafic plutonic complexes may often have ultramafic parent liquids. In sedimentary successions both the proportions and nature of the rocks are different. For instance, ironstones usually occur as banded ironstones ('banded iron-formations', in North American terminology). Carbonates are relatively rare, and many common types of biogenic Phanerozoic limestone are absent. To work in an Archaean terrain requires an eye for Archaean rock types and an appreciation of the differences and similarities between Archaean rocks and the more familiar Phanerozoic lithologies.

Finally, in considering Archaean mapping, there is the predilection of Archaean rocks to outcrop in remote inhospitable places, especially in the Anglophone extremes. Although small areas of Archaean rocks outcrop in the USA and United Kingdom and have been intensively studied, the bulk of exposed and investigated Archaean rocks exist in the Canadian Shield, in Western Australia, in Zimbabwe, in South Africa, in India and also (in territory not once occupied by Scots) in the USSR, Brazil and Finland. In many of these areas the primary problem of mapping is logistic – to get into the area and to move around in it. Huge areas have indeed been mapped, but in general on a large scale, in comparison to the detailed knowledge of the Phanerozoic cover of most continents. Much of the mapping was carried out during the waning days of the Empire and is generally of very high quality, but it is reconnaissance work. In this, Archaean geology has been lucky: the standard of mapping in many areas (e.g. work by Bruce (1926) in Ontario, Maitland (1906) in Western Australia, Macgregor (1928) in Southern Rhodesia and by the Indian Survey) has been very high indeed. Most early geologists worked in these areas without either topographic maps or air photography, yet for the most part they rapidly produced work which is still of value today. However much of the work is of a regional nature, and many areas have not been investigated at all. Thus the Archaean geologist has the chance of truly unknown areas to map, of discovering new rock types such as the komatiites, or at the least of identifying new supergroups whereas the Phanerozoic geologist may be content with the redefinition of a member or bed.

2 Geochronology and other uses of isotopic analysis

> ...it is fearful then
> To steer the mind in deadly solitude
> Up the vague stream of probability
> To wind the mighty secrets of the past
> And turn the key of time.
>
> H. Kirke White (1785–1806), *Time*

2.1 Introduction

The discovery that fossil assemblages could be used in setting up a stratigraphic column was the cornerstone of Phanerozoic geology. In Archaean rocks some 'fossils' do exist, but they are of very little stratigraphic use. Isotope geochronology is used instead: inevitably, radiometric dates cannot be used as an exact substitute for a fossil assemblage and the philosophical basis is subtly different. But just as the study of fossils had implications far beyond their narrow stratigraphic use, so geochronology provides information of great significance in understanding the early history of the Earth (Rutherford 1907).

Fossil assemblages provide a very precise (i.e. reproducible) timescale, with a resolution of perhaps 0.3 Ma at best (e.g. in ammonite zones). This enables the Phanerozoic stratigrapher to fix the relative age of strata very precisely, and occasionally even to identify lithological horizons deposited diachronously. Fossil ages are not very *accurate* – often the age of an assemblage is not known to within 10–20 Ma since fossil 'ages' are interpolated between known radiometric ages – but their great *precision* makes them extremely useful to the stratigrapher.

In contrast, Archaean strata must be dated by radiometric geochronological techniques. In most cases this means that strata can be dated to, say, ± 50 Ma, and it is impossible in the absence of mapping information to tell relative stratigraphic levels of horizons. Error analysis is very important, and errors are usually quoted to two σ levels (i.e. 95% confidence that the quoted answer is within the error bounds). If the error is greater than the random instrumental error in analysis, the isotopic ratio samples cannot be used to provide a 'date'. The Archaean geologist is thus often faced with the problem of mapping a terrain where the dating error is greater than the likely age range of the strata. In fossiliferous Phanerozoic strata, there are often many lithological horizons where relative ages can be fixed: in con-

12

trast, to obtain a radiometric date involves a great deal of effort and expense and as a result, radiometric dates are generally rare even in intensively studied Archaean terrains. It is not uncommon for a whole stratigraphic sequence extending through 1000 Ma to be hung on a handful of 'good' dates (e.g. Wilson *et al.* 1978).

Fortunately, radiometric studies can provide not only the age of a rock or rock suite, but much other information. It is worth examining dating techniques to assess their relative value and the information they provide. A detailed and lucid discussion of isotope geology is given by Faure (1977). This method is based on the work of Rutherford and Soddy (1903), who found that the number of atoms of a radioactive isotope that decay in unit time is proportional to the number present:

$$dN/dt = -\lambda N \qquad (2.1)$$

where N is the number of atoms at time t and λ is a constant for that particular decay. From a time $t = 0$ (with N_o atoms present) to time t, integration gives at time t:

$$N = N_o e^{-\lambda_t} \qquad (2.2)$$

2.2   K–Ar and ^{40}Ar/^{39}Ar Methods

Potassium–argon methods of dating were very popular in the earlier days of the application of radiometric dating to the Archaean, but it has since been realised that there are many problems in interpreting the results. More recently, ^{40}Ar/^{39}Ar dating has become a standard technique in dating Archaean terrains. The methods are based on the branching decay of ^{40}K to ^{40}Ca and to ^{40}Ar; although ^{40}Ca is of little radiometric use as it is so common, ^{40}Ar is trapped in many minerals. The method is of very broad applicability since K is so common in crustal minerals, yet there are major complications as the radiogenic product is a gas that escapes at a rate dependent in part on the temperature of the rock.

The equation for the ^{40}Ar in the sample is, from (2.1) and (2.2)

$$^{40}\text{Ar}_m = {}^{40}\text{Ar}_o + \frac{\lambda_e}{(\lambda_e + \lambda_\beta)} \, {}^{40}\text{K} \, [e^{(\lambda_e + \lambda_\beta)t} - 1] \qquad (2.3)$$

where ^{40}Ar$_m$ is the total ^{40}Ar measured in the sample, ^{40}Ar$_o$ the original ^{40}Ar in the sample, λ the total decay constant for ^{40}K, λ_e the constant for decay to ^{40}Ar and λ_β to ^{40}Ca. Commonly used values are $\lambda_e = 0.581 \times 10^{-10}$ yr^{-1} and $\lambda_\beta = 4.962^{-10}$ yr^{-1} (Steiger & Jaeger 1977). The age t of the sample is 'true' only if no radiogenic argon has escaped since the formation of the sample, if no excess ^{40}Ar has been introduced, and no ^{40}K has been added or removed. Normally ^{40}Ar$_o$ is assumed to be zero, which means that an age can be obtained from a single whole-rock or mineral. This is the great attraction of K–Ar dating, since virtually any Archaean rock can be analysed and will produce an answer. Many 'dates' can be produced with comparatively little effort, in contrast to the laborious business of constructing a Rb–Sr or Sm–Nd isochron. Unfortunately, it is often exceedingly difficult to interpret the significance of a 'date' measured in a laboratory: natural rocks and minerals are complex objects with complex histories. Much depends on the time when the minerals in the sample became closed to argon diffusion.

Diffusion of any chemical species in a mineral is thermally activated, and the process can be described in terms of a diffusion constant D, where $D = D_o \exp(-E/RT)$, D_o being a factor that depends on the species and mineral, E an activation energy, R the gas constant and T the absolute temperature. Clearly, D depends very strongly on temperature, and for geological materials can vary by an order of magnitude with a change in temperature of a few tens of degrees. As a result, it is generally valid to introduce the concept of a closure temperature, below which a species (such as argon) no longer is lost from a crystal (Fig. 2.1).

Dodson (1973) derived the following expression for closure (or blocking) temperature:

$$\frac{E}{RT_c} = \ln\left(A \frac{D_o}{a^2} \frac{RT_c{}^2}{E(-\dot{T})_c}\right) \tag{2.4}$$

where T_c is the blocking temperature, a the dimension of the crystal, A a geometrical factor depending on the geometry of the system, and $(-\dot{T})_c$ is the rate of cooling when the system passes through the closure temperature. The date given by conventional K–Ar analysis is that at which the mineral was at the closure temperature T_c.

Closure temperatures depend on the mineral involved and the rate of cooling, but as an approximation, typical closure temperatures in amphiboles are *circa* 600°C, and 300°C in micas, ranging to as low as *circa* 100°C in apatite.

2.2.1   The ^{40}Ar/^{39}Ar method

In the traditional K–Ar dating method, the ^{40}Ar and ^{40}K concentrations in a sample are measured in two quite different experiments, and the age is calculated from Equation 2.3. In the ^{40}Ar/^{39}Ar method (York 1984), the daughter/parent ratio is measured in one experiment and an age *spectrum* is derived, instead of a single age.

In the ^{40}Ar/^{39}Ar method the specimen is irradiated in a nuclear reactor,

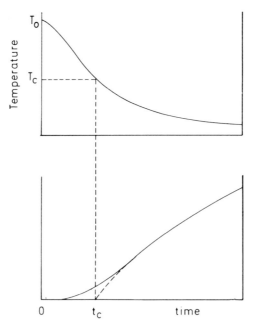

Figure 2.1 Relationship between geochronological closure of a mineral and its cooling history from Dodson (1973). Top diagram shows the cooling history of a typical mineral (with a steady increase in $1/T$. In the lower diagram the vertical axis is related to the diffusion coefficient and approximates the rate of escape of the radiogenic daughter product (e.g. Ar). T_c is the radiometric closure temperature, which is reached at time t_c. Curves are calculated for identical diffusion parameters: in a natural rock, each mineral phase would have a different set of diffusion coefficients, giving a variety of closure temperatures and times.

in which fast neutrons convert some ^{39}K to ^{39}Ar. In the age determination, the sample is gradually heated in a vacuum in a series of steps, and at each step the ^{40}Ar/^{39}Ar ratio of the gas given off is determined by mass spectrometry. As the ^{39}Ar content is proportional to ^{39}K in the sample, and ^{39}K is proportional to ^{40}K, so ^{40}Ar/^{39}Ar is proportional to ^{40}Ar/^{40}K in the sample. Thus a date can be calculated for each temperature step.

The result of the step heating is usually a series of dates, which must be interpreted in the light of the closure temperature of the system (Eqn 2.4). The age spectra obtained from natural rock samples are very varied, and in general reflect the thermal history of the sample. A detailed exposition of the problems and power of the method is given by York (1984).

2.3 Application of K–Ar data

K–Ar methods provided the first radiometric techniques to be widely available in most Archaean cratons, and were used in several areas to set up stratigraphic frameworks or to correct and amplify earlier purely lithostratigraphic columns. Two good examples are those provided by the important work of Wilson (1973) and Wilson and Harrison (1973) in Zimbabwe, and Stockwell (1982) in Canada. Wilson used a large number of K–Ar dates (together with a few ages by other methods) to revise the lithostratigraphic column set up by earlier mapping in the Rhodesian craton. The K–Ar ages served to identify several 'events', at 3300 Ma, 2900 Ma and 2650 Ma and to assign a *circa* 3000 Ma age to primitive life forms in the Bulawayo area. Since 1973, detailed Rb–Sr and Sm–Nd work has shown that many of the rocks thought to be of 3000 Ma age are more probably of *circa* 2700 Ma (Wilson 1979). This later work has consequently cast considerable doubt on the usefulness of *all* K–Ar data from the craton.

In Canada a similar process occurred. Until recently, most dates were established by K–Ar and in a series of classic studies, Stockwell (1961, 1973) identified several major 'orogens' in the Canadian Shield, each being marked by a distinct cluster of K–Ar results. In the Superior Province (north and east of Lake Superior) a cluster of K–Ar dates around 2480 Ma was used to identify a late Archaean 'Kenoran' event thought to represent a period of mountain building accompanied by folding. Later work revised this substantially (Stockwell 1982 gives a superb summary catalogue of geochronological work in Canada), but the concept of several major orogens (each followed by profound erosional intervals) remains firmly entrenched as the basis of the Canadian Precambrian stratigraphic column. Newly mapped strata tend to be ascribed to one orogen or another, with the implication that periods between orogens were quiet.

This pioneering work by Wilson and by Stockwell was of very great importance in reducing the previous chaos of Archaean stratigraphy to some sort of order, but as Wilson (1979) has pointed out, recent results 'have not upheld (the earlier work) and there is no consistency of age among intrusions previously assigned to (a specific) event..At this stage K–Ar results must be considered unreliable due to some as yet unexplained redistribution of argon on local and regional scales.' Certainly experience in Zimbabwe has tended to invalidate the simplistic concept of Precambrian crustal history as a sequence of orogens separated by long, quiet periods of erosion. Indeed, many K–Ar dates are now interpreted as representing periods of erosional unroofing: those 'good' K–Ar dates, which are unaffected by argon redistribution, in the main probably represent the erosional and post-metamorphic cooling. It is thus often rather difficult to interpret K–Ar information from Archaean rocks. However, it should be stressed that K–Ar, and especially Ar–Ar data (in particular, the results of mineral ages and incremental heating experiments) provide an extremely powerful tool for investigating the metamorphic and erosional history of Archaean

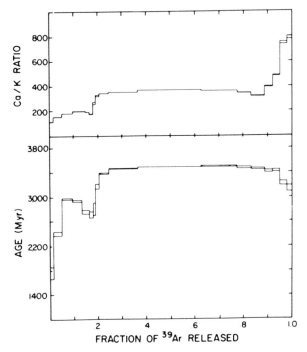

Figure 2.2 Age and Ca/K spectra of a vacuum-stored komatiite sample from the Komati Formation in the Barberton Mountain Land, South Africa. The sizes of the boxes represent 1σ errors, where they are large enough to be shown. (From Lopez-Martinez *et al.* 1984).

terrains. This is probably the greatest use of the K–Ar techniques in the Archaean, and K–Ar measurements are likely to be used increasingly as detailed studies of Archaean metamorphism and sedimentation are carried out.

In contrast to the problems in interpreting K–Ar dates, $^{40}Ar/^{39}Ar$ techniques are able to provide good results in Archaean rocks. For instance, Lopez-Martinez *et al.* (1984) report $^{40}Ar/^{39}Ar$ ages for komatiites and komatiitic basalts from the Barberton Mountain Land. Their results indicate a period of metamorphism in the 3450–3490-Ma range, close to a date of 3540 ± 15 Ma thought to represent eruption. Their step heating analysis (Fig. 2.2) of komatiitic argon provides much useful information about the post-depositional history of the rocks. Similarly, Hanes *et al.* (1985) have used $^{40}Ar/^{39}Ar$ step-heating to obtain a precise primary age of 2703 ± 22 Ma (2σ or 95% confidence in error limits) for a sill in Munro Township, Ontario. This is in excellent agreement with U–Pb zircon dates of 2700–2712 Ma and an Sm–Nd age of 2622 ± 60 Ma for the sill.

2.4 Rb–Sr dating

Rubidium and strontium occur widely in common crustal rocks, dispersed in small concentrations usually of the order of 10–1000 ppm. Rb is an alkali metal chemically similar to K and usually formed in small but easily detectable amount in K minerals. Sr is roughly analogous to calcium and occurs typically in Ca-bearing minerals. Consequently, most Archaean rocks are accessible to Rb–Sr dating, and the Rb–Sr method was until recently the standard 'workhorse' of Archaean geochronology. In general, Rb–Sr isochrons are much more reliable than K–Ar dates: isochrons can be reset or mixed, but usually if an isochron *is* obtained from a suite of rocks, the date can be attributed to a definite event such as metamorphism or alteration.

^{87}Rb decays by β emission to ^{87}Sr. The total number of atoms of ^{87}Sr in a mineral or sample which has behaved as a closed system whose age is t years is given by

$$^{87}\mathrm{Sr}_m = {}^{87}\mathrm{Sr}_o + {}^{87}\mathrm{Rb}_m \, (e^{\lambda t} - 1) \tag{2.5}$$

where ^{87}Sr$_m$ is the total number of atoms of ^{87}Sr present in unit weight of the sample today, ^{87}Sr$_o$ the number of atoms of ^{87}Sr present when the sample was first formed and closed to Rb and Sr movement, ^{87}Rb$_m$ is the number of atoms of ^{87}Rb present today in unit weight, λ is the decay constant, and t the time elapsed (the 'age' of the sample). The presently accepted value for λ is $1.42 \times 10^{-11} \mathrm{a}^{-1}$ (Steiger & Jaeger, 1977) but until recently $\lambda = 1.39 \times 10^{-11} \mathrm{a}^{-1}$ was used. To convert, simply multiply by previous/new. For example, an age of 2500 Ma using $\lambda = 1.39 \times 10^{-11} \mathrm{a}^{-1}$ becomes 2447 Ma using $\lambda = 1.42 \times 10^{-11} \mathrm{a}^{-1}$.

The equation for the number of ^{87}Sr atoms can be modified by dividing by the number of stable ^{86}Sr atoms, which has remained constant

$$\left(\frac{^{87}\mathrm{Sr}}{^{86}\mathrm{Sr}}\right)_m = \left(\frac{^{87}\mathrm{Sr}}{^{86}\mathrm{Sr}}\right)_o + \left(\frac{^{87}\mathrm{Rb}}{^{86}\mathrm{Sr}}\right)_m (e^{\lambda t} - 1) \tag{2.6}$$

This is the equation of a straight line. If a suite of samples is chosen from an area, in each sample ^{87}Sr and ^{86}Sr can be measured, as can ^{87}Rb. The results are plotted on a graph of ^{87}Rb/^{86}Sr vs. ^{87}Sr/^{86}Sr. If the results from the suite of samples do indeed fall on a straight line within the random errors of the analytical method, an isochron has been obtained (Fig. 2.3). The slope of the line is $(e^{\lambda t} - 1)$, or very nearly λt, and the intercept of the line on the ^{87}Sr/^{86}Sr axis is the initial strontium isotope ratio.

Both the age and the initial ratio are of extreme importance to the Archaean geologist. If the isochron has been reset, or if the samples have

18

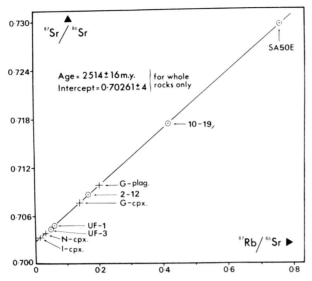

Figure 2.3 Example of an Rb–Sr isochron plot (from Hamilton 1977). Data points include whole rock (circles) and mineral (crosses) measurements from the Great Dyke, Zimbabwe. Calculation is for $\lambda_{Rb} = 1.39 \times 10^{-11} a^{-1}$.

been derived by a two-stage process (e.g. by remelting of crustal rocks), the initial ratio will be relatively high. Many Archaean mafic extrusive suites give initial ratios in the range 0.700–0.703 (a number which evolves with time), reflecting the Sr isotopic ratio of the Archaean mantle. Archaean granites and gneisses which appear to be derived from or formed at relatively deep levels give initial ratios of 0.700–0.704. In contrast, crustally derived and altered rocks (e.g. those subject to Archaean hydrothermal processes) may give initial ratios as high as 0.711 or more. Figure 2.4 shows $^{87}Sr/^{86}Sr$ evolution diagrams for groups of rocks from Zimbabwe. The figure shows a growth line for the mantle (from Peterman 1979) and the growth lines of a variety of granitoids and volcanic rocks emplaced in the crust. The sample suites in groups *A* and *B* appear to represent juvenile addition to the crust from the mantle or melts derived from a source depleted in Rb (e.g. a granulite). In contrast, the altered granite represented by *C* has a much higher $^{87}Sr/^{86}Sr$ initial ratio, and may have been derived as a partial melt of somewhat older continental material. Early alteration may also have occurred. In most cases, rocks showing strong alteration do not give isochrons: at best an 'errorchron' is obtained, in which points fall further away from a straight line than the analytical error. In other words, the samples have not behaved as closed systems relative to Rb and Sr. (The wider significance of isotopic initial ratios is discussed further in Sections 2.8 and 6.11.)

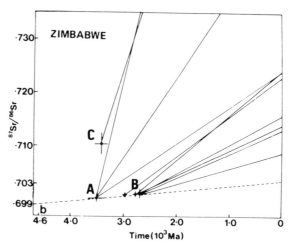

Figure 2.4 Sr isotope evolution diagram for Zimbabwe. A = early Archaean gneisses; B = late Archaean gneisses; C = Mont d'Or granite. (From Moorbath and Taylor 1981, the growth line for the mantle is from Peterman, 1979).

For the most part, Rb–Sr work is done with the primary purpose of obtaining a date for a rock unit. Since the analytical work is tedious, and isochrons are relatively difficult to obtain, it is important that rock suites be carefully selected to be as useful as possible. Ideally, the rock unit chosen should be one whose position in the local lithostratigraphic column is well understood, and whose structural and metamorphic history is relatively well known. A wide variety of rock types can be dated by Rb–Sr, but the most commonly used in Archaean terrains are extrusive mafic sequences, granites and gneisses, depending on local stratigraphic needs. In younger rocks, lithologies are chosen to give a wide spread in Rb/Sr ratios, but this is less important in Archaean rocks as the time span is so great. Limestones, however, rarely give good dates as Rb is usually very low, and the rocks are often altered by fluid movement.

Samples should be large (2 kg), as little altered as possible, and preferably taken from a small, stratigraphically coherent area. Alteration is a major problem in many Archaean terrains: both in Australia and Africa, relatively recent groundwater movement may have altered Rb and Sr content in rocks to a depth of 50 m, or more. Samples chosen are usually in suites of 'whole rock' samples, which usually give the date of extrusion, intrusion or metamorphism of the suite. Mineral separates are also commonly studied, either to give 'model ages' calculated by assuming initial $^{87}Sr/^{86}Sr$ or to calculate 'mineral isochrons' using data from one or more minerals with or without whole-rock results. Often although the 'whole-rock' samples have behaved as closed systems, minerals within the rock have recrystallised. In some cases the dates of metamorphic events can be inferred, as well as the original age of the system. Such mineral dates are subject to constraints similar to those applying to K−Ar systems, with closure temperatures of around 600−200°C, depending on the mineral and rate of cooling. Detailed Rb−Sr work can thus in good cases provide the age of metamorphic cooling.

Bridgwater and Collerson (1977) and Schiotte *et al.* (1985) have drawn attention to major problems which can arise in the interpretation of apparent Rb−Sr isochrons in very old rocks. In such rocks, Rb metasomatism occurring after the development of primary Rb/Sr ratios would lead to a scatter on an isochron drawn during the first 1000−2000 Ma after the event took place. However, 3.5 Ga or so after the metasomatism, the effects of this scatter would be difficult to distinguish from actual scatter in an isochron. What would have been rejected as a 'mixed' system, say, 500 Ma after migmatisation would produce a very passable errorchron 3 Ga later if the average amount of rubidium added was large compared to the amount originally present.

In good cases, Rb−Sr isochrons provide high quality Archaean age data, with 2σ errors typically around 50 Ma and sometimes as low as 10−20 Ma. All depends on the quality of the samples and the quality of the analysis; Wilson (1979) provides an excellent example of how the geological history of an Archaean craton can be deduced from the interpretation of good lithostratigraphic data in the light of a small number of good Rb−Sr isochrons. One of these is illustrated in Figure 2.3.

2.5 Sm−Nd, Lu−Hf and Re−Os methods

Several isotope decay schemes are similar to the Rb−Sr geochronometer, but with the added potential that the isotopes involved are far less mobile and less likely than Rb and Sr to be separated during alteration of the host rock. Unfortunately, the range of relevant interelement ratios in normal geological specimens is typically very small, and decay constants are also small; as a result very fine chemical work and high precision of measurement is required, and few laboratories outside the major centres are capable of producing age and initial ratio data from these isotopes.

2.5.1 Sm−Nd

Sm−Nd techniques are described by Lugmair (1974), Lugmair *et al.* (1975) and Hamilton *et al.* (1977). The basic equation is of the same form as the

21

Rb–Sr isochron equation, ^{147}Sm decaying by alpha emission to ^{143}Nd:

$$\left(\frac{^{143}\text{Nd}}{^{144}\text{Nd}}\right)_m = \left(\frac{^{143}\text{Nd}}{^{144}\text{Nd}}\right)_o + \left(\frac{^{147}\text{Sm}}{^{144}\text{Nd}}\right)_m (e^{\lambda t} - 1) \qquad (2.7)$$

where m refers to measured values, o to values when the system was set up, λ is the decay constant and t the time since the system was created. The decay constant of ^{147}Sm is usually taken as $\lambda = 6.54 \times 10^{-12}\,\text{a}^{-1}$. This value is so small that instrumentation capable of very high precision is necessary. The ^{147}Sm/^{144}Nd values typically range from 0.1–0.2, with Sm and Nd levels around 1–10 ppm, so high precision is also required for this measurement.

A powerful way of looking at the Sm–Nd data is the comparison of results from terrestrial rocks with models of the isotopic evolution of possible source reservoirs from which the rocks may, ultimately, have been derived. Two such models are the *chondritic uniform reservoir* or CHUR, which is an undepleted model source, and a model *depleted mantle* or DM. Figures 2.10a and 2.10b show how a chondritic reservoir would have evolved over time. Today, oceanic mafic liquids appear to have been derived not from a primitive mantle like CHUR, but from a depleted mantle source like DM, which evolved away from CHUR as shown in the upper curves in Figures 2.10b and 2.11. It is standard for initial ^{143}Nd/^{144}Nd ratios to be reported as deviations in parts per ten thousand (ε_{Nd}) from the CHUR or DM reference reservoirs (DePaolo & Wasserburg 1976). For CHUR,

$$\varepsilon_{\text{Nd}} = \left[\frac{(^{143}\text{Nd}/^{144}\text{Nd})_{\text{INITIAL}}^{T}}{(^{143}\text{Nd}/^{144}\text{Nd})_{\text{CHUR}}^{T}} - 1\right] \times 10^{4} \qquad (2.8)$$

where T is the reference time, and

$$(^{143}\text{Nd}/^{144}\text{Nd})_{\text{CHUR}}^{T} = (^{143}\text{Nd}/^{144}\text{Nd})_{\text{CHUR}}^{T=0} - (^{147}\text{Sm}/^{144}\text{Nd})_{\text{CHUR}}^{T=0}(e^{\lambda_{\text{sm}}T} - 1)$$
$$(2.9)$$

Different laboratories have different normalisations for calculating these various ratios, but the results are comparable. Some laboratories use an effective normalisation of $(^{146}\text{Nd}/^{144}\text{Nd}) = 0.7219$, which leads to $(^{143}\text{Nd}/^{144}\text{Nd})_{\text{CHUR}} = 0.512638$ and $(^{147}\text{Sm}/^{144}\text{Nd}) = 0.1966$, while others use values equivalent to 0.724134, 0.511847 and 0.1967 respectively for the three quantities. The decay constant λ_{Sm} is, $6.54 \times 10^{-12}\,\text{a}^{-1}$. For the similar depleted mantle DM curve, parameters again vary according to laboratories. Goldstein *et al.* (1984) use a present-day depleted mantle with $(^{143}\text{Nd}/^{144}\text{Nd}) = 0.51316$ when normalised to $(^{146}\text{Nd}/^{144}\text{Nd}) = 0.7219$.

Model ages can be calculated to estimate the time of derivation of the rock from the parent reservoir (see Fig. 2.7):

$$T_{\text{CHUR}}^{\text{Nd}} = \frac{1}{\lambda_{\text{Sm}}} \ln\left[1 + \frac{(^{143}\text{Nd}/^{144}\text{Nd})_{\text{measured}} - (^{143}\text{Nd}/^{144}\text{Nd})_{\text{CHUR}}^{T=0}}{(^{147}\text{Sm}/^{144}\text{Nd})_{\text{measured}} - (^{147}\text{Sm}/^{144}\text{Nd})_{\text{CHUR}}^{T=0}}\right] \qquad (2.10)$$

$$T_{\text{Dm}}^{\text{Nd}} = \frac{1}{\lambda_{\text{Sm}}} \ln\left[1 + \frac{(^{143}\text{Nd}/^{144}\text{Nd})_{\text{measured}} - (^{143}\text{Nd}/^{144}\text{Nd})_{\text{Dm}}^{T=0}}{(^{147}\text{Sm}/^{144}\text{Nd})_{\text{measured}} - (^{147}\text{Sm}/^{144}\text{Nd})_{\text{Dm}}^{T=0}}\right] \qquad (2.11)$$

A similar notation can be used to express deviations of an Rb–Sr system from bulk reservoirs, giving an ε_{Sr}, which can be compared with ε_{Nd} (Allègre *et al.* 1979). For the Lu–Hf system, ε_{Hf} can likewise be defined (Patchett *et al.* 1984).

Hamilton *et al.* (1977) demonstrated the great advantages of Sm–Nd dating by attempting to date a rock suite which had proved to be too heavily altered to yield useful Rb–Sr data. An Sm–Nd isochron was indeed obtained, thereby demonstrating the considerable stability of Sm and Nd in circumstances where Rb and Sr had proved to be mobile. To the Archaean stratigrapher this is a most important feature of the Sm–Nd method. Hamilton *et al.* (1979) have obtained a good Sm–Nd isochron from the Barberton area, a notoriously difficult set of rocks to date. However, Chauvel *et al.* (1983) have shown that some Sm–Nd ages can be anomalously old. The use of Sm–Nd isochrons in Archaean mafic suites is in fact exceedingly complicated, and often it is difficult to assess what exactly the isochron represents. (The further implications and complications of Sm–Nd information will be examined in detail in Sections 2.7, 5.6 and 6.11.) Lu–Hf and Re–Os methods have similar problems and potential: the elements involved appear to be relatively stable during metamorphism and alteration, so that, on the whole, isotopic systematics are preserved in circumstances where K–Ar and Rb–Sr systems would be thoroughly disturbed. However, element concentrations and decay constants are very small, so difficult chemical procedures and high-precision measurement are needed.

2.6 U, Th–Pb dating methods

The decay of uranium and thorium to various lead isotopes provides a variety of dating techniques. The isotopic systematics are the most complex of all geochronologically useful decay series, but correspondingly they offer what are potentially the most informative and the most powerful of geochronological tools. Faure (1977) gives a detailed description of the methods used; what follows is only a brief and partial summary.

Each of the naturally occurring uranium isotopes and also the main natural thorium isotope is individually the parent of a specific and distinct chain of daughter isotopes that ends in a particular lead isotope.

^{238}U constitutes 99.27% of natural uranium, and has a half-life of 4.47×10^9 a. Its decay gives rise to the uranium series, through a variety of isotopes including isotopes of Th, Pa, Ra, Rn, Po, At, Bi, Tl and Hg, eventually leading to ^{206}Pb. The decay can be summarised as

$$^{238}_{92}U \rightarrow {}^{206}_{82}Pb + 8^4_2He + 6\beta^- + Q \qquad (2.12)$$

where $Q = 47.4\,\text{MeV/atom}$, or $0.71\,\text{cal gm}^{-1}\text{a}^{-1}$ in heat terms. During the decay, relatively long-lived isotopes include ^{234}U, ^{230}Th and ^{226}Ra. Thorium is chemically an actinide and analogous to the rare earths in reactivity, while Ra is analogous to Ba, Sr and Ca. Thus, provided major fluid movement through the rock does not occur, it is probable that most of the intermediate isotopes in the chain are geologically relatively stable: the chance of loss during decay is low except at high temperatures.

$^{235}_{92}U$ makes up 0.72% of natural uranium, and has a half-life of 7.04×10^8 a in its ground state. Its decay gives rise to the actinide series, to stable $^{207}_{82}$Pb, as

$$^{235}_{92}U \rightarrow {}^{207}_{82}Pb + 7^4_2He + 4\beta^- + Q \qquad (2.13)$$

where $Q = 45.2\,\text{MeV/atom}$ or $4.3\,\text{cal gm}^{-1}a^{-1}$. Most of the time during the decay is spent as ^{231}Pa, analogous to platinum.

$^{232}_{90}$Th is the main natural isotope of thorium, with a half-life of 1.4×10^{10}a. Its decay can be written as

$$^{232}_{90}Th \rightarrow {}^{208}_{82}Pb + 6^4_2He + 4\beta^- + Q \qquad (2.14)$$

where $Q = 39.8\,\text{MeV/atom}$ or $0.20\,\text{cal gm}^{-1}a^{-1}$. The intermediate daughter isotopes are all short-lived by Archaean standards.

The lead isotope composition in minerals containing uranium and thorium can be expressed in the usual equations

$$\left(\frac{^{206}Pb}{^{204}Pb}\right)_m = \left(\frac{^{206}Pb}{^{204}Pb}\right)_o + \left(\frac{^{238}U}{^{204}Pb}\right)_m (e^{\lambda_1 t} - 1) \qquad (2.15)$$

$$\left(\frac{^{207}Pb}{^{204}Pb}\right)_m = \left(\frac{^{207}Pb}{^{204}Pb}\right)_o + \left(\frac{^{235}U}{^{204}Pb}\right)_m (e^{\lambda_2 t} - 1) \qquad (2.16)$$

and

$$\left(\frac{^{208}Pb}{^{204}Pb}\right)_m = \left(\frac{^{208}Pb}{^{204}Pb}\right)_o + \left(\frac{^{232}Th}{^{204}Pb}\right)_m (e^{\lambda_3 t} - 1) \qquad (2.17)$$

where m refers to measured, present-day contents, and o to original contents, λ_1, λ_2, λ_3 are the relevant decay constants, and t is time elapsed. The ^{204}Pb isotope is treated as a reference, 'stable' isotope, although it is weakly radioactive with a very long half-life. Equation 2.15 can be rewritten

$$\left(\frac{^{206}\text{Pb}^*}{^{238}\text{U}}\right)_m = e^{\lambda_1 t} - 1 \tag{2.18}$$

where

$$\left(\frac{^{206}\text{Pb}^*}{^{238}\text{U}}\right)_m = \frac{\left(\dfrac{^{206}\text{Pb}}{^{204}\text{Pb}}\right)_m - \left(\dfrac{^{206}\text{Pb}}{^{204}\text{Pb}}\right)_o}{\left(\dfrac{^{238}\text{U}}{^{204}\text{Pb}}\right)_m} \tag{2.19}$$

^{206}Pb* is thus the *radiogenic* ^{206}lead.
Similarly

$$\left(\frac{^{207}\text{Pb}^*}{^{235}\text{U}}\right)_m = e^{\lambda_2 t} - 1 \tag{2.20}$$

where ^{207}Pb* is the radiogenic ^{207}lead.

A uranium-containing system will give concordant dates from both the ^{238}U $\rightarrow$ ^{206}Pb and the ^{235}U $\rightarrow$ ^{207}Pb systems, if: (a) the system has remained chemically closed with respect to all the elements of the chain, throughout its history; (b) correct values are used for the initial lead isotope ratios; (c) the original isotopic composition of the uranium was normal; and (d) decay constants and analytical results are accurate.

Since λ_1, and λ_2 are known, Equations 2.18 and 2.20 can be used to define a curve on a plot of

$$\frac{^{206}\text{Pb}^*}{^{238}\text{U}} \quad \text{vs.} \quad \frac{^{207}\text{Pb}^*}{^{235}\text{U}}$$

This curve (Fig. 2.5a) is known as *concordia*–the locus of all concordant U–Pb systems. To see its application, consider a mineral that ideally contains very little Pb, but that contains U and is retentive to U, Th and Pb. At the time of crystallisation the mineral contains no radiogenic lead and plots at the origin. As time elapses, the system will have Pb and U isotopic ratios as represented by the curve. While the system remains closed it will stay on concordia, and the U–Pb contents are concordant and give the age of the system.

If the system loses lead or gains uranium during some geological event,

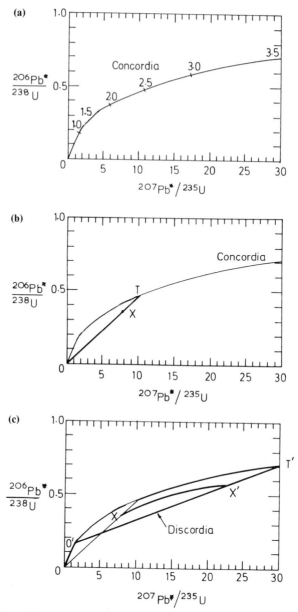

Figure 2.5 Concordia and Discordia. (a) Concordia curve, illustrating the evolution of an initially lead-free U-bearing system as it ages (numbers are age in Ga since closure of the system). (b) Effect of lead loss episode at time T: one mineral loses all its radiogenic lead and returns to the origin, another loses some lead and moves to X, and a third suffers no lead loss and remains at T. (c) Further evolution of systems in (b). First mineral is reset and moves again along concordia: mineral at X evolves to X'; third mineral continues along concordia. Line 0^1-X^1-T^1 defines discordia: point $0'$ gives time since lead loss event and T' time since original crystallisation.

it will move off concordia. Loss of radiogenic lead will move the system back toward the origin. Consider three minerals, one of which at time T loses all its radiogenic lead and returns to the origin, a second that loses only some of its lead and moves to X (Fig. 2.5b) and a third that suffers no lead loss. The minerals will now evolve as in Figure 2.5c: the first mineral has been reset and is now represented by O' as it moves again along concordia; the second moves to X' according to Equations 2.18 and 2.20, and the third continues to evolve along concordia to T'. The three minerals and any others that suffered lead loss in the same event define a chord $O'-X'-T'$, known as *discordia*, which intersects the concordia curve at two points. One point, T', represents the time elapsed since original crystallisation of the system and the other point, O', ideally represents the age of the resetting event. This, of course, is in ideal cases, but the method does offer an exceedingly powerful way of attacking the history of altered rocks.

Zircon is ideal for the U–Pb method of dating. Typically, zircons contain a few hundred to a few thousand parts per million of U and Th respectively. Pb tends to be low in zircon at the time of crystallisation because the Pb^{2+} ion has a larger ionic radius and lower charge than Zr^{4+}, while U^{4+} and Th^{4+} substitute more easily. Krogh (1973) has developed methods for analysing and dating single zircons with very high precision, giving analytical errors of $\pm 2\,Ma$ in some cases. Krogh and Davis (1973) contrasted U–Pb systems in zircon with Rb–Sr in the same whole rock. Their study illustrates well the many pitfalls in interpreting both zircon and Rb–Sr information. In general the zircon technique is one of the most precise and powerful of all tools in Archaean stratigraphy.

2.6.1 *Pb–Pb isochrons*

By combining Equations 2.11 and 2.12, the relationship

$$\frac{\dfrac{^{207}Pb}{^{204}Pb} - \left(\dfrac{^{207}Pb}{^{204}Pb}\right)_o}{\dfrac{^{206}Pb}{^{204}Pb} - \left(\dfrac{^{206}Pb}{^{204}Pb}\right)_o} = \frac{^{235}U}{^{238}U}\left(\frac{e^{\lambda_2 t} - 1}{e^{\lambda_1 t} - 1}\right) = \frac{1}{137.88}\left(\frac{e^{\lambda_2 t} - 1}{e^{\lambda_1 t} - 1}\right) \qquad (2.21)$$

is obtained. A suite of cogenetic rocks and minerals would thus have $^{207}Pb/^{204}Pb$ and $^{206}Pb/^{204}Pb$ ratios lying along a straight line whose slope would be equal to $(1/137.88)[e^{\lambda_2 t} - 1/e^{\lambda_1 t} - 1]$. As a result, Pb–Pb isochrons can be plotted. These often provide very valuable information about the age of events which may otherwise be difficult to date, and are applicable to systems as diverse as granites, volcanic rocks (altered by hydrothermal events on eruption) and carbonates.

Besides allowing isochrons, Equation 2.21 can be used to estimate the age of the earth

$$\frac{\left(\dfrac{^{207}Pb}{^{204}Pb}\right)_{present} - \left(\dfrac{^{207}Pb}{^{204}Pb}\right)_T}{\left(\dfrac{^{206}Pb}{^{204}Pb}\right)_{present} - \left(\dfrac{^{206}Pb}{^{204}Pb}\right)_T} = \left(\frac{^{235}U}{^{238}U}\right)_{present} \left(\frac{e^{\lambda_2 T} - 1}{e^{\lambda_1 T} - 1}\right) \qquad (2.22)$$

where T is the age of the Earth. The modern lead composition of the earth is estimated from analyses of various rocks and minerals, and the initial composition is assumed to be that of troilite (FeS) in iron meteorites, which has negligible uranium and thorium. This gives results in the range 4.55 Ga or more, depending on the value taken for modern lead. For a more detailed discussion of the use of lead isotopes to find the age of the earth – a method originally developed by Rutherford (1929), Holmes (1913, 1946) and Houtermans (1946) – see Albarède and Juteau (1984) and the references cited therein, and Faure (1977).

2.6.2 Examples

An excellent example of stratigraphically useful U–Pb dating is that reported by Pidgeon (1978), where a single very good zircon date served to fix the stratigraphic age of a major early Archaean cratonic series. Pidgeon collected 100 kg of sample from a 200-m square area of dacite from the Duffer Formation of the Warrawoona Group in the Pilbara Block, Western Australia. From this large sample he isolated 0.16 g of zircon. In a parallel study he collected a suite of 2–4-kg samples for Rb–Sr analysis.

From the zircon analysis, Pidgeon obtained a single discordia chord, which intersected concordia at 3452 ± 16 Ma, quoting errors at 2σ (95% confidence) and 778 ± 160 Ma. The older age was interpreted as the age of extrusion of the dacite and original crystallisation of the zircon. Since the stratigraphic succession in the area was relatively well known, this single age on a well-chosen rock fixed the age of a major stratigraphic sequence. Analysis of Sm–Nd ratios (Hamilton *et al.* 1981) later served to confirm the ages that Pidgeon obtained. It is worth noting that Rb–Sr work on whole rock samples collected from the same site gave an apparent age around 2290 Ma. Clearly the Rb–Sr systems had been opened during a later geological event. In contrast, the U–Pb dating of zircon 'saw through' this later event to the earlier age – a clear demonstration of the power of the zircon dating technique.

Another very important application of zircon dating is illustrated by the work of Krogh *et al.* (1976), followed by Hinton and Long (1979). Krogh *et al.* studied zircons from gneiss in the English River Belt in the Archaean of the Superior Province, northwestern Ontario. Analysis of zircon separates indicated a minimum age of formation of the gneiss of 3008 ± 5 Ma, with a probable subsequent metamorphism of 2680 Ma. The high precision of this measurement indicates what potentially can be obtained: in good cases 2σ errors of 1–2 Ma are possible. Stratigraphically this precision is extremely valuable, as it may make possible precise chronostratigraphic correlation with a resolution not much poorer than that of Phanerozoic zonal assemblages. This can be extremely important in the analysis of greenstone belt successions (see Davis & Edwards 1982, and Gariépy *et al.* 1984).

Zircons from the Krogh *et al.* study were later taken by NBW Harris to be studied by Hinton and Long (1979), using an ion microprobe. The ion microprobe microanalyser permits the mass spectrometric analysis of selected parts of single grains, with a spatial resolution of the order of 20 μm. This high resolution permitted the 'dating' of cores and margins of the zircons, which showed euhedral form, intact cores and extensive peripheral cracking. The results were interpreted as implying an intrusion age of the tonalite of 3.3 ± 0.1 Ga. The cores showed a peak which appeared to represent a metamorphic event at 2.93 ± 0.05 Ga, the higher 'formation' age having only survived in a few resistant areas. A second event which removed lead from the cracked and more susceptible rims implied an age around 2.7 Ga. This interpretation was entirely consistent with the results of Krogh *et al.*, and the combination of the two techniques led to a deep insight into the history of the rock.

Ion microprobe techniques have also been used on zircon collected from metamorphosed sandstones near Mount Narrayer, Western Australia. Of 102 zircon grains examined, the ages of four were fixed between 4.1 and 4.2 Ga, about 500 to 600 million years older than the whole-rock age of the sandstone (Froude *et al.* 1983). Thus the ion microprobe appears to have penetrated a zircon record which goes back past the deposition of the rock and the erosion of the zircon grains to give some idea of the terrain which acted as a source for the detritus. It is very interesting that even as long ago as 3.6 Ga, the source terrains from which sediment was derived may have been so much older: the modern equivalent is a river sand containing reworked Cambrian detritus. However, there remains much controversy about the results obtained (Scharer & Allègre 1985): only a very few of the zircons in the sandstone appear to have been derived from the 4.2 Ga terrain. Recently, a zircon grain close to 4.3 Ga old has been found in the Jack Hills area near Mount Narrayer (Compston & Pidgeon 1986).

Pb–Pb isotopic data are also extremely useful in Archaean terrains especially when used in conjunction with other techniques. Dupré *et al.* (1984) obtained a Pb–Pb isochron data of 2690 ± 15 Ma for two Archaean komatiitic flows from Alexo, Ontario (Fig. 2.6). This date is in excellent agreement with zircon ages of 2725 ± 2 and 2710 ± 2 Ma from underlying rocks, and 2710 ± 2 Ma from overlying strata. Dupré *et al.* argue that the

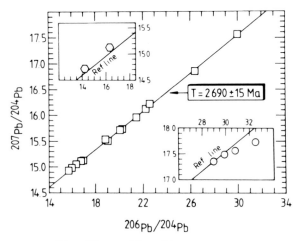

Figure 2.6 Example of ^{207}Pb/^{204}Pb vs. ^{206}Pb/^{204}Pb diagram (from Dupré *et al.* 1984). Most of the data points, obtained from an olivine spinifex flow at Alexo, Ontario, in the Abitibi Belt, define an isochron with an age of 2690 ± 15 Ma. Upper inset shows two samples whose isotopic composition has been disturbed by sedimentary sulphides. Lower inset shows how samples from an underlying clinopyroxene flow deviate from the isochron.

spread in U/Pb that defines the isochrons probably took place as a result of hydrothermal alteration of the lavas immediately after eruption, and thus the Pb–Pb data provide a measure of the time of eruption. In contrast, Sm–Nd data appear to reflect the varied effects of differences in the conditions of melting and contamination of the lava. In a study of mafic volcanics from Kambalda in Western Australia, Roddick (1984) reached similar conclusions. He obtained a Pb–Pb isochron date of 2720 ± 105 Ma, which contrasts with Sm–Nd data (Chauvel *et al.* 1985, Claoue-Long *et al.* 1984) which give a much older date. Possibly the Pb–Pb date is close to the real age of eruption, while the Sm–Nd date reflects contamination of the magma on ascent. This problem is further discussed in Section 6.10.

2.7 Choosing a dating technique

Most field geologists do not have the option of choosing a dating technique. Unless they work for a well-equipped geological survey, they are far more likely to be in the position of trying to persuade any overworked isotope colleague they can find that a particular rock suite is of great stratigraphic interest. Ideally, though, a range of techniques should be exploited.

Mafic volcanic rocks are best dated by using Rb–Sr, Sm–Nd, ^{40}Ar/^{39}Ar or Pb–Pb techniques. The Rb–Sr dating technique is very useful and many laboratories carry it out but, in general, precision is too low (errors of

10–100 Ma) to allow detailed use of dates for stratigraphic correlation. As most Archaean mafic suites are altered, much depends on the careful selection of fresh material from a coherent, well-defined stratigraphic unit. Pb–Pb dating has similar constraints but can in good cases give excellent precision. $^{40}Ar/^{39}Ar$ dating, at best, can offer good precision too, with 1σ values around 10 Ma. All three techniques generally date the age of eruption of the lava or, in many cases, some post-eruptive event such as hydrothermal alteration or metamorphism. In contrast, Sm–Nd dating can give good precision and isochrons are relatively robust against post-eruptive metamorphism, but in many cases Sm–Nd results appear to reflect contamination of magma on ascent and eruption, producing a mixing of isotopes: the date obtained may be too old.

In felsic and intermediate extrusives and also in granitoids – wherever zircons can be extracted – the U–Pb zircon method is exceptionally powerful. In routine cases analytical precision is as good as ± 1–2 Ma. Although this precision may in some cases be rather better than the true accuracy of the age of the rock, it is far superior to that obtained in other dating methods. In the best constrained cases, it is good enough to allow individual older and younger stratigraphic units in an Archaean sequence to be distinguished: other techniques simply give the general age of a stratigraphic sequence. Carbonate sedimentary rocks are sometimes dated by the Pb–Pb methods; ore deposits are generally dated by Pb methods.

2.8   The isotopic record of planetary evolution

Gast (1968) realised that the fractionation of trace elements and the consequent effects on their isotopic distribution offers an extraordinarily powerful set of tools for investigating the early history of the Earth. Element pairs

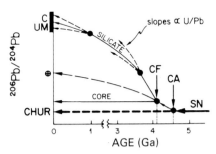

Figure 2.7   Growth of $^{206}Pb/^{204}Pb$ isotope ratio with time (from DePaolo 1981). SN = solar nebula; CA = condensation of nebula and accretion of solid planetary bodies; CF = core formation in the Earth; present day values of isotope ratio shown for continental crust (C), upper mantle (UM) and chondritic meteorites (CHUR). Dashed line is to bulk earth composition (circle with cross).

31

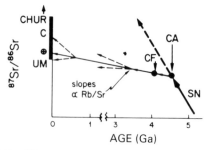

Figure 2.8 Growth of $^{87}Sr/^{86}Sr$ isotope ratio with time (from DePaolo 1981). Symbols as for Figure 2.7.

such as Rb and Sr, Sm and Nd, U and Pb are particularly important because variations in the distributions of their stable and radiogenic isotopes are controlled by the evolution of the mantle and continents, and isotopic half-lives are such that the record is accessible. Isotopic information can in principle tell us not only the age of specific rock suites but also the age of the Earth itself, and much about the way in which it has evolved to produce the continents and mantle.

Figure 2.7 illustrates how this type of information is obtained. The isotope ^{206}Pb is produced by the decay of ^{238}U, so over time the slope of an evolution line of $^{206}Pb/^{204}Pb$ depends on the $^{238}U/^{204}Pb$ ratio in the rock. As the uranium isotope decays, ^{206}Pb increases. The $^{238}U/^{204}Pb$ ratio was very small in the early solar nebula (*SN*), as present day solar abundances show, so the evolution curve for the nebula has a very small slope. When the Earth accreted, it probably did so with a higher U/Pb ratio than the solar nebula as a whole: thus the evolution line of the Earth diverges above the meteorite line about 4.5 Ga ago, following condensation and accretion (*CA*). Later, core formation (*CF*) could have preferentially con-

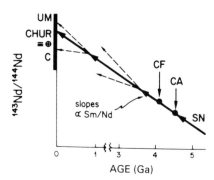

Figure 2.9 Growth of $^{143}Nd/^{144}Nd$ ratio with time (from DePaolo 1981). Symbols as for Figure 2.7.

32

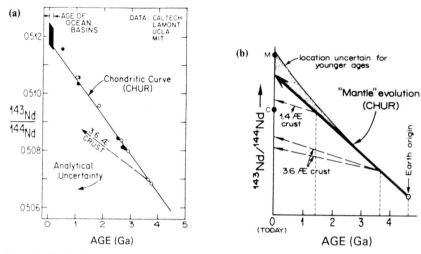

Figure 2.10 (a) Comparison between measured Nd initial ratios in crustal rocks and the CHUR curve, showing the close fit of old samples to the curve and increasing scatter at more recent times (from DePaolo 1981). (b) Model for crust and mantle Nd isotope evolution (from DePaolo 1981). Crust forms by extraction of chemically fractionated material from the mantle, and thereafter evolves along lines of lower slope since it has lower Sm/Nd than the source. The residual mantle evolves away from CHUR in the opposite direction.

centrated Pb to the core, giving a higher still U/Pb ratio in the silicate mantle and crust (evolution line after *CF*), although the bulk earth ratios are not known. During formation of the crust and upper mantle, minor further U–Pb fractionation would have occurred, but since this fractionation was minor the evolution curves of upper mantle (*UM*) and crust (*C*) would not diverge greatly. In consequence, the U–Pb system provides an estimate of the age of the Earth (Section 2.6.1), but is not a sensitive indicator of the time of separation of crust and mantle.

In contrast, the Rb–Sr system shows a very different history (Fig. 2.8). In the accretion of the earth, the Rb/Sr ratio acquired by the Earth was apparently about ten times smaller than that of the solar nebula. Furthermore, fractionation of Rb from Sr during the separation of the core from the mantle seems to have been limited, so the Rb–Sr system gives an excellent indication of the time of the Earth's formation. Magmatic processes fractionate Rb and Sr strongly, so that the system is useful in giving information about the age of the crust. Evolution curves for $^{87}Sr/^{86}Sr$ are nearly straight lines since the half-life of ^{87}Rb is long.

The Sm–Nd system is powerful in a different way. There seems to have been little fractionation of Sm from Nd in the formation of the earth or during core formation, so the system is not very useful in dating these events. However, Sm is fractionated from Nd in magmatic processes, so the

33

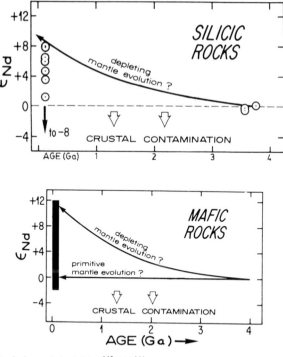

Figure 2.11 Deviations of the initial ^{143}Nd/^{144}Nd ratios from the CHUR curve, expressed in terms of ε_{Nd} (from DePaolo 1981). Top diagram shows range of silicic rocks, which include strongly negative examples (typical of modern continental material). Mafic rocks, especially those derived from mantle with little or no crustal contamination, include examples with increasingly positive ε_{Nd} as the Earth has aged.

system is enormously valuable in unravelling the history of magmatic differentiation in the Earth without also having to disentangle the complexities of the earliest history of planetary accretion.

Figures 2.9, 2.10 and 2.11 show the evolution of the ^{143}Nd/^{144}Nd ratio in terrestrial rocks compared against the CHUR curve. If this line is taken as a baseline, than the complementary nature of the Earth's upper mantle and continental crust can be seen. Initial ratios of mantle-derived volcanics in older rocks (over 2 Ga) are close to CHUR, suggesting a fairly uniform, well-mixed mantle. In bulk, the silicate part of the Earth probably has an Sm/Nd ratio within a few per cent of a chondritic model.

Continental crust generally has an Sm/Nd ratio about half that of the mantle (Ben-Othman *et al.* 1984) and is enriched in both elements relative to the mantle, by a factor of 25 for Nd and 16 for Sm. Thus crustally derived rocks evolve off the CHUR curve to lower ^{143}Nd/^{144}Nd (Fig. 2.10). As the continental crust formed, the Sm/Nd ratio of the mantle increased

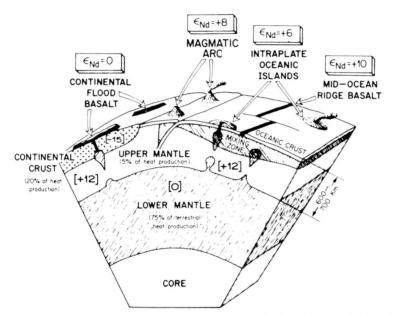

Figure 2.12 Earth structure model, based on Nd isotopic data (from DePaolo 1981).

(Fig. 2.11). At present (Fig. 2.12), the ε_{Nd} value of the crust is around -15, and for the mantle ε_{Nd} is around $+12$ if it is assumed that the upper mantle and continental crust are complementary, while the lower mantle retains a chondritic Sm/Nd ratio (De Paolo, 1981). The further implications of this type of use of isotopic information are explored in Chapters 5 & 6.

35

3 Archaean terrains: the available geological evidence

Nemi makomo eGunguhwe! Harahwa dzemhanza dzakare
Pasi pamakatu kunyudza, pasi pevu pasichigare;
[–And you, Gunguhwe Hills! Bald-headed omens
Eroded, hard granitic, residual humps, aeons old;]

Mutswairo, *Poems from Mazoe*, trans. Herdeck

3.1 Introduction

The strictly geological evidence to support and to test ideas about the nature of the Archaean Earth comes from mapping Archaean terrains. Models, inferences from the modern Earth and mathematical calculations are all useful in reconstructing the Archaean, but it is in the rocks that most information lies. Archaean geology is based first on evidence gathered in the field: only when field relationships are properly understood can the various tools of geochemistry, geophysics and the like be applied.

Archaean rocks are exposed in many but widely scattered terrains. The largest areas of exposure include the Canadian Shield, with its extensions into Greenland and the outer Scottish margins; the Yilgarn and Pilbara Blocks in Western Australia; parts of South Africa and Zimbabwe; parts of South India and extensive regions of Russia, China, Finland, Brazil, Guyana, Central Africa and Antarctica (Fig. 1.1). Individual areas of Archaean crust are termed 'cratons' if they have remained relatively undisturbed since the end of the Archaean.

In this chapter a few well-studied examples are described, in order to give some 'feel' as to the nature of Archaean terrains. No individual Archaean terrain can be described as 'typical', yet collectively Archaean rocks have a distinctive character which sets them apart from the assemblages of younger terrains. Condie (1981) has given a detailed description of much of the world's Archaean geology: the discussion in this chapter is much more limited in scope and is intended to illustrate specific types of terrain.

3.2 Transects through the Archaean crust

3.2.1 Vredefort

In several places, tectonic accidents have exposed sequences from which transects through much of the Archaean crust can be reconstructed. Figure

3.1 shows the regional geology around the Vredefort Dome, in South Africa. Beneath the Mesozoic cover, much of the area consists of rocks of the Transvaal Supergroup (Proterozoic) which overlie the late Archaean Witwatersrand Supergroup (See Ch. 7). Around the little town of Vredefort is an extraordinary domal structure which shows, from edge to core, a section through the crust from Transvaal Group central granulites. Figure 3.2. shows a cross section across the structure. Around the edge is a ring of steeply dipping to overturned rocks of the Witwatersrand and Transvaal sequences. This stratified succession is up to 15 km thick. Inward from the basal contact of the stratified rocks is granitic basement. In this basement, Bisschoff (1972) has described a mafic sill which has an inverted sequence of differentiates: the sill must have been intruded in a near-horizontal attitude and then updomed and overturned. Furthermore, strong geochemical gradients exist in the granitic basement. For instance, the abundance of heat producing elements falls off from the outer edge of the granitoid for the first 7 km inwards, and then stabilises (Fig. 3.3). Rb/Sr ratios decrease towards the centre of the dome, while K/Rb ratios increase. Geologically, the core of the Vredefort structure consists of a ring of granite–gneiss surrounding a central core of granulite facies rocks which includes both mafic metasediments and metavolcanics as inclusions within predominantly felsic rocks. Hart *et al.* (1981) have studied the age of the metamorphic rocks forming the core. They found that the outer granite–gneiss ring gave a very good Pb–Pb age of 3080 ± 20 Ma, an Rb–Sr age of 3000 ± 30 Ma and a Th–Pb age of 3060 ± 50 Ma (all errors at 1σ). The central granulitic assemblages were rather more complex isotopically, but appeared to have a history dating back to 3.5–3.6 Ga. Mafic samples give an Rb–Sr age of 3480 ± 130 Ma, and some felsic and mafic samples give together a Th–Pb age of 3450 ± 70 Ma. Welke and Nicolaysen (1981) used U–Pb data to infer the possibility of an earliest episode of differentiation at *circa* 3860 Ma.

Bisschoff (1982) recognised four phases of metamorphism in the rocks of the Vredefort Dome. The last phase, probably a shock metamorphic event, is represented by shatter cones and pseudotachylite, and marks the post-Archaean formation of the dome structure. In the penultimate phase, rocks of the Witwatersrand Supergroup were metamorphosed thermally in the albite–epidote–hornfels and hornblende–hornfels facies, with retrograde metamorphism of core rocks. This phase too was probably post-Archaean and related to the dome. The second phase of metamorphism is represented by low grade assemblages occurring in the Witwatersrand rocks, and probably reflects the result of loading in the sedimentary basin. Finally, the oldest period of metamorphism is recorded by relict granulite minerals and pseudomorphs in the central core of the structure. This early granulite assemblage may have formed under conditions of 6–8 kbar (Schreyer & Araham 1979).

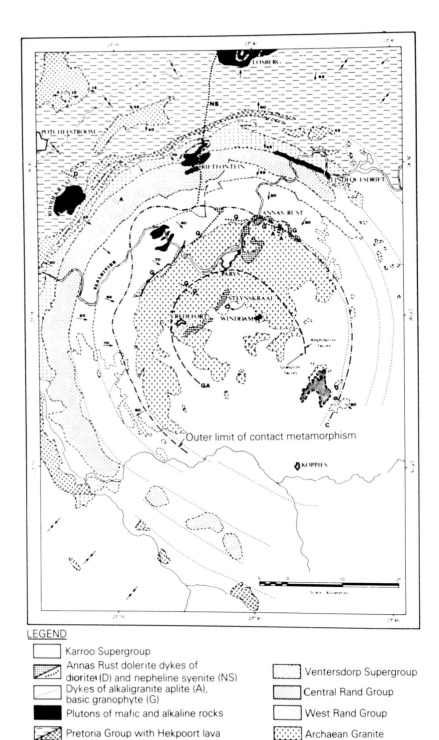

Outer limit of contact metamorphism

Amphibolite facies

Granulite facies

LOSBERG

POTCHEFSTROOM

GRIETFONTEIN

LINDEQUESDRIFT

ROOIKRAAL

ANNAS RUST

HARTBIESFONTEIN

VREDEFORT

STEYNSKRAAL

WINDDAM

KOPPIES

NS

Scale Kilometres

<u>LEGEND</u>

☐ Karroo Supergroup

▨ Annas Rust dolerite dykes of diorite (D) and nepheline syenite (NS)

▤ Dykes of alkaligranite aplite (A), basic granophyte (G)

■ Plutons of mafic and alkaline rocks

▨ Pretoria Group with Hekpoort lava

▦ Malmani dolomite and Black Reef Groups

▨ Ventersdorp Supergroup

▦ Central Rand Group

☐ West Rand Group

▨ Archaean Granite

▨ Swaziland Supergroup

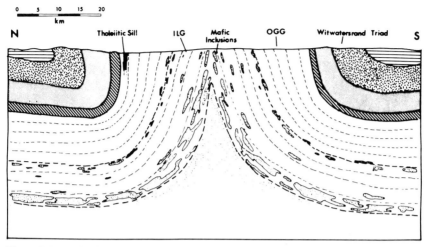

Figure 3.2 Geological cross section across the Vredefort structure. OGG = outer granite gneiss of the basement core. ILG = Inlandsee Leeucogranofels felsic rocks of central core. (From Nicolaysen *et al.* 1981).

Vredefort thus preserves a section through the Archaean crust (Slawson 1976), from deep-level granulites, both felsic and mafic, to granite–gneiss, overlain by thick stratiform sediments of the Witwatersrand Supergroup. The stratiform Archaean sequence is roughly 6 km thick, and overlies 14 km of exposed middle crustal rocks: thus, perhaps half the Archaean crust is seen at Vredefort.

Not much is known about the processes which produced the Vredefort structure, but Simpson (1981) and Lilly (1981) consider that, although coesite and stishovite were formed in the shock event, deformation was from within the Earth and not the result of an external impact; possibly the structure formed as a result of explosive intrusion. The event is thought to have taken place about 2 Ga ago. There is an interesting analogy between the Vredefort structure and the much smaller, higher-level young structure of the Little Rocky Mountains, Montana (Knechtel 1959).

3.2.2   The Kapuskasing transect and an African parallel

In central Superior Province, Canada, around Kapuskasing there is preserved an apparent section through the Archaean crust which, although

Figure 3.1 Geology of Vredefort structure and surrounding terrain, South Africa (from Bisschoff 1982).

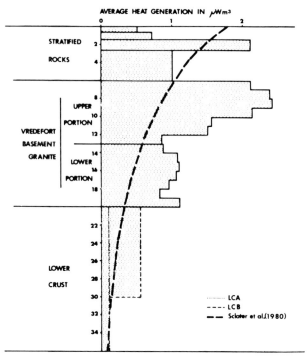

Figure 3.3 Vertical distribution of heat generation in the stratified cover and Vredefort basement profile. Dashed line is a model distribution taken from Sclater *et al.* (1980). Vertical scale in km. (From Nicolaysen *et al.* 1981.)

exposed by a very different set of tectonic events, is broadly similar to the Vredefort section.

Figure 3.4 shows the regional geology of the central Superior Province, which includes a wide variety of little-metamorphosed volcanic and sedimentary rocks ('supracrustals'), as well as some high-grade metamorphic rocks formed under conditions of deep burial. The province is composed of east–west trending belts or subprovinces of alternate volcanic-rich and sediment-rich character, interrupted by a north-east trending zone of high grade metamorphic rocks, the Kapuskasing structural zone. This zone is fault bounded on the south-east, but towards the west its margin is gradational over 120 km to low grade rocks of the Michipicoten Belt.

Percival and Card (1983, 1985) interpreted this transition as an oblique cross section through the Archaean crust (Fig. 3.5). To support this interpretation, they used several distinct arguments. First, the metamorphic grade increases eastwards from low greenschist facies in the Michipicoten Belt through amphibolite facies in the Wawa domal gneiss terrain to upper

40

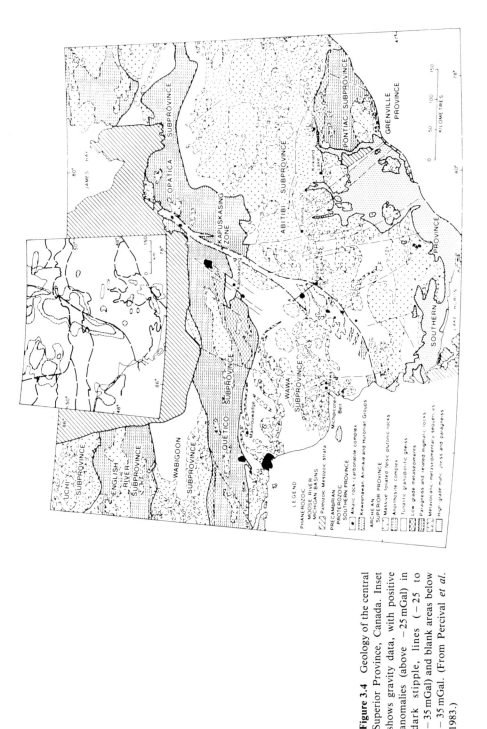

Figure 3.4 Geology of the central Superior Province, Canada. Inset shows gravity data, with positive anomalies (above −25 mGal) in dark stipple, lines (−25 to −35 mGal) and blank areas below −35 mGal. (From Percival *et al.* 1983.)

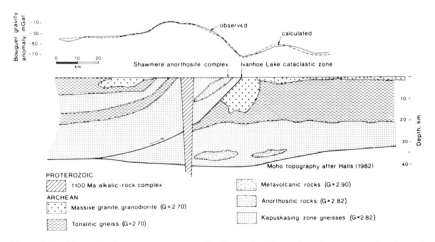

Figure 3.5 Generalised west–east cross section from the Wawa domal gneiss terrain, through the Kapuskasing zone into the Abitibi subprovince (from Percival *et al.* 1983). The gravity model is based on an average density of 2.7 gcm^{-3} for tonalitic rocks, 2.90 for metavolcanics and 2.82 for rocks of the Kapuskasing zone and lower crust.

amphibolite and granulite facies in the Kapuskasing Zone. Second, the proportion of plutonic to supracrustal rocks increases in the same direction across the Wawa subprovince. Third, the oldest rocks are at the inferred base of the section; and finally, gravity data are well modelled by using a west-dipping crustal slab. Each piece of evidence is interesting but not conclusive, but the hypothesis is nevertheless most attractive. Figure 3.6 shows a restored vertical section through the Archaean crust. In the Kapuskasing, Percival and Card (1983) estimate from geobarometric evidence that the granulitic assemblages represent a depth of equilibration of 18–28 km. Their generalised crustal cross section has at its base a sequence of gneiss and anorthosite in the upper amphibolite to granulite facies, of which 5–10 km are exposed in the Kapuskasing Zone. Structurally above this are 10–15 km of tabular batholiths of gneissic and xenolithic tonalite, with massive granitic sheets and plugs. In the upper 5–10 km both granitic rocks and gneissic migmatitic haloes surround the remaining low-grade supracrustal strata of the Michipicoten Belt. Hall and Brisbin (1982) have recognised two seismic discontinuities in the western Superior Province, at 16–19 and 21–22 km. Percival and Card suggest that these discontinuities defining upper, middle and lower crust correspond to lithological transitions in the crustal model, the upper discontinuity being the boundary between high-level granites and gneisses and an underlying high-grade gneiss complex, and the lower discontinuity may represent a metamorphic change, such as the orthopyroxene isograd within the gneiss.

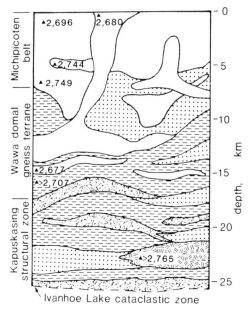

Figure 3.6 Restored model of the Archaean crust (from Percival *et al.* 1983). Numbers are zircon dates. Key: fine stipple = metavolcanics; light stipple = xenolithic tonalite gneiss; white = massive to foliated granite to tonalite; dashed horizontal lines = gneissic tonalite granodiorite; paired randomly oriented lines = anorthositic rocks; shading = paragneiss and mafic gneiss.

The major thrust in Figure 3.5, which produced the modern exposure of deep crustal components, is of unknown age. Percival and Card suggest that major thrusting could have taken place around 2.65–2.45 Ga ago, possibly with a later Proterozoic activity as well, and uplift around 1100–1000 Ma. Preliminary seismic reflection work supports this model, and suggests that the fault zone has a shallower dip at depth.

Robertson (1973) has described a somewhat similar lithological assemblage on the margin of the Limpopo Belt, in Zimbabwe. North-west of the margin are supracrustal rocks with low-grade to amphibolite facies assemblages: southeast of the margin are granulites passing southeastwards across a transitional zone to supracrustals. Coward and Fairhead (1980) and Coward and Daly (1984) used structural and gravity data to support the notion (Coward *et al.* 1976) that this region too was the site of a major thrust, which today exposes the granulites of the deep Archaean crust (Fig. 3.7). This hypothesis has been tested seismologically by Stuart *et al.* (1986) who found that the contact between the Zimbabwe craton and the Limpopo Belt is sharp and dips at about 45° under the belt. Under the belt, the crust is about 34 km thick, thinning to the south.

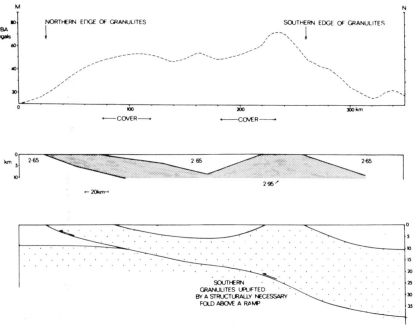

Figure 3.7 Section through the Limpopo Belt (from Coward 1984). Top figure shows observed Bouguer gravity data, middle section a possible model of the gravity data assuming densities as shown, and bottom section a preferred cross section, showing uplift of granulites on a stepped shear zone.

In each of these examples the preserved crustal sequence includes, in broad terms, a high-level suite of volcanic or sedimentary rocks, an underlying suite of granitoid and gneissic material and, below that, high-grade metamorphic assemblages, typically felsic or mafic granulites. Figure 5.18 illustrates a simple crustal model. What is striking about these conclusions is how similar they are to our preconceptions of the modern crust, which are based on transects through younger mountain belts and on models of seismological results. Possibly Archaean geologists are finding what they choose to find, but more likely these transects of Archaean crust do indeed imply a more general truth: that the Archaean continental crust was rather similar to the modern crust. It was of comparable thickness to today's crust – geophysical data suggest 'normal' Moho depths under Archaean low-grade strata; it was dominantly granitic or gneissic, and reworked crustal rocks appear as metamorphic material at considerable depths in the sequences.

In the following description, examples are given of both high-grade (mainly granulitic) and low-grade (granite–greenstone) terrains, to illustrate further the nature and diversity of this Archaean crust.

3.3   Archaean 'cover' successions

Most Archaean geologists tend to regard little-deformed overlying sequences of 'cover' rocks with disfavour, a nuisance to be mapped in at the boundary and coloured a featureless white. In a few places, however, the cover is itself of Archaean age. In these cases, the cover is often dismissed as being of Proterozoic aspect, and the Archaean/Proterozoic boundary is placed at the base of the cover; indeed, this is the cause of much of the disagreement about the definition of the top of the Archaean. If a strictly chronostratigraphic division is used, as in this book, certain little-deformed cover sequences become part of the Archaean sequence.

Three of the most interesting of those cover sequences are the mid-Archaean Pongola succession, South Africa, which is sufficiently ancient to be regarded as Archaean by most workers, and the late Archaean Witwatersrand and Fortescue successions, in South Africa and Australia respectively, which are often classified as 'Proterozoic' because of their little-deformed character.

3.3.1   The Pongola Supergroup

The Pongola Supergroup outcrops around the junctions of the borders of Swaziland, the Transvaal and Natal in southern Africa, over a depositional area of at least $32\,500\,km^2$. Its stratigraphy has been summarised by Button (1981). In the north of its outcrop area it is up to 11 km in apparent stratigraphic thickness, thinning to about 2.5 km in the south (Matthews & Scharrer 1968). Its age has been straddled by dating of the basement, of volcanic rocks in the succession and of intrusions into it, and it is probably close to 2.9 Ga old (Hegner *et al.* 1984, Button 1981). It has been only gently deformed since deposition by flexing into gentle folds, with dips of $0-30°$.

One of the most interesting features of the Pongola Supergroup is the presence of a basal unconformity (see Section 5.3.1), which has been described in detail by Matthews and Scharrer (1968). The basal sediments of the supergroup rest in clear unconformity on older granitoid basement. At the contact there is a palaeoregolith 1–8 m thick of altered granitic material, apparently produced by Archaean weathering. Above this are arkosic sandstones and siltstone (Matthews & Scharrer 1968). Further up in the stratigraphic sequence are basic volcanic rocks intercalated with sediments, and alternating argillaceous and arenaceous layers, with some ironstones and stromatolites (see Section 4.1.4). Figure 3.8 summarises the stratigraphy of the supergroup, which was intruded about 2.9 Ga ago by a set of major mafic igneous bodies, including the Ushushwana Complex.

The Pongola Supergroup is of great tectonic interest, in that its existence

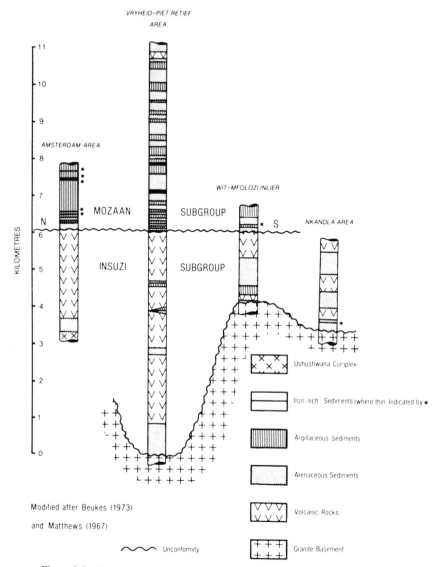

Figure 3.8 Stratigraphic columns for the Pongola Group (from Button 1981).

demonstrates unequivocally that regions of stable continental crust have existed, little deformed, since the mid-Archaean. Much controversy has surrounded this. Were the continental nuclei created by some great event or events which marked a transition from 'Archaean' to more stable 'Protero-zoic' tectonics, or did some or many of the continents develop early as granitic rafts, upon which cover sequences were deposited, later to suffer

46

the chances of fortune? Were most Archaean sequences later disrupted by the tectonic accident of happening to be close to a plate margin, while a very few sequences, such as the Pongola Supergroup, by chance evaded the active edges of plates for the most part and survived intact?

3.3.2 Late Archaean cover sequences

Perhaps the best known of the late Archaean cover sequences is the Witwatersrand Supergroup (see Section 3.2.1 & Fig. 7.8). This is discussed in Sections 5.3.1 and 7.1.5. Another interesting example is the Lower Fortescue Group, above the Pilbara craton in Western Australia (Blake 1984a, 1984b). The Fortescue Group rests unconformably on the older deformed and metamorphosed granitoid–greenstone terrain of the Pilbara craton (Section 3.6.2). Deformation within the Fortescue Group is minor, and strata for the most part dip gently. Burial metamorphism has reached prehnite–pumpellyite facies. The basal rocks are at least 2.8 Ga old and the top older than 2.5 Ga (Blake & McNaughton 1984, Richards & Blockley 1984).

Blake has recognised three early Fortescue Group sedimentary basins which developed on the eroded Pilbara surface. In the Marble Bar basin, the lower clastic sequence (Unit 1) is dominated by braided fluvial sandstones and lesser conglomerate of local derivation. Significant local topographic highs existed within the eroding greenstone belt terrain. The basins seem to have been initiated in a regional tensional regime, indicated by thick early flood basalts. Above the lower sequence the succession passes to a unit of cyclic coarsening-upward sequences of material derived from granitoids, in contrast to the local provenance of Unit 1. Unit 3, above Unit 2, seems to have been laid down in a regime of passive regional subsidence (Blake 1984a), with sediments covering higher-lying parts of the basement high.

Blake (1984b) suggested that major stabilisation of the Pilbara granitoid–greenstone terrain took place before deposition of the lower Fortescue Group, and compared the style of volcanism and sedimentation in the Fortescue with that of similar Phanerozoic successions. The Pilbaran continental nucleus was clearly well established by Fortescue time. One very interesting facet of the Fortescue basins is the presence of well-preserved stromatolitic structures and microfossils (reviewed by Walter 1983 – see Section 4.1.7).

3.4 Granite–greenstone terrains

Archaean granite–greenstone terrains are very widespread, occurring in every continent as a component of structural blocks which range in size from a few to hundreds of thousands of square kilometres. These blocks, especially those which contain stratigraphic assemblages little disturbed since the Archaean, constitute the cratons. Granite–greenstone terrains have a characteristic tectonic 'style', in which elongate belts of greenstone (volcanic and sedimentary rocks often at low metamorphic grade) wrap around granitic batholiths. In some places the granites are intrusive, and have metamorphosed the greenstones; elsewhere the granitoids are really gneisses which were the basement on which the greenstones were laid down; in many other examples the contact is tectonic and difficult to interpret. Although this style (see Fig. 3.4) is typically Archaean, it is not uniquely so: the Sierra Nevada range of northern California has a very similar juxtaposition of granites and volcano-sedimentary suites.

There are many good examples of granite–greenstone terrains, and Condie (1981) has provided a detailed and comprehensive description of most of them. Here, a few examples are taken to illustrate specific areas.

3.4.1 The Zimbabwe craton

The formal stratigraphic name for the Archaean rocks exposed in most of Zimbabwe, eastern Botswana and west central Mozambique is the Rhodesion craton (Vail 1968, Wilson 1973), but since 1981 the craton's name has slowly metamorphosed to Zimbabwe – a process contrary to the rules of nomenclature but consistent with common sense. The craton is made up of rocks ranging in age from 3.8 Ga to 2.5 Ga, including high grade metamorphic rocks, gneisses, older granites, various distinct sets of greenstone belts, intrusive complexes, younger granites and the Great Dyke (Wilson et al. 1978, Wilson 1979). It and the Pilbara are amongst the few granite–greenstone successions where craton-wide correlation has been attempted.

3.4.2 Older Basement

The oldest rocks in Zimbabwe include a wide variety of gneisses and assorted metamorphic rocks exposed on the craton proper, and various granulites and amphibolites in the Limpopo Belt (Fig. 3.9). The area around Beitbridge in southern Zimbabwe and immediately to the south in South Africa includes gneisses which may be of early Archaean age, dykes, a metamorphosed supracrustal sequence perhaps older than 3.3 Ga and various intrusive bodies of the same general age. Several points are of great interest: (a) the old supracrustal metasediments appear to have been laid down on a continental basement (Barton & Key 1981); (b) the metasediments include carbonate-bearing rocks, and (c) some early Archaean metamorphic

88JAN76 C S20-13/E030-01 N S20-13/E030-05 MSS 5   R SUN EL50 RZ100 189-4000-A-1-N-D-2L NASA ERTS E-2351-07150-5 01

Figure 3.9 LANDSAT image of central southern Zimbabwe. Compare with Figure 3.11. Running north–south in the centre of the image is the Great Dyke, with two mafic complexes clearly visible (centre and north). Parallel to the dyke are the mafic satellites: the West Dyke and the East Dyke (most visible in the north centre). Note the late faults cutting the dykes. All terrain cut by the dykes is Archaean. In the south-centre of the image is the Belingwe Belt (dark); on the east-centre edge are the Fort Victoria Belt and Mashaba Complex. The Selukwe Belt is north-centre. The 2.6-Ga Chibi Batholith is clearly visible running from south-centre edge to the north-east; south-east of it is the Mweza-Buchwa Belt. Featureless terrain showing river drainage in centre of image is 3.6 to 2.9-Ga gneiss and tonalite. Straight-line boundaries between light and dark areas are fences bounding forested farmland from degraded communal land. In south-east corner is the granulitic terrain of the northern margin of the Limpopo Belt.

assemblages imply temperatures of *circa* 600°C at 12 kbar (Chinner & Sweatman 1968; see Section 3.8.4).

On the craton proper (Figs. 3.10 & 3.11) 3.6 Ga old gneisses are common and often appear to incorporate relicts of earlier supracrustal volcanic or sedimentary rocks.

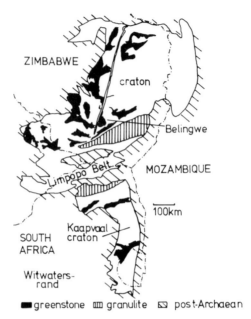

Figure 3.10   Archaean cratons of Southern Africa (from Nisbet 1984d).

3.4.3   Older greenstone belts

The older greenstone belts of the craton are collectively termed the Sebak-wian succession (Wilson 1979). They include assemblages of lavas and sediments best developed in the Selukwe, Lower Gwelo, and Mashaba regions, with scattered examples elsewhere mostly as remnants infolded with gneisses. The degree of deformation and metamorphism of these rocks varies from area to area: in a few places they are little strained, although the metamorphic grade is generally in the amphibolite or, in some areas, greenschist facies.

The Selukwe Belt near the town of Shurugwe (formerly Selukwe), is of great significance. Cotterill (1976, 1979) and Stowe (1968, 1984) have shown that the Sebakwian sequence here includes a variety of lavas and metasedimentary rocks (Ch. 7.5.2). A lower sequence (Table 7.1) includes magnesian basalts and possible komatiites (lavas with over 18% MgO) with

Figure 3.11   Geology of central Zimbabwe (from Wilson 1981). (a) Subdivisions of greenstone belts. Note that 'lower Bulawayan' is also referred to as 'lower greenstones' or here, as 'Belingwean'. (b) Distribution of late granitoids: (1) Sesombi tonalite, (2) Somabula tonalite, (3) Chilimanzi batholith, (4) Victoria porphyritic granitoid, (5) Zimbabwe batholith, (6) Mashaba igneous complex, (7) Shabani intrusion, (8) Gurumba Tumba – Filabusi intrusion, (9) Shangani intrusion.

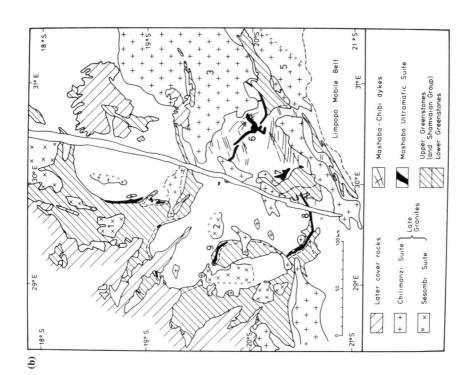

(a)

Later cover rocks

Shamvaian Group

Upper Greenstones (Bulawayan)

Lower Greenstones (Belingwean)

~ 3 500 Myr Greenstones

Granites and Gneisses

Approximate division between western and eastern
successions of Upper Greenstones

* Stromatolites

(Belingwe = Mberengwa)

Chegutu

Kadoma

Kwekwe

Gweru

Shurugwe

Gwenoro

Shangani

Fort Rixon

Filabusi

BULAWAYO

Belingwe

Zvishavane

Mashava

Mvuma

Felixburg

Chivhu

Limpopo Mobile Belt

Africa

Archaean Craton

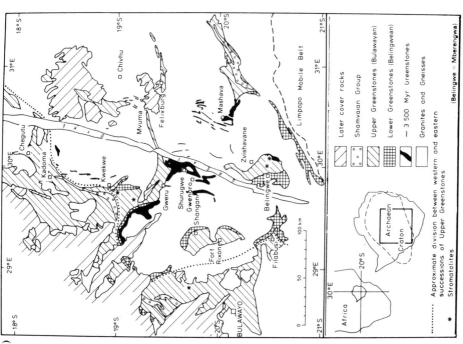

(b)

Later cover rocks

Chilimanzi Suite

Sesombi Suite

Mashaba - Chibi dykes

Mashaba Ultramafic Suite

Upper Greenstones
(and Shamvaian Group)

Lower Greenstones

Late Granites

Limpopo Mobile Belt

SELUKWE NAPPE LONGITUDINAL SECTION

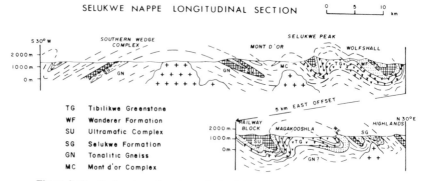

TG Tibilikwe Greenstone
WF Wanderer Formation
SU Ultramafic Complex
SG Selukwe Formation
GN Tonalitic Gneiss
MC Mont d'or Complex

Figure 3.12 Regional section through the Selukwe nappe (from Stowe 1984).

minor metapelite and banded ironstone, and was intruded by a major suite of ultramafic bodies, some with chromitite. Unconformably above this is the Wanderer Formation, a very diverse assortment of sediments showing rapid lateral facies variation from conglomerates to pelites and ironstones. The conglomerate includes clasts of talc-carbonate rocks, chromitite, metabasalt, jaspilite chert, granite and gneiss, showing how varied the 3.6-Ga surface was.

Cotterill (1976, 1979) and Stowe (1968, 1984) have shown that at least part of this Sebakwian terrain around Shurugwe is inverted, and was emplaced as a nappe or a series of nappes (Fig. 3.12). Movement on the nappe may have been 20 km or more (Cotterill 1976), and took place prior to intrusion of the Mont d'Or granite 3.35 ± 0.06 Ga ago (Moorbath *et al.* 1976). Elsewhere, in the Mashaba/Mushandike area, the upper, uninverted surface of the nappe may be preserved (Wilson 1979).

3.4.4 ?2.9 Ga granite–gneiss terrain

An extensive 2.9 ± 0.1 Ga granite–gneiss suite has been identified within the area between Mberengwa (Belingwe) and Mashava (Mashaba) (Wilson *et al.* 1978, Hawkesworth *et al.* 1979), and this may extend into the Limpopo Belt (Hickman 1976, 1978). Rocks of the suite include tonalites and gneisses. Not much is yet known about the distribution or the origin of these rocks; while it is tempting to erect a 2.9-Ga 'event', and to identify a 2.9-Ga 'terrain' on the basis of the few available dates and some reconnaissance mapping, such grouping is premature. Yet it is also needed; how else can one map? This illustrates one of the perennial problems of Archaean stratigraphy – the data are so fragmentary, and the error margins of geochronology so wide, that any bold attempt to group the stratigraphy runs the risk of lumping together unrelated strata.

3.4.5   The main greenstone successions

The main greenstone successions were laid down on the varied granite
–gneiss terrain described above. They consist of two discrete sequences, the
lower greenstones which are here *informally* termed 'Belingwean', and the
overlying 'Bulawayan' strata.

A. 'Belingwean' succession   The greenstones of the Belingwean succession have been correlated across a large part of the craton (Fig. 3.11, Table
3.2) through the work of Wilson (1981, 1979), and Wilson *et al.* (1978)
(Note: these authors refer to the Belingwean as 'Lower Greenstones' or in
some cases as 'Lower Bulawayan'). The lower part of the succession contains dacitic rocks – pyroclastics, flows and related intrusions. These are
overlain by an extensive and varied suite of coarse clastic sedimentary
rocks, siltstones and ironstones, thick komatiitic basalts and komatiites
associated with banded ironstone. Figure 3.13 shows the geology of the
type area, the Belingwe greenstone belt. The Belingwean succession is
almost certainly unconformable upon older basement (Fig. 3.14): the
contact is not clearly exposed but can be mapped as an unconformity; and
sedimentary facies in the basal deposits of the succession (Fig. 3.15) imply
the existence of a very proximal basement source terrain. It is possible that
some of the pyroclastic volcanism may have been coeval with the 2.9-Ga
tonalites.

B. Bulawayan succession   The 'Upper Greenstones' include the bulk of
the strata in the greenstone belts of the Zimbabwe craton, and have been
described variously (as the stratigraphic column has been refined) as
Bulawayan, Upper Bulawayan, and Upper Greenstones. They and the
locally developed Shamvaian succession which overlies them are about
2.7 Ga old. Wilson *et al.* (1978) and Wilson (1979) have shown that a correlation may be set up between the various remaining fragments of the
Bulawayan across the Zimbabwe craton over a lateral distance of over
200 km and a length of perhaps 700 km. In the east and in the lower part
of the western succession (Fig. 3.11) the bulk of the succession is a thick
sequence of komatiites, komatiitic basalt, tholeiites and associated
sediments. In the west of the craton the upper part of the succession is interbedded with dacite flows and pyroclastic material and is overlain by a
thick, mainly andesitic 'calc-alkaline' suite.

The Belingwe Belt provides the stratigraphic basis of the correlation. The
unconformity at the base of the Bulawayan succession is very clearly
exposed in several places (Fig. 3.16), with Bulawayan strata laid down
variously on Belingwean greenstones and older gneisses.

Many of the greenstone belts in Zimbabwe, especially in the west of the

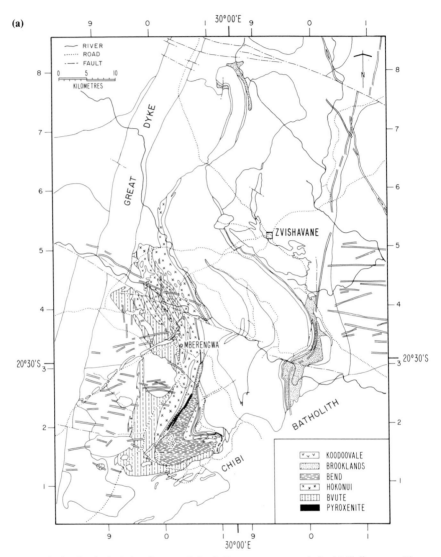

(a)

Figure 3.13 Geological sketch map of the Belingwe greenstone belt. (a) Belingwean ('lower

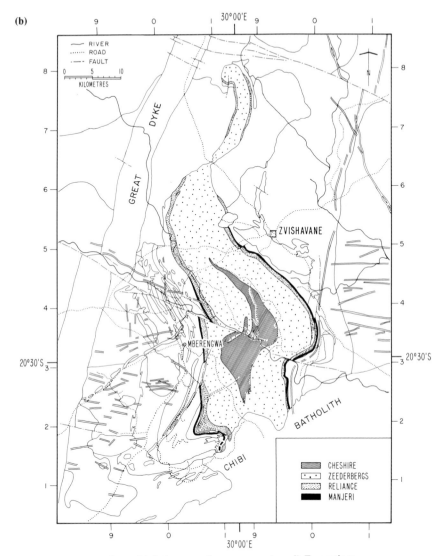

(b)

greenstones') Formations. (b) Bulawayan ('upper greenstones') Formations.

Figure 3.15 Coarse conglomerate with inverse grading, Brooklands Formation, Belingwe Belt.

Figure 3.14 Basement gneisses, Belingwe greenstone belt.

craton, contain thick sedimentary successions in their upper parts. This upper facies assemblage of sediments and minor volcanic rocks (often andesitic or dacitic) was termed the 'Shamvaian' by Macgregor (1947, 1951); its stratigraphic significance is now being reassessed, and it is not clear whether it is best treated as an upper division of the Bulawayan or as a separate succession.

3.4.6 Mafic intrusions

The main Bulawayan greenstone belts have been dated as *circa* 2.7 Ma (Wilson 1979, 1981). Associated with these belts, but poorly dated, are several major intrusive bodies, including the Mashaba ultramafic suite and various dyke swarms. The Mashaba Complex is a major layered intrusion of predominantly ultramafic composition. Nisbet (1982b) has suggested that it may be representative of the magma chambers which fed the Bulawayan lavas. The dykes may in part be feeder systems between the crustal magma chambers and the overlying lavas.

3.4.7 Younger granites

Most of the greenstone belts have been intruded and to some extent metamorphosed by younger granitoids (Fig. 3.11b). In the west the largely tonalitic Sesombi suite may have been derived from the mantle or from deep crustal granulites (initial $^{87}Sr/^{86}Sr = 0.701$), while in the east and the south the more potassic Chilimanzi suite may have had a major crustal component in its source (initial $^{87}Sr/^{86}Sr = 0.7025–0.7045$, Hawkesworth *et al.* 1979). The *circa* 2700 Ga ages and low initial ratios of the Sesombi suite make them indistinguishable from the andesitic volcanics of the western Bulawayan greenstone belts: it is tempting to suspect that tonalites and andesites were produced by the same melting process caused by the same tectonic event.

3.4.8 Great Dyke

The last major event on the Zimbabwe craton was the intrusion of the Great Dyke. The Dyke cross cuts all the older terrain (Fig. 3.9). It is a layered, dominantly ultramafic body, probably fed by a parental liquid with 15–16% MgO (Wilson 1982), closely comparable to some komatiitic basalts from the Belingwe Belt (Nisbet *et al.* 1977). In outcrop it appears to be a connected series of intrusions, rather than a continuous dyke. It is discussed in more detail in Chapter 7.

(a)

(b)

3.5 Construction of the Zimbabwe craton

How was the craton assembled? How did the continental crust grow? Nisbet *et al.* (1981) have shown that a continental nucleus has been present since the early Archaean, and from the earliest time there is sedimentological evidence for shallow-water deposition in some areas and for local high relief on land. Fresh material has been added to the crust from the mantle in a variety of events: several periods of greenstone belt volcanism probably derived magma from parental komatiitic melts ascending from the mantle; and an assortment of ultramafic and granitic intrusions has been added, with granitic material derived either from reworking of the lower crust or, perhaps, from partial melting in the lower lithosphere. At each stage, deformation, metamorphism, erosion and sedimentation have reworked the

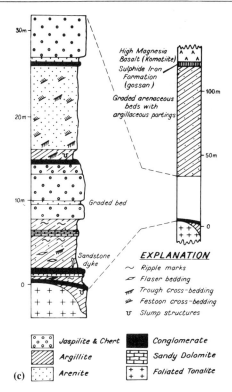

Figure 3.16 Basal unconformity beneath Bulawayan ('upper greenstone') succession. (a) General view: To left, weathered tonalitic gneiss. Hammer close to contact, which is marked by a line of white quartz clasts. To right, overlying tidal and shallow-water deposits. (b) Detail: to right weathered gneiss. Hammer-head on contact. To left, quartz-rich sediment. (c) Sketch section across unconformity (from Bickle *et al.* 1975).

pre-existing cratonic nucleus to weld it together as continental crust. The present craton has been largely undisturbed since 2.5 Ga ago: apart from the chance of its preservation and exposure, its history is probably representative of that of much of the world's older continental crust. Other areas were probably constructed by similar processes, but have undergone post-Archaean reworking or cover.

3.6 Other Archaean low-grade terrains

3.6.1 Barberton

The Barberton belt is important, because of its great age (*circa* 3.5 Ga), as the type locality of komatiites and as the location of important early evidence for life. *Komatiites* are defined as ultramafic lavas, or in other words, lavas with more than 18% MgO (Arndt & Nisbet 1982). *Komatiitic basalts* are magnesian lavas with less than 18% MgO. The Onverwacht Group, which contains the komatiites, has been dated as 3540 ± 30 Ma by Hamilton *et al.*, 1979, using the Sm–Nd technique. The Barberton Belt thus provides a window through which to view the early Archaean: in places the strata are not highly metamorphosed or strained (though elsewhere in the belt they are highly deformed), and they include a diverse array of unusual rock types.

Figure 3.17 shows the geology of the Barberton area, after Viljoen *et al.* (1982), who first discovered the komatiite succession (Viljoen & Viljoen 1969), The lavas and sediments of the greenstone belt are set in a granite–gneiss terrain (Jackson 1984) and intruded by a variety of ultramafic complexes (Anhaeusser 1985). The relationship between the greenstones and the gneisses and the structure within the greenstones is complex and controversial (de Wit 1982, 1983), in contrast to the much simpler story in the Belingwe belt. Parts of the gneiss complex are certainly as old as the Onverwacht Group (Barton 1981), but it is not at all clear whether or not the gneisses acted as a basement, and what controlled deformation (Lamb 1984, Anhaeusser 1984).

The Onverwacht Group contains a variety of komatiitic, basaltic and felsic lavas. A thin but important sedimentary horizon separates the lower lavas, which are dominantly komatiites or komatiitic basalts, from the overlying basalts and felsics. The ultramafic magmas have been emplaced as a variety of flows, dykes and sills. Flows are 0.3–20 m thick, sometimes massive and sometimes containing well-developed olivine spinifex texture, now preserved as pseudomorphs in serpentine. This texture, which is characteristic of komatiites, is a skeletal crystal form in which crystals

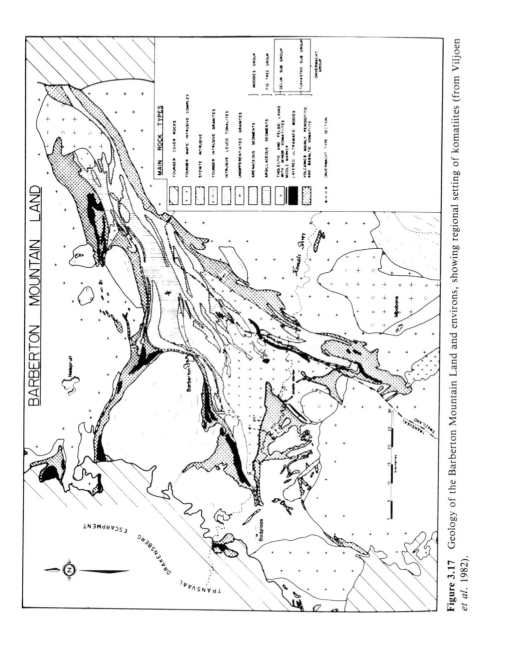

Figure 3.17 Geology of the Barberton Mountain Land and environs, showing regional setting of komatiites (from Viljoen *et al.* 1982).

display random or parallel grouping. Clinopyroxene also forms spinifex textures, characteristically in komatiitic basalts, but with elongate needles as compared to the plate-like olivine crystals.

The structure of the komatiitic sequence in the Barberton Belt is complex, and thus it is difficult to interpret the tectonic setting in which the lavas were erupted. Williams and Furnell (1979), and de Wit (1982), de Wit *et al.* (1982) and Lamb (1984) have shown that major tectonic discontinuities exist in the sequence, with large-scale thrusting. Both de Wit *et al.* (1986) and Hoffman *et al.* (1986) have suggested that part of the Onverwacht Group represents an Archaean ophiolite complex. If the implications of some of their work are correct, then the Barberton Belt may be one of the very few places where some information is preserved as to the nature of the Archaean ocean floor. It is very difficult to prove this, though, as the evidence is very circumstantial, and extremely controversial: Lowe and Byerly (1986) consider the succession to be of shallow-water origin.

In the upper parts of the Onverwacht Group in the Barberton Belt are assorted sedimentary rocks which include cherts and carbonates, and also sedimentary units which resemble turbidites. These rocks too have been the source of considerable controversy (Lowe & Knauth, 1977, Stanistreet *et al.* 1982, Heinrichs 1984). It is possible that the chert was deposited by turbidity currents from a felsic ash precursor. Accretionary lapilli in the rock may be indicators of sub-aerial eruption.

Overlying the Onverwacht Group are the Fig Tree Group and Moodies Group, containing thick sedimentary sequences (Tankard *et al.* 1982). The Fig Tree Group includes a northern facies development of graywackes and shales with minor cherts and ironstones, and a southern facies of coarse clastics. Lowe and Byerly (1986) consider that the bulk of the Fig Tree succession represents a volcanic interval, with extensive dacite volcaniclastic deposits as well as intercalated chert–pebble conglomerate and sandstone of local derivation. Interbedded ultramafic lavas and stromatolites also occur. These rocks pass up into the generally coarser conglomerates and arkoses at the base of the Moodies Group in the south, with subarkose and quartz arenite more common northwards. Other rocks in the Moodies Group include lavas, ironstones and shales. Very shallow water facies are common (Fig. 3.18).

In reconstructing the palaeogeographic setting of these rocks much depends on the interpretation of the complex structures. Which units are contemporaneous facies equivalents? Which units are structurally juxtaposed but widely separated in age? Textural interpretation within the sedimentary rocks is also difficult. What do the ironstones represent? At what depth were the chert deposited? The solutions to these problems can only be provided by detailed structural studies of a terrain where tectonic style may have been very different from modern analogues, and by 'boot-

Figure 3.18 (a) Olivine spinifex textures, komatiite, Komati Formation, Barberton Mountain Land. (b) Trough cross-bedding, Moodies Group, Barberton Mountain Land.

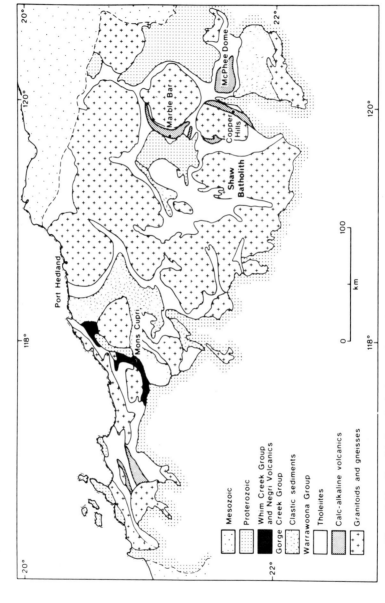

Figure 3.19 Simplified geological map of the Pilbara Block, Western Australia (from Barley *et al.* 1984).

strapping' sedimentological analysis, going from known facies or texture to facies or textures with no modern analogues.

3.6.2 The Pilbara

The Pilbara Block (*circa* 3.5 Ga) in the north of Western Australia contains strata of almost exactly the same age as the Barberton Belt. The block is large (Fig. 3.19) and contains perhaps the most extensive early Archaean greenstone sequence preserved (Fig. 3.20). There is an extensive literature on the Pilbara: good review discussions include those by Hickman (1981), Hallberg and Glikson (1981), Barley and Bickle (1982), Hickman (1984) and Blake and McNaughton (1984).

Detailed mapping, especially in the early 1970s, has enabled the

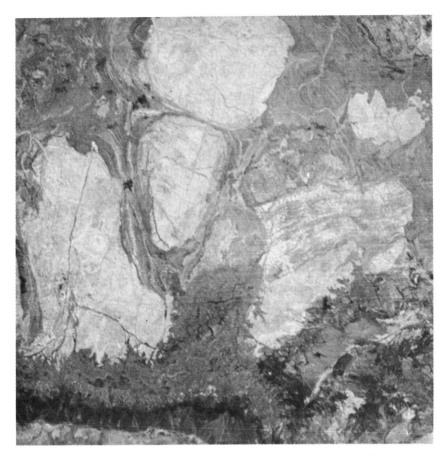

Figure 3.20 LANDSAT image of part of the Pilbara Block, Western Australia. Image approx. 170 km across, Marble Bar top left.

Geological Survey of Western Australia to set up a regional stratigraphic correlation across the entire Pilbara Block. Only in the Zimbabwe (Wilson *et al.* 1978, Wilson 1979) and Pilbara cratons (Hickman & Lipple 1978) has large-scale regional correlation been attempted in an Archaean greenstone terrain. The details of these correlations (and indeed of any correlation in Archaean terrains) may remain in dispute, but the work nevertheless demonstrates that even in greenstone belts, Archaean geology is subject to the same basic rules that William Smith used: despite structural complexity and difficult facies variations there is yet hope for the Archaean stratigrapher. Part of the significance of the studies by Hickman and Lipple (1975) in the Pilbara and by Wilson *et al.* (1978) in the Zimbabwe craton lies in the message that the problem *can* be tackled (although the solutions proposed may be disputed).

Figure 3.21 and Table 3.1 give details of the stratigraphy of the Pilbara. The greenstone sequence includes the dominantly volcanic Warrawoona

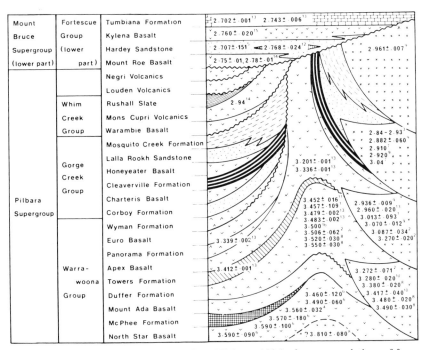

Figure 3.21 Diagrammatic illustration (from Hickman 1984) of common relations of formations and ages in the Pilbara Block. Symbols: bricks = limestone and tuff; vvv = basalt; inverted v = felsic; cross-hatch = ultramafic; dots = sandstone and conglomerate; dashes = turbidite, lines = pelites; heavy lines = banded ironstone; diagonal lines = chert; vertical lines = porphyry; crosses = granite; wavy line = unconformity; zigzag line = facies change; dashed line = uncertain.

Table 3.1 Simplified stratigraphy of the Pilbara Block (from Hickman and from Bailey *et al.* 1984)

Pilbara Supergroup	Formations	Lithology	Approximate thickness (km)
unconformity	Negri volcanics	basalt and andesite	0.2
unconformity	Louden volcanics	basalt and ultramafics	0.10
Whim Creek group (Cover 3 Ga – Barley *et al.* 1984)	Rusball slate	slate, minor tuff	0.2
	Mons Cupri volcanics	felsic volcanics	0.5
unconformity	Warambie basalt	basalt	0.2
	Mosquito Creek Fm.	psammite–pelite	5
	Lalla Rookh sandstone	sandstone, conglomerate	3
Gorge Creek group	Honeyeater basalt	basalt	1
	Cleaverville Fm.	banded ironstone	1
Soanesville Subgroup	Chateris basalt	basalt	1
	Corboy Fm.	metasediments	1.5
local unconformity	Wyman Fm.	rhyolite	1
Salgash Subgroup	Euro basalt	basalt, komatiite	2
	Panorama Fm.	felsic volcanics	1
Warrawoona Group (3.5 Ga)	Apex basalt	basalt, komatiite	2
	Towers Fm.	chert, basalt	0.5
	Duffer Fm.	felsic volcanics	5
Talga Talga Subgroup	Mount Ada basalt	basalt	2
	McPhee Fm.	carbonate schist, chert	0.1
	North Star basalt	basalt	2

Group, overlain by the dominantly sedimentary Gorge Creek Group. In the western Pilbara the younger volcanic Whim Creek Group overlies the Gorge Creek Group, although it is possible that some Whim Creek strata may be lateral equivalents of parts of the Gorge Creek Group (Barley & Bickle 1982). Zircon from the Duffer Formation has been dated at 3453 ± 16 Ma (Pidgeon 1978 – see Section 2.6.2), a date confirmed by Hamilton *et al.* (1981) and Barley and de Laeter (1984). Barley and de Laeter also showed that Rb–Sr systems had been extensively disturbed around 3 Ga ago.

The Warrawoona Group contains thick tholeiitic lavas together with cherty sediments and calc-alkaline volcanic rocks. In the eastern Pilbara the tholeiitic lavas appear to have floored a shallow-water platform or basin in which partly sub-aerial calc-alkaline centres were built up (Barley 1981; Barley *et al.* 1984). Calc-alkaline pyroclasts and volcanogenic sediments are interfingered with mafic lavas. In some areas komatiitic lavas occur in the

Warrawoona Group, both in the eastern Pilbara near Marble Bar, and in the western Pilbara (Nisbet & Chinner 1981) in rocks generally ascribed to the Warrawoona Group although the correlation is rather tenuous. Magnesian basalts are present in most mafic volcanic sequences in the Warrawoona Group.

Cherty sedimentary units in the Warrawoona Group are used as marker horizons for stratigraphic correlation, as they are readily identifiable in a generally mafic terrain. Some sediments in the Warrawoona Group include altered carbonates and evaporites, and locally sedimentary textures indicate local subaerial exposure. Possible stromatolites have been reported from a variety of outcrops (e.g. Buick *et al.* 1981).

The overlying Gorge Creek Group (Fig. 3.21) contains a sequence of platform to trough sediments (Eriksson 1981), minor magnesian basalts and ironstones. In the eastern Pilbara alluvial sediments occur in the same general area that contains shallow water Warrawoona sequences, while in the southeastern and central Pilbara, turbidite troughs are developed. Possibly granitic crust was being eroded to the north of the greenstone basin during this period. The Whim Creek Group is dominantly a sequence of calc-alkaline lavas with associated sediments of shallow to deep-water facies; the group is overlain in the west by magnesian lavas displaying spinifex textures.

What was the basement to the Warrawoona Group, if any? Much of the evidence hinges on sedimentological interpretation. Barley *et al.* (1979) describe extensive shallow-water environments existing in the eastern Pilbara throughout the evolution of the Warrawoona Group. They postulate the existence of a large shallow basin studded with calc-alkaline volcanoes and locally with evaporitic lakes (Dunlop & Buick 1981). Almost certainly the basement to this basin was continental, though the argument is circumstantial and based mainly on isostatic logic. Hickman (1981) has pointed out that quartz sandstones near Marble Bar could provide evidence of a granitic continental source. The Gorge Creek Group contains granitic pebbles which appear to have been derived from a continental land mass. The uppermost formation, the Lalla Rookh Sandstone, was laid down in an intracratonic basin which seems to have been unrelated to a continental margin but instead formed a discrete basin within a continent (Krapez 1984). In strong contrast to this picture of the east Pilbara, some mafic and ultramafic lavas of the west Pilbara (Nisbet & Chinner 1981) may have been extruded as new crust, without pre-existing basement.

3.6.3 The Yilgarn

The Yilgarn craton, in the south of Western Australia, is a huge but for the most part rather poorly exposed Archaean continental block, containing rocks which range in age from at least 3300 Ma to late Archaean greenstones (Fletcher *et al.* 1984). The regional geology has been reviewed by Hallberg and Glikson (1981). Detailed geophysical work has been carried out to determine the present crustal structure, as shown in Figure 3.22. This structure has presumably not changed very greatly since late Archaean times; possibly it provides a glimpse of the structure of late Archaean continents.

The Yilgarn includes material of very great age; in the 3.3–3.5 Ga Mount Narryer quartzites and nearby Jack Hills area, Compston and colleagues (Froude *et al.* (1983)) have found detrital zircons which have been identified by ion microprobe as 4.1–4.3 Ga old (Section 2.6.1), although Scharer and Allègre (1985) failed to confirm the discovery. About 60 km north-east of Narryer, Compston and Pidgeon (1986) have found more evidence of very old material in the Jack Hills area, including one zircon which gives 4276 ± 6 Ma as a minimum age. Presumably a terrain of this age was formed, and then at *circa* 3.0–3.5 Ga exposed and eroded. Moorbath (1983) discussed the implications of this observation. One explanation, and much the most probable, is that the 4.2-Ga terrain was a continental region: however, Moorbath cautions that zircon occurs in Icelandic granophyre – 'four zircon grains do not necessarily make a continent'. Nevertheless, the implication is very strong that silicic differentiates did occur on the earliest Archaean crust. Continents are essentially aggregates of silicic differentiates from the mantle, but how extensive the earliest silicic differentiates were is unknown. Chemical differentiation from part of the early mantle is not necessarily synonymous with continental crust formation.

The Yilgarn is not discussed further here, although some economic deposits in the province are described in Chapter 7. For more stratigraphic detail, the reader is referred to Hallberg and Glikson (1981).

3.6.4 Cratons in the Canadian Shield

The Canadian Shield contains three major Archaean cratons: the Slave, Superior (Ayres & Thurston 1985) and West Greenland/Nain provinces. The bulk of the rocks in the first two provinces are *circa* 3.0–2.5 Ga old. The West Greenland/Nain Province, on the other hand, is known to contain rocks up to 3.8 Ga old.

The Slave Province (Padgham 1985) contains several large supracrustal belts set in a sea of plutonic metamorphic rocks ('supracrustal' is often used by Northern-Hemisphere geologists to describe the same relatively low-grade assemblages of lavas and sediments which are more often termed 'greenstones' in the Southern Hemisphere, although the term also includes high grade assemblages derived from material once laid down on the Earth's surface). In the Yellowknife 'basin', the largest of the supracrustal belts, extensive lavas are associated with a thick suite of turbidites and

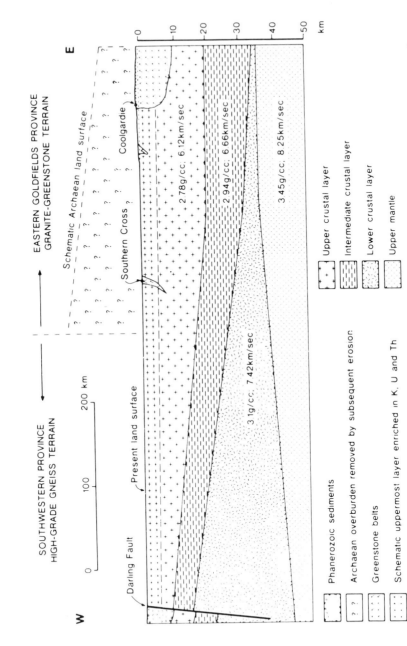

Figure 3.22 Cross section across the Yilgarn Block between Perth and Kalgoorlie (from Archibald *et al.* 1981). The section shows the Archaean greenstone belts in relation to major crustal features of the region.

mudstones. Figure 3.23 is a speculative reconstruction of the original depositional environment, from Henderson (1981). It should be noted that the mafic volcanics are restricted to the edge of the fault-bounded basin, in contrast to the distribution inferred from Belingwe or Barberton, where lavas are thought either to be close to the floor of the succession, to constitute the bulk of the succession, or to occupy the centre of the basin. In contrast to this 'basinal' model, Hoffman (1986) has suggested that the succession is the record of a prograding trench–arc system. The greenstone belts are seen in Hoffman's model as being synformal remnants of a formerly continuous complex of tectonically accreted seamounts, remnant arcs, aseismic ridges, submarine plateaux and microcontinents. Hoffman's model has the interesting property that it accounts for both unconformable (trench inner-slope) and subconformable (trench outer-slope) relations between volcanics and overlying turbidites, and allows the existence of older basement (microcontinents) and syn-greenstone plutons (accreted arc roots). In this context, one of the most interesting outcrops in the Slave Province is at Point Lake. Here a clearly exposed unconformable basement is seen (Henderson, 1975a, Easton 1985), with conglomerates and sandstones overlying granitic basement (Fig. 3.24).

A third model of the Yellowknife greenstone belt is different yet again. Helmstaedt *et al.* (1986) draw a comparison between mafic rocks at the base of the Kam Group in the Yellowknife Supergroup and sheeted dyke complexes in young ophiolites. On the basis of this comparison they suggest that the Yellowknife belt formed as a consequence of sea-floor spreading in an Archaean marginal basin setting.

The term 'basin' has often been abused in the Archaean literature, especially in description of the Canadian Shield. Walker (1978) pointed out very strongly that a basin cannot be identified without detailed sedimentological analysis. The Yellowknife Belt is one of the few Archaean supracrustal successions in Canada where sedimentary facies variations (from fluvial sandstones to conglomerates to turbidites) may eventually allow the depositional setting to be identified. The debate between proponents of basinal or rifting models (Henderson 1981, Easton 1985) and supporters of trench–arc models (such as Hoffman's) is of general interest in Archaean terrains. Often the record has been much obscured by deformation (which may or may not be of much later age), and it is very difficult to be certain of what really happened. In the circumstances, Occam's razor – *essentia non sunt multiplicanda praeter necessitatem*' (hypotheses should not be multiplied unnecessarily) –usually rules, until precise zircon dating upsets the pretty and simple notions.

Before leaving the Slave Province, it is also worth noting that stromatolites occur in it (Henderson 1975b).

The southern Canadian Shield contains the vast Superior Province,

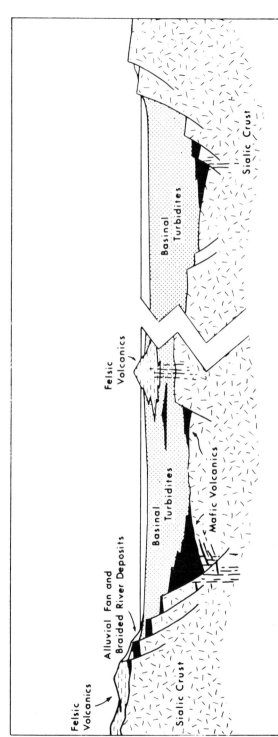

Figure 3.23 Model of a fault-bounded Archaean basin (Yellowknife) in which greywacke–mudstone turbidites derived from the basement and felsic volcanics on the uplifted basin margin are the main basin fill (from Henderson 1981). Contrast this with the Belingwe Belt (Fig. 3.40).

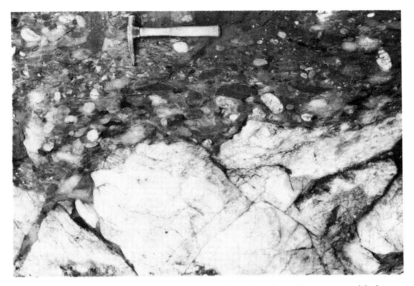

Figure 3.24 Basal unconformity at Point Lake, Slave Province, between granitic basement and overlying granitic and volcanic pebble conglomerate. Fractures in the unconformity surface are filled with pebbles. Scale is 43 cm long. (From J. B. Henderson.)

nearly 1 million km^2 of granite–greenstone terrain. Most of the terrain (80%) is granitic, but it includes several very extensive belts of volcanic and sedimentary rocks (Fig. 3.4). The largest of these is the Abitibi Belt, 650×225 km and perhaps the largest greenstone belt extant (see map in Ayres *et al.* 1985). It contains a very extensive sequence of lavas, with an apparent stratigraphic thickness of 20 km or more. Much of this thickness may be the result either of tectonic stacking or of deposition on a subsiding, tilting basement, but nevertheless the belt does contain some very major volcanic piles. Lavas include komatiites, such as those at Munro Township (Arndt *et al.* 1977), basalts, andesites, rhyolites and even leucite-bearing rocks (Goodwin 1979). The latter are almost unique in the Archaean record. The associated thick sedimentary units include greywackes, conglomerates, shales and ironstones. Although extensive submarine fans probably exist, detailed basin analysis is only beginning. Ludden *et al.* (1986) have interpreted the Abitibi Belt as the result of a superimposition of younger rift basins upon an older terrain of massive basaltic to andesitic to dacitic volcanics. The older terrain is approximately 2720 Ma or older. Between 2710 Ma and 2700 Ma a series of rift basins, dominated by komatiites and tholeiites, formed in a setting which may have been similar to modern North Island, New Zealand, or the Hokuroko basin of Japan. Further descriptions of parts of the Abitibi sequence are given in Chapters 6 and 7.

3.6.5 Greenland/Nain Province

Finally in this section of brief descriptions of some 'classic' supracrustal Archaean terrains, comes the Archaean Gneiss Complex of the North Atlantic region, which is best developed in West Greenland, although related rocks occur in eastern Greenland, Labrador, northwestern Scotland and northern Norway. It contains a variety of both high-level and deeper-level rocks. In particular, the Isua supracrustals, which occur in a small belt north-east of Nuuk (Godthaab), contain the oldest Archaean supracrustal rocks known. Figure 3.25 outlines the major components of the Archaean of the West Greenland/Labrador region. In Labrador, the geological evolution was similar to that in West Greenland (Korstgard & Ermanovics 1985).

The Isua belt (Fig. 3.26) contains a variety of supracrustal rocks, now deformed and metamorphosed. The sequence is approximately 3.8 Ga old (Moorbath & Taylor 1981) with igneous activity dated at $3769 \pm {}^{11}_{8}$ Ma by

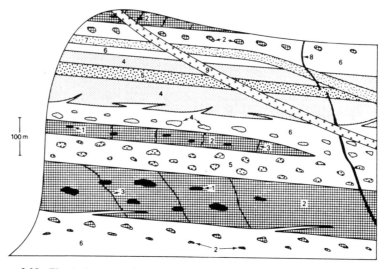

100 m

Figure 3.25 The Archaean continental crust. Hypothetical vertical section through part of the Archaean gneiss complex, West Greenland and Labrador (from Bridgwater *et al.* 1978). All contacts are either tectonic or intrusive and individual rock units are highly deformed (except the youngest granites), and their conformable nature is due to tectonic rotation. (1) Amphibolites, layered basic complexes, ultrabasic masses and metasediments. Isua supracrustals (3.76 Ga). (2) Tonalitic and granodioritic gneisses (Amitsoq and Uivak gneisses), 3.7 Ga. (3) Amphibolite dykes. (4) Amphibolites, ultrabasic rocks, metavolcanics and metasediments (e.g. Malene supracrustals *circa* 2.9 Ga, and Upernavik supracrustals older than 3.1 Ga). (5) Layered anorthosite complexes (2.8 ± 0.2 Ga). (6) Tonalite, granodioritic and locally granitic gneisses emplaced as subconcordant sheets into gneiss complex (e.g. Nûk gneisses, 2.8–3.0 Ga). (7) Igneous complexes emplaced at least in part under granulite facies conditions (*circa* 2.8 Ga). (8) Basic and intermediate dykes. (9) Late to post-tectonic potash-rich granites and pegmatites (*circa* 2500 Ga).

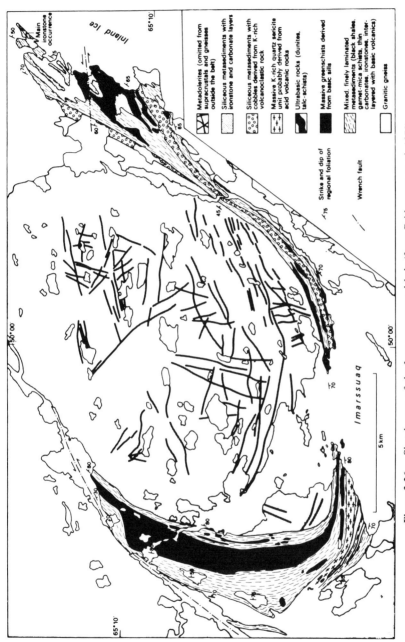

Figure 3.26a Sketch map of the Isua supracrustal belt (from Bridgwater *et al.* 1978).

Metadolerites (omitted from supracrustals and gneisses outside the belt)

Siliceous metasediments with ironstone and carbonate layers

Siliceous metasediments with cobbles derived from K-rich volcaniclastic rock

Massive K-rich quartz sericite unit probably derived from acid volcanic rocks

Ultrabasic rocks (dunites, talc-schists)

Massive greenschists derived from basic sills

Mixed, finely laminated metasediments (black shales, garnet-mica schists, thin carbonates, ironstones, inter-layered with basic volcanics)

Granitic gneiss

Strike and dip of regional foliation

Wrench fault

Main ironstone occurrence

Inland Ice

Imarssuaq

5 km

65°10'

50°00'

65°10'

50°00'

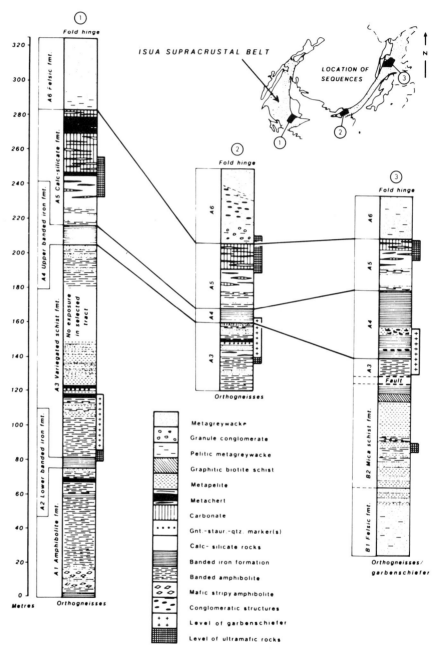

Figue 3.26b   Stratigraphic columns, Isua supracrustal belt (from Nutman *et al*. 1984).

Sm–Nd whole-rock analysis (Hamilton *et al.* 1978) and at 3770 ± 42 Ma by U–Pb zircon studies (Michard-Vitrac *et al.* 1977).

The Isua Belt is of great importance in view of its remarkable age: many of its aspects are discussed in later sections of this book. Nutman *et al.* (1984) and Nutman (1984) summarise the stratigraphy of the belt, which is a fragment of a more extensive early Archaean sedimentary and volcanic succession, intruded by and perhaps tectonically intercalated with gneisses, and metamorphosed to amphibolite facies assemblages. Over half of the belt (Fig. 3.26) consists of layered sequences of sedimentary and probably volcanic rock, associated with intrusive mafic and ultramafic rocks. Two layered sequences can be distinguished, in faulted contact. Well-preserved graded layering is present in felsic metasediments, and overall the succession changes upwards from mainly basic to mainly felsic volcanism; from the products of this volcanism the clastic sediments were derived. Interlayered chemical sediments include banded ironstones, metachert, and calc-silicate rocks. Some sedimentary structures such as the lateral facies changes and possible flat pebble conglomerates imply shallow water conditions with occasional shoals. The sediments could all have been locally derived – there is no necessary implication that a continent (in the modern sense) existed, since the Isua suite could have been a small silicic fragment in a dominantly simatic crust. Nevertheless, the existence of silicic fragments would imply that at least in some places there was a topographic dichotomy: some regions did stand out of the water (as the sedimentary facies show). The continents were, at least, beginning, if only as fragments comparable to modern island arcs; how extensive they were is not known.

Other extensive Archaean greenstone terrains exist in India, Brazil, the Soviet Union, Finland, China and Guyana, amongst other places. These are not discussed here, in what is simply a brief survey of a few areas, but Condie (1981) gives many details, as do Salop (1982), Windley and Naqvi (1977) and Bernasconi (1983).

3.7 Gneiss terrains

Most Archaean greenstone belts are closely associated with large domains of foliated to gneissic tonalite–granodiorite. Often the relationship between the relatively high-level greenstones and the granitoids is complex. In some cases, the granitoids are at high structural level, have suffered little deformation and are clearly post-greenstone (e.g. the younger granitoids discussed in Section 3.4). In other cases, the granitoids are older and more deformed, and their contacts with the greenstones may be difficult to interpret (e.g. as in the Older Greenstone Belts discussed in Section 3.4.3). The relationship between greenstones and gneisses was touched on in the last section: in this section it will be explored in more detail with examples of rocks formed at intermediate levels in the crust.

3.7.1 The problem of gneiss domes: Wabigoon and Chinamora

Schwerdtner (1984) and Schwerdtner *et al.* (1985) have described the intimate association between anastomosing Archaean metavolcanic belts and large regions of foliated or gneissic tonalite and granodiorite in the Wabigoon subprovince of the Canadian Shield, west of Lake Superior. The term gneiss 'dome' is used by the author in a purely morphological sense.

The typical domes consist of tonalite–granodiorite, surrounded by concentric bands of supracrustal remnants. Foliation is horizontal at the centre of the domes and dips outwards at other localities (Fig. 3.27). The margins of the domes are hard to define: Schwerdtner regards the gneiss domains as oval structures bounded by amphibolite-rich zones. The margins and leucocratic cores of many ovals are characterised by oblique foliation and are far from domical.

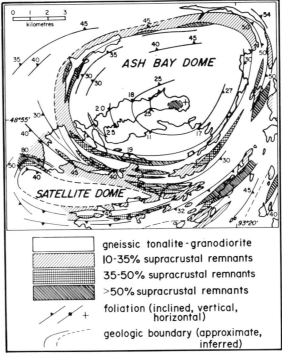

Figure 3.27 Structure of the northwestern part of the Rainy Lake gneiss domain, Northwestern Ontario, Canada (from Schwerdtner 1984).

There is considerable controversy about the origin of these structures. They may have been formed by diapiric uprise of granitic material (Macgregor 1951) or by polyphase deformation. Snowden and Bickle (1976) and Snowden (1984) have demonstrated that in the Chinamora batholith, Zimbabwe (one of Macgregor's original examples), the latter explanation is more likely to be correct. Figure 3.28 shows the local structural setting and Snowden's explanation of the development of the batholith. Field mapping in the 'batholith' has demonstrated its complex and composite nature, including old gneisses, gneissic granites and late granites. The Chinamora Porphyritic Granite was one of the last granites to be intruded: within it, Snowden has shown that K-feldspar megacrysts are oriented in a fabric which implies that emplacement of the granite was syntectonic with a deformational event. Megacrysts grew with preferred orientation during the final stages of magma crystallisation. During this compression the sheet-like Chinamora Porphyritic Granite was buckled about northeasterly trending axes. Structures formed in this deformation were later refolded in a further event, marked by minor folds defined in late veins and dykes. A consequence of the interference of structures formed during the two events was the formation of a roughly circular composite 'batholith', called a 'structural batholith' by Snowden (1984) encircled by and infolded with greenstone belt rocks.

3.7.2 Horizontal structures in the crust: The Pilbara, Yilgarn and Limpopo

Figure 3.12 shows the Selukwe nappe, a high-level structure in the Rhodesian craton (see also Table 7.1). Many Archaean terrains show evidence for major horizontal movement, sometimes with nappe-like structures forming (Anhaeusser 1984, Myers 1984, Jackson 1984). There is extensive evidence at intermediate to deep levels in the gneiss terrains for major horizontal movement. In the Pilbara (Fig. 3.19), the old gneisses and granites are extensive and in places well exposed, but the problem of their relationship to the greenstones is not simple. For many years the granite–greenstone terrain around Marble Bar (Fig. 3.20) was cited as a classic example of groups of granite diapirs rising as 'gregarious batholiths', after the model of Macgregor (1951), now reinterpreted in the Zimbabwe craton (Snowden 1984). Detailed work by Bickle et al. (1980, 1985) has shown this model is incorrect in the Pilbara too. Instead, the batholiths are complex bodies whose shape is structurally controlled by polyphase deformation. The Shaw batholith has been studied in considerable detail (Fig. 3.29). The oldest events so far deciphered involve interleaving of extensive granitoid rocks with supracrustal components including metasediments. This early gneiss terrain was extensive and the present outline of the batholith bears no relationship to the distribution of gneiss components. Gneiss–greenstone interleaving may have involved subhorizontal movement (Fig. 3.29, 3.30). At this later stage, some diapirism may indeed have occurred (Hickman 1984).

Myers and Watkins (1985) have suggested a similar process in the Yilgarn Block, where they interpret the granitoid–greenstone outcrop pattern to be a result of large scale dome-and-valley fold interference structures rather than diapirism. Granitoids and greenstones were initially deformed together in a subhorizontal tectonic regime. This produced a gneissosity in the granitoids subparallel to the stratigraphy of the greenstones. Later deformation produced two successive sets of folds with vertical axes at high angles to each other, giving interference structures up to 50 km in diameter.

Coward (1984) has contrasted major shear zones in Precambrian (mainly Archaean, but with late Archaean to Proterozoic deformation) crust from northwestern Scotland and the Limpopo Belt. The intensity of deformation

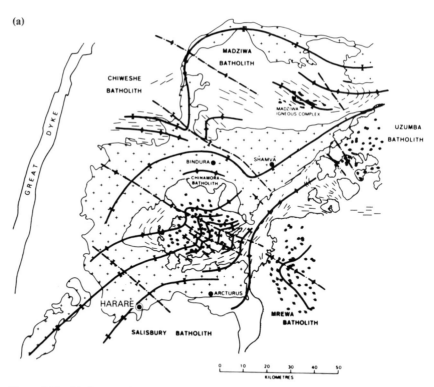

Figure 3.28 (a) Structural map of the north-central part of the Zimbabwe craton (from Snowden 1984). (b) Cartoons to show stages in the development of the batholiths of the northern part of the Zimbabwe craton (from Snowden 1984).

in Precambrian orogenic belts is very variable, and the model of large scale heterogeneous simple shear is most applicable. Within the shear zones Coward demonstrates how the shear direction and thus the relative plate movement vector can be estimated from fabric orientations, from folds such as sheath folds and from lateral ramps or steps in the shear zone (Fig. 3.7). Both in the example Coward describes in northwestern Scotland and also in the Limpopo Belt, deformation took place on gently dipping shears associated with crustal compression developing structures rather analogous to those seen in high level, thin-skinned regions. Coward's work and Bickle *et al.*'s (1985) conclusions are characteristic of the conclusions arrived at by many Archaean structural geologists: very major horizontal motions took place within the Archaean crust. These motions are most simply interpreted as the result of plate motions.

(b)

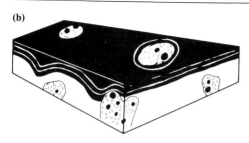

STAGE 1

Greenstones deposited on a gneissic basement and then intruded by tonalite diapirs

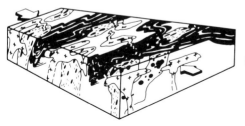

STAGE 2

Greenstones are infolded with various syntectonic granites and basement in a regional compressive deformation

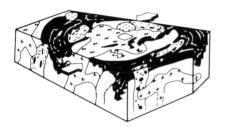

STAGE 3

A second regional compressive deformation causes cross folding. This results in a composite granitic dome or batholith surrounded by greenstone belts

81

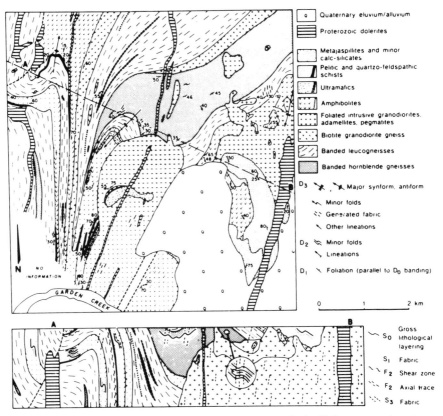

o	Quaternary eluvium/alluvium
	Proterozoic dolerites
	Metajaspilites and minor calc-silicates
	Pelitic and quartzo-feldspathic schists
	Ultramafics
	Amphibolites
	Foliated intrusive granodiorites, adamellites, pegmatites
	Biotite granodiorite gneiss
	Banded leucogneisses
	Banded hornblende gneisses

D₃ — Major synform, antiform

— Minor folds

— Generated fabric

— Other lineations

D₂ — Minor folds

— Lineations

D₁ — Foliation (parallel to D₀ banding)

0   1   2 km

So — Gross lithological layering

S₁ — Fabric

F₂ — Shear zone

F₂ — Axial trace

S₃ — Fabric

Figure 3.29 Geology and schematic cross section of the Fairwig Well area, southwestern Shaw Batholith, Pilbara. Note the complexity of the interleaving between granitic and 'greenstone' components. (From Bettenay *et al.* 1981.)

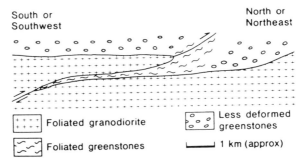

South or Southwest   North or Northeast

Foliated granodiorite   Less deformed greenstones

Foliated greenstones   1 km (approx)

Figure 3.30 Schematic section illustrating possible thrust mechanism responsible for intercalation of greenstones within gneisses in the Shaw batholith (from Bickle *et al.* 1980).

3.8 Archaean high-grade terrains

3.8.1 The Charnockites of South India

Job Charnock appears to have been a most interesting if execrable individual. Apart from fathering the city of Calcutta (a city which later gave us isostasy) and numerous other progeny, and acquiring a wife by rescuing her from metamorphosis by self-immolation on her former husband's funeral pyre, he attained immortality by being himself buried under a tomb of charnockite. An excellent illustration of a thin section cut by some devious means from this solemn slab is given and discussed by Chinner, in Nockolds *et al.* (1978). Charnockite is the granulite facies anhydrous equivalent of the granitoid (quartz–two feldspar–mica ± hornblende) mineralogy, and has the characteristic assemblage quartz–orthoclase–plagioclase–hypersthene. The presence of mesoperthite intergrowths of equal amounts of exsolved sodium and potassium feldspar indicates that the original crystal crystallised at temperatures above the alkali feldspar solvus. Garnet is present in more aluminous charnockite such as that derived from muscovite granite. More sodic rocks with quartz–plagioclase–pyroxene mineralogy ('dioritic') are termed 'enderbites', while 'syenitic' charnockite, with potash feldspar, is called 'mangerite'.

South India consists mainly of a very extensive late Archaean granulite terrain (Fig. 3.31). The Archaean of South India can be divided into a northern greenschist–amphibolite facies terrain, and a southern granulite facies terrain. South of Bangalore a progressive metamorphic tract has been recognised, culminating in granulite assemblages (Hansen *et al.* 1984), and many lithological and structural features of the gneiss–greenstone association can be traced southwards into the granulites (Harris *et al.* 1982).

The granulite terrain consists of a very varied association of metasedimentary and meta-igneous rock. The original compositions of the rocks probably varied from assorted basic rocks, now mafic granulites, through tonalites and trondhjemites to granites, now charnockites. Metasedimentary rocks are represented by pelitic gneisses interlayered with quartzites and calc-silicates. Several crustal blocks can be identified, divided from each other by Proterozoic shear zones, which allow the exposure of different crustal levels (Harris *et al.* 1982). The Nilgiri Hills are composed of acid to intermediate charnockites and rare pyroxenites; the Kodiakanal Massif contains charnockites (in part extensively retrogressed) and interlayered metasediments; and the Nagercoil Massif contains metapelites interlayered with both garnetiferous and non-garnetiferous charnockites.

Harris *et al.* used geothermometry and geobarometry to obtain fields of pressure–temperature equilibration. High pressure granulites, with $P = 8.3 \pm 1$ kbar and $T = 760 \pm 40°C$, occur in the charnockites and mafic

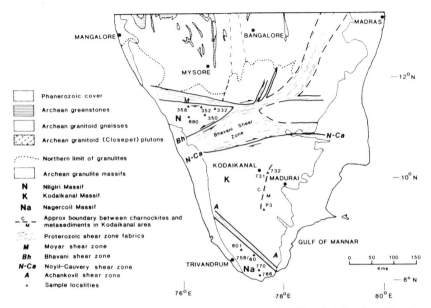

Figure 3.31 Geological sketch map of the high-grade terrain of South India (from Harris *et al*. 1982).

granulites in the north slopes of the Nilgiris, and indicate that the Archaean crust was at least 30 km thick (Harris *et al*, 1982; Janardhan *et al*, 1982). Metamorphosed mafic and ultramafic rocks from the Sargur supracrustal series nearby give similar P–T results, and suggest a minimum crustal thickness of 35 km (Srikantappa *et al*. 1985).

3.8.2 Enderby Land, Antarctica

A very extensive Archaean granulite terrain is preserved in the Australian Antarctic Territory and provided rocks suitably intractable and attractive to engage the attention of Mawson and Tilley in the 1930s. Sheraton *et al*. (1980) and Sandiford (1985) have summarised the results of Australian and Soviet research in the area.

Enderby Land is part of the East Antarctic Shield, and contains two major metamorphic complexes – the Napier Complex, including material 3.9 Ga old (Black *et al*. 1986), and the Proterozoic Rayner Complex. The Napier Complex mainly consists of pyroxene–quartz–feldspar and garnet–quartz–feldspar gneiss, associated with mafic granulite, pyroxenites and assorted silica, aluminum and iron-rich metasediments. Parts of the complex reached conditions of at least 900–980°C at 8–10 Kbar, in the intermediate pressure granulite facies (Ellis & Green 1985; see also Harley 1985). Potassic

84

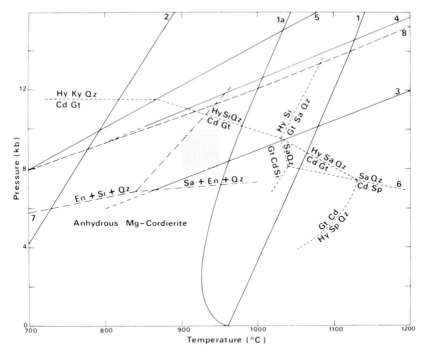

Figure 3.32 P–T diagram, with stippled area showing estimated conditions of metamorphism in the Tula Mountains, Enderby Land, Antarctica (from Sheraton *et al.* 1980). (1) Dry granite solidus (1a) Estimated granite solidus for $P_{H2O} = 0.25\ P_{Total}$. (2) Crest of alkali feldspar solvus. (3) Appearance of garnet in mafic rocks of olivine tholeiite composition. (4) Appearance of garnet in rocks of quartz tholeiite composition. (5) Kyanite/sillimanite boundary. (6) Univariant phase boundaries for reactions in pelitic rocks. (7) Stability limits of enstatite and sillimanite and quartz, sapphirine and enstatite and quartz and anhydrous magnesian cordierite. (8) A possible Archaean geotherm.

mesoperthite charnockite gneiss predominates in part of the area, including the Tula Mountains, while more sodic, enderbitic gneiss is abundant around Casey Bay in the southern Scott and Ragatt mountains. The presence of sapphirine, which occurs in the metapelites associated with quartz, orthopyroxene and osumilite, and common calcic mesoperthites indicates very low water pressures in metamorphism. Figure 3.32 shows estimated pressures and temperatures of metamorphism in the Tula Mountains of the Napier complex. Sandiford (1985) estimates the peak metamorphic crustal thickness at 35–56 km. Though thick, this is less than the sum of the present crustal thickness (35 km) and burial depths indicated by exposed assemblages. Possibly there has been post-Archaean addition to as well as erosion of the crust.

3.8.3 The Pikwitonei domain

Next, an example from Canada. Arima and Barnett (1984) have investigated sapphirine-bearing granulites in the Pikwitonei granulite terrain in northern Manitoba. Sapphirine occurs in orthopyroxene–cordierite and in feldspar–sillimanite granulites. In the orthopyroxene–cordierite rocks conditions of metamorphism are estimated to have been 860–890°C and 3–11.2 kbar. In the feldspar–sillimanite granulites, sapphirine is a relict phase mantled by sillimanite or by successive coronas of sillimanite and garnet. The compositions of the minerals imply metamorphic conditions of 780–880°C and about 9 kbar. In comparison, Ellis (1980) estimated rather hotter (900–980°C at 8–10 kbar) conditions for osumilite-bearing assemblages in Enderby Land. Osumilite appears to be absent from the Pikwitonei rocks.

In general, Archaean granulites often preserve mineral assemblages which crystallised under about 30 km of crust, at about 700–1000°C.

3.8.4 The Limpopo Belt

The Limpopo Belt links the Zimbabwe and Kaapvaal cratons in Southern Africa, with as its limiting boundaries the orthopyroxene isograds at the flanks of the cratons (Watkeys 1983). Figure 3.33 shows the distribution of metamorphic facies, from Robertson and du Toit (1981) who describe the granulite terrain in Zimbabwe as consisting of a sea of granitic granulite gneiss (a Zimbabwean field term used for a granitic gneiss which is pyroxene-free but appears to have undergone granulite-grade temperatures) in which are islands of charnockites, enderbites and scattered deformed and folded metasedimentary and metaigneous inclusions.

The inclusions appear to represent remnants of greenstone belt material. Most common are mafic granulites with pyroxene–plagioclase ± hornblende ± biotite assemblages. Metamorphosed banded ironstones also occur, as well as calc-silicates and sapphirine-bearing assemblages presumably derived from limestones and argillaceous sediments. Some metamorphosed mafic–ultramafic complexes occur. Parts of the Limpopo Belt are of very great age, possibly older than 3 Ga (Barton & Key 1981, see also Harris 1985).

In the Beitbridge region, Watkeys (1979) and Broderick (1979) have mapped an extraordinarily diverse terrain including garnetiferous paragneisses of pelitic and arkosic origin, magnetite quartzites, mafic granulites and calc-silicates, which may be younger than associated (early Archaean) old basement gneisses. The metamorphic assemblages preserved in the supracrustals are extremely varied, including sapphirine and kornerupine-bearing assemblages. Chinner and Sweatman (1968) found

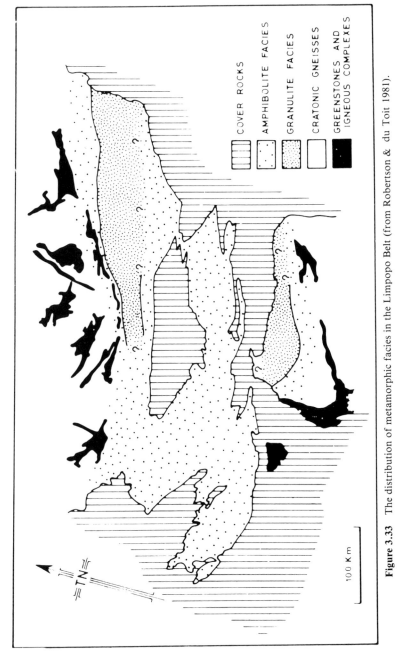

COVER ROCKS

AMPHIBOLITE FACIES

GRANULITE FACIES

CRATONIC GNEISSES

GREENSTONES AND
IGNEOUS COMPLEXES

TN

100 Km

Figure 3.33 The distribution of metamorphic facies in the Limpopo Belt (from Robertson & du Toit 1981).

evidence for an early kyanite–enstatite assemblage, indicating pressures of 10–12 kbar and temperatures perhaps as low as 600°C. However, equilibria recorded in the preserved supracrustal assemblages imply conditions of 4–5 kbar, and temperatures above 670°C (Harris & Holland 1984). Possibly the rocks underwent rapid decompression from 40 km depth to 15 km, at a time prior to 2.6 Ga (Harris 1985). These rocks are further discussed in Section 5.7.3.

3.9 The information available in Archaean terrains

Each type of Archaean terrain contains a characteristic set of clues to the nature of the young Earth. The greenstone terrains tell us about the surface of the Earth, the environment in the shallow seas and the beginnings of life. They also have much to say about the state of the mantle and the tectonic regime, through the information contained in the volcanic rocks. In contrast, the information in the gneiss and granulite terrains is mostly about the history of the continents, how they grew and the processes of metamorphism and mountain building that went on. Each topic and each terrain is interesting in itself, yet the Archaean Earth is best seen as a whole, reconstructed piece by piece from the fragments of information locked up in the individual rocks and rock assemblages. The chapters which follow attempt to use this fragmentary information to reconstruct aspects of the whole, in order to describe in a coherent fashion what is known or can be guessed at. In exploring unknown territory false steps and bad guesses are common: much that is speculated upon today will be shown to be wrong tomorrow, and even more disturbingly, the commonly accepted 'facts' of the Archaean have a habit of being disproven. The solid ground turns to quagmire. Nevertheless, without exploration, nothing can be found.

It is worth considering in detail an example of the diversity of rocks which can be found in an Archaean terrain. The Belingwe Belt in Zimbabwe contains a splendid assortment of rocks, problems and information about the Archaean Earth, and is described here in some detail to show the types of challenges the field geologist can meet in a good area: one day it may be stromatolites and thoughts about early life, the next komatiites and complicated pictures of mantle evolution.

3.10 An example of an Archaean field area: the Belingwe Belt, Zimbabwe

3.10.1 Stratigraphy

The Belingwe Belt and surrounding rocks (Table 3.2) include an extraordinary variety of strata; they constitute what is almost a microcosm

Table 3.2 Simplified stratigraphy of the Belingwe greenstone belt

Great Dyke (2.5 Ga)		
Younger Granites (2.6 Ga)		
	Cheshire Fm.	conglomerate, limestone, siltstone, shale up to 2.5 km
Ngezi Group	Zeederbergs Fm.	basalt up to 5.5 km
	Reliance Fm.	komatiite and komatiitic basalt 0.5–1 km
	Manjeri Fm.	shallow water–deeper water sediments 100 m
unconformity		
	Koodoovale Fm.	conglomerate, agglomerate
Mtshingwe Group	Bend and Brooklands Fm.	komatiite, komatiitic basalt, assorted sediments
	Hokonui Fm.	intermediate to felsic lavas and pyroclastics
unconformity?		
Chingezi gneiss, Mashaba tonalite (2.9 Ga)		
Shabani gneiss (3.5 Ga)		
schist inclusions		

of the Zimbabwe craton, or of the Archaean in general. They range in age from 3.6 Ga or more to 2.5 Ga, and include widely assorted igneous, metamorphic and sedimentary rocks. Of the 'older' rocks, there are assorted gneisses and tonalites (Fig. 3.34) dated at *circa* 3.6 Ga and 2.9 Ga, with Limpopo granulites a few kilometres to the south-east. Of the supracrustals, there are actually two distinct greenstone belts, one overlying the other; and there is also a major ultramafic body and various younger instrusions.

3.10.2 The 'Basement'

Those rocks which underlie the greenstones are collectively termed 'Basement'. They include a wide variety of gneisses of *circa* 3.6 Ga which have undergone polyphase deformation and general amphibolite facies metamorphism. To the south-east the metamorphic grade rises to granulite facies. The gneisses include a great variety of rock types: in some places, pelitic assemblages imply that the rocks were originally sedimentary; elsewhere the more common mafic stringers must have been derived from igneous parents – dykes and lavas. Clearly the gneisses are the deformed and metamorphosed product of a long sequence of events including eruption of lavas, deposition of sediments and intrusion of granites. In most respects the gneisses are little different from Proterozoic or Phanerozoic gneisses except that pelitic assemblages are relatively rare. Although it has

Figure 3.34 Agglomerate, Hokonui Formation, Belingwe Belt.

been suggested that temperatures may have been slightly higher at given pressures than in younger examples, there are no striking differences. Yet this is some of the oldest continental crust extant in Africa. In Hutton's dictum, there is here no 'vestige of beginning'; apparently all that is preserved is a repeated sequence of greenstone belt formation, deformation and intrusion by granitoid melts derived from a variety of crustal and mantle sources.

Intruding into the 3.6-Ga terrains is a set of *circa* 2.9-Ga tonalites and gneisses. Apart from being younger, these are not obviously different from the 3.6-Ga strata. It is quite probable that this 2.9-Ga terrain is coeval with the formation of the lower part of the older greenstones.

3.10.3 Older greenstones

The older greenstones of the Belingwe Belt constitute the Mtshingwe Group, here informally termed the 'Belingwean' succession. There are four formations (Table 3.2). The Hokonui Formation, which is probably the lowest stratigraphically, contains 2–3 km of dacitic pyroclasts, and andesitic flows. At the base of the formation is a spectacular vent agglomerate (Fig. 3.34) which includes huge blocks of surrounding 2.9 Ga tonalitic country rock: elsewhere this tonalite is apparently intrusive into the Hokonui. Quite possibly the tonalite is the plutonic equivalent of the pyroclastics: similar problematic time relationships occur elsewhere in the

Zimbabwe craton and present extremely difficult mapping problems to the field geologist. It is probable that most of the major granitic intrusions were broadly contemporaneous with overlying dacitic or andesitic volcanism.

In the south of the belt, apparently unconformable on the Hokonui Formation, is the Bend Formation. This is a remarkable pile of komatiites (Fig. 3.35), komatiitic basalt and banded ironstones 2–5 km thick. From the absence of clastic sediment it is possible that volcanism took place well away from any source of detritus. In contrast, to the east of the belt, the Brooklands Formation contains very thick coarse conglomerates and breccias, passing to an assortment of komatiitic and komatiitic basalt lavas, shales and ironstones. The Brooklands Formation may be laterally equivalent to the Bend Formation: if so, a facies transition is preserved, from trough edge, through coarse proximal sediments, to distal sediments to komatiites and ironstones. Overlying the Bend Formation is the Koodoovale Formation, which consists of 1 km of coarse conglomerates and felsic volcanics.

The entire Mtshingwe Group succession was warped and partly eroded prior to deposition of the younger greenstones in the Belingwe Belt: there are thus two quite distinct greenstone successions in the belt. This is seen across much of the craton – obviously, the older greenstones stood a much better chance of preservation where they underlay younger greenstones. Part of this 'chance' must be in the erosional history, since if a younger

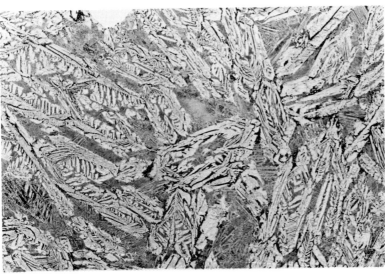

Figure 3.35 Wholly altered komatiite, preserving skeletal olivine textures (now serpentine), tremolite–actinolite after pyroxenes between crystals, and fine-grained groundmass after glass (with thanks to J. L. Orpen and W. E. Cameron).

greenstone is preserved, what is underneath it will also be preserved; but part may reflect some general crustal weakness where the greenstone belts are now preserved. This would explain why the older greenstones were *not* eroded just in that place where the younger greenstones were later deposited.

Problems of this sort are not easily answered, since the evidence is so fragmentary. Yet they are the typical problems of Archaean geology. They irritate the mind of the field geologist; they demand models. Occasionally those models can be tested and lead to theory.

3.10.4 Younger greenstones

The younger greenstones form the Ngezi Group, part of the Bulawayan succession. They overlie all the older strata with marked unconformity (Figs. 3.13, 3.16). The unconformity can be traced right round the belt, stepping across older gneisses and older greenstones. This is perhaps the best example known of a greenstone belt laid down wholly on continental crust. Before the contact was described in detail (Laubscher 1963, Oldham 1968, Bickle *et al.* 1975), many geologists thought greenstone belts to be in some way analogous to modern ophiolites. In other words, greenstone belts were seen as possible Archaean oceanic material. This is still a tenable hypothesis in some belts (e.g. Barberton; Ruth Well, Pilbara), but the Belingwe Belt very clearly demonstrates that at least one belt (and, by correlation, most of the belts in the Zimbabwe craton) was laid down on old, established continental crust (Bickle *et al.* 1975).

The basal formation of the Ngezi Group is the Manjeri Formation (0–100 m). This contains basal conglomerates and beach sands lying on the basement (Fig. 3.16), which pass up to a variety of shallow-water sediments. These often display intertidal sedimentary structures (Fig. 3.36), and include stromatolitic limestones. The facies changes upwards to deeper water deposits (Fig. 3.37), overlain by lavas of the Reliance Formation (*circa* 1 km thick). These lavas include komatiitic basalts and komatiites, erupted as flows, pillow lavas and tuffs. They include some very unusual outcrops of komatiitic pillow lavas (Fig. 3.38).

Above the Reliance Formation are roughly 5 km of basaltic lavas, the Zeederbergs Formation, mostly pillows and flows with little or no interbedded sedimentary material. Suddenly there is a major break and the uppermost formation of the belt, the Cheshire Formation, is dominantly sedimentary. It begins with basal conglomerates derived from the Zeederbergs Formation, which pass laterally into ironstones. These pass into shales and siltstones and an assortment of shallow-water sediments, including very extensive limestones which in places are profusely stromatolitic (Fig. 3.39). The top of the formation is not seen.

(a)

Figure 3.36 Ripple marks in the Manjeri Formation, Belingwe Belt, above the unconformity outcrop. (a) Bedding surface. (b) Normal to bedding.

(b)

Scattered around the edges of the Belingwe Belt are several major mafic to ultramafic intrusions (Fig. 3.11). The most important of these is the Shabani ultramafic body, but several of the others are also of considerable size. Much of the granite–gneiss country rock is cut by mafic or komatiitic dykes, which may or may not be related to the intrusions. It is extremely

Figure 3.37 Upper Manjeri Formation, unconformity locality, deeper water facies.

difficult to date the intrusions, except by the use of cross-cutting dykes, and there is as yet little to suggest or to refute the suggestion that the intrusions are in some way related to the lavas within the greenstone belt.

The Shabani Complex is a huge slab mainly of ultramafic rock, exposed on the north-east edge of the Ngezi Group. It consists of a simply differentiated, sill-like igneous body of layers of dunite which give way upward through peridotite and pyroxenite to gabbro. It outcrops over an area of 15 km × 2.5 km, dips at 60° southwards and is 1500 m thick. Seventy per cent of the sill is dunite, 20% peridotite and pyroxenite and 10% gabbro. The question obviously arises: is the Shabani Complex in some way a magma chamber from which some eruptive lava suite was derived? The massively ultramafic nature of the complex suggests an origin as a magma chamber fed from below by ultramafic liquid – a stratified chamber in which doubly diffusive processes operated to produce voluminous low-density basalt lava overlying major ultramafic cumulate deposits (Fig. 3.40). Whether or not such a model is viable, whether or not the Shabani Complex is representative of the type of magma chamber which fed the Zeederbergs lavas is a matter for speculation; but it is this type of question which provides some of the interest and challenge to Archaean petrologists – and also to economic geologists, since the economic potential of huge ultramafic bodies is considerable (see Section 7.6).

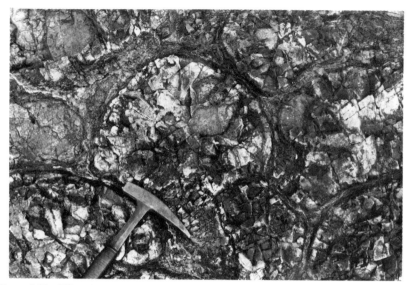

Figure 3.38 Pillow lavas in komatiite, Reliance Formation, Belingwe Belt (from Bickle *et al.* 1975).

3.10.5 Younger granitoids

To the south-east of the Belingwe Belt and cutting off its southern tip is the Chibi Batholith. This is a 2.6-Ga body of adamellite and granodiorite which may have been derived by partial melting of deeper-level gneisses (Hawkesworth & Bickle 1976). This batholith is similar to many in the south and east of the Zimbabwe craton: the bodies are probably huge sheets of granitoids emplaced at high levels in the crust and giving the upper crust its characteristic appearance of 'greenstone belts set in a sea of granite'. Macgregor (1951) suggested that the granitoids were 'gregarious', rising like bubbles from below. Recent mapping elsewhere in Zimbabwe (Section 3.7.1) has shown this hypothesis to be incorrect, but it is nevertheless true that an enormous volume of granitoids was rapidly emplaced in sheet-like bodies at high level. A possible modern parallel would be the emplacement of high-level plutons in the Sierra Nevada, California. The granites were then deformed with the greenstone belt rocks in two regional tectonic events. Thus, although individual plutons within the batholiths intruded as diapirs, the 'batholiths' did not, and the granitoid–greenstone belt relationships now seen are a result of multiple regional deformation (Snowden 1984).

Figure 3.39 Stromatolites, Cheshire Formation, Belingwe Belt (from Bickle *et al.* 1975).

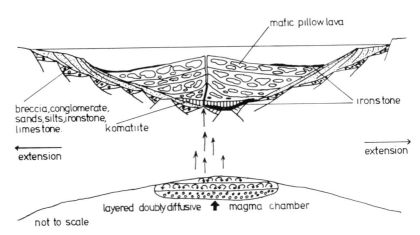

Figure 3.40 Cartoon to show possible development of thick mafic lavas succession in Belingwe Belt.

3.11 The Archaean record: a basis for interpretation

The various examples given in this chapter show some of the diversity of
the Archaean record, and how information can be extracted from what are
usually very complex and often poorly exposed rocks. Many other well-
known Archaean terrains have not been discussed here: each is unique and
important, and omitted not because of insignificance but rather because of
a desire to illustrate some of the less famous areas. In general, though,
the Archaean record preserves for us a complex set of information about
the nature of the Archaean surface, crust and mantle, and it is from this
information that we must attempt to reconstruct the Archaean Earth. In the
following three chapters this attempt is made, using the various lines of
evidence to reconstruct the Archaean surface, crust and mantle, descending
through the Archaean Earth. In the last chapter the reconstruction is
further developed, from mantle to surface, showing how each part of the
Earth influences and is dependent on the others.

PART II
Reconstructing the Archaean Earth

4 The beginnings of life

...drawing from its rocky bowels palaeontological treasures
which have caused no little degree of astonishment here, more
especially as the rocks were generally supposed to be Primary and
non-fossiliferous

A. G. Bain to Sir Henry de la Beche,
1844, Fort Beaufort, Cape of Good Hope

Bain, the first Southern African geologist, was studying what are now known to be Phanerozoic rocks, yet his successors have indeed drawn convincing evidence from the Archaean that life *did* exist, and flourished, in the early part of the Earth's history. 'How life began' is one of the great questions of natural science: a geologist cannot presume even to approach the problem, which is in the domain of the molecular biologists, geneticists and mathematicians. What geology *can* do, though, is to 'set the stage'. The study of Archaean rocks can provide central evidence as to *when* life began, under what conditions, and in what environment the miracle took place. There is much evidence, discussed in this and the following chapters, that the existence of life is of crucial significance to the geological evolution of the planet: life has played an important role in shaping the development of the atmosphere and in much of the history of the oceans. All sedimentary geology has been controlled or influenced in some way by the activity of living organisms. More than that, by helping to constrain CO_2 levels in the atmosphere and hence the surface temperature of the planet, life may have exerted a profound influence on the metamorphic and tectonic development of the crust and upper mantle.

4.1 Geological evidence for life

What geological evidence is available? There are several sources of information: stromatolites – structures built by algal and bacterial colonies; microfossils – the microscopic relics of life preserved in the rock (which must be disembowelled in the laboratory); organic residues in the rocks; and finally, those isotopic signatures in sediments (e.g. of carbon) which imply biological control. Detailed reviews of the available evidence are given in Schopf (1983).

101

Much of this evidence is contradictory and difficult to interpret (Nisbet 1980, Nisbet & Pillinger 1981). As a consequence, great controversy surrounds most claims of evidence from Archaean life. Many rock structures of inorganic origin can be misinterpreted as stromatolites, rocks can be contaminated during weathering or in the laboratory, with the introduction of 'modern' microscopic objects, or of modern organic chemicals (not to mention fingerprints and dandruff), and isotopic ratios can be reset by metamorphism or misinterpreted. Geology is a science, and the answer to every question is either 'yes' or 'no', yet in the study of Archaean life as in so many other aspects of geology the answers can only be 'I think so, because...'. The problem is similar to that of the zoo keeper confronted by a fat gorilla whom he thinks may be pregnant. The evidence is inconclusive, and the keeper can only balance the probabilities, yet either she is or she is not. But perhaps all is not lost: as medical science improves, more tests become available. Perhaps they can wait... Cloud and Morrison (1979) pointed out that the evidence for the existence of Archaean life should be weighted according to its reliability. They divided the evidence into three categories, best described here as 'possible', 'probable' (or 'presumptive'), and 'almost certain'. Only in a handful of Archaean localities is there almost certain evidence for the existence of life, but there is a considerable body of 'presumptive' evidence, including evidence from rocks as old as 3.5 Ga. Such evidence – for instance, a stromatolite, a microfossil or an isotopic signature – if found in a Mesozoic rock, would be accepted without question, but in the early Archaean the burden of proof is much greater as it has not yet been fully accepted that life did definitely exist before 3.5 or even 2.7 Ga ago. We *think* there was life in early Archaean time; many of our models of the development of the atmosphere and the oceans *demand* the existence of life from very early on in the Earth's history; but even a large body of 'presumptive' evidence is not equal to a single really convincing piece of 'almost certain' evidence. Only in the late Archaean (2.7 Ga) is there this sort of unequivocal evidence, though there is very strong presumptive evidence from 3.5-Ga strata.

4.1.1 Stromatolites

Much of the evidence is from stromatolites (Fig. 4.1), which are worth considering in detail. Buick *et al.* (1981) have discussed the definition of the term 'stromatolite', which was introduced by Cloud (1942), after Kalkowsky (1908). Most geologists consider that stromatolites are structures in sedimentary rocks (usually carbonates or chert) that have been constructed or put together as a result of the activities of living organisms such as bacteria or algae. However, the term has been variously used to describe either (a) structures of diverse shapes but all accreted by organic activity,

Figure 4.1 Modern stromatolitic growths, Shark Bay, Western Australia. (Photo by G.A. Chinner.)

or (b) in a morphological sense, to describe any sedimentary accretionary structure composed of hemispheroidally or spheroidally shaped laminae. Buick *et al.* (1981) sought to resolve this conflict by using two terms. 'Stromatolite' describes organosedimentary structures predominately accreted by sediment trapping, binding and/or *in situ* precipitation as a result of the growth and metabolic activities of benthic, principally pro-caryotic micro-organisms. 'Stromatoloid' on the other hand, they reserved for 'structures which are morphologically similar to stromatolites, but of uncertain origin' (i.e., possibly abiological).

Buick *et al.* went on to set up criteria for recognising stromatolites. Although not every stromatolite satisfies every one of these criteria, they form a useful set of tests to apply. Loosely stated, the criteria are that the structures must occur in what were once sedimentary rocks, and the structures must be proven to be synsedimentary. If so, there should be a preponderance of convex-up structures (see Fig. 4.2; this is characteristic of stromatolites), and laminae should thicken over the crests of structures (since growth is fastest in the best-lit areas on the top of stromatolites). Laminae should typically have wavy, wrinkled or strongly curved shapes

Figure 4.2 Typical convex-upward structures in Archaean stromatolites. 10 cm across photo. Note that often it is difficult to distinguish in the field between small stromatolitic hemispheres and local small-scale folding. Field criteria used to discriminate between these possibilities include the continuity, regularity and shape of the structures, which should young consistently and coherently. Petrographic examination is necessary to support field opinion. (From Bickle *et al*, 1975).

(Fig. 4.3). Sometimes microfossils or organic remnants occur in association with the stromatolites. Finally, and critically, there should be solid evidence that a synsedimentary microbiota accreted the structure.

4.1.2 Growth of stromatolites

Modern sediments laid down by the activity of algae or cyanobacteria are very varied in structure. Material composing the sediment may include the remains of micro-organisms, trapped detrital material, and material introduced during endolithic boring by metabolically controlled precipitation or by migrated pore fluids. The best evidence in ancient rocks that a rock is stromatolitic is the identification of filaments binding the sediment, or structures such as bores or fenestrae which are evidence of organic activity. It is this sort of evidence which can provide the critical final criterion for the recognition of a stromatolite.

4.1.3 Possible and probable early Archaean stromatolites

Rocks which may be stromatolites have been described from 3.5-Ga strata in three areas: the Pilbara, the Barberton Mountain Land and the Zim-

Figure 4.3 Stromatolitic laminae, Steep Rock Lake, Ontario.

babwe craton. Strong early Archaean evidence comes from the Pilbara (Buick *et al.* 1981, Lowe 1980, 1982, Walter *et al.* 1980) in rocks discovered by R. Buick and J. Dunlop. Many of the structures in the area which are morphologically similar to stromatolites and have been interpreted as such do not meet the stringent criteria set up by Buick *et al.* (1981), and are best described as stromatoloids: nevertheless, Buick *et al.* consider that some structures from the area do indeed meet enough of the tests to be termed 'possible' stromatolites. A few structures contain kerogen-rich laminae and are considered to be 'probable' stromatolites. However, Buick *et al.* stress that none of the structures yet discovered at North Pole (an exceedingly hot locality in Australia) can be proven to satisfy the critical criterion that a synsedimentary microbiota accreted the structure.

Byerly *et al.* (1986) have discovered a morphologically variable group of

Figure 4.4a) 3.3–3.5-Ga old stromatolites directly overlying brecciated top of komatiitic lava flow. Barberton Mountain Land, South Africa (from Byerly *et al.* 1986). Small basal domes are covered by large, slightly asymmetric domes. These are in turn overlain by very low-relief laminae with high inheritance. Coin is 2.5 cm (1 inch).

Figure 4.4b) Pseudo-columnar stromatolites in a thin (1 m) chert between komatiitic lava flows, Barberton (from Byerly *et al.* 1986).

probable stromatolites in the Fig Tree Group, Barberton Mountain Land, South Africa. The host rocks are thought to be at least 3.3 Ga old. Probable stromatolites occur in at least three areas, preserved in grey–black finely laminated chert. The stromatolitic structures are made up mainly of microcrystalline chert, laminae being defined by alternation in grain size and by the presence of other minerals such as tourmaline, sericite and iron oxides.

Most commonly, the stromatolitic structures are low-relief, laterally linked domes (Fig. 4.4a). Elsewhere, pseudo-columnar structures occur (Fig. 4.4b), and in general there is a considerable variety of apparently organic morphology in the rocks. Byerly *et al.* did not find any evidence for microfossils in the rocks, but concluded that the diversity and detail of the morphology of the structures was good evidence that the features were of organic origin, accreted by synsedimentary microbiota.

In outcrop the stromatolites are closely associated with silicified komatiite flows showing well-developed spinifex textures (Fig. 4.5). The surface of the flows is irregular: in some places stromatolites grew directly on pinnacles of komatiite, elsewhere 1–18 m of sediment separate the stromatolites from the lava.

Elsewhere in the Barberton Belt, de Wit *et al.* (1982) have recognised a variety of probably abiogenic and also some biogenic structures, *circa*

107

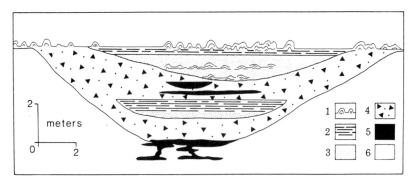

Figure 4.5 Cross section showing general setting of stromatolites in Figure 4.4, from an individual outcrop. 1 = stromatolites; 2 = banded cherts, 3 = sandstone, 4 = breccia, 5 = massive black chert, 6 = komatiite lavas. Up to 18 m of relief existed on top of the lava flows, which may have been eroded. Channels were filled with breccia and sandstone. (From Byerly *et al.* 1986).

3.5 Ga old. The abiogenic structures are composed of a variety of concentric, millimetre-thick laminae, and are similar to structures which have elsewhere been used as supposed 'evidence' for stromatolites (Fig. 4.6).

De Wit *et al.* conclude that the structures were most probably formed abiogenically in hydrothermal mud pools (Fig. 4.6). Other fascinating structures in the area are also probably of inorganic origin (Fig. 4.7). However, de Wit *et al* do identify other structures in the areas as possible stromatolites (Fig. 4.8). These structures meet most but not all of the set of criteria established by Buick *et al.* 1981, and they are closely comparable in fabric to the better-established late Archaean stromatolites from the Belingwe greenstone belt (see below). In particular, de Wit *et al.* describe domical laminated forms which may very well be the metamorphosed equivalents of some structures seen in the Belingwe Belt. Walter (1983) pointed out that if the Barberton fabrics are accepted as stromatolitic, analogies can be drawn between structures described by Muir and Grant (1976) and pustular mat structures built today by cyanobacteria in Shark Bay, Western Australia.

Finally, in this catalogue of early Archaean evidence, there are structures (Fig. 4.9) reported by Orpen and Wilson (1981) from the Mushandike Sanctuary, Zimbabwe. The rocks have been metamorphosed, and in thin section there is no clear evidence for algal filaments although well developed laminae and fenestrae are present. However, most of the other criteria of Buick *et al.* are met, and thus the Mushandike structures are 'probable' stromatolites (Abell *et al.* 1985). The problem is in the dating of the structures; field work (Orpen & Wilson 1981) implies that they may be *circa* 3.5 Ga old, but the rocks are close to a major unconformity, the area

Figure 4.6 Possible 'mudpool' structure, formed abiogenically by emanation of gas, Barberton Mountain Land (from M. J. de Wit).

Figure 4.7 Cavity infill, probably abiogenic but possibly not, Barberton Mountain Land (collection C. M. R. Fowler).

Figure 4.8 Stromatolite-like structures, Barberton Mountain Land (from A. Martin).

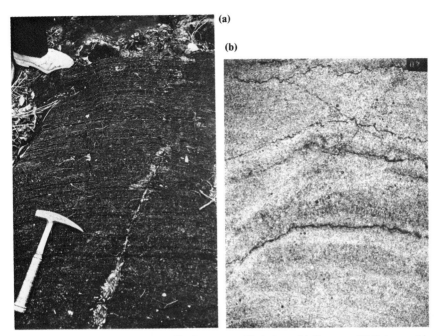

Figure 4.9 Stromatolites, Mushandike Sanctuary, Zimbabwe. (a) Outcrop. (b) Petrographic detail. Field of view 17 mm × 13 mm.

is structurally complex, and it is possible that the carbonates have been isotopically reset, making them difficult to date. The available information is contradictory and it is not certain that these are early Archaean strata. The problem is fascinating and typical of the difficulties faced by Archaean field geologists in general.

4.1.4 The mid-Archaean

One of the most interesting reports of evidence for life in the mid-Archaean (*circa* 2.9 Ga) is that of Mason and von Brunn (1977). They report 'probable' stromatolites in a shallow-water sedimentary sequence in the Pongola Supergroup (Section 3.3.1) of northern Natal, South Africa, laid down unconformably upon an older granitoid basement (Matthews & Scharrer 1968). The rocks include a repetitive sequence of quartz arenites and dolomites with subordinate siltstone–mudstone units. There is considerable evidence that deposition took place in a tidal setting, and the wide variety of sedimentary structures reported by Mason and von Brunn (1977) includes evidence for dessication. The 'probable' stromatolites are generally of low relief, rarely rising more than a few centimetres above their contemporary substrates, and set in host dolomite. They are generally low domes.

111

In thin section they show fine lamination, fenestrae and are generally very similar to modern 'blue–green algal' or, more properly termed, cyanobacterial mats. Walter (1983) has compared these structures with similar structures formed by the modern cyanobacteria *Phormidium hendersoni*, *Rivularia haematites* and *Phormidium tenue*. The similarity suggests that these mid-Archaean stromatolites were built by finely filamentous microorganisms which grew up towards the light.

4.1.5 Late Archaean stromatolites

In the late Archaean geological record (mostly around 2.7 Ga) there are several examples of undisputed stromatolites. These include rocks from the Slave Province (Henderson 1975a,b), from the Fortescue Group, Australia (Walter 1983) and Ushi (Hofmann *et al.* 1985) and from Steep Rock in the Superior Province (Jolliffe 1955, Wilks & Nisbet 1985), Canada, as well as at least six examples from the Zimbabwe craton. Good specimens of these – indeed, amongst the best preserved of all evidence for the existence of life in the Archaean – are from the Belingwe greenstone belt (Bickle *et al.* 1975, Martin *et al.* 1980, Abell *et al.* 1985a).

The Belingwe stromatolites are approximately 2.7 Ga old. There is no doubt about the Archaean age of the strata as there is good isotopic and

Figure 4.10 2.7-Ga stromatolites, Manjeri Formation, Ngezi Group in the Belingwe greenstone belt, Zimbabwe.

structural evidence that the Belingwe Belt is older than the Great Dyke. Stromatolites occur in the Ngezi Group both in the basal Manjeri Formation and in the uppermost Cheshire Formation. In the Manjeri Formation they are only locally developed (Fig. 4.10), but they are widespread in the Cheshire Formation. Figure 4.11 shows some examples of the stromatolites and the associated sedimentary rocks. The stromatolites themselves are very varied in size and shape, and range from wavy laminations to large domes with radii up to 400 mm. In some cases the inheritance is several metres ('inheritance' refers to the height across which a set of concentric laminae can be traced, while 'synoptic height' is the relief of an individual lamina in a dome above its substrate). In outcrop, Martin *et al.* recognised 33 distinct stromatolitic beds, which they grouped together in 22 cyclic units (Fig. 4.12). In thin section the rocks are extremely well preserved, with little or no optically detectable metamorphic recrystallisation in some samples.

(a)

Figure 4.11 (a) 2.7-Ga stromatolites, Cheshire Formation, Ngezi Group in the Belingwe greenstone belt, Zimbabwe (from Nisbet 1985b; photo M. J. Bickle). (b) Large domical stromatolites, built by clotty lamination (horizon 29, Fig. 4.12). (c) Domical or nodular stromatolites produced by radiating crystal structures. White square is approximately 4 cm across. (d) Well-developed radiating crystal structures in polished slab. Approximately 50 cm across photograph. (e) Small branching stromatolites similar in morphology to *Baicalia*. (f) Polished block, showing unusual conophyton-like stromatolites. (g) Ripple marks with trilete cracks in argillaceous troughs between silty ripple crests. Scale in centimetres. (h) Coquina-like breccia with clasts set in a recrystallised and sparry calcite matrix. (Figs. b-h from Martin *et al.* 1980.)

(b)

(c)

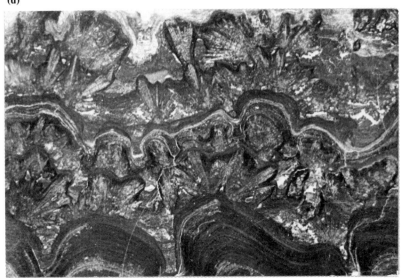

(f)

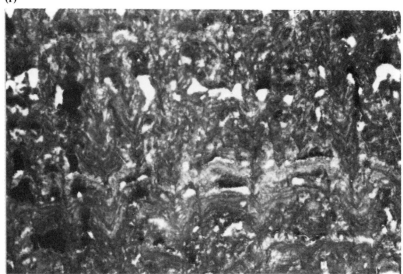

(g)

(h)

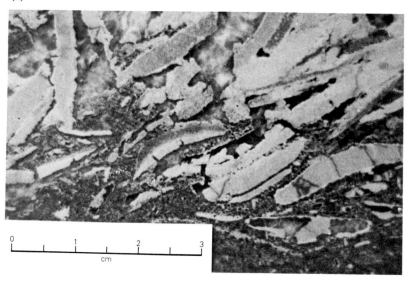

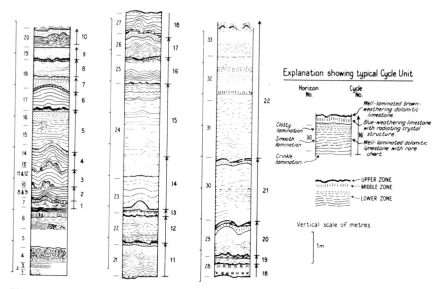

Figure 4.12 Stratigraphic column of main stromatolite outcrop, Cheshire Formation, Belingwe Belt (from Martin *et al.* 1980).

They show a wide variety of sedimentary and diagenetic textures (Fig. 4.13); these textures include finely defined lamination, layers rich in organic material, abundant fenestrae and finely preserved algal textures (Abell *et al.* 1985). The surrounding sedimentary rocks are of intertidal facies, and include siltstones with mud cracks and ripple marks. Martin *et al.* (1980) concluded that the rocks were possibly deposited in a lagoonal or intertidal setting (Fig. 4.14), and that the cyclic units reflected changing local conditions. Figure 4.15 illustrates this. The lower zones of each cycle suggest quiet growth of planar mats, with a minimal contribution of ferruginous detritus. The middle zones may represent evaporative conditions, in a closed lagoon, followed by catastrophic influx of detritus and then growth of nodular stromatolites.

Martin *et al.* recognised a wide variety of stromatolite *shapes* in the Belingwe outcrops. These ranged from large domes to small nodules to rare branching forms. Among the shapes recognised are forms similar to

(a)

Figure 4.13 Petrographic textures in thin section, Cheshire stromatolites. (a) Edge of small dome. Field of view 17 mm × 13 mm.

118

Baicalia, Conophyton, Irregularia, and *Stratifera,* all of which have been widely recognised in younger rocks. The nomenclature of stromatolites is a vexed and controversial problem not worth entering into here, but it *is* worth noting that the presence of these forms in Archaean strata means that they are of little stratigraphic use as dating tools in the Proterozoic where they occur more widely. However, within the Zimbabwe craton the stromatolites are useful as a facies marker horizon as a part of the general lithostratigraphic correlation across the craton (Ch. 3).

Walter (1983) has pointed out that if *Conophyton*-like forms are present in the Belingwe strata, then analogy with extant examples would suggest that the stromatolites were constructed by filamentous, positively phototactic organisms that may have been microaerophilic.

In the Steep Rock Group, northwest Ontario, late Archaean stromatolites are present in a thick carbonate succession lying above an unconformity (Fig. 7.30) on older tonalitic basement (Wilks & Nisbet 1985). The

(b) Middle to upper zones (see inset in Fig. 4.12). Radiating spar at base, finer at top. Field of view 2 mm × 1.5 mm.

119

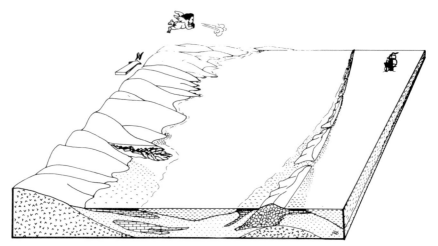

Figure 4.14 Possible palaeoenvironmental reconstruction, Cheshire Formation stromatolites (from Martin *et al.* 1980).

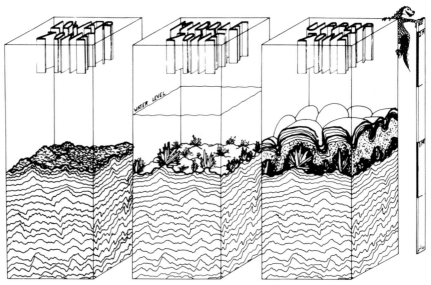

Figure 4.15 Model of formation of cyclic units, Cheshire formation stromatolites (from Martin *et al.* 1980). See text for explanation. Diagrams by G. Burton.

Figure 4.16 Large domal stromatolites, steeply dipping, Steep Rock Group, Ontario (from Nisbet 1985b).

stromatolites vary greatly from large domal bodies 5 m long or more (Fig. 4.16), to small columnar structures, including branched and walled forms (Fig. 4.17). The carbonate rocks are capped by pyroclastic mafic rocks, which include carbon-rich sulphide veins, possibly of hydrothermal origin; this close association of stromatolites with volcanic rocks containing possible hydrothermal deposits is an intriguing feature of the Archaean geological record found in Canada, Africa and Australia.

Martin *et al* present evidence which implies that the stromatolites grew in very shallow-water, protected conditions. In Belingwe, they appear to have grown wherever the appropriate conditions were available, sheltered

Figure 4.17 Small-scale stromatolitic structures, Steep Rock Group, Ontario (from Wilks & Nisbet 1985). (a) Linked domes, exposed on surface parallel to overall bedding. (b) Branching columns. Some structures are walled.

from terrigenous detritus. It is likely that wherever the correct environmental conditions were present, stromatolites grew, and that they were widespread on the surface of the late Archaean Earth. The present rarity of Archaean stromatolites is probably mainly a consequence of the fragmentary nature of the Archaean stratigraphic record. Most recognisable Archaean sedimentary rocks are preserved in greenstone belts, generally in association with volcanic rocks and in settings where major tectonic events took place. Quite probably, these preserved rocks do not provide a representative sample of the typical Archaean cratonic shallow-water environments (now lost), in the same way that platform carbonate successions are not common in the Mesozoic of California: the tectonic and sedimentological setting is wrong, although carbonates are indeed common elsewhere in the Mesozoic. It is tempting to speculate that by late Archaean time the Earth's shallow-water environment was widely populated by cyanobacteria. Perhaps the entire oceanic photic zone, including both coastal water and also the water close to the surface in the oceans, was densely populated by a diverse population of procaryotes.

4.1.6 Other evidence for life in the Archaean

The geologist – in the company of the chemist and the biologist – has a variety of other ways of investigating the remains of Archaean life. These include the search for microfossils, the search for chemical residues of organic life, and the search for evidence of the isotopic signature of life, using C, O, and sometimes N and H isotopes.

4.1.7 Microfossils

The search for microfossils is a difficult business – even the most painstaking research is not necessarily believed by a properly sceptical scientific community (Muir 1978). The problems include the possibility of contamination, and the likelihood that many microscopic structures thought to be microfossils may really be of inorganic origin. The term 'microfossil' has been variously applied to a wide variety of small (0.1 mm or less), generally circular structures in Archaean rocks.

To be preserved, a micro-organism must become incorporated into a sediment in such a way that it is not immediately broken down physically or chemically, and it must then be replaced in very fine detail by the fossilisation process. Muir (1978) pointed out that initial preservation could only occur in quiet conditions, and where the organic matter was rapidly incorporated into sediment (i.e. bottom-living bacteria would be favoured over planktonic forms), probably in a relatively acid and reducing setting. Typical sediments which seem to favour preservation are cherts, evaporites, etc. Bacteria are very small – typically less than $10\,\mu$m across, although cyanobacteria can reach $100\,\mu$m – and replacement must be on a very fine scale to preserve initial morphology. Margulis *et al.* (1983) have studied a variety of modern micro-organisms to investigate how they are preserved and what structures they produce. The micro-organisms, from a flat laminated microbial mat, produced a wide variety of distinctive structures and morphologies associated with varying conditions of growth, mat burial and degradation. Their work implies that it will be extremely difficult to identify specific pre-Phanerozoic mat building organisms without a very detailed understanding of the morphologies and ecological habitats in modern mats, and then a full knowledge of the environment in which fossil organisms grew. For instance, the identification of cyanobacteria in Archaean or Proterozoic rocks must remain very tentative, as modern mats produce a variety of similar-sized structures from other organisms. Similarly, some manganese-oxidizing bacteria form colonial structures which might be mistaken for individual organisms in the tens to hundreds of microns size range.

However, more difficult tests yet must be passed by the microfossil hopeful of immortality. Even relatively low-grade metamorphism usually leads to recrystallisation and chemical transport within the rock: for instance, low greenschist metamorphism of a carbonate might destroy all textures on a scale finer than $100–1000\,\mu$m, while amphibolite-grade metamorphism might rearrange the rock on a scale of the order of 1 cm, destroying all fine detail. Simultaneously, residual organic matter would be cracked and broken down to kerogen, and eventually to graphite. Thus the metamorphic constraints are very rigorous indeed.

Deformation must also be avoided – simple shear and flattening can rapidly erase microfossils, and, indeed 'microfossils' were first studied in Barberton for their strain ellipses (Ramsay 1965). A good example of these problems is in the debate over supposed microfossils in the 3.8-Ga Isua greenstone belt, Greenland (summarised by Nisbet & Pillinger 1981). In this case a claim that microfossils had been found was contested, initially on the grounds that nothing could survive the high grade of metamorphism displayed by the host rocks. Later this intuitive scepticism was confirmed by detailed evidence (Bridgwater *et al.* 1981): the moral to be drawn is that one should not search for microfossils in deformed or metamorphosed strata – even if they exist, the evidence will not be believed!

What then of the evidence? Buick (1984) and Schopf and Walter (1983) have summarised the available information. Much work has concentrated on the Barberton and Pilbara belts. In Barberton, various workers (e.g. Strother & Barghoorn 1980, Muir 1978, Knoll & Barghoorn 1977, Muir & Grant 1976, Barghoorn 1971) have described carbonised spheres preserved in cherts laid down in conditions likely to promote preservation.

Examples of supposed microfossils include *Archaeosphaeroides barbertonesis* (Schopf & Barghoorn 1967, Strother & Barghoorn 1980). These consist of spherical objects, about 20 μm in diameter, consisting of a spherical pattern of carbonised organic matter preserved in a chert made of quartz with a 1-μm grain size. There has been considerable scepticism about the biogenicity of these objects (Cloud & Morrison 1979). Perhaps the general opinion (Schopf & Walter 1983) is that these morphologically very simple forms *may* be objects of biogenic origin, but they are certainly *not proven* to be so. They have thus been consigned to the ambiguous limbo of 'dubiomicrofossils'. Recently, more complex forms were discovered at North Pole, in the Pilbara (Awramik *et al.* 1983), but the precise field relations of the samples are controversial (Buick *et al.* 1981); a post-depositional origin cannot be ruled out. The problem has been discussed at length by Schopf and Walter (1983), Awramik *et al.* (1983), Buick *et al.* (1981) and Buick (1984). Microfossils occur in two localities, both of which have uncertain field settings. Buick *et al.* conclude that, 'to date, no certain microbes are known ... from North Pole. No microfossils that are even moderately convincing are known from any other contemporaneous Archaean rocks.' Possibly some material from Barberton (Muir & Grant 1976) is indeed of biological origin, but the evidence is as yet not conclusive (Schopf & Walter 1983).

Schopf and Walter (1983) describe microfossils from the Fortescue Group in the Hamersley Basin of Western Australia. The succession contains well preserved cherty limestones, displaying both domical and stratiform stromatolites, with abundant microstructural evidence of microbial activity and poorly preserved filaments, possibly representing evidence for cyanobacteria. The age of the strata is uncertain, but is most probably late Archaean (Blake 1984a,b). Of similar age are supposed plant fossils from the Witwatersrand succession in South Africa (Hallbauer *et al.* 1977). These have been interpreted by Schopf and Walter as non-fossil artefacts of preparation or as modern contaminants.

4.1.8 Chemical residues

The problems involved in searching for chemical residues of life are similar to those discussed above: organic matter, even if preserved by sedimentation, is rapidly 'cracked' during diagenesis and metamorphism (Nagy *et al.* 1981). The extent of the degradation of organic matter depends exponentially on the temperature and pressure of burial: reactions which may take 10^{10} years at 50°C may take a few days at 200°C. The main chemical product seen in Archaean rocks is kerogen, which includes a wide variety of insoluble organic debris.

There are very major problems involved in analysing organic matter in Archaean samples. First, there is the problem of contamination. For instance, optically active amino acids have been reported in Archaean rocks. These must be recent introductions to old rocks, since amino acids cannot survive at geologically reasonable temperatures for more than a few years (at the most, 10^6a). Similarly, hydrocarbons may be introduced to Archaean rocks by circulating fluids: it is usually improbable that they could have survived the metamorphic history of the rocks as they would have been destroyed (McKenzie & McKenzie 1983). In a recent summary of the evidence, des Marais (1980) discussed the contamination problems and concluded that more rigour is needed to avoid them. Perhaps some alkanes and porphyrins found in Archaean rocks may be original biogenic compounds. Sklarew and Nagy (1979) have reported relatively 'tough' organic compounds from the Manjeri Formation stromatolites, Belingwe greenstone belt.

Most of the reduced (i.e. non-carbonate) carbon in Archaean rock is present as amorphous kerogen, which, being insoluble and relatively abundant, was probably not introduced by contamination. Hayes et al. (1983), after a survey of the problems of Archaean organic geochemistry, concluded that the answer to the problems of the survival of chemical fossils could be based on understanding the geochemistry of kerogen. Unfortunately, although most kerogen is almost certainly part of the rock and probably was derived from organic residues, by its nature kerogen is not particularly informative. Kerogen is usually highly modified by diagenesis and metamorphism. In some cases it preserves the shapes of supposed microfossils, in other cases molecular fragments can be removed from the kerogen. Kerogen also serves as an index of the grade of metamorphism, as its chemistry changes as metamorphism proceeds. Initially, H/C ratios of organic matter are around 1.5, and O/C ratios around 0.5. As degradation occurs, H/C ratios drop to 0.5 (a value found in very well preserved Proterozoic rocks) and then eventually to less than 0.2 in good Archaean specimens (Hayes et al. 1983). In such rocks, surviving organic compounds are generally uninformative about the organisms which originally produced their precursors.

4.1.9 Isotopic evidence

The study of stable isotope systematics in Archaean sediments is perhaps the most powerful, yet also the most complex and potentially the most misleading contribution the geologist can make to the study of the origin of life. Biologically derived rocks contain the isotopic signatures of the biologically controlled reactions which produced them; thus, in principle, the analysis of rocks for suitable isotopic ratios – $^{12}C/^{13}C$, $^{16}O/^{18}O$, $^{14}N/^{15}N$, $^{34}S/^{32}S$ and H/D – can provide information about the process and hence the organic reactions which controlled the Archaean biosphere.

126

Schidlowski *et al.* (1983) and Hayes (1983) have summarised the biological effects involved and described the various isotopic signatures of organisms.

The problems, of course, are many. First, there are the familiar barriers of diagenesis and metamorphism. Inorganic reactions during these processes can radically alter isotopic ratios. For instance, in Archaean geology, hydrogen isotopes are generally of little use because hydrogen diffuses rapidly, and the isotopes are generally remobilised quickly in metamorphism, alteration and exposure. Isotopes of other elements are more interesting. Although they are generally reset, they are reset according to the grade and nature of the metamorphism, and in some cases the metamorphic effect can be allowed for and subtracted, to give a notion of the original sedimentary (or at least diagenetic) ratio. In a few cases nearly unaltered stable isotopic systems may be preserved in Archaean strata.

Stable isotope measurements are usually expressed in delta values, where

$$\delta = \frac{\text{(isotopic ratio of sample)} - \text{(isotopic ratio of a standard)}}{\text{(isotopic ratio of the standard)}} \times 1000$$

In other words, δ is the per mil difference in ratio between the sample and the arbitrary standard (which is usually Standard Mean Ocean Water (SMOW) for oxygen and hydrogen, a now-exhausted belemnite from the Peedee Fm (PDB) for carbon and sometimes oxygen, and troilite from the Canyon Diablo meteorite (CD) for sulphur. To convert from PDB to SMOW for oxygen,

$$\delta^{18}O_{SMOW} = 1.03086 \, (\delta_{PDB}) + 30.86$$

(Friedman & O'Neil 1977). Since isotopic fractionation in reactions depends on temperature, it may be possible to use a pair of simple, known inorganic reactions to calibrate both the temperature of the Archaean ocean and its isotopic composition.

The literature on the subject is large; recent reviews include those of Schidlowski (1980a) on the carbon isotope record and Schidlowski (1979) on sulphur isotopes, work by Veizer *et al.* (1982) on carbon and oxygen, and a general review by Schidlowski *et al.* (1983). Much of this work is on the border between bacteriology, chemistry and geology – the practising Archaean geologist can only contribute the raw material of the rocks, and point out the hazards of preservation. Figure 4.18 shows carbon isotope ratios in modern materials.

4.1.10 Isotopic study of stromatolites

To take an example of the study of isotopes in Archaean rocks of biological origin, Abell *et al.* (1985a,b) have investigated the stromatolites from the

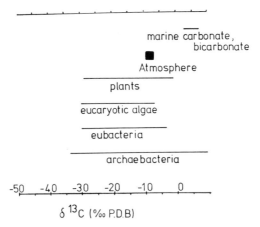

Figure 4.18 Carbon isotope compositions in modern plants, bacteria, carbonates and atmosphere.

Cheshire Formation of the Belingwe Belt (see Ch. 3). Palaeomagnetic data imply that these stromatolites probably grew in tropical or subtropical latitudes. They are texturally well preserved (see Section 4.1.5). Abell *et al.* suggested that the grade of metamorphism suffered by the rocks is so low that the oxygen and carbon isotopic ratios in the rocks have not been substantially reset since sedimentation. In contrast to the stromatolites from the Cheshire Formation in the upper part of the Belingwe succession, stromatolites from the Manjeri Formation near the base of the Ngesi Group display slightly more recrystallised textures. This appears to be recorded in their stable isotopic ratios, which are slightly different from the Cheshire material. Samples from the Mushandike Formation (see Section 4.1.3) are even more recrystallised and have stable isotope ratios which appear to have been substantially shifted by metamorphism (Fig. 4.19).

The oxygen isotope ratios measured in the stromatolite carbonates from the Cheshire Formation are around $\delta = 19.5‰$ SMOW, and the carbon isotope ratios are about $\delta = -0.3‰$ PDB. The interpretation of these results hinges on the isotopic composition assumed for sea water. If Archaean sea water were similar in oxygen isotopic composition to today (Beaty & Taylor 1982) then the carbonate–water fractionation would imply a sea temperature of around $80°C$. However, some data from cherts suggest (Chase & Perry 1972) that the Archaean sea had $\delta^{18}O$ around -10 to $-15‰$ SMOW. If so, temperature as low as around $25°C$ would be implied. Temperatures as high as $50°C$ are not uncommon in modern stromatolite-growing lagoons: the Archaean ocean was not necessarily hotter than today. In fact it is one of the most remarkable aspects of life on Earth that the

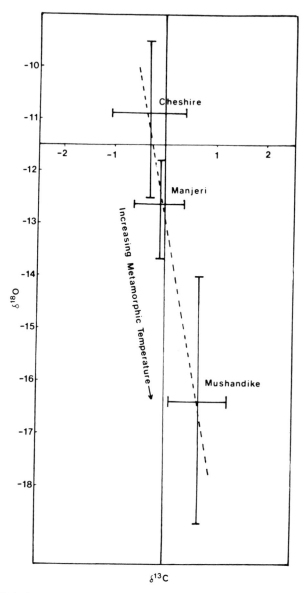

Figure 4.19 Variation of carbon and oxygen isotope ratios with increasing metamorphic temperature in Archaean stromatolites from Zimbabwe (from Abell *et al.* 1985b). Oxygen isotope ratios quoted against PDB standard.

surface temperature has remained within the stability field of liquid water for perhaps 4×10^9 years – uniformity indeed!

Carbon isotope ratios in the kerogen of the Cheshire Formation range from $\delta = -26‰$ to $-35‰$ PDB. These values are similar to values obtained in modern hot springs from algae growing in water with high CO_2 pressures (Fig. 4.18). Finally, the Belingwe material includes residues substantially enriched in ^{15}N, possibly implying important denitrification reactions.

Another and potentially more powerful method towards working out the temperature of the Archaean oceans is by identifying organic reactions which are known to have taken place. For instance, diazotrophy, or the ability to 'fix' atmospheric nitrogen by converting it to a metabolically available form, occurs in most eubacteria in the temperature range up to $35-40°C$, although some cyanobacteria can manage to fix nitrogen up to $60°C$. Some archaebacteria can fix nitrogen at rather higher temperatures (Belay et al. 1984, Postgate 1984). Were we able to identify which bacteria managed to fix nitrogen and when, we could infer much about the sea temperature. Most probably, the sea temperature has not exceeded about $60°C$ since nitrogen fixation began.

4.1.11 The diversity of Archaean life

What sort of life existed in the Archaean? There are two ways to find out: one is to make morphological comparisons between Archaean stromatolites and microfossils and modern equivalents; the other is to use the information preserved in the genetic code of modern procaryotes in an attempt to discover their ancestral history. This second, molecular approach is discussed in Section 4.2; here the geological evidence is considered. Schopf and Walter (1983) and Walter (1983) have reviewed the information available. Stromatolites are commonly assumed to have been built by cyanobacteria (blue–green algae), by analogy with modern examples. Most probably this was the case in the Archaean, but Walter (1983) has pointed out that the evidence suggesting that cyanobacteria were the building organisms is only circumstantial, even though the conclusion is plausible. Even if stromatolites are interpreted as cyanobacterial, the use of water as an electron donor is not obligatory for all cyanobacteria; many can use H_2S and thus not release oxygen to their environment. The existence of stromatolites in association with local Archaean shallow-water and intertidal sedimentological facies demonstrates that the organisms were photosynthetic: most probably, the principal stromatolite builders were phototactic and photoautrophic, although a complex and diverse microbial community probably existed in the mats. Fenestrate fabrics occur in the Belingwe stromatolites, possibly indicative of heterotrophic decomposition.

The microfossil record is extremely difficult to decipher, especially in view

130

of how little is known about preservation of microbial structures in modern mats.

4.1.12   The Garden of Eden

Schidlowski (1979, 1980b), Schidlowski *et al.* (1983) and various others have tried to use isotopic and chemical data to build up models of the diversity of Archaean life. It is fairly generally accepted that photosynthesis

$$2H_2O + CO_2 \overset{\text{light}}{\underset{\text{energy}}{\rightarrow}} CH_2O + H_2O + O_2 \quad \Delta G^0 = + 112 \text{ Kcal}$$

helps to control the present oxygen-rich atmosphere and that bacteria, probably cyanobacteria, have been synthesising organic matter in this way at least since the late Archaean – indeed, Schidlowski (1980a, 1984) has suggested from the carbon isotope record of Isua sediments that this form of photosynthesis commenced as early as 3.8×10^9 years ago. In the late Archaean the available shallow-water environments (on continental margins and in basins on cratons) probably provided homes for abundant and flourishing communities of stromatolite-building cyanobacteria.

There is some evidence to show that these were not the only form of life present on earth. For instance, there is tenuous evidence from nitrogen isotopes that some variety of denitrifying bacteria was at wotk in shallow-water settings, amongst the stromatolites. Possibly this was in the presence of oxygen, produced by photosynthesis, or, by an alternative pathway, in a reducing setting. The presence of primary sulphates in evaporitic horizons implies that mildly oxidising conditions were common, at least on the surface.

However, the shallow seas close to coastlines were probably not the only homes for life. Many greenstone belts contain mineral deposits in what are probably extinct hydrothermal systems (see Ch. 7). Characteristically these deposits consist of veins of sulphide minerals, often closely associated with 'graphite' (optically identified, dark, carbon-rich material). The 'graphite' is often finely laminated and probably consists of 'cracked' organic residues, after kerogen. 'Thucolite', or carbon compounds of uncertain composition, is common in many gold mines, both in sedimentary sequences (Mossman & Dyer 1985) and especially also in alteration zones produced by hydrothermal fluxing. In the Hoyle Pond occurrence, Ontario, Downes *et al.* (1984) identified amorphous carbon, some of which may have been organic, possibly as thermally resistant highly condensed aromatic polymers. Various authors (e.g. Berry & Wilde 1983) have pointed out that these deposits are closely analogous to organic deposits associated with modern black smoker deposits on mid-ocean ridges. As yet, there is little

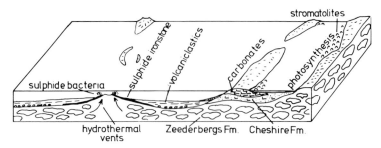

Figure 4.20 Schematic reconstruction of regional setting of Cheshire Formation. Note that while photosynthesis was taking place on stromatolite banks, other organisms may have been active at hydrothermal vents around active volcanoes. World-wide, a biological control on sea-water chemistry may have been imposed by oxidation–reduction reactions occurring at such sites and in the deposition of ironstones.

or no proof that the Archaean 'graphite' was biogenic (although isotopic evidence may be forthcoming), but the analogy is fascinating.

Consider the Cheshire Formation of the Belingwe Belt (Fig. 4.20). The formation consists of tuffs and limestones; the limestone is clearly biogenic and probably formed in an environment inhabited *inter alia* by photosynthetic cyanobacteria and by denitrifying bacteria. Elsewhere in the formation tuffs predominate, except for thin banded ironstones. At the nearby Agincourt gold deposit (and presumably at similar places elsewhere) hydrothermal vents existed, probably in fairly shallow water. These probably provided a home for flourishing communities of bacteria, now preserved as 'graphite'. These bacteria would have been for the most part chemoautotrophs – in other words, they provided their own food by chemical synthesis. The vent would be the main source of chemicals.

Much depends on the amount of oxygen available. If the sea water above the vent were oxygenated, then bacteria could utilise the H_2S in the vent fluids

$$2H_2S + O_2 \rightarrow 2S + 2H_2O$$

$$2S + 2H_2O + 3O_2 \rightarrow 2SO_4{}^{2-} + 4H^+$$

$$S_2O_3{}^{2-} + H_2O + 2O_2 \rightarrow 2SO_4{}^{2-} + 2H^+$$

in a sulphur-oxidising chemoautotrophic system, with parallel sulphate reduction

$$SO_4{}^{2-} + 8e^- + 8H^+ \rightarrow S^{2-} + 4H_2O$$

The products eventually preserved in the rock would be a vent deposit rich in sulphide, sulphate and 'graphite' (from dead organic material, 'cracked' by the heat of the hydrothermal system and by later local or regional metamorphism).

The energy chain outlined above depends on the presence of oxygenating water above the hydrothermal vent. In the Cheshire Formation, Belingwe, it is easy to invoke this as flourishing stromatolite communities must have existed very close by, in what may have been a restricted basin or lagoon, and there is evidence for sulphate deposition. In other words, there was probably a very primitive ecosystem in operation. The hydrothermal vent bacteria would have controlled the pH of the water, and to some extent would have governed the influx of new mineral species from the vent to the water. Simultaneously they would have devoured oxygen and sulphate ions from the water. For their part, the cyanobacteria in the stromatolites would have produced the oxygen by photosynthesis (Fig. 4.20). Possibly other reactions took place too, e.g.

$$5S + 6NO_3 + 2H_2O \rightarrow 5SO_4{}^{2-} + 3N_2 + 4H^+$$

eventually to form gypsum-rich layers.

Most of this is speculation, but there is some evidence that bacterial sulphate reduction, at least, is of great antiquity. Schidlowski (1979) has used sedimentary $\delta^{34}S$ patterns in an attempt to trace the history of sulphur bacteria. He suggests that photosynthesis by sulphur bacteria began early on

$$\tfrac{1}{2}H_2S + CO_2 + H_2O \rightarrow CH_2O + H^+ + \tfrac{1}{2}SO_4{}^{2-}$$

followed later by oxygen-releasing cyanophytic processes. Similarly, Schidlowski *et al.* (1983) concluded that the biological nitrogen cycle was also established at a very early date.

4.2 Molecular palaeontology and the History of Life in the Archaean: 'à la recherche du temps perdu'

> Weighs not the dust and injury of age
> Nor gives to necessary wrinkles place
> But makes antiquity for aye his page
> Finding the first conceit of love there bred
> Where time and outward form would show it dead
>
> Shakespeare, *Sonnet* CVIII

What of that first 'conceit', or conception of life? We have another route to the past, a route that is complementary to the geological route, and in-grained in the heritage of all modern life. Consider three modern languages:

French, German and English. They are recognisably different, yet even a superficial analysis would class them together when compared with Chinese or Xhosa. An extraterrestrial visitor, knowing nothing of history, would deduce that the three European languages are in some way related. It might even deduce that English was descended from a cross-breeding of a German-like parent and a French-like parent. As with languages, so (approximately) with living cells. The genetic code of each cell is a historical document, representing the assembled surviving genes of its parentage, and much of that document is of great antiquity. For instance the homoeobox, which is a part of the DNA sequence which directs the organisation of segmented animals during growth has been so conserved that it is obviously related in organisms as distant as humans and insects, and even yeast has similarities in its DNA.

Shortly after the discovery of the structure of DNA, Crick (1958) conceived a new approach to understanding the origin of species. Many proteins in living organisms – and, more fundamentally, the nucleic acids which determine these proteins – have been dynamically conserved by evolution over long periods of time. They thus contain the most powerful information available to us which records the lines of evolutionary descent of species (Zuckerkandl & Pauling 1965). Since much of the terminology of molecular biology is obscure to geologists, Table 4.1 lists some of the

Table 4.1 Selected biological terms for geologists

nucleotide	a chemical compound consisting of a base, a 5-carbon sugar and one or more phosphate groups
base	in nucleotides, a nitrogen-containing ring compound, either pyrimidine (cytosine (C), thymine (T) or uracil (U)), or a purine (adenine (A) or guanine (G))
nucleic acid	sequences of nucleotides linked together to carry genetic information (a polynucleotide)
RNA	ribonucleic acid, a polynucleotide containing a string of the bases U, A, C, G
DNA	deoxyribonucleic acid, the double helix, containing the bases A, C, G, T
amino acid	simple organic compound containing a carboxylic acid group and an amino group (-COOH and -NH$_2$) linked to a single carbon atom
polypeptide	a string of amino acids linked by peptide bonds
protein	a polypeptide; there are 20 common amino acids in proteins
cytochrome-c	a small protein (about 60 amino acids) containing an iron atom capable of changing oxidation state
ferredoxin	a small iron-containing protein involved in electron transport (e.g. in photosynthesis)
globins	a family of proteins – e.g. haemoglobin

134

Table 4.1 (*continued*)

enzyme	a protein with a unique three-dimensional conformation which allows it to act as a very efficient and specific catalyst; enzymes are essential in the rapid formation of polynucleotides
gene	information-containing element in the cell, carried in specific lengths of nucleic acid; in most life, information is carried in DNA, then copies to RNA (which in eucaryotes and archaebacteria is then spliced to delete introns); these 'mRNA' molecules are then read at ribosomes, to direct the synthesis of protein
exon	length of DNA or RNA which carries genetic information which is expressed in the body of the organism by being read and translated into amino acids
intron	length of DNA or RNA which is not expressed in the body of the organism and which must be deleted prior to translation: eucaryotes and archaebacteria (but not eubacteria) generally contain introns in their DNA
genetic code	the rules by which base sequences in DNA are translated into sequences of amino acids in proteins; this code is common to bacteria, plants and animals, and indicates our joint descent from an early ancestor
genome	the hereditary information of an organism
phenotype	the expression of the genome (i.e. the body of the organism, on whose characteristics natural selection operates)
cell	small, membrane-bounded compartment filled with assorted aqueous solutions − the building block of life; *procaryotes* are single cells with relatively simple internal structure; *eucaryotes* possess a nucleus and include complex, multicelled organisms such as geologists
ribosome	a large multienzyme complex, composed of protein and RNA molecules, at which the information in RNA is processed and proteins are synthesised; 5S RNA molecules are short RNA molecules, about 120 nucleotides long, which make up part of the ribosome
chloroplast	organelle found in cells of higher plants, bounded by a double membrane and containing chlorophyll and responsible for photosynthesis; contains its own DNA, and may originally have been descended from cyanobacteria
mitochondrion	organelle, about the size of bacteria, that acts as the power plant of the eucaryotic cell and carries out most cellular oxidations; like a chloroplast, it contains its own DNA and may be descended from originally symbiotic bacteria
autotrophs	bacteria which do not require organic substances either for energy or as a source of carbon
hetrotrophs	bacteria needing organic substances for carbon and energy

commonest terms discussed below. Each species has a distinctive sequence of nucleotides in its genetic material, which codes for a peculiar assortment of specific proteins. Human proteins, for example, are almost (though not exactly) the same as chimpanzee proteins, but both are very different from kangaroo proteins. Behind the proteins, the underlying DNA sequences in humans and in chimpanzees are very similar, but substantially different from kangaroo DNA, yet all three are clearly related when compared to frogs.

This method of deducing evolutionary descent by comparison of genetic material is particularly powerful since it can be quantified. It is very difficult to compare languages because it is hard to quantify small differences in phonemes (how does one measure the differences between 'one', '*un*' and '*ein*'?). Equally, it is hard to compare animals by their bodies or bones. In contrast, genetic and protein sequences are written in simple lists, such as the four-letter code of DNA or the 20 amino acids in proteins. It is easy to quantify statistically the similarities and differences between sequences and thus to classify species in groups according to similarity. For instance, part of comparable RNA sequences from *E. coli* (a bacterium) reads *GUUUGAUCAU*, from *H. volcanii* (another procaryote) reads *GGUUGAUCCU* and from *Xenopus laevis* (a South African toad) reads *GGUUGAUCCU* (Gupta *et al.* 1983). From this it is obvious that the first bacterium diverges by two letters in ten, or 20%. Of course, a longer sequence may give a different story; the danger of misinterpretation is comparable to that faced by a blind man who examines a Manx cat, a Siamese cat and a sheep: if he simply examines the tail he will classify the sheep and Siamese together (with tails) and the Manx separately (no tail). Recently there has been an explosion in sequence data, since it is now possible to read nucleic acid sequences rapidly (and, through them, protein sequences). Available sequences ran into millions of characters. A respectable chunk of the cat is now becoming available for examination. Thus, this method is now the most important of all tools in evolutionary palaeontology, and the only way in which the descent of Archaean life will be elucidated.

4.2.1 The tree of early evolution

The geological evidence indicates that Archaean life consisted of single-celled procaryotes (organisms without a nucleus) and possibly eucaryotes (with a nucleus). However, even this interpretation is stretching the available morphological evidence to the limits of uniformity and allowable analogues with modern equivalents. The phylogeny of the simplest organisms is best worked out from genetic information, and it can then be geologically calibrated.

Fox *et al.* (1980) and Schwartz and Dayhoff (1978) have identified the major lines of procaryotic descent. Fox *et al.* (1980) and Woese (1983) distinguished between three major lines of procaryotic organisms: the eubacteria which include the cyanobacteria (blue–green algae) and most of the commoner species of bacteria; the archaebacteria, a quite distinct primary kingdom which contain bacteria such as the methanogenic bacteria, the extreme halophiles and some thermoacidophiles (in other words, a variety of organisms, some of which exist in hot, acid or salty environments); and finally, there may have existed a set of organisms ancestral to modern eucaryotes (Garrett 1985).

Dayhoff (1983) has reviewed the evidence used to construct evolutionary trees in simple organisms. Early work was based on sequences from proteins, especially the ferredoxins (George *et al.* 1985) and C-type cytochromes. This work has been supplemented more recently with information from ribosomal RNA sequences. Ferredoxins are small iron-

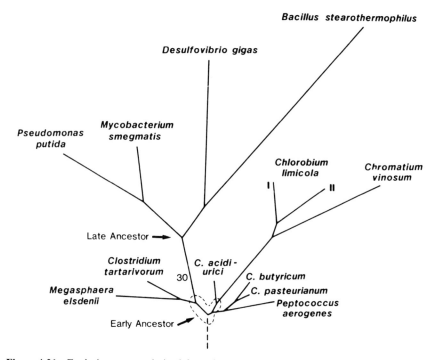

Figure 4.21 Evolutionary tree derived from ferredoxins (from Dayhoff 1983). *Clostridium, Megasphaera* and *Peptococcus* are anaerobic heterotrophic bacteria; *Chromatium* and *Chlorobium* are anaerobic bacteria capable of photosynthesis using H_2S as an electron donor, *Pseudomonas putida* and *Mycobacterium smegmatis* are aerobes and *Bacillus stearothermophilus* is a facultative aerobe, while *Desulfovibrio gigas* is a sulphate-reducing bacterium that respires anaerobically using sulphate as a terminal electron acceptor.

137

containing proteins which participate in fundamental biochemical processes such as photosynthesis, oxidation–reduction respiratory reactions, nitrogen fixation and sulphate reduction. Amino acid sequences from these proteins demonstrated that all of the eubacteria studied descended from a common ancestor which contained a doubled gene sequence (Fig. 4.21). From this ancestor arose several lines of descent. Anaerobic, heterotrophic bacteria (*Clostridium*, *Megasphaera*, *Peptococcus*) still contain protein apparently similar to the very ancient protein that duplicated. Another line leads to *Chlorobium* and *Chromatium*, which are anaerobic bacteria capable of photosynthesis using H_2S as an electron donor. A third line leads to a 'late bacterial ancestor' of aerobes such as *Pseudomonas* and sulphate-reducing bacteria such as *Desulphovibrio*.

The evidence from the protein sequences thus implies that certain types of bacteria are older than others, and that certain chemical reactions were utilised later than others. Some of the steps may be dated by using stable isotopic analysis of rocks whose age is known by radiometric techniques. For instance, Schidlowski (1979) in his study of the antiquity of bacterial sulphate reduction, concluded that isotopic evidence from the Archaean of the Aldan Shield, Siberia (3 Ga approx.) and from banded ironstone on the Canadian Shield (2.75 Ga) suggested that sulphate reduction became important at least by around 3 Ga ago. Prior to that, the early Archaean may have been the 'golden age' of photosynthetic sulphur bacteria. If this is correct, some guesses may be made as to the age of the late ancestor in Figure 4.21. But the evidence is still very, very thin: older sedimentary successions may well turn out to have sulphur isotopes of modern aspect.

4.2.2 More detailed information: the RNA record

The initial work on the molecular record of early life was based on proteins. More recently, our knowledge of the succession of the procaryotes has been greatly improved by work not on proteins, but directly on RNA molecules themselves. This study of RNA has deepened and amplified the results of protein sequencing (Woese 1981, 1983, Dayhoff 1983).

Short RNA molecules from the ribosomes, or 5S RNA molecules (the shortest of the three RNA molecules formed in the bacterial ribosomes, the places where genetic information is translated into proteins) are about 120 nucleotides long. Analysis of their sequences provides the evolutionary tree shown in Figure 4.22. In one sector of the diagram are the aerobic bacteria, near the base are the blue–green algae or cyanobacteria. In another sector are the Archaebacteria, and in the centre the eucaryotes, including animals and plants.

4.2.3 Symbiosis

Figure 4.22 was devised from relatively short RNA molecules, and so is subject to the Manx cat problem. Nevertheless, it shows clearly the distinction between the main groups of organisms present. One of the most interesting features on the diagram is the position of chloroplast and mitochondrial DNA. Margulis (1971, for example) suggested that the chloroplasts (which are where the chemical events of photosynthesis in plants take place) and the mitochondria (where foodstuffs are oxidised to produce ATP (adenosine triphosphate), the fuel of biochemical reactions) were originally independent organisms, which became symbiotically incorporated into the eucaryotic cell. Both chloroplasts and mitochondria contain DNA which is not related to the cell nucleus and is handed down from the mother in sexual reproduction. Evidence from cytochrome-c, an electron transport protein found in blue–green algae and chloroplasts shows the similarity between the two (Dayhoff 1983). Thus it is possible that the plants include symbiotic organelles which were originally related to blue–green algae (cyanobacteria): the eucaryotic ancestor of the plants somehow engulfed and attained symbiosis with a photosynthetic eubacterium. Similarly, mitochondria were engulfed by the eucaryotic chimaera. The plant mitochondrion probably originated as a purple

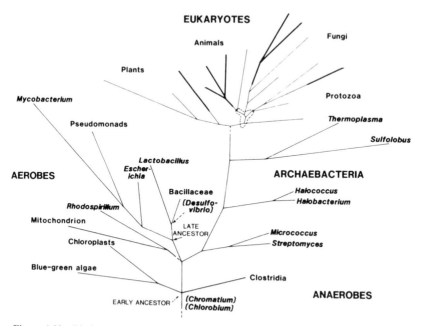

Figure 4.22   Phylogenetic tree derived from 5S RNA sequences (from Dayhoff 1983).

photosynthetic bacterium (Villanueva *et al.* 1985). Eventually, much of the genetic information in the mitochondrial DNA may have been incorporated in the nucleus (Obar & Green 1985), since, for example, the human mitochondrial DNA is only responsible for encoding a few proteins and ribosomal nucleic acids (Dayhoff 1983). Incidentally, mitochondrial evidence also suggests (Cann *et al.* 1987) that all humans share descent from one woman: a point worth pondering.

4.2.4 Clocks and trees

Margulis and Stolz (1983) have summarised what is known about the descent of the bacteria (Fig. 4.23). To what extent can the growth of this tree be calibrated in time? One method is based on the measurement of the rate of change of DNA in species which are palaeontologically well understood. For instance, globin genes can be used to time the development of eucaryotes. Globins are widespread, including haemoglobins in vertebrates, as well as a variety of globins in invertebrates and even in root nodules of nitrogen-fixing plants (Jeffreys *et al.* 1983). Since the evolu-

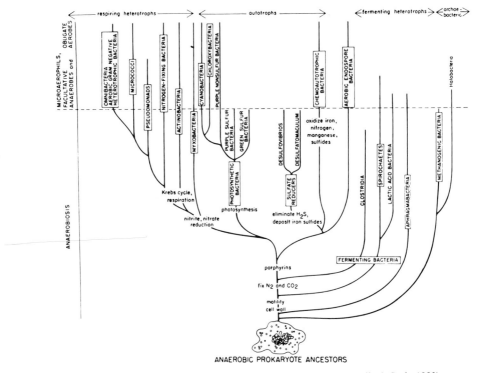

Figure 4.23 Phylogeny of the Monera kingdom (from Margulis & Stolz 1983).

tionary history of vertebrates and invertebrates is relatively well understood palaeontologically, the rate of divergence of globin genes can be measured by comparing, for instance, two species which diverged 100 Ma ago. A pair of species which diverged 200 Ma ago will have globin sequences about twice as far apart as the 100-Ma pair. In fact, the clock is more complex than this, since different genetic sites diverge at different rates. Sites where substitutions of new nucleotides cause amino acids replacements diverge at 0.1% per Ma. Nevertheless, the clocks seem to be regular. A molecular clock can thus be used to measure the degree of divergence of any pair of species; and, from that, the time of divergence, once the clock has been successfully calibrated against well-known species. Other genetic information can be used to calibrate other clocks.

It is relatively easy to calibrate such a molecular clock in the well-understood Phanerozoic; it is much more difficult to calibrate a Precambrian, and specifically an Archaean clock. Although rates of genetic change may have been reasonably steady in the past few hundred million years, they may have been very different in the past (Kimura 1979, 1981a, 1981b), especially in the early Archaean when both the inorganic environment (e.g. ultraviolet flux, cosmic-ray flux) and the organic environment (the selection pressure from the organisms, and the chance of change in less complex and perhaps less stable organisms) may have been quite different from today. Furthermore, in the Archaean record the geological information is extremely sparse. As was mentioned above, morphological information is almost useless in the Precambrian: a few Proterozoic microfossils may be identifiable, but in the Archaean we can only be certain that stromatolites were photosynthetic and guess that they were built by cyanobacteria; we can also guess that organic material in hydrothermal veins was produced by thermo-acidophilic organisms (archaebacteria?). Perhaps some characteristic sediments, such as the banded ironstones, also are of biological origin and were produced by specific bacterial lines, but we cannot be certain.

Schidlowski's (1979) approach is thus our best route to calibrating the evolutionary clock. Stable isotopic signatures would indicate that sulphate respiration began possibly about 3 Ga ago or perhaps earlier, and that bacteria processed nitrogen in some way at least 2.7 Ga ago. Both eubacteria and archaebacteria (Murray & Zinder 1984) are able to fix nitrogen. On the tree of Figure 4.22 the 'late ancestor' must have existed prior to 3 Ga. The apparent consistency of stromatolite morphology from 3.5 Ga onwards would suggest that the 'early ancestor' was at least 3.6 Ga ago. If it becomes possible to pin down the time of two or three divergences in the tree, it will then be possible to calibrate the clock and to date the other steps by measuring the genetic change between each step. It should thus be possible to date the major events in the development of the archaebacteria and eubacteria with considerable precision and moderate accuracy.

4.2.5 *The Eucaryotes and their ancestors*

From the anthropic point of view, one of the more interesting questions in Archaean palaeontology is how the eucaryotes, our ancestors, began. As discussed above, there is strong evidence that the eucaryotes are chimaeras which include genetic material from a variety of sources. One distinctive feature of the genetic information in all eucaryotes including ourselves is that the information contains long sequences of nucleotides which need to be cut out of the message in order to encode the amino acids of a protein (Darnell 1983). DNA is read off to a primary RNA transcript; then 'introns' are deleted, and a much shorter, messenger RNA is produced by splicing together the remaining strips of RNA which carry the message. This messenger RNA can then be translated into protein. The gene in its most basic form in eucaryotes is a series of 'exons' which are read and translated, separated by 'introns', which are not, determining a polypeptide. Genes occur in gene clusters, or collections of adjacent genes related in evolutionary history and function. On a grander scale, the gene clusters make up the chromosomes and the genome (Bodmer 1983), and are the basic functional genetic units.

Unlike the eucaryotes, eubacterial RNA does not generally carry the 'introns', splitting the genes, which must be deleted prior to translation. Of the eubacterial line of descent only mitochondria and chloroplasts have introns, but they may have acquired them from their eucaryotic hosts. Instead, RNA transcripts can be directly translated by eubacteria without splicing in a much more streamlined process. In contrast, however, archaebacteria do carry split genes (Kaine *et al.* 1983), although in detail the introns are slightly different from eucaryote introns. Thus there is further evidence for the existence of three distinct lines of descent: eubacteria, with streamlined genetic sequences and related ribosomal RNA; archaebacteria, with introns and markedly different ribosomal RNA; and eucaryotes. The latter, like archaebacteria, have split genes; have ribosomal RNA which has some characteristics in common with archaebacteria, some in common with eubacteria and some distinct characteristics; and include separate organelles which appear to be descended from symbiotic eubacteria.

Woese (1981, 1983) has suggested that these were three early and distinct branches to the tree of life, representing eubacteria, archaebacteria and 'urcaryotes'. This last branch may have been ancestral to the organisms which later engulfed bacterial material to produce the eucaryotes. Each branch retains some characteristics of a very early ancestor, and has evolved some distinctive features. Split genes, for instance, may be a very old characteristic which has been lost by the more streamlined eubacterial genetic material. The eucaryotic ancestral line is particularly complex, since even at the level of the nucleus it may be a disparate entity assembled from a variety of sources, some archaebacterial, some eubacterial and some from another primitive line.

Before all this, what? Since all life shows a common method of reproduction involving strings of nucleic acids, and since there is a universal genetic code, it is highly unlikely that there was more than a single ancestor (but see Ch. 8 for a discussion of the nature of this being). This 'universal ancestor' seems to lie before the various lines of descent: Woese has named the postulated ancestors 'progenotes'. It is widely thought (Darnell 1983) that the earliest coding nucleic acid was RNA, not DNA. Since primitive RNA chains can be synthesised, possibly the earliest RNA may have been a random nucleotide chain without enzymes, with discontinuous pieces of information which could have been spliced together. Jacob (1983) has suggested that it all began with strings of 30–50 nucleotides, each able to code for 10–15 amino acids. New and longer genes may have arisen by a process of molecular tinkering, through internal duplications in the sequence or through a mechanism of joining pre-existing sequences at random. Some of these longer polypeptide chains would be useful, and favoured by natural selection; most would be discarded. Much of the excess DNA in eucaryotic cells could be useful new material for this sort of process.

Duplication of genes seems to have been a principal mechanism leading to the evolution of new proteins and organisms. In this process, a single copy of a gene is duplicated to two or more copies, and the new copies evolve separately, either by mutation or by minor insertions or deletions, to give new proteins with new functions. In some cases, genes may have fused together to produce larger proteins. Phillips *et al.* (1983) have shown that the three-dimensional structure of these proteins is more strongly conserved over time than the underlying amino-acid sequence, so that a study of protein structure may provide the best intimation of evolution available. The timescale of gene duplication is rather slow: human globin genes have apparently fixed only six duplications over the past 500 Ma, although some may have been lost (Jeffreys *et al.* 1983).

Two possible mechanisms for gene evolution may account for the complexities of the split structure of eucaryotic genes. It is possible that each exon of a gene specifies a distinct structural part of a protein and evolved as an individually discrete element. Reshuffling of these elements could create new proteins containing already stable standard domains. It may also be that introns contain 'selfish' mobile or transposable elements which have no phenotypic function and are, in a sense, parasitic. On occasion, however, this 'junk' DNA may have been useful in evolutionary tinkering with the genome (Jacob 1983). On occasion, bizarre horizontal transfer of information can occur – soybeans may have acquired animal DNA, while ponyfishes seem to have given an enzyme to symbiotic bacteria. Over 4 Ga,

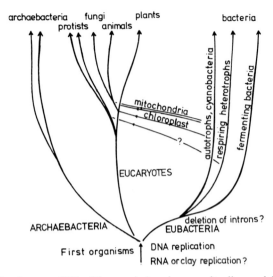

Figure 4.24 The descent of life. Diagram is based on results discussed in text. Origin of eucaryote line is not known. It may come directly from ancestral 'urcaryotes' descended from first progenote, but may also include archaebacterial information. Order of eucaryote kingdoms from Hasegawa *et al.* 1985, who found that fungi and animals are relatively closely related, with plants more distant. Separation of these groups from the protists took place earlier. Several symbiotic incorporations of bacterial origin into the eucaryotes may have taken place. There is evidence to suggest that the mitochondria of plants and animals came from different sources within the purple bacteria (Fox 1985). The chloroplasts of plants are probably derived from the cyanobacterial lineage. Within the bacteria, at least ten major families can be identified, and at least two archaebacterial families are known (Fox 1985). Transfer of genetic material probably also took place between these families. The timing of divergence within the eucaryote line is unknown. It may have been as late as mid–late Proterozoic, but it is also possible that divergence may have taken place much earlier. Note that the diagram represents the "orthodox" view of the position of the archaebacteria, after Woese and coworkers. Lake *et al.* (1984) and Lake (1986) have suggested an alternative possibility based on an analysis of ribosome structure. In this model eucaryotes are related to eocytes (classified in the archaebacteria in the orthodox model), while halobacteria and methanogens (also classified in the archaebacteria in the orthodox model) are associated with eubacteria. Which model is correct is not yet resolved, but with luck soon will be.

this complex array of processes has served to produce from a simple ancestral reproducing organism the whole extraordinary modern array of living organisms, via the accidents of mutation and genome reshuffling and the driving force of natural selection in an increasingly disparate and individually competitive yet collectively co-operative population (Lovelock & Margulis 1984).

To return finally to the geological evidence: what can the geologist contribute? In the period 3.5–2.5 Ga we can calibrate the clocks, by using stable isotopes to discover the time of first appearance of specific lines of bacteria. We may, if we are good enough chemists, be able to identify the products (limestones, ironstones) of biological activity. Life is disequilibrium, and the biosphere has been growing in disequilibrium ever since it began. We may be able to measure the extent of that disequilibrium. We can, with some security, put the origin of life prior to 3.5 Ga; we can, with some imagination, suggest that life began at least 4 Ga ago. With further imagination, we can perhaps look to Archaean hydrothermal organic matter for the remains of thermoacidophilic organisms, especially archaebacteria, and look to Archaean limestones for the remains of photosynthetic eubacteria. We may even be able in the next few years to construct simple models of Archaean ecology – the exchange of chemical species between water, hydrothermal life, inorganic hydrothermal reactions, photosynthetic life, material eroded from the continents, and the atmosphere.

5 Archaean continents

but a mist went up from the earth and watered
the whole face of the ground.

Genesis 2:6

Thou didst cover it with the deep as with a mantle:
the waters stood above the mountains.
At Thy rebuke they fled. The mountains rose, the valleys
sank down to the place which thou didst appoint to them.

Psalm 104

5.1 Continents and oceans

By about 3.5 Ga ago there may have existed on Earth an assortment of well-defined 'continents' and distinct 'oceans'. The sedimentological record is our main source of evidence for the existence of this dichotomy and for the attendant development of the erosional cycle, mountains, rivers, shallow seas, abyssal depths and all that went on above the Moho.

Consider first the extent to which continents project above sea level, their 'freeboard' (Hess 1962). Various lines of evidence, including seismic surveys of old continental nuclei (Gane *et al.* 1956), electrical studies (van Zijl 1977) and studies of metamorphic assemblages (Harris & Holland 1984) as well as the interpretation of transects through the crust (see Ch. 3) suggest that old continental crust was roughly the same thickness (35 km approximately), or in places even thicker, than today's continental crust (Nisbet 1984b). On this crust, rugged terrain must have existed (since coarse clastic detritus is common in Archaean strata), but extensive areas of shallow water also occurred (Barley *et al.* 1979). Deep-water conditions may also be recorded in some greenstone belts (Stanistreet *et al.* 1981, but see also Lowe 1982a, Stanistreet *et al.* 1982 and Heinrichs 1984) and the hypsographic curve must have had roughly the same shape as today. This 35 km or greater thickness of continent would have been in isostatic balance with the oceanic lithosphere then and now: were the continents to be thickened they would 'float' up, be eroded, and the eroded material would be redeposited on the continental margin. If any process of segregation from the mantle had the effect of adding to the vertical thickness of continental crust, the material would rapidly be redistributed and the continents would grow laterally instead.

The isostatic problem has fascinated geologists from Pliny onwards, in recent times most notably and most profoundly Hess (1962). The upper surface of the continents is adjusted to equilibrium with sea level by erosion. If material is removed, the continent rises isostatically, to re-equilibrate. For instance, if sea level drops by 100 m, then

$$100 \text{ m} \times \frac{\rho_m - \rho_w}{\rho_m - \rho_c}$$

(where ρ_m = density of mantle, ρ_c = density of continent, ρ_w = density of water) or, choosing typical values, $100 \times [(3.3 - 1.01)/(3.3 - 2.83)] =$ 487 m of continental surface is removed to restore equilibrium. A simple isostatic balance between continent and oceans gives the relationship shown in Figure 5.1, derived by Hess and by Wise (1974), and adopted by McLennan and Taylor (1982), who give

thickness of continental crust (km)
$$= 12.3 + [5.75 \times (\text{depth of oceans in km})] \qquad (5.1)$$

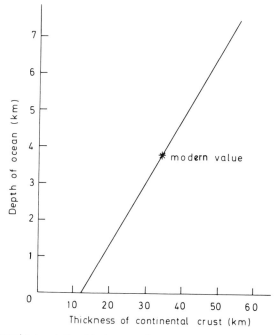

Figure 5.1 Approximate relationship between depth to the Moho under the continents and depth of the abyssal sea floor, calculated from isostatic balance assuming crustal compositions as today (from Hess 1962 and McLennan & Taylor 1982).

147

Figure 5.2 illustrates the isostatic balance between continents and oceans, where d = depth of sea above the mid-ocean ridge, ρ is the density of the asthenosphere a, subcrustal lithosphere l and continent c, with water assumed to have a unit density, h_r is the height of the ridge above the base of the continental lithosphere, h_l the thickness of the subcontinental lithosphere, h_c the thickness of the continent, e the elevation of the continent above sea level and d the depth of water above the mid-ocean ridge axis

$$d + \rho_a h_r = \rho_c h_c + \rho_l h_l \qquad (5.2)$$

$$d = \rho_c h_c + \rho_l h_l - \rho_a h_r$$

Now, lithosphere is cooled asthenosphere, so $\rho_l = K\rho_a$ where $K \simeq 1 + \alpha(T_a - T_l)$, α being the coefficient of expansion, T_a and T_l the temperatures of asthenosphere and subcrustal lithosphere, respectively. Thus

$$d = \rho_c h_c + K\rho_a h_1 - \rho_a h_r$$

Also $h_r = h_c + h_l - e - d$

Thus $d = \rho_c h_c + K\rho_a h_l - \rho_a(h_c + h_l - e - d)$

$$d(1 - \rho_a) = \rho_c h_c + \rho_a h_l(K - 1) - \rho_a h_c + \rho_a e$$

Since $1 - \rho_a$ is negative, but $K > 1$

$$\rho_a h_c > \rho_a e + \rho_a h_l(K - 1) + \rho_c h_c$$

$$h_c > e + h_l(K - 1) + \frac{\rho_c}{\rho_a} h_c \qquad (5.3)$$

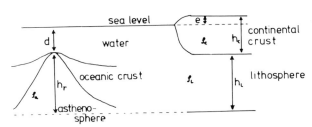

Figure 5.2 Isostatic balance between continents and the oceanic column (sea over rising asthenosphere) at the mid-ocean ridge axis (from Nisbet 1984d). For definition of terms see text.

Or, for typical values of density,

$$h_c > [e + h_l(K - 1)] \, 15 \qquad (5.4)$$

Since K is marginally greater than 1 (say, $1 + 3.10^5 \times (300) = 1.01$), roughly

$$h_c > (e + 0.8) \, 15$$

which for an 80-km thick Archaean subcrustal lithosphere and for $h_c \sim 35 \, km$, gives $e < 1.5 \, km$. An interesting point to consider is the evolution of K with age, as the mantle may have cooled. T_l is the 'average' lithosphere temperature, which depends in part on the composition (i.e. in propensity to melt) of the lithosphere. Assuming that to be constant (i.e. that the roots of modern continents are frozen Archaean material), then $T_a - T_l$ would be much greater in the Archaean than today and thus ($K - 1$) would be greater, implying thicker continents for comparable, erosion-controlled freeboard (e). Other assumptions obviously give other answers.

Have the mid-ocean ridges always been sub-aqueous (i.e. was d positive)? The available evidence strongly implies that they were. Quite apart from arguments derived from continental freeboard, there is presumptive evidence for calc-alkaline volcanism in the Archaean (see Ch. 6), which would imply that there was a subducted supply of water beneath the volcanic arcs (for a discussion of this point, see Campbell & Taylor 1983). By further implication, the new oceanic crust must have been hydrated. It is possible that this hydration could have taken place subaerially, by meteoric water as in modern Iceland, but it is much more probable that hydration was sub-aqueous. Secondly, there is the observation that both basalts and, more significantly, komatiites (which were presumably derived directly from the mantle) were erupted subaqueously: they characteristically formed pillow lavas and sub-aqueous flows (e.g. in the Belingwe Belt − see Ch. 6). Since eruption was sub-aqueous in rifting settings such as Belingwe or Barberton, then isostatic arguments would imply that similar liquids would also erupt sub-aqueously at mid-ocean ridges. Thirdly, it has been suggested that the modern oceans appear to be steadily losing water by return to the mantle down subduction zones (Ito et al. 1983). If so, the volume of Archaean oceans would be greater than today's oceans, all other things being equal, and, most probably, the depth of those oceans would also be greater. All of these are very circumstantial arguments, and each can be attacked: nevertheless, the strong implication is that Archaean oceans did indeed cover the mid-ocean ridges.

The volume of the oceans depends on the area of the oceans, the depth above the ridge, and the age–depth subsidence curve of the oceanic floor away from the ridge crest. The area of the oceans is today about $3.3 \times 10^8 \text{km}^2$ (compared with a continental area of $1.8 \times 10^8 \text{km}^2$): it is possible that in the Archaean the oceanic area was somewhat greater, if there has been growth in continental area since then, either by thinning of the continents or by differentiation. The depth above the ridge has been discussed above: if the oceanic water is indeed being steadily subducted as Ito *et al.* claim, then the depth may have been greater in the Archaean. A good approximation to the age–depth curve of the oceanic floor is, today, given by (Dahlen, 1981)

$$s = 2\left(\frac{\rho_m}{\rho_m - \rho_w}\right)\alpha\ T_m\left(\frac{\varkappa t}{\pi}\right)^{\!1/2} \qquad (5.5)$$

where s is the subsidence below the mid-ocean ridge crest, ρ_m, ρ_w densities of mantle and water, α the volume coefficient of thermal expansion, T_m the asthenospheric temperature under the ridge axis, $\varkappa$ the thermal diffusivity, and t the lithospheric age. For a modern ridge, with $T_m = 1350°C$, this gives $s = 350\,m/(\text{my})^{1/2}$, while, to take an extreme end-case for a komatiitic Archaean ridge, using $T_m = 1700°C$, $s = 440\,m/(\text{my})^{1/2}$. Thus Archaean ocean floor, if komatiitic, would lie more deeply below the ridge axis than modern ocean floor of comparable age, Figure 5.8 shows other estimates of Archaean depth–age curves from McKenzie *et al.* (1980). However Bickle (1978) has used heat flow arguments to show that there is good reason to suppose that Archaean mid-ocean ridges had higher spreading rates than today: thus, Archaean ocean floor would be younger and shallower than modern ocean floor at comparable distance from the ridge. In sum, the likelihood is that the volume of the ocean below the ridge crest was less then than now: thus, if oceanic volume has been constant or decreasing as the Earth ages, Archaean sea level would have been higher above the ridge crest than today. The implication of Hess's equation is that Archaean continents were thicker than today, though perhaps not by much, since thicker continents would mean a smaller continental area and hence more oceanic area (which would restrain deep oceans).

Schubert and Reymer (1985) have assumed that the oceans have had constant volume, the upper mantle constant density, the mean age of subducted plate is constant, and the subsidence of the ocean floor away from the ridge is inversely related to mean oceanic surface heat flow (see Section 5.11). Given these assumptions, the apparent constancy of the continental freeboard (Section 3.3) implies net growth of continental crust at a rate of about $1\,km^3\,a^{-1}$.

How old are the oceans? As far as the geological record indicates, deep oceans with water lapping onto the edges of the continents have existed since 3.6 Ga, and most probably since prior to 4 Ga. The Beitbridge assemblages and also the Isua suite include a variety of metamorphosed sediments, from clastics to carbonates to highly aluminous pelitic rocks. Such assemblages suggest that neither were the continents totally flooded, nor were the ocean floors dry. Most probably the oceans are almost as old as the Earth itself. Indeed, Allègre *et al.* (1983) suggest that major degassing took place at least 4400 Ma ago. Furthermore, some of the oceanic water may have collected during the late bombardment of the planet by water-rich material.

5.2 Archaean sediments

The study of Archaean sediments provides many of the clues to the puzzle of how the continents grew. The problem is varied: How old are the continents? What were they made of? Did they contain high mountains? How rapidly were they eroded? Did extensive stable platforms exist, and if so, what controlled global tectonics? All these are just a few of the more tectonically biased questions. The sedimentary record contains the debris of the continents, and much of what we know of the composition and environment of the continents comes from studying sediments. Sediments are critically dependent in their depositional sites and their erosion upon isostatic movement, which in turn is related to the thermal and tectonic factors which produce metamorphism. Investigating the metamorphism of the Archaean crust thus may produce an understanding of what controlled much of the sedimentation. The two subjects and the problem of Archaean tectonics are simply different facets of a central question: how did the Earth manage its thermal budget in Archaean time?

5.3 The sedimentological record: stratigraphic examples

The Archaean sedimentological record is very diverse. As a gross simplification it can be divided into three major associations:
(a) extensive shallow water and alluvial sequences,
(b) successions showing evidence for major local relief changes and,
(c) non-clastic associations.
   The clastic record is dominant: in the Canadian Shield, Ojakangas (1985) distinguishes a subordinate Alluvial Fan–Fluvial facies association, of cross-bedded sandstones and associated conglomerates; a dominant resedimented (Turbidite) facies association of greywacke, mudstone–siltstone and conglomerate, and a minor non-clastic record.

5.3.1 Shallow-water (platform) successions

It is often and erroneously supposed that the early Archaean continental surface was entirely unstable – mountains of jelly through which squirted monstrous effusions of lava: a terrestrial analogue of Io. Perhaps in part, but even some of the oldest strata show evidence for stable platform successions. In Chapter 3, several stratigraphic successions were described: here it is worth investigating their sedimentology in more detail.

A. Pilbara (3.5 Ga) In the Pilbara, Barley *et al.* (1979, 1984) have identified a major shallow-water succession approximately 5–8 km thick. Rocks of the 3.5 Ga old Warrawoona succession (see Ch. 3) include thin but laterally extensive cherty metasediments intercalated with ultramafic–mafic metavolcanic sequences. The cherty metasediments consist of black carbonaceous and pyritic units, banded grey and white units, and minor graphitic and pyritic shales. A wide variety of sedimentary structures has been recorded. Cherty sedimentary units tend to be roughly 5 m thick. They are massive, or finely laminated (0.5–1 mm), or sometimes show parallel or cross laminations. Ripple marks occur in places. The cherts grade laterally and vertically into silicified coarse-grained arenitic metasediments with graded bedding (Fig. 5.3). Cross-bedding and scour-and-fill structures, as well as small lenticular edge-wise conglomerate beds, and intraformational pebble and cobble conglomerates indicate contemporaneous reworking.

Around the North Pole dome is a bedded barite and chert unit, which contains possible or probable stromatolites (see discussion in Ch. 4). In many localities there is good evidence for pseudomorphs after gypsum. This deposit is interpreted as an Archaean evaporite sequence.

Lowe (1983) has described a study of the Strelley Pool chert near the top of the Warrawoona Group. He recognizes a regressive sequence of chert, stromatolites and evaporite deposited in a large hypersaline lake or a marine basin. Barley *et al.* (1979, 1984), summarising the work in the area by various workers of the University of Western Australia, pointed out that the cherty metasediments and associated metamorphosed felsic volcaniclastics, apparently of shallow water to sub-aerial origin, are continuous for tens of kilometres in well-documented localities, although lateral facies changes are common and cherts cannot be used for correlation. The lateral extent of thin (< 20 m) shallow-water horizons indicates deposition in an area of gentle topography. They concluded that the landscape during deposition of the Warrawoona Group was fairly flat, with felsic vents forming local topographic highs in the basin. Buick and Barnes (1984) describe the cherts of the Warrawoona Group in detail. Most are secondarily silicified, after dolomitised or baritised diagenetic precursors, but primary fabrics are well

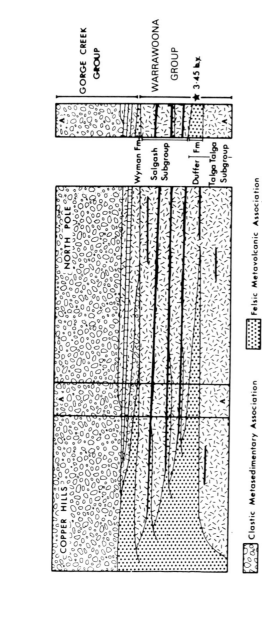

Figure 5.3 Composite lithostratigraphic section of the Archaean greenstone succession in the eastern Pilbara Block (from Barley *et al.* 1979).

preserved, and lithofacies display evidence of deposition in shallow sub-aqueous or intermittently exposed settings.

B. Pongola Supergroup (circa 3.0 Ga) A similarly subdued topography can be inferred from the work of Matthews and Scharrer (1968) and von Brunn and Hobday (1976) in the 2.5–7.0 km thick Pongola Supergroup of Southern Africa (see Section 3.3.1). The base of the Supergroup is marked by a graded unconformity, passing from granite, the top of which displays an extensive Archaean weathering profile, to stratified sediments which are generally feldspathic and display considerable lateral facies variation with breccias, grits and silt. Von Brunn and Hobday describe two sections in detail and show that an extensive shallow marine–tidal flat milieu existed with intermittent fluviatile influx. All this was laid down on what was apparently a relatively stable Archaean craton (Tankard *et al.* (1982).

C. The Witwatersrand Sea The Witwatersrand Supergroup is approximately 2.5–2.6 Ga old (von Niekerk and Burger 1978) and has a stratigraphic succession 7–10 km thick, or more. Its geological character has often been compared more closely to Proterozoic than to Archaean rocks. It is perhaps the most intensively studied of all Archaean sedimentary successions (Tankard *et al.* 1982). A major part of the supergroup (see Table 5.1) is the West Rand Group, which occupies a roughly oval area of 42 000 km², 350 km long and 200 km across. Most of the sediments were laid down in marine shelf and tidal environments with minor fluvial episodes, upon a substrate of earlier Witwatersrand deposits and, below them, of granite. In thickness the Group averages about 4.5 km, varying from 1 km to 7 km. Above it is the Central Rand Group, consisting of alluvial fan deposits up to 3 km thick, preserved today in a smaller basin than that of the West Rand strata. There is good local evidence to suggest that the pre-

Table 5.1 Composite stratigraphy of the Witwatersrand Supergroup (from Pretorius 1981).

Supergroup	Group	Subgroup	Approx. thickness (m)	Lithology
Witwatersand	Central Rand	Turffontein	1700	coarse clastics
		Johannesburg	1500	coarse clastics, minor volcanics
	West Rand	Jeppestown	1400	subgreywacke, shales
		Government	2000	subgreywacke, shales
		Hospital Hill	1700	orthoquartzite ironstone, shales
	Dominion	Syferfontein	2100	rhyolites, andesite
		Rhenosterhoek	600	andesites, tuffs, basal conglomerates

sent margin probably corresponds closely to the original basin edge (Tankard *et al.* 1982), and that the basin progressively closed. Individual major fluvial fans can be identified – the group consists of a diverse set of mainly fluvial and fan–delta sediments. The Witwatersrand is amongst the most important of all Archaean sedimentary sequences. It is the chief source of the livelihood of millions of people (see Ch. 7); to the Archaean geologist it represents something less tangible, a *fin de siècle*. The basin is a huge depository laid down on what was clearly stable, strong lithosphere. The thickness of the 'lithosphere' can be defined by choosing an isotherm: for instance, one way of defining the thickness is to equate the lithosphere with the cool and thus mechanically strong layer above, say, the $500°C$ isotherm. The depth of this isotherm depends on the square root of the time since the last major thermal event (e.g. igneous intrusion and volcanism). Other isotherms, such as $1100°C$, can also be chosen, depending on the purpose of the definition. As the lithosphere thickens, its strength increases, and thus its ability to sustain load (i.e. thick sediment) becomes greater. The enormous thickness of the Witwatersrand Supergroup seems to be a witness to this: in this part of Southern Africa the local lithosphere was thick enough in the late Archaean to allow the development of such a basin. Diamonds have been found in Witwatersrand sediments and have been produced in some numbers from the gold mines, implying a lithosphere perhaps 150 km thick (see Section 5.7.4).

The Warrawoona and Pongola sequences, as preserved, are thinner and appear always to have been thinner. Thicknesses are almost impossible to estimate in the Pilbara. Even in the Pongola and Witwatersrand it is very difficult to judge maximum vertical thickness, as opposed to heights of stratigraphic columns. It is tempting, though not safe, to say that the Warrawoona and Pongola sequences are part of a general trend. Below many early Archaean continental nuclei the lithosphere was probably thin, so only thin shallow-water sedimentary successions could be sustained. In the mid-Archaean there is evidence that diamonds were forming in some areas: this would imply that at least in a few cratons the cooling had progressed, so a greater load could be carried. However, there may be other explanations; perhaps the continental lithosphere was stabilised chemically from very early on. More of this later.

5.3.2 *Successions showing evidence for major local relief*

Most Archaean sedimentary successions are not like those described above. Instead, they consist of an assortment of rock types which were laid down in a wide depth range. Often there is evidence for a progressively deepening sequence of depositional environments, terminated by volcanism. It is in this setting that some of the most interesting of all Archaean rocks occur.

155

The stratigraphy of the Belingwe greenstone belt, and the sedimentology of other Archaean belts have already been discussed (Ch. 3). It is now appropriate to move from stratigraphic data to speculative interpretation. McKenzie *et al.* (1980) and Bickle and Eriksson (1982) have proposed a simple model which can account for most of the observed features of the succession in the Belingwe Belt (Nisbet 1984). Models are very dangerous things in geology since the evidence can so easily be twisted to fit a presupposed requirement, yet they are also essential and stimulative; even in default they can contribute by drawing attention to previously unrecognised unpleasant facts requiring explanation. Darwin once observed that incorrect 'facts' are the death of Science but incorrect hypotheses are its lifeblood.

McKenzie *et al.* (1980) pointed out that some Archaean sedimentary basins can be understood if they are interpreted in terms of subsidence caused by lithospheric extension, as illustrated in Figure 5.4. This type of model was originally developed for modern basins such as the North Sea.

Figs. 5.5–5.7 illustrate the geological consequences of this model. In the initial protobasinal stages (Bickle & Eriksson 1982) the crust and lithosphere

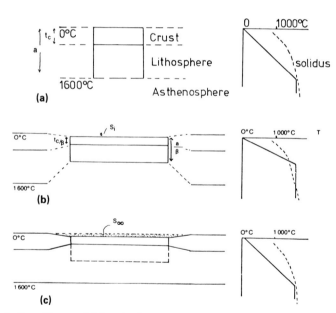

Figure 5.4 Stretching model for the formation of some Archaean greenstone belts (from Nisbet 1984a). (a) Initial state. Solid line on graph shows thermal gradient. Solidus very approximate. (b) Immediately after stretching. Note thinning of lithosphere and zone of potential melting at base of lithosphere. Initial melts may come from great depth (komatiites) during early rapid extension, followed by formation of high-level magma chambers and high-level melting. (c) Thermal re-equilibration, infilling of basin, decay of thermal gradient.

156

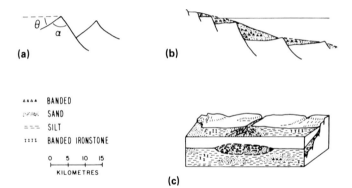

BANDED
SAND
SILT
BANDED IRONSTONE

0   5   10   15
KILOMETRES

Figure 5.5 Early stages of rifting in a developing basin (proto-basinal stage). (From Nisbet 1984a.) (a) Configuration of tilted blocks (rotational). (b) Development of rifted margin. Note rotational faults. (c) Depositional facies. Features include braided rivers, debris flow and rockfall deposits, construction of sub-aerial and sub-aqueous fan, local cliffed shoreline, local oxide and carbonate ironstones in protected environments. Likely host strata for gold deposits include the clastic fans, the ironstones and algal mats.

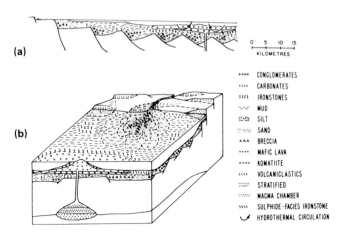

0   5   10   15
KILOMETRES

CONGLOMERATES
CARBONATES
IRONSTONES
MUD
SILT
SAND
BRECCIA
MAFIC LAVA
KOMATIITE
VOLCANICLASTICS
STRATIFIED
MAGMA CHAMBER
SULPHIDE-FACIES IRONSTONE
HYDROTHERMAL CIRCULATION

Figure 5.6 Late initial phase of development of an Archaean sedimentary basin (from Nisbet 1984a). (a) Initiation of volcanism as subsidence continues with hydrothermal activity along axis of eruption. (b) Volcanic and depositional environments. Development of deltas and submarine fans, with grain size ranging from conglomerates to fine distal silts. Local coastal stromatolite growth. Oxide and carbonate ironstones in sheltered areas. Sulphide ironstones near lava flows. Formation of stratified magma chamber at lithosphere/asthenosphere boundary. Likely host strata for gold deposits (see Ch. 7) include the clastic fans, coastal carbonate mats and sulphide ironstones near lava flows. The latter would however have a low potential for preservation.

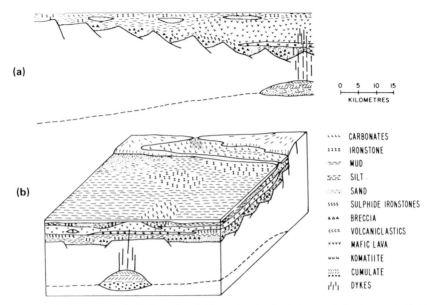

KILOMETRES

0 5 10 15

ʟʟʟʟ   CARBONATES
ɪɪɪɪ   IRONSTONE
═══   MUD
▂▂▂   SILT
       SAND
ssss   SULPHIDE IRONSTONES
▲▲▲   BRECCIA
cccc   VOLCANICLASTICS
vvvv   MAFIC LAVA
ᴜᴜᴜ   KOMATIITE
       CUMULATE
ıʼıʼı DYKES

Figure 5.7 Long period of thermal subsidence in the final stages of development of an Archaean sedimentary basin (from Nisbet 1984a). Likely host strata for gold deposits (Ch. 7) would include ironstones at the interface between terminal lavas and the first clastic sediments to accumulate in the post-volcanic phase. (a) Cessation of volcanism, leaving ultramafic cumulate bodies at depth. Infill of slowly subsiding basin by fine-grained, shallow-water clastic sediments, ironstones and carbonates. (b) Formation of extensive shallow basin, slowly infilling, as sedimentation matches subsidence, with lagoonal coastline.

is rapidly extended, while isostatic compensation is maintained. During this phase the stretched crust subsides very rapidly and a basin forms, into which coarse detritus is rapidly poured. Sedimentation does not keep up with subsidence: the basin deepens. As stretching continues, hot asthenospheric material upwells to occupy the space left by the lithosphere. Eventually, if stretching is great enough, volcanism begins (Fig. 5.6), in the centre of the subsided basin.

In the extreme case, stretching continues until the lithosphere parts, and new oceanic crust is generated in the gap. In other cases, stretching does not progress so far, or even is so small that no volcanism at all takes place.

In the final stage of the model, stretching ceases. The hot asthenosphere then cools, slowly. As it cools it becomes more dense. The isostatic consequence of this is a slow subsidence, with which the sedimentation can easily keep up. A thick shallow-water succession slowly accumulates (Fig. 5.7).

The thermal time constant of this late subsidence was calculated by McKenzie *et al.* (1980) to be about 24 Ma in latest Archaean times, and only about 8 Ma in the early Archaean (3.8 Ga ago), in contrast to the modern value of over 60 Ma. In this modelling, much depends on very poorly constrained assumptions about the thickness of the lithosphere (see Section 5.10). Figure 5.8 shows calculated subsidence curves. The curves show that initial subsidence in a stretching basin was probably faster in the early Archaean than in later times if the lithosphere was thinner, but total sediment thickness was very much less (*circa* 4.2 km, if the density of the sediment was 2.5 gm/cc). In the late Archaean, if the lithosphere had thickened, initial subsidence would have been slower, but total sediment thickness greater (over 7 km). If dense volcanics were present in the succession, greater thicknesses would accumulate as the basin sank under the heavier load.

McKenzie *et al.* (1980) and Bickle and Eriksson (1982) applied this model with some success to a variety of Archaean greenstone belts, but it appears that the model is not very successful in belts which have significant andesitic–felsic volcanics. The assumptions of the models are great, and they only properly apply to greenstone belts of purely tensional origin.

McKenzie *et al.* (1980), Bickle and Eriksson (1982) and Nisbet (1984a) all applied the model to a facies analysis of the Ngezi Group of the Belingwe greenstone belt. There is a close correspondence between the order of most of the sedimentary and volcanic facies predicted by the model and the rock types that actually exist in the belt (see details of the stratigraphy in Ch. 3), although the protobasinal stage is poorly developed. In the lower, Mtshingwe Group the protobasinal stage is much better developed. A warning though: thermal models are generally very non-unique, in the sense that many models give similar solutions. Thus the stretching model is not necessarily correct. However, it does give the right general order of events.

Other successions showing evidence for major local relief are not nearly as simple as the Belingwe sequence. In western Zimbabwe, extensive and varied late Archaean sediments are associated with andesitic volcanism and the intrusion of major granite plutons. In the Pilbara, very extensive associations of coarse clastic sediments form the Gorge Creek Group. Above the Witwatersrand sequence, the Ventersdorp Supergroup includes extensive volcanogenic horizons which do not easily fit into a simple extensional model. Instead, many Archaean successions are probably broadly analogous to sedimentary and volcanic suites found today above subduction zones, but in few cases has detailed modelling yet been attempted to describe the facies distribution, subsidence rates and style of volcanism. Modern sedimentary basins close to subduction zones often show components both of extensional subsidence and also subsidence due to lithospheric flexure, as in the modern Queen Charlotte Basin, off the coast

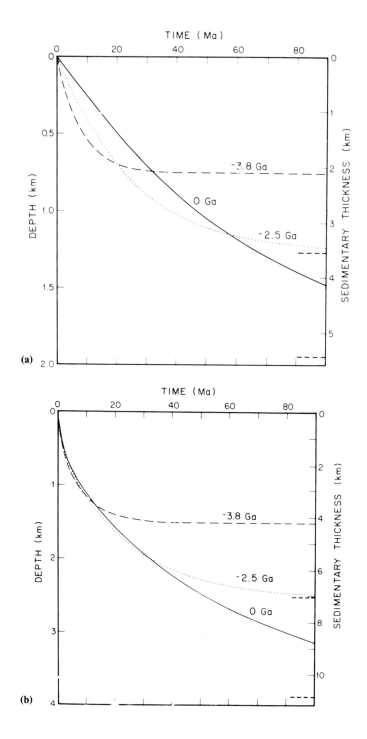

(a)

(b)

of British Columbia (Yorath & Hyndman 1983). In other areas, extension may occur by simple shear, greatly thinning the lithosphere but not necessarily the crust (Wernicke, 1985).

Thus, stretching models can usefully be applied to Archaean sedimentary successions, but should be used with much caution. Most probably, the majority of Archaean sedimentary accumulations formed in complex tectonic environments, often with a component of stretching. Modelling of these complex suites is only just beginning; much needs to be learnt (Fig. 5.9). Simple shear models of extension have not yet been applied to

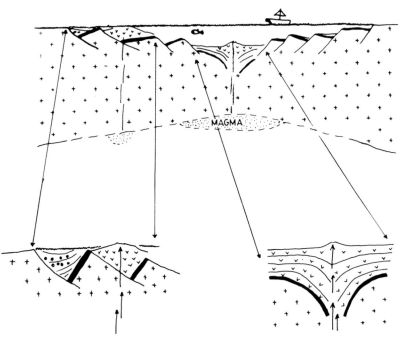

Figure 5.9 Cartoon to show possible settings in which some greenstone belt successions may form as a result of extension of continental crust. Left: deposition of clastic sediment (ooo) and volcanoes (vvv) on rifted blocks. Subsequent deformation would lead to a homoclinal belt. Right: deposition in centre of rift, with basement further depressed by load of volcanics and sediment. Deformation would tighten dips to produce a very tight to isoclinal syncline.

Figure 5.8 Subsidence as a function of time for a basin stretched by a factor of two, when full of sediment of density $2.5 \, g \, cm^{-3}$ and full of seawater. The dashed line corresponds to a possible early Archaean model lithosphere below young continent; the dotted line to a similar late Archaean model and the solid line to a modern model lithosphere. Heavy dashed lines in (b) show the depth to which the curves will eventually tend after infinite time. (From McKenzie et al. 1980).

Archaean belts, but may prove to be widely relevant, especially in explaining apparently monoclinal successions.

5.3.3 Possible deeper water associations

Very few deep water Archaean sediments have been identified, and those that have been so described are controversial. Yet these facies, although unusual, are of great importance in identifying possible relicts of oceanic crust.

For the Barberton Mountains, several authors (e.g. Anhaeusser 1981a, 1969, de Wit *et al.* 1980) have drawn analogies between the *igneous* rocks of the greenstone belt and possible Archaean oceanic crust, but interpretation of the sedimentary sequence is very controversial. Stanistreet *et al.* (1981) described the Msauli Chert, at the contact between the lower mainly mafic and komatiitic lavas of the Onverwacht Group and the upper sedimentary Fig Tree Group. This chert is characterised by interspersed 2-cm and 30-cm thick units of spheroidal grains, which appear to be laid down in graded units. Stanistreet *et al.* (1981) draw analogies between the observed fabric of the rocks and the typical Bouma sequence of turbidites, and conclude that the chert was laid down in deep water, in a deep oceanic basin. More recently, Heinrichs (1984) has confirmed the identification of turbidites, but suggested that the chert probably represents the deposit of a major phreatoplinian volcanic event.

De Wit *et al.* (1980) considered that the underlying Onverwacht Group (including the type succession of komatiites) was laid down in deep water, possibly in oceanic conditions. Perhaps, if they are right, the komatiites of the Onverwacht Group are a sample of the elusive Archaean oceanic crust: one must always remember, though, that eruption in deep water does not automatically mean eruption as oceanic crust – the ophiolite debate has shown up this fallacy in modern rocks. But, nevertheless, the matter is of great interest and potential import. Nothing, of course, is simple: for example, the work by Stanistreet *et al.* (1981, 1982) has been vigorously disputed by Lowe *et al.* (1982).

A rather similar example, both stratigraphically and geochemically (in the details of the alumina content of the komatiites) is the Ruth Well sequence, West Pilbara (Nisbet & Chinner 1981). Although the area has not been subject to expert sedimentological scrutiny, the very thin intercalations of chert and of volcaniclastic material in the komatiitic sequence all have a very deep-water aspect. Perhaps this area contains another possible mine for that rare and elusive philosopher's stone: the Archaean oceanic crust. As yet, however, no convincing case has been made to prove that Archaean oceanic material is anywhere preserved.

5.4 Archaean sedimentary facies: some deductions from evaporites, stromatolites, cherts and ironstones

Sedimentology provides a set of immensely powerful tools for breaking open the two great puzzles of the Archaean – the tectonic style of the Earth and the origin of life. The brief analysis in the preceding pages has shown that despite the fragmentary state of the record, some very important information has been preserved. The continents were distinct, even by 3.6 Ga; they probably had high mountains and also extensive lowlands or areas of shallow water on continental crust. We may even have left to us some fragments of the oceans, in which cherts and volcaniclastic sediments were being laid down on komatiitic crust.

The shallow seas were floored by evaporites, stromatolites and cherts and ironstones, as well as silts and clay. The evaporites show us that the sea was not fresh: quite probably its composition was in part controlled by hydrothermal circulation through the komatiitic mid-ocean ridges, in part by the erosion from the continents, and in part by the activity of life. Magnesite deposits occur in Archaean strata – they are usually of very controversial origin (Macgregor & Bliss 1968), but may be a variety of evaporite precipitated from the magnesium-rich waters. The presence of sulphate in the evaporites suggests at least mildly oxidising settings.

Life by its nature has a habit of rapidly filling any available niche: since it has existed it must have been very widespread indeed, and also diverse (within the limits of the procaryota). Almost all modern sediments are in some way influenced by life (even the triggering of debris flows depends on occasion on the failure of binding vegetation); it is thus reasonable to assume that many Archaean *sub-aqueous* sediments were similarly influenced. What then of carbonates, and why do they appear to be uncommon in the Archaean? Presumably part of the answer lies in the absence of an 'inventory': today the erosion of limestones supplies abundant calcium to the oceans. In the early Archaean the source of calcium would have been dominated by the erosion of igneous rocks. On the other hand, limestones do occur, so presumably where sedimentological conditions were right, carbonate precipitation did indeed occur.

From this comes the implication that the pH of Archaean oceans was not radically different from that of today's oceans (Walker 1983a), and thus the deduction that a massively CO_2-dominated atmosphere comparable to that of modern Venus has not been present on Earth during the period of the geological record. Presumably, as CO_2 degassed at mid-ocean ridges and above subduction zones, it went into solution in the seas (in equilibrium with the atmosphere). Most degassed CO_2 would have been rapidly returned to the oceanic crust, carried in by hydrothermal fluids at mid-ocean ridges and deposited as carbonates in the altered mafic and ultramafic rock of the ocean floor. At subduction zones, some CO_2 would be driven off to return to the atmosphere via calc-alkaline volcanism; other CO_2 would descend with the host oceanic crust to the mantle; yet other CO_2 would go to the sub-continental mantle wedge. Degassed CO_2 would return, via atmosphere and oceans and hydrothermal fluids, to the oceanic plate.

To quantify this, today there is an inventory of *circa* 5×10^{22} g of carbon on the surface (Javoy *et al.* 1982). This inventory may represent the small fraction of CO_2 captured in the supracontinental sediments during the cycle. The modern flux of degassed carbon from the mantle is about 2×10^{14} g per year (Javoy *et al.* 1983); in the Archaean this flux may have been much greater. Much of this flux may be recaptured by the oceanic plate almost immediately. The modern surface inventory of carbon, in carbonate and hydrocarbons, represents only 10^8–10^9 yr of degassing, or, stated in another way, represents the capture (by weathered Ca, Mg etc. and biological precipitation) on the continents and continental shelves of somewhere between 2% and 25% of the degassed CO_2 over the past 4 Ga. The apparent rarity of Archaean carbonates thus becomes a matter both of the absence of inventory to be reworked and the original tectonic setting of those few rocks that have been preserved, and is not necessarily more surprising than the rarity of carbonates in California. What *is* surprising, though, is that a substantial proportion of the few preserved Archaean carbonates are limestones, not dolomites, though the Proterozoic record is dominated by dolomite. There is as yet no satisfactory explanation of this: perhaps it is related to sea level, circulation processes in mid-ocean ridges, and Ca/Mg balance.

Many of the sediments which chance has preserved for us are intertidal, and in some places (e.g. Belingwe and Barberton) very close comparisons can be drawn between Archaean and modern intertidal sedimentary structures. Since solar tides are very small, the deduction from this is that the Moon has been present for at least the past 3.5 Ga, and that during this period there is no evidence to suggest any catastrophically close approach by the Moon to the Earth (although, of course, the record is very discontinuous). Not much can be said about how high the Archaean tides were, except that they produced sediments similar to those of today and were presumably comparable to modern tides in the size order of their range. There is no ubiquitous evidence for very great or very small tidal ranges; in many areas, intertidal facies seem quite 'normal'. We have no idea if the Archaean record has selectively preserved deposits from small, closed basins with comparatively low tidal ranges or, alternatively, from areas of the sea more similar to the Bay of Fundy or the Bristol Channel; all that can be deduced is that the Moon *was* present.

Panella (1976) has attempted to use stromatolite laminae to measure day length, which is related to lunar distance: this work is extremely interesting but solid conclusions are probably as yet beyond the sedimentological resolution left to us in the available stromatolites, although it might be worth attempting in the very best preserved examples (e.g. Fortescue, Belingwe) if modern stromatolites could be understood better. Similarly, stromatolite synoptic heights are to some extent related to tidal height: if it could be proved that a particular morphology of giant stromatolites was intertidal and its height was indeed tidally controlled, possibly some deductions could be made about the history of the lunar orbit. However, many modern stromatolites are subtidal, so this type of approach to the tidal problem is rather unreliable.

The cherts and ironstones present different problems: again, the existence of life may have been important, at least in the precipitation of some rock associations. Archaean ironstones are very varied and are present throughout the record from Isua onwards, but their mineralogy falls into four main classes: carbonates (siderite), silicates, oxides (haematite and magnetite) and sulphides. In North America, Precambrian ironstones are called 'iron formations'. This term is not used here, as it is easily confused with formal stratigraphic nomenclature: instead, the older Southern Hemisphere usage of 'banded ironstone' is preferred, as being explicit and unambiguous – 'banded', because the iron minerals are characteristically interbedded with chert, and 'ironstone', because they are true ironstones, and not perhaps quite as distinct from their Phanerozoic counterparts as is commonly held.

Banded ironstones come in a wide variety of sedimentological facies from intertidal or shallow water settings to deep water associations, as is illustrated by the succession immediately above the unconformity at the base of the Ngezi Group, Belingwe greenstone belt. Near the base, in an intertidal or shallow-water setting, iron-rich carbonates occur and then oxide-facies banded ironstones, jaspilites and cherts, which display superb textures (Fig. 5.10). The clasts appear to be intraformational rip-ups – the ironstone must have been partly lithified when it was ripped up in large tabular clasts in an erosional channel. Field observations in the Manjeri Formation suggest that many of the banded ironstones were laid down in protected settings, in lagoons or perhaps in what would today be marshes and waterlogged flats. Oxide-facies banded ironstones generally contain very little in the way of detrital material – they were clearly laid down only in highly protected areas. Cloud (1983a,b) suggested that much of their deposition was controlled by the metabolism and death of micro-organisms, and Goodwin *et al.* (1985) considered that organic activity was a vital catalyst in carbonate–sulphide precipitation.

Up-section from the intertidal and shallow-water ironstones of the Manjeri Formation, Belingwe, the sedimentary facies change rapidly and deeper-water clastics occur. At the top of the formation is a sulphide-facies

Figure 5.10 Brecciation, apparently penecontemporaneous, in banded ironstone and chert, Manjeri Formation, Belingwe greenstone belt.

banded ironstone, rich in pyrite, and above it the major komatiitic succession begins. This is the characteristic association of sulphidic banded ironstones which usually occurs close to volcanic rocks. Many sulphide-facies banded ironstones are also associated with small 'graphite-rich' bodies (usually containing complex organic molecules, rather than graphite). It is very tempting to think that these are of organic origin, and that the whole association (sulphide-facies banded ironstone, 'graphite' and volcanics) was produced during active microbial growth around hydrothermal vents at the sea surface during volcanism.

Banded ironstones are often thought of as being typical Precambrian rocks, but many Archaean rift settings are dominated by coarse clastic rocks. It is conventional wisdom that there was no vegetation on the

Archaean land except possibly lichen or fungi, and erosion would have been quite different, dominated by mechanical and inorganic chemical weathering. Catastrophes – debris flows, landslips and assorted coarse clastic flows – may have resulted in the coarse clastics which are commonly displayed in the Archaean record. Mountains probably were eroded rapidly, more in the way that is today apparent in the desert volcanic islands of the Atlantic than in the way one associates with the rounded luxuriant tops of Pacific volcanoes. Yet relief existed, and the continents did most certainly have a freeboard to provide the landslips of coarse clastic detritus transported as debris flows, and turbidity currents which spread out the continental material onto the continental shelves and slopes.

In the deep oceans we do not know what went on. Mid-ocean volcanism *must* have existed in some form (Bickle 1978) to balance the Earth's thermal budget, and new oceanic crust would have subsided according to a function of the square root of its age (Carslaw & Jaeger 1959; see also Section 5.1). On this crust would be laid down the ridge deposits, and then the pelagic sediment. When did life first penetrate the black smokers of the (presumably) komatiitic ridges, or did it indeed begin there? We have no information, yet if we can show that life existed in hydrothermal systems in greenstone belts then it would almost certainly have occupied the exotic habitat of the ridge-axis black smokers. The product would be an assortment of sulphides, precipitates and perhaps 'graphite' extracted, by a variety of stages, eventually from the mantle. In the deep ocean basins the sediment would probably consist of chert, wind-blown dust (there would have been a lot of that) and perhaps the debris of periodic procaryotic blooms on the ocean surface. Input of carbon to the system from the mantle at the ridges and to a lesser extent from continental volcanoes must have been sufficient to have allowed life to have maintained the CO_2 levels of the atmospheres and oceans to its liking.

Walker and Brimblecombe (1985) have constructed tentative geochemical cycles for the young Earth by comparing the relative fluxes of oxygen, dissolved iron, and sulphide to the atmosphere and ocean. They conclude that the flux of iron exceeded both the oxygen and sulphide fluxes. Because of the insolubility of iron oxides and sulphides they infer that dissolved iron was fairly abundant and oxygen and sulphide were rare in the young atmosphere and ocean. Sulphide was the most abundant sulphur species in the ocean, produced by the oxidation of volcanogenic sulphur gases, but they conclude that its concentration was low compared to modern levels. This latter conclusion depends on the assumption that the river-borne flux of dissolved sulphate was very small, and that the continents were not, in the early Archaean, significant suppliers of dissolved sulphate. The validity of this assumption is discussed in Section 5.5.

Figure 5.11 illustrates their models of the geochemical cycles of oxygen

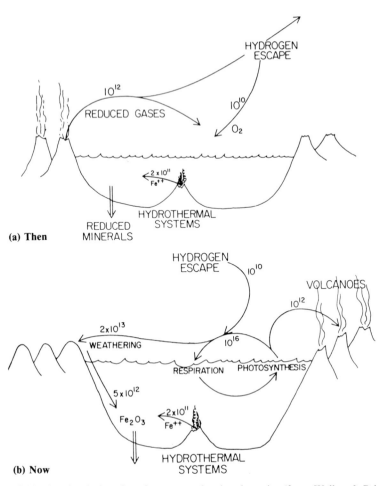

Figure 5.11 Geochemical cycles of oxygen and reduced species (from Walker & Brimble-combe 1985). Annual rates are expressed in moles of oxygen or equivalent reducing power. (a) Presumed geochemical cycles of oxygen and reduced species on the prebiological Earth. (b) Schematic representation of the biogeochemical cycles of oxygen on the modern Earth.

and reduced species on the prebiological Earth, compared with the biologic-ally dominated cycles today, and Figure 5.12 compares the presumed cycles of sulphate on the prebiological Earth with the modern Earth. The contrast is a striking example of the importance of life, and demonstrates the massive impact the beginning of life had on the atmosphere and oceans. It is worth repeating that these models for a prebiological Earth also assume an almost continent-free surface, on which assumption more follows below. Wholly different models can be constructed from other assumptions which imply much higher levels of oxygen in the biosphere (see Sections 8.4, 8.5).

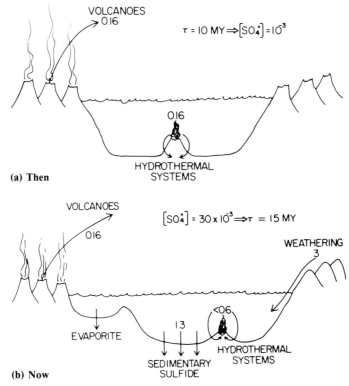

Figure 5.12 Geochemical cycles of sulphate (from Walker & Brimblecombe 1985). Rates of exchange are expressed in units of 10^{12} gm S per year. (a) Presumed geochemical cycles of sulphate on the prebiological Earth. A residence time of 10 Ma against the removal of sulphate in sea floor hydrothermal systems would imply a concentration of sulphate in sea water equal to 10^{-3} mol L^{-1}. (b) Schematic representation of the modern cycles. The present day concentration of sulphate in sea water, equal to 30×10^{-3} mol L^{-1} implies a residence time of sulphate in the ocean of 15 Ma. The modern budget may be unbalanced, and sulphate appears to be accumulating slowly in the ocean.

5.5 The composition of the sedimentary mass

Sedimentary piles represent the eroded and often well-mixed detritus from large areas of continental crust. Thus, the geochemistry of Archaean and younger sediments can be used to attempt to constrain the chemical evolution of the continental crust and, perhaps, to document the history of the cratons. One of the most interesting problems is whether the volume of the continental crust has grown steadily over the Earth's history (curve b in Fig. 1.2), or has grown by a process of catastrophic additions (curve c in Fig. 1.2) or whether it has remained constant over geological time (curve a in

169

Fig. 1.2). This last case would imply that the crust underwent recycling to the mantle, so that addition to the crust by volcanism and intrusion of material from the mantle would have balanced the loss of crustal components to the mantle by subduction of sediments lying on oceanic crust, by loss of components such as calcium through their precipitation in altered ocean basalt, and by erosion of the base of the continental edges above subduction zones. Arguments in favour of the assorted models of crustal growth and evolution have been put forward by various authors (Fig. 6.27), including Armstrong (1981), O'Nions *et al.* (1979), Moorbath (1977), Jacobsen & Wasserburg (1979) and Taylor & McLennan (1985).

McLennan and Taylor (1982, 1980) compared rare earth element (REE), U and Th abundances in a variety of post-Archaean and Archaean clastic sedimentary rocks. In post-Archaean rocks they concluded that the trace element abundances were broadly similar and little dependent on the age of the sediments. This would indicate that if there had been any additions to the post-Archaean upper crust, these additions must have had similar compositions to the upper crust itself. In contrast, Archaean sediments appear to have been derived from a considerably more mafic crust than that which existed later. The most striking feature of this contrast is that samples of post-Archaean upper crust appear to show consistent negative Europium anomalies, irrespective of age, while Archaean samples do not display Eu anomalies in their REE patterns (Fig. 5.13). This observation has been disputed by Naqvi (1986), who obtained both positive and negative Eu anomalies in samples from the Chitradurga schist belt in India. Negative Eu anomalies occurred especially in shales interbedded with greywackes.

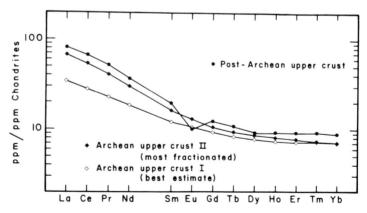

Figure 5.13 Chondrite-normalised REE diagram, showing average Archaean and post-Archaean upper crust compositions (from McLennan & Taylor 1982). Data are derived from REE distributions in sedimentary rocks. Two Archaean patterns are shown: one is a 'best estimate' and the other an extreme 'most fractionated' or conservative model.

The data were interpreted by McLennan & Taylor (1982) as implying a major change in the nature of the continental crust, around the Archaean/Proterozoic boundary, when a vast volume of granitic material, representing a new crustal addition from the mantle (not recycled ancient crust) was intruded and unroofed, to generate major Eu anomalies. Models of the abundances of REE and Th in sedimentary rocks suggest that the minimum ratio of post-Archaean to Archaean upper crustal composition needed to remove the Archaean upper crustal trace element signature is around 4:1. By implication, 65–75% of the continental crust formed during the period 3.2–2.5 Ga, and most (70–85%) of the continental crust had formed by the end of the Archaean. If this is correct, the Earth in early Archaean time would have had a few small continental nuclei scattered across a global ocean like water-beetles; by the end of the Archaean, after a splendid late Archaean pandemonium, the bulk of the continental crust would be fractionated and sailing as huge stately floes across the simatic sea.

5.6 The crustal residence times of the sedimentary mass

Today virtually all of the Earth's surface is covered by sediment, and erosion of old sediment on the continents for the most part supplies the new sediment accumulating on the continental margins. Thus there is very extensive reworking, and only a relatively small part of the vast mass of detritus collecting in the oceans comes directly from new igneous rock. Even this igneous rock often has a large component of crustally derived material, and only a minor amount of the total amount of sediment being transported is derived from a 'first-cycle' or new mantle-derived parent.

Isotopic evidence in sediments is a powerful way of attacking this problem. For instance, the Sm–Nd system can be used to discriminate the origin of sediments (Section 2.8). The Sm/Nd and Nd isotope ratios measured in a sediment sample can be used, if the sediment's depositional age is known, to calculate ε_{Nd} of the sample (see Section 2.5.1) at the time of deposition. Alternatively, model ages termed *crustal residence ages* can be calculated to give the length of time the sample has been apart from a source reservoir (O'Nions *et al.* 1983). Since the continental crust is very different from the upper mantle in its Nd isotopic composition and Sm/Nd ratio, the technique is a powerful tool in deciphering the history of the continents (Jacobsen & Wasserburg 1979, Allègre & Rousseau 1984). Other isotope systems such as Lu–Hf are similarly interesting (Patchett *et al.* 1984).

Hamilton *et al.* (1983) studied metasediments from the Archaean of West Greenland. Sm–Nd data obtained from pelitic and greywacke-like samples gave T_{CHUR} model ages of 3.5–3.6 Ga, slightly less than ages estimated

171

stratigraphically from other dated rocks. However, if the precursors to the sediments separated from a reservoir which had a $^{143}Nd/^{144}Nd$ ratio corresponding to $2\varepsilon_{Nd}$ units greater than CHUR, then their model ages T_{CHUR+2} are around 3.8 Ga, which is stratigraphically correct. Similarly, younger (3.0 Ga) sedimentary samples, also from West Greenland, appeared to be derived from a source of $\varepsilon_{Nd}^{3.0}$ between $+2$ and $+5$. These sediments appear to be 'first-cycle' sediments, in that their T_{CHUR} ages are comparable to or younger than their stratigraphic age, something not true for most modern sediments which are dominantly derived from recycled crustal material.

The positive ε_{Nd} values obtained by Hamilton *et al.* from their Greenland samples, and which are also shown by meta-igneous rocks, are a not unusual feature of Archaean crustal material. If this is a general characteristic, then either the CHUR model is inappropriate for the bulk Earth or fractionation of Sm/Nd had occurred in the source of these Archaean crustal components prior to their generation, most likely by the formation of continental crust prior to 3.8 Ga ago. Hamilton *et al* (1983) commented that a differentiation event that left a depleted mantle source with $\varepsilon_{Nd}^{3.8} = +2$ could have occurred at any time ranging from close to the time of the Earth's formation to as little as 300 Ma prior to the Isua crust-forming event at 3.8 Ga. In the first extreme, if depletion had taken place early in the Earth's history, the Sm/Nd ratio of the source could have increased by almost 10%, giving a present-day ε_{Nd}^{0} of about $+10$, comparable to that inferred for sources of modern mantle-derived melts. Alternatively, in the latter extreme, the sources supplying the Isuan crust may have been more heavily fractionated, with Sm/Nd increased by about 30% at a time 300 Ma prior to 3.8 Ga, but these sources may have only occupied a relatively minor proportion of the mantle.

Goldstein *et al.* (1984) and Allègre & Rousseau (1984) have used Sm/Nd ratios and isotopic compositions to investigate the source and average 'crustal residence age' of the whole sedimentary mass – in other words, how long, on average, the sedimentary mass has been separated from the source mantle. Figure 5.14 shows $^{147}Sm/^{144}Nd$ and $^{143}Nd/^{144}Nd$ for a variety of different rock types of different ages. A striking feature of the diagram is that recent river and aeolian particulates have the same Sm/Nd ratios as Isuan metasediments and grey gneisses and also material from the Canadian Shield and the Scottish Precambrian. This similarity of Sm/Nd ratio implies that there has been little variation in the composition of the continental crust through time. The implication is that overall, the early continental crust was broadly similar (i.e. more silicic than basaltic) to today's, and that there has been no major secular trend from an early basaltic to a later granitic crust, in contradiction to the conclusions drawn from REE analyses (see above).

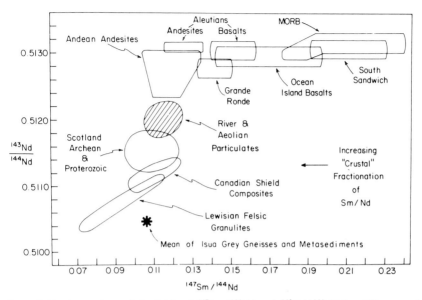

Figure 5.14 Comparison of the fields of ^{147}Sm/^{144}Nd and ^{143}Nd/^{144}Nd for different rock types (from Goldstein *et al.* 1984). Variations in Sm/Nd primarily reflect magmatic processes, while ^{143}Nd/^{144}Nd ratios reflect both Sm/Nd ratios and time. The near constancy of Sm/Nd ratios in Recent particulates and Archaean granulites and gneisses implies the absence of secular trends varying the composition of the continental crust through time. Note that basalts and mantle-derived magmatic rocks have higher Sm/Nd ratios than the continental material.

The mean age of the sedimentary mass is about 1.9 Ga. Today the stratigraphic age distribution of the sedimentary mass shows an exponential range, with a half-mass age of about 500 Ma. 'Crustal residence' ages (t_{CR}) can be calculated by calculating the time since the sample possessed the same ^{143}Nd/^{144}Nd ratio as the mantle which supplied its crustal precursors; or the time the sediment has resided in the continent, separate from the evolving mantle reservoir. For Archaean sediments the crustal residence age is typically close to the 'stratigraphic' age (t_{STRAT}), as for the Greenland material discussed above, but sediments with stratigraphic ages less than about 2.0 Ga typically have crustal residence ages substantially greater than their stratigraphic age.

Figure 5.15 illustrates this. Sediments deposited soon after their crustal source was derived from the mantle fall close to the $t_{CR} = t_{STRAT}$ line. However, as the sedimentary mass has built up, the two ages have increasingly diverged. If continents had not grown at all, t_{CR} would remain constant. Line *A* in the diagram represents the mean age of the sedimentary mass through time for a uniform rate of input of new sediment, presumably from new continental crust derived from the mantle, and line *B* represents the evolution of the sedimentary source, assuming that sediments are

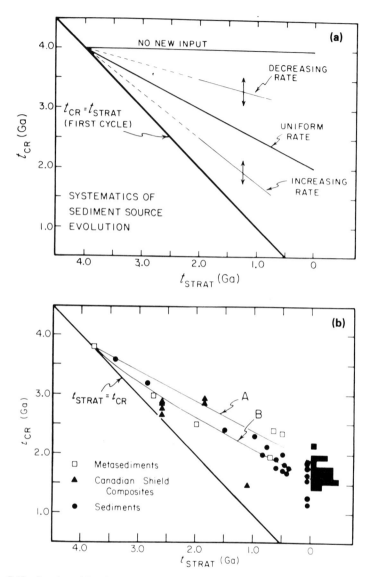

Figure 5.15 Stratigraphic (t_{STRAT}) and crustal residence (t_{CR}) ages of sediments, metasediments and composites (from Goldstein *et al.* 1984.) (a) Upper diagram illustrates the systematics of the evolution of the source of sediments. 'First-cycle' sediments, which are deposited soon after emplacement of their source into the crust without mixing in of older crustal material, would fall close to the line of $t_{CR} = t_{STRAT}$. In contrast, a horizontal (t_{CR} constant) line implies that no new material is added to the source, and sediment is simply reworked pre-existing crust. A uniform input of new material to the continental crust would give a trend with a slope of -0.5. An increasing rate of input would mean that new material from the mantle dominated the sedimentary inventory, while a decreasing rate of input would give a

formed by mixing new continental crust with pre-existing material. As the bulk of accumulated sediment grows, the contribution from new continental crust becomes less important in proportion.

From this Goldstein *et al.* (1984) estimate the mean $^{143}Nd/^{144}Nd$ ratios of the upper crust as 0.5118, or $\varepsilon_{Nd} = -17$, and further estimated values for the whole crust as 0.5122 or $\varepsilon_{Nd} = -9$ and the lower crust as 0.5127 or $\varepsilon_{Nd} = +1$, using data from Taylor and McLennan (1981). Figure 5.16 shows the comparison between $^{147}Sm/^{144}Nd$ and $^{143}Nd/^{144}Nd$ ratios and lines of equal model age based on a depleted mantle (DM) which has evolved in a single stage from CHUR at 4.6 Ga to $\varepsilon_{Nd} = +10$ today.

Miller and O'Nions (1985) used Nd isotopic data in an attempt to search for evidence of continental crust pre-dating 4 Ga. They concluded that Archaean clastic sediments (or at least, those available for sample) were generally derived from precursors with short previous histories of crustal residence, usually no more than 200 Ma prior to deposition. No major input of relatively old crust into clastic sediments can be observed until less than 3 Ga ago. If a significant quantity of continental crust existed, before 4.0 Ga, than either it must have been recycled back to the mantle by 3.8–3.5 Ga, or else sediments derived from it have not been sampled. There is also no evidence for the derivation of Nd in banded ironstones from sources older than 3.5 Ga. The Nd in the ironstones comes from the water masses, and originally from continental sources: thus, any Nd contribution to Archaean sea water by ancient (pre-4 Ga) crust must either have been negligible, or masked by input from more juvenile crustal sources. However, there may be a sampling problem here: the older samples are not from sediments derived from representative areas, and are often closely associated with volcanism.

Several continental growth models can be accommodated within this Sm–Nd data (Fig. 6.27). In general, the older the mean age of the continental crust, the greater the required amount of recycling of sediment out of the crust–sedimentary mass system (Goldstein *et al.* 1984). Armstrong (1981) has suggested that the continents were created early on (3.5–4 Ga), and have had near-constant mass ever since then. This model would demand initially very fast but constantly decreasing rates of continental recycling. Alternatively, Allègre and Rousseau (1984), amongst others,

---

trend with shallow slope. (b) Lower diagram shows data from Archaean to recent sediments, metasediments and composites. Line A represents the evolution of a sedimentary mass which has grown since 3.8 Ga by addition of new material derived from the mantle at a uniform rate. Line B represents the evolution of the source of sediments for the condition that the sedimentary mass as a whole follows line A, but the half-mass stratigraphic age of the sediments is always 500 Ma, as a result of erosion and redeposition of older material. The 'age' of the source of sediments at any point in time reflects mixing of new crust derived from the mantle with the old sediment. (From Goldstein *et al.* 1984.)

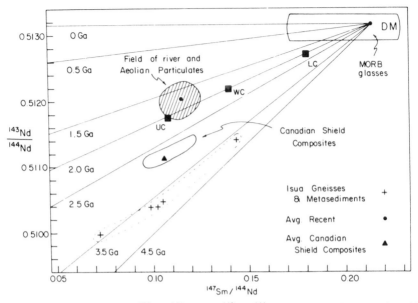

Figure 5.16 Comparison of ^{147}Sm/^{144}Nd and ^{143}Nd/^{144}Nd ratios in various samples with lines of equal model age calculated assuming a depleted mantle (DM) which has evolved in a single stage from CHUR at 4.6 Ga to the modern value of ε_{Nd} at about $+10$. The upper crust is estimated to have ε_{Nd} about -17. Similarly, using estimates of Sm/Nd at from Taylor and McLennan (1981) for the whole crust (WC) and the lower crust (LC), the ratios of these reservoirs can be estimated as 0.5122 or $\varepsilon_{Nd} = -9$ (WC) and 0.5127, or $\varepsilon_{Nd} = +1$ (LC) if the mean age of these reservoirs too is about 2 Ga. (From Goldstein *et al.* 1984).

discuss the possibility of increasing rates of continental growth in the Archaean, followed since by decreasing rates. This is possible if the evolution of the source of the sediments directly reflects that of the continental crust, but it is more likely that recycling of older sediment would be effective in causing the sediment source to diverge from the whole continent.

DePaolo (1983) used Nd and Hf data in an attempt to model continental growth. He suggested that the divergence of ^{143}Nd/^{144}Nd and ^{176}Hf/^{177}Hf ratios from chondritic ratios over the past 2 Ga has been much less than would be expected from the Sm/Nd and Lu/Hf ratios of the mantle source of mid-ocean ridge basalts. One explanation of this would be that continental material has been regularly recycled back into the mantle at a rate of about a third of the continental mass per Ga (2.5 km^3/yr), implying that the continental mass has been roughly constant since the late Archaean, and that the modern upper mantle has an important component of recycled continental material.

Patchett and Chauvel (1984) have disputed some of DePaolo's conclusions. From their analysis of the available evidence they showed that it is not possible to determine the degree of crustal recycling into the mantle, or even whether it occurred. The isotopic data for Nd and Hf are consistent with a wide variety of models of mantle evolution, from those which allow crustal growth with no recycling of crust back to mantle, to, at the other extreme, models of constant mass continental crust with extensive recycling. Patchett *et al.* (1984) did however show that some very interesting deductions can be made from the Lu/Hf fractionation. In contrast to the Sm/Nd ratio, the ratio Lu/Hf is strongly fractionated in the Earth's sedimentary system, because of the high resistance to chemical weathering of zircon. Zircon-bearing sandy sediments have very low Lu/Hf, while deep-sea clays have up to three times the chondritic ratio. Patchett *et al.* showed that a recycling model involving pelagic sediments alone could not explain the Hf/Nd isotopic array. The only way in which the array could be generated by a recycling process is if subduction of turbidite sandstone well mixed with pelagic sediment occurred in the ratio of 1.2:1. Today these components are not especially well mixed, but possibly mixing may have been better in the young Earth.

If subduction zone magmatism has indeed been the principal mechanism of continental growth, then mantle evolution curves for Hf and Nd isotopes do not solely reflect the isotopic evolution of depleted mantle but instead reflect both this and the extent of continental crust recycling via sediment subduction. Some sediment subduction clearly occurs, probably enough to account for the existence of various different parcels of mantle with distinctive isotopic ratios, which may perhaps later be sampled by ocean island basalts (Patchett *et al.* 1984), but there is as yet no evidence as to whether or not enough subduction of sediment occurs to satisfy the no-growth continental model. (Of all this more in Section 6.12).

5.7 The thermal regime of the continental crust: metamorphism and intrusion

It seemed that out of battle I escaped
Down some profound dull tunnel, long since scooped
Through granites which titanic wars had groined...

Wilfred Owen, *Strange Meeting*

The oldest rocks known are now incorporated as fragments in the continental crust – not unnaturally, since oceanic crust is rapidly recycled. The dichotomy that exists today between the topography of the sialic continental crust and the topography of the simatic oceanic crust is certainly as old as 3.5 Ga, and may possibly be almost as old as the Earth.

These oldest rocks known include high-pressure metamorphic assemblages from various terrains (Ch. 3) including the 3–3.5 Ga assemblages of the Limpopo Belt (Chinner & Sweatman 1968; Harris & Holland 1984). Evidence such as this, together with the assorted geophysical, isostatic and stratigraphic clues discussed earlier leads us to suspect quite independently of other lines of reasoning that the continental crust was thick (say, 30–35 km) even in the Archaean: thus continents were *not* thinly smeared across the global surface, and the seas were deep.

Oceanic crust probably covered much of the surface of the Earth, then as now. We can still only guess at the nature of the oceanic crust, but from a study of the continental crust we can attempt to estimate the global heat flow, and hence to attempt to quantify the heat dissipation and temperatures of the mid-ocean ridges. Thus a study of the metamorphism of the continental crust can, perhaps, tell us not only how the continents developed, but also what went on at Archaean mid-ocean ridges. But it must always be remembered that the fragments of identifiable Archaean continent remaining – though they are all we have – do *not* necessarily represent the generality of the Archaean continental crust. Indeed, perhaps they were special, since they alone are preserved. Morgan (1985) has argued that terrains with low radiogenic heat production, and thus a relatively cool geotherm, are less susceptible to magmatic and tectonic reactivation than terrains with higher heat production and a hotter geotherm. The argument to support this is simply that cooler crust is thicker and thus less likely to be perturbed than hotter crust: a matter of debate, since the perturbations are so poorly understood. Nevertheless, any preserved Archaean crust which has remained undeformed since 2.5 Ga is, by its existence, unusual (since most Archaean crust has been reworked or perhaps reconsumed).

What *is* preserved is an assortment of metamorphic and plutonic rocks set in various Archaean 'cratons'. The rocks, as illustrated in Chapter 3, include greenstone suites, granites, amphibolites and gneisses, granulites and associated plutonic bodies. Glikson (1979), Rutland (1981) and especially Condie (1981) and Windley (1984) have written comprehensive reviews of the development of these early continental nuclei: instead of repeating their work it is worth considering in detail informative specific areas.

5.7.1 Western Australia

Archibald *et al.* (1981) considered the evolution of Archaean crust in the eastern Goldfields Province of the Yilgarn. The terrain includes greenstones, granitoids and granulites, the first two being commoner at higher levels and (by inference from gravity data) the proportion of granulite increasing with depth. The granitoids include banded gneisses and migmatites, foliated intrusions, unfoliated post-kinematic bodies and minor adamellites. The banded gneiss component probably predominates. Intrusive granitoids are thought to have been derived as water-saturated melts, which crystallised close to their source, by partial melting of banded gneisses at 4–5 kb and 650–680°C. Some of the intrusive granitoids may have been emplaced by solid-state deformation as synkinematic diapirs (Archibald *et al.* 1981, also Schwerdtner *et al.* 1979; see Section 3.7.1). In other words, the continental crust shows a long, complex history of reworking and remelting. Archibald *et al.* consider that the intrusive granitoids were probably derived from pre-existing granitic crust; that the greenstones were laid down on a basement of banded gneisses, followed perhaps by thickening of the crust to 50 km and uplift.

Metamorphic studies indicate a range of facies from prehnite–pumpellyite to the high amphibolite facies (Fig. 5.17). Archibald *et al.* consider that thermal gradients in the low-grade areas were around 30–40°C/km. Such gradients would require a steady-state heat flow of 1.8–2.4 hfu (1 hfu = 10^{-6} cal cm^{-2} s^{-1}). Bickle and Archibald (1984) used a study of the stability of quartz–chloritoid–staurolite–almandine–cordierite and aluminium silicates to constrain both metamorphic conditions and pressure–temperature trajectories for two localities in the Yilgarn Block.

A lower amphibolite facies locality from the margin of a lower strain area gave a history of heating to 530-560°C at 4.2 kbar. In contrast, a sample from the mid- to upper-amphibolite facies was heated isobarically from conditions similar to the other sample (560°C at 4.2 kbar) to temperatures of 600–650°C. The higher-grade sample occurs in the thermal aureole of a granitoid dome, which locally superimposed a higher grade of metamorphism on regional conditions. Estimates of the radioactive heat production of the Archaean crust allowed Archibald *et al.* to guess that the heat flow from the mantle into the base of the crust was 1.2–1.8 hfu, with gradients of 20–30°C/km at the base of the crust under equilibrium conditions. This would imply temperatures of *circa* 1250°C at the base of an anhydrous granulitic crust. O'Hara and Yarwood (1978) suggested similar conditions (1150 ± 100°C at 15 ± 3 kbar) for the Scourian Archaean metamorphism.

Further north in Western Australia, Bickle *et al.* (1985) have published a description of the metamorphic regime in the Shaw Batholith, in the Pilbara Block. They describe metamorphic conditions not greatly dissimilar to those in much younger orogenic belts such as the Scottish Dalradian. In part of the Shaw region, mineral assemblages crystallised at *circa*. 5 kb, at 525–650°C, with some enclaves recording 650–670°C. A few areas record pressures of 6–8 kb at *circa*. 660°C.

This metamorphic record implies that about 25 km of crust has been eroded from the Shaw Batholith and its margins, or probably more if metamorphic assemblages closed during uplift. The thermal gradients of 25–35°C/km on the margins of the batholith and 25–45°C/km within the batholith are not significantly different from those recorded in the Caledo-

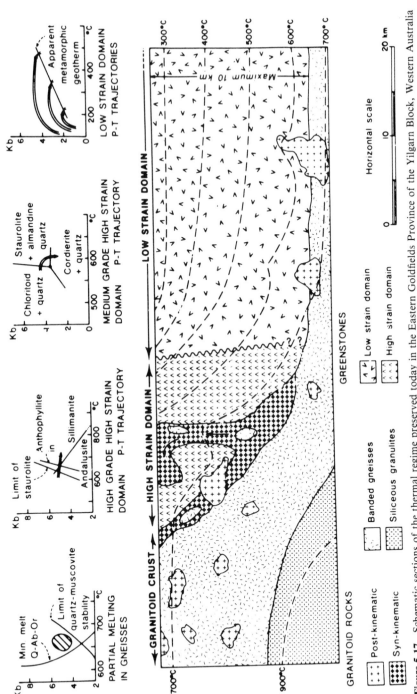

Figure 5.17 Schematic sections of the thermal regime preserved today in the Eastern Goldfields Province of the Yilgarn Block, Western Australia (from Archibald *et al.* 1981). Metamorphic temperatures and *P–T* trajectories are inferred from available evidence.

nian or Alpine belts. The presence of a modern crust 35 km thick from which 25 km has been eroded implies a maximum Archaean crustal thickness in the area of about 60 km. Bickle *et al.* (1985) further argue, more generally, that the Pilbara crust overall may have been up to 55 km thick at least. Possibly the crust was initially thickened by thrusting, which may have produced the earlier high pressure metamorphism in the mid-Archaean.

5.7.2 Greenland

Wells (1979) studied gneisses from West Greenland, slightly to the south of Isua, and part of a crust which crystallised under prograde granulite facies conditions 2950–2750 Ma ago. The granulite gneisses were severely depleted in some lithophile and heat-producing elements (Si, Na, Sr, Rb, U and Th) during metamorphism, which were transferred upwards in the crust, possibly by a migrating vapour phase. This upward transport of volatiles and heat production is characteristic of granulite terrains, and has been a very important factor in stabilising the continental crust against melting. Wells estimated temperatures and pressures of 800°C, 10.5 kbar for granulite and 630°C, 7.3 kbar for amphibolite facies assemblages, implying that the West Greenland crust was at least 30–40 km thick by 2800 Ma ago. Water vapour pressures in the amphibolite were very low, at 0.3 to $0.1 P_{total}$; prograde granulite facies metamorphism could have taken place either under strongly dehydrating conditions and falling temperatures, or during a phase of rising temperature in the lower crust.

5.7.3 Zimbabwe craton and Limpopo Belt

The section from the southern edge of the Zimbabwe craton to the centre of the Limpopo Belt, and across into the Kaapvaal craton, South Africa, contains another very informative collection of Archaean rocks (Coward & Fairhead 1980, Barton 1981, Barton & Key 1981, Nisbet *et al.* 1981, Nisbet, 1984d).

Assemblages from Beitbridge have been studied by many authors, including Chinner and Sweatman (1968), Harris and Holland (1984) as well as Huebner *et al.* (1986). From cordierite-bearing assemblages, Harris and Holland derived conditions of $P = 4.5$ kbar, $T > 670°C$, assuming $a_{H_2O} = 0$, from phases present in Limpopo metapelites. Cordierite-free thermobarometers in pelites and mafic granulites gave similar conditions ($P = 3.5$–5 kbar, $T = 750 \pm 50°C$), indicating virtually dry metamorphism. In nearby rocks, Chinner and Sweatman (1968) report sillimanite pseudomorphing kyanite in association with enstatite, implying early decompression from pressures in excess of 10 kbar. The history emerging from the rocks is thus rather complex and polymetamorphic, and Harris and Holland (1984) inferred a period of essentially isothermal uplift, raising crustal blocks rapidly from depths of around 40 km to 15 km. Huebner's work suggests major isotopic disequilibrium in the rocks, with some lower-temperature mineral pairs implying perhaps an episode of catastrophic loss of fluid due to the emplacement of a nearby granitoid.

Let us return to the problem of how thick the continental crust was, especially if it could undergo such decompression. There is considerable geophysical evidence that the crust under the Southern African cratons is about 35 km thick today (Gane *et al.* 1956, Van Zijl 1977), and Nisbet (1984d) argues that the Archaean crust when in erosional equilibrium was probably at least of similar thickness. Geochemical studies of the sedimentary cover, of greenstone belts and of granitoids and granulites imply that in erosional equilibrium, heat production and crustal structure was probably as shown in Figure 5.18. Transient events of granitoid emplacement, massive overthickening and decompression by erosion or extension probably disrupted this picture.

If assumptions are made about the mantle-derived heat flow, then an equilibrium geothermal gradient can be calculated. Figure 5.19 shows three possible equilibrium gradients, each calculated for varying assumptions about mantle heat flow and conductivity in the late Archaean Zimbabwe craton. These gradients are calculated on the assumption that erosional and thermal equilibrium had been roughly attained, or, in other words, they would apply in places where several hundred million years had passed since the last thermal disturbance. Elsewhere, such equilibrium gradients would

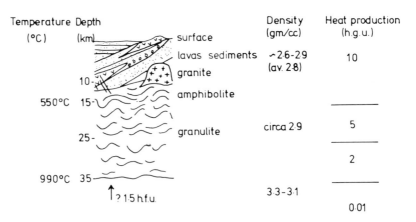

Base of lithosphere (thermal) at circa 80 km (2.7 Ga)

Figure 5.18 Simple model of the Archaean crust in Zimbabwe in late Archaean time. 1 h.g.u. = 0.418×10^{-3} mWm^{-3} = 10^{-13} cal cm^{-3} s^{-1}. (from Nisbet 1984d).

182

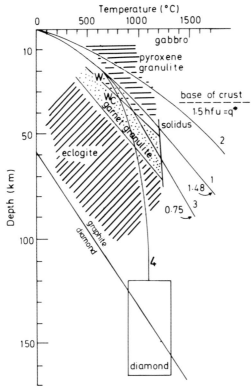

Figure 5.19 Some possible 'equilibrium' Archaean geotherms for stable continent, from the crustal model of Figure 5.18. Note that the equilibrium assumption is most unlikely to be valid (see text). 1 h.f.u. + 41.8 mW m^{-2} + 10^{-6} cal cm^{-2} s^{-1}. (1) Model with conductivity = 0.008 cal cm^{-1}°C^{-1} sec^{-1} and $T = 550$°C at 15 km, from metamorphic assemblages. This gives a heat flow of 1.48 hfu into the base of the continent, and a thermal base of the lithosphere (1600–1700°C) at approximately 75–80 km. (2) Similar model, but with conductivity = 0.006 cal cm^{-1}°C^{-1} sec^{-1} and a 1.5 hfu heat flow into the base of the crust. (3) Model similar to (2) but constrained by a temperature of 550°C at 15 km, which gives a basal heat flow of 0.75 hfu. W = Greenland assemblages (from Wells 1979), C = Beitbridge (from Chinner & Sweatman 1968). (4) Possible geotherm in old continental lithosphere, as implied by the existence of Archaean diamonds. Box shows P, T field of mineral assemblage associated with diamonds.

have meant little: the metamorphic record is a record of disequilibrium rather than equilibrium.

5.7.4 The Kaapvaal

In section 5.3.1 the Witwatersrand diamonds were mentioned. These diamonds have had an unfortunate history, since the preserved examples were stolen from the collection of the University of the Witwatersrand, but their existence (if only in geological memory – McIver, personal communication) demonstrates unarguably that by about 2.5 Ga (the approximate age of the Witwatersrand sequence) the continental lithosphere in the region (probably the northern Transvaal) which supplied the Witwatersrand basin had a lithosphere sufficiently cool and thick to allow diamonds to be stable (at least locally). Kramers (1979) and Richardson *et al.* (1984) have confirmed the case of the missing diamonds by dating diamonds from South African mines (in the northern Cape) at *circa*. 3.1–3.3 Ga. They further showed that the diamonds must have been less than 4.0 Ga old: they are not some sort of relic from planetary accretion. Melton and Giardini (1980) obtained a similar age from a North American diamond. This demonstration that diamonds were crystallising in the deep Archaean lithosphere, which implies temperatures around 1150°C at depths of about 150 km, supported as it is so strongly by both stratigraphic and isotopic proof, is perhaps the single most important metamorphic constraint in our understanding of the thermal structure of the continents.

5.8 Archaean granitoids: the substance of the continents

Granitoids of various types constitute over 91% of the exposed area of Archaean basement on the Kaapvaal craton (Anhaeusser 1981b): although this proportion is lower in some other cratons, granitoids and gneisses in general form the fabric of the Archaean continental cores.

In general, Archaean granitoid terrains are dominated by gneisses, which are typically tonalitic. For example, flanking the Barberton greenstone belt is the Ancient Gneiss Complex (Hunter 1970) including: (a) a bimodal suite of interlayered leucotonalites and amphibolites; (b) homogeneous tonalitic gneiss; and (c) a suite of metamorphites including quartzites, quartzo–feldspathic gneisses, siliceous and biotite-rich garnetiferous gneisses, quartz–diopside and diopside–plagioclase granulites and assorted high-grade metasediments. Relationships between the various components of the gneiss complex are very complex, and there has been considerable controversy about the age and nature of the early crust (Glikson 1979, Glikson & Jahn 1985).

Similarly, in West Greenland by far the most voluminous rocks in the Archaean are grey gneisses with tonalitic–trondhjemitic–granodioritic compositions. However, minor potassic granites do occur, including the granites and associated granite pegmatites of the Qorqut granite complex, which occur in a linear belt over 150 km long (Brown *et al.* 1981).

Most Archaean cratons correspond in their fabric to these two examples. They are composed of a sea of granitoids set in with greenstone belts, and the granitoids are dominantly tonalitic gneisses, with minor granite.

Although some greenstone belts are very large indeed (e.g. Abitibi), it seems that the upper half of the continental rafts was dominantly tonalitic gneiss, probably overlying extensive granulite terrains. How did this come to be? Moorbath & Taylor (1981) suggested that irreversible chemical differentiation of the mantle commencing prior to 3700 Ma ago has produced new continental crust during a series of short episodes in which melts derived from the mantle underwent a process of igneous, metamorphic and geochemical differentiation to produce thick, stable continental crust of tonalite and granodiorite. More potassic granites, which tend to have high $^{87}Sr/^{86}Sr$, may have been derived by crustal reworking.

Wyllie (1983) has shown that very high temperatures are needed to produce a tonalitic or andesitic magma. Andesite is not primary from subcontinental depths, and can be generated as liquid in continental crust only above $1100°C$. Calc-alkaline magmas may contain components from mantle peridotite, subducted oceanic crust and continental crust, while in continental crust, in contrast, hydrous granite liquid is generated at depths of less than 30 km. Possibly the tonalite and trondhjemite could have been made by partial fusion of sinking basic crust, with moderate H_2O content and high temperature. Subsequent partial melting of tonalites would yield potassic granites. However, most Archaean batholiths, dominated by tonalites, probably included heat and material transported from the mantle. The possible mechanisms of this process are further discussed in Section 8.2.2.

The continents may have been put together by a series of calc-alkaline events, each producing voluminous tonalitic melts and each reworking previous crust, metamorphosing it in the granulite facies and producing potassic granite melt. Eventually the continental crust may have changed from an initial assortment of tonalitic blobs to a complex amalgam of gneiss, derived potassic granites, and metamorphosed sediments and volcanic rocks overlying a granulitic lower crust.

Ben-Othman et al. (1984) have used the Sm–Nd and Rb–Sr isotopic composition of granulites to constrain the evolution of the lower continental crust. They concluded that the lower crust is varied in the extent of its depletion in Rb while similar to the upper crust in Sm–Nd. Possibly the lower continental crust has a larger proportion of mafic components than the upper crust. Isotopic evidence clearly shows that recycling processes have had a major role in constructing the lower continental crust. Internal differentiation of the crust often followed external differentiation by a major time interval, and metasediments are often involved in the granulites (e.g. see Section 3.8.4). The lower crust is a complex, reworked collage of material derived from mantle and surface, and it has itself by partial melting given birth to much of the granitoid (and by erosion, sedimentary) material overlying it.

5.9 Metamorphism: the problem of 'equilibrium' gradients

What then of the metamorphism in the upper crust? How was it produced? So-called 'metamorphic geotherms', derived from $P-T$ estimates from mineral phases, are quite different from equilibrium thermal gradients, and are exceedingly difficult to interpret. A metamorphic geotherm (England & Richardson 1977) is essentially the $P-T$ curve obtaining by plotting P, T data from an assortment of rocks collected from a terrain which has had a coherent tectonic and thermal history. Figure 5.20 illustrates as an example a piezothermal array defined by assemblages from South India (Harris *et al.* 1982, Drury *et al.* 1984). There are several problems with interpreting such arrays: first, it is almost impossible in Archaean outcrop to identify metamorphic terrains which are structurally coherent; and secondly, and more important, even in a terrain which has had a coherent tectonic history, the $P-T$ assemblages which make up the metamorphic geotherm are all of different ages. The metamorphic geotherm represents the erosional and thermal history of the rock pile, *not* the P, T gradient at any particular time. Detailed discussions of this point are given by England and Richardson (1977), Nisbet and Fowler (1982) and Fowler and Nisbet (1982).

In particular, England and Richardson showed that for tectonically thickened continental crust or subducted sediment wedges, the polychronic metamorphic geotherm will often be concave towards the temperature axis. Maximum pressures recorded on the metamorphic geotherm are signific-

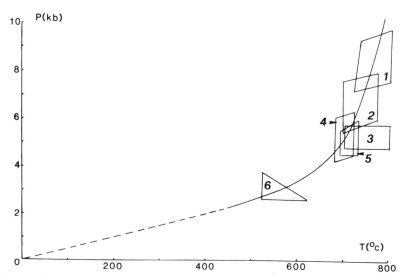

Figure 5.20 Pressure–temperature fields determined from Archaean terrains throughout South India. Numbers refer to individual localities. (From Drury *et al.* 1984).

186

antly less than maximum pressures experienced by the rocks during the early stages of recrystallisation. In contrast, crust thickened by the addition of hot magma is likely to yield a metamorphic geotherm convex to the temperature axis. Wells (1980) stressed that the array of $P-T$ estimates from exhumed mineral assemblages such as are found in Archaean granulite terrains must be used with extreme caution in inferring thermal gradients during equilibration of minerals and in determining or constraining mantle heat flows. Indeed, in metamorphic events which are caused by accretion of magma above or below the crustal pile, the maximum temperatures may be very poorly recorded (Figs. 5.21, 5.22).

Even if a rock pile did equilibrate thermally, and from its assemblages a P, T gradient could be established for a rock pile at a particular time, that gradient would be most unlikely to represent mineralogical 'equilibrium' conditions. Metamorphic facies as preserved in ancient granulite facies rocks are best understood in terms of time–temperature-transformation $(T - T\text{-}t)$ curves: chemical equilibrium is most unlikely in dry deep crustal rocks except over times of 10^9 years or more (Fig. 5.21a). Relatively 'hot' mineral assemblages are formed in the country rock around plutons or near heat sources; high-pressure, low-temperature assemblages typically occur in major thrust piles, buried under kilometres of tectonically emplaced material. Thus metamorphic gradients (°C/km) can only be interpreted in their tectonic and erosional context: very high gradients occur today in some places close to intrusions ($\geqslant 300$°C/km on mid-ocean ridges), while very low gradients occurred in the early Archaean (*circa.* 15°C/km, according to Chinner & Sweatman 1968, or less to give diamonds).

Each metamorphic geotherm reflects the particular circumstances which created it. Those Archaean metamorphic geotherms which record over-accretion (i.e. vast outpourings of magma on the continental surface above the rocks undergoing metamorphism) or underaccretion (i.e. intrusions of magma into the base of the crust and thickening by addition of magma beneath the crust) will inevitably record geotherms which depend on the temperature of the magma and the subsequent erosional history of the pile. Since Archaean calc-alkaline and basaltic magmas are, in general, closely comparable in overall chemistry to modern magmas, their magmatic temperatures will also have been similar. Thus it is not too surprising that Archaean geotherms from deep continental crust are comparable to younger geotherms from similar tectonic or magmatic settings, if the source of heat was the intrusion of, for example, granitic magma. Indeed, even if the magmatic heat source were substantially hotter (e.g. a komatiite), the temperature of the crust would be limited by partial melting of the precursor rock to the granulites. Since partial melting presumably occurs today in the deep crust, which is more or less the same in composition as the Archaean deep crust (being controlled by the chemistry of partial melting

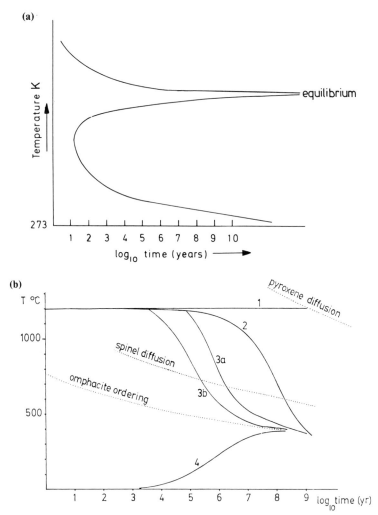

Figure 5.21 (a) Schematic representation of time–temperature-transformation controls on dry metamorphic equilibration. Time axis gives the time taken by reaction. Note that at the equilibrium temperature, transformation is slow in dry systems although the presence of volatiles greatly speeds reactions, increasing the rate by several orders of magnitude. (b) Some examples of cooling histories of deep crustal bodies in a dry crust. Dotted lines show the times taken by various metamorphic reactions in dry rock. Path 1: the rather improbable case of a mafic body intruded at depth at high constant temperature. Re-equilibration would be slow if the temperature were close to reaction equilibria, otherwise it would be fast. Path 2: mafic body intruded into the base of hot crust, which then cools as a pile together. Path 3a: 10-km thick intrusion at base of already cool crust. Path 3b: 4-km thick intrusion at base of already cool crust. Path 4: heating curve of an initially cool slab of mafic crust, thrust under base of continental crust. All calculations purely conductive. Diffusion times shown are those for metamorphic re-equilibration in minerals in dry rocks. (From Fowler & Nisbet 1985.)

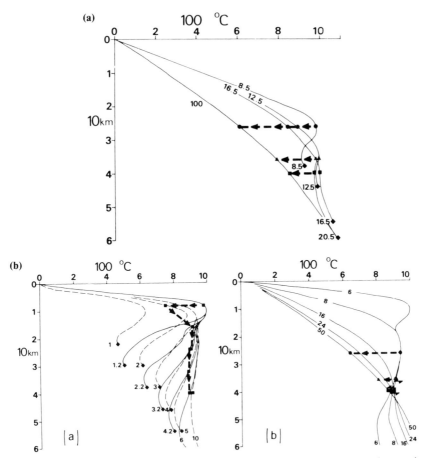

Figure 5.22 Example of temperature–depth curves for crust undergoing magmatic accretion (from Wells (1980), who studied the development of the Archaean crust in Greenland). (a) Accretion of magma at 1000°C to base of the crust, each of a set of intrusive events adding an 8-km thick layer, with accretion lasting 20 Ma. The temperature–depth curves are labelled with times (in Ma) from the start of accretion. Individual temperature–time paths shown by thick arrowed lines at selected levels in the crustal pile. (b) Overaccretion model, in which magma is poured out on the surface over 20 Ma. A temperature–depth–time line for the 40-km level is shown in (a), which shows conditions after accretion. Static relaxation paths are shown in b for 26, 36 and 40 km levels.

and the density of rising liquids), maximum temperatures attained in modern belts may be broadly similar to those attained in the Archaean. Possibly the volume of melt at given depth was greater in the past (but melts rise); possibly melts are now wetter and hence can be slightly cooler; nevertheless, the difficulty in interpreting metamorphic geotherms makes it dangerous to come to far-reaching conclusions about Archaean geotherms from deep crustal metamorphic assemblages alone. Similar strictures apply to the interpretation of overthrust assemblages. England and Richardson (1977) point out that even if Archaean blueschists had existed, erosion would have removed them, and they would not be likely to be preserved today. Indeed, it is remarkable that assemblages such as Chinner and Sweatman's (1968) kyanite–enstatite rock exist at all, even in pseudomorph. Cool, high-pressure rocks most probably *did* exist in places, but they have been eroded or overprinted during decompression. Diamonds, of course, can survive erosion.

5.10 Archaean continental geotherms: how thick was the subcontinental lithosphere?

How then to tackle the problem of understanding Archaean continental thermal regimes? One possible approach is to study those rocks which appear to have approached most closely to equilibrium under anorogenic conditions over very long periods (for it takes hundreds of millions of years for a column of crust to attain thermal equilibrium and often even longer to attain mineralogical equilibrium in dry rock). In modern North America, temperatures at the base of the crust range from 200–800°C (Black & Braile 1982). Archaean granulites may perhaps give some comparative information. Typical temperatures obtained from granulites are *circa* 600–700°C at 5–7 kb, ranging to 900°C at 8–10 kb (Horrocks 1980). The temperature data probably set upper limits on the 'equilibrium' state. Even then, there is no information as to whether the preserved granulites come from what was *then* old cool crust (equivalent to modern 200°C Moho temperatures in old lithosphere) or hotter crust (equivalent, say, to crust under western North America close to regions of recent volcanism).

Newton *et al.* (1980) have discussed the stability of the crust. Partial melting would begin around 11 kb/1190°C to 15 kb/1230°C for a two-pyroxene granulite of basaltic composition. Geotherms of the sort illustrated in Figure 5.19 (no. 1) would limit crustal (as opposed to lithospheric) thickness to 40–50 km. Newton *et al.* showed that in the early Archaean, water and heat-producing elements would rapidly be flushed upwards to create a refractory anhydrous lower continental crust, made of low-radioactivity granulite. Streaming CO_2 vapour probably played a major role in this metamorphic process, and nitrogen, sulphur and chlorine (which may have been crustally derived) were probably also important (Glassley *et al.* 1984).

Thus the continental crust is self-stabilising. It is less dense than the material beneath it, and heat production and early melting fractions are concentrated upwards. Beneath it the mantle may have cooled slowly to produce a subcontinental lithospheric 'keel'. If so, in the very early Archaean, the lithosphere and the crust were probably of similar thickness, perhaps even with the base of the crust fringing on the asthenosphere. In such conditions the Moho would become very sharply defined by repeated upward transport of the light, early-melting fraction to give a silicic crust over a mainly solid peridotitic residue in the uppermost mantle. As time continued, the lithosphere may have thickened and the lithosphere/asthenosphere boundary would have descended into the upper mantle. Possibly the base of the lithosphere was defined by a similar chemical process, which produced a light, depleted bottom to the continents rich in olivine. The continental 'keels' would form as the earth cooled. The 'water-beetles' would be replaced by 'ice floes' with deep roots. But is this simple model valid?

The most interesting evidence we have for the growth of the subcontinental lithosphere is the stratigraphic and geochronological proof that diamonds formed in the Archaean lithosphere. Richardson et al. (1984) considered that diamonds in the Kimberley field of the northern Cape probably formed at temperatures in the 900–1300°C range (probably below 1150°C) by enrichment of mantle residues or high-pressure cumulates in the deep lithosphere after an episode of komatiite generation, as now preserved in Barberton (3.5 Ga), over a widespread region. By implication, the major Archaean continental regions may have had lithospheric keels up to 150 km or deeper in places, to allow diamond stability at temperatures in the ranges found. In a very simple half-space cooling model, with a mantle temperature (T_m) of 2000°C, a surface temperature (T_s) of 0°C, crystallisation of diamond at 150 km (z) and 1150°C (T_d), and diffusivity, $K = k/\rho C_p$, or 0.75 mm^2 s^{-1} for $k = 0.007$ cm^{-1} K^{-1} s^{-1} and $\rho = 3.35$ gm cm^{-3},

$$\frac{T_d - T_s}{T_m - T_s} = \text{erfc}\left(\frac{z}{2\sqrt{Kt}}\right),$$

where t is time taken to cool the continental lithosphere from its last major thermal disruption by material at asthenospheric temperatures. This gives a time of around 0.5 Ga needed to allow simple conductive cooling from the surface to produce a subcontinental lithosphere capable of containing diamonds (see Fig. 5.23).

In cratons which have no evidence for the formation of diamonds, the metamorphic data help to constrain this process, but not tightly. Cool modern cratonic areas (e.g. parts of mid-continental North America) probably today have lithospheric keels descending several hundred kilometres into the mantle (Anderson & Dziewonski 1984). In contrast, a geotherm such as no. 1 in Figure 5.19 would imply that the thermal base of the lithosphere was at *circa* 80 km. Very roughly, the late Archaean lithosphere may have had a thermal base ranging from perhaps 150–200 km in old, cool stabilised

191

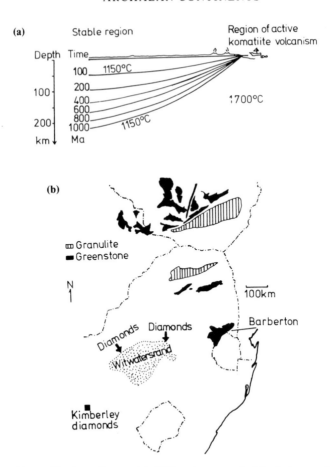

Figure 5.23 (a) Simple cooling model of lithosphere growth. Mantle temperature is taken as 1700°C, surface temperature as 0°C. Lines show descent of 1150°C isotherm with time into diamond stability field. Note that this model is oversimplified: more realistically, the last thermal event to affect the continent would leave a temperature of about 1100°C at the base of the crust (e.g. at 40 km) where melt would accumulate, rather than a mantle temperature at the surface. (b) Region of thick late Archaean continental lithosphere, as outlined by distribution of diamonds in Kimberley area (3.3 Ga – Richardson *et al.* 1985) and in Archaean sediments in Witwatersrand basin, derived from northern and western Transvaal.

areas (e.g. the Kaapvaal craton) to, say, 40–50 km or less in young hot areas. Today the equivalent thicknesses may range from 40–50 km to 400–500 km. It is possible that eventually the base of the Archaean continental lithosphere was chemically stabilised (see Section 8.1.1) at 150 km.

Next, a comment on the top end of the geotherm. On Venus the surface has stabilised at *circa* 500°C. Consequently the whole metamorphic regime in the Venerian crust must be different from the Earth's crust, and virtually all crustal rocks on Venus must be anhydrous below depths of a few kilometres, to avoid melting. Mantle temperatures too may be quite different. This dehydration of the crust is a consequence of the high surface temperature. On Earth, in contrast, the fine control on CO_2 levels in the atmosphere (which is possibly mediated by biological activity at the surface) has maintained a surface temperature of slightly above $0°C$ over 4 Ga, and has allowed the upper crust to remain hydrous. Thus, all terrestrial metamorphic assemblages to some extend depend on the stability of the atmosphere and hydrosphere. It is possible that ultimately the state of the crust may depend on the organic or 'Gaian' constraint that life is able to maintain a state of disequilibrium on the surface.

5.11 Plate tectonics: an Archaean necessity

Bickle (1978) demonstrated that if 'modern' plate tectonics did not take place in the Archaean, then some other very vigorous process of plate creation must have occurred to account for the metamorphic record. He also used the Archaean metamorphic record to allow some estimate to be made of the rate of Archaean plate creation.

In the modern Earth, about 65% of the total heat lost is through the formation of plates and their subsequent destruction (Sclater *et al.* 1981). Some is lost by heat flow from the mantle through the crust, with this heat flow (q^*) averaging about 0.7 hfu. The rest of the heat lost (17%) is lost from radiogenic heat production in the crust, mainly in the continents. The bulk of the lost heat thus comes from the mantle, lost either directly or through plate tectonics, and the Earth is slowly cooling as heat production in the mantle does not keep up with heat loss.

Total heat production in the Earth 2.8 Ga ago was around three times present heat production, depending on which estimate is chosen for the bulk K/U ratio of the Earth. If a bulk Earth K/U ratio of 10^4 is chosen, then heat production at 2.8 Ga was 2.65 times, and at 3.5 Ga 3.25 times the modern production. If plate tectonics did *not* operate 2.8 Ga ago, and if this heat were lost by conduction from the asthenosphere into the lithosphere, the equilibrium heat flow would be around 3.4 hfu at the base of the lithosphere (Bickle 1978). This would give a thermal gradient of around $50°C/km$ in the continents with very high Moho temperatures, perhaps sufficient to liquefy the continental base if it were not chemically stabilised. If plate tectonics did not operate 3.5 Ga ago, the heat flow into the base of the lithosphere would be about 4.5 hfu and temperatures as high as $80°C$ would be typical at depths of 10 km (Bickle 1978).

This is *not* what the geological record appears to be telling us: despite the difficulty of interpreting them, assemblages seem to be cooler, especially in those rocks which appear to have taken longest to crystallise (and are therefore perhaps slightly closer to thermal equilibrium). The continents *were* solid, at least after 3.7 Ga. Diamonds existed.

Somehow, the heat must have been dissipated or stored; and the most likely solution is that it was dissipated by massive volcanic eruption, or, in other words, some process of plate creation (and hence destruction), either chaotic or ordered. The metamorphic assemblages in the Archaean cratons and the existence of large cratons (stable, and thus 'plates' or part of plates, since 2.5 Ga) are thus very strong evidence indeed that some sort of plate tectonics operated. At this point, however, Bickle's paradox arises. To dissipate so much heat, plate creation must have been very rapid. But rapid plate creation means rapid spreading, which means rapid subduction. Subduction of young oceanic crust is thermally inefficient, as young crust is hot. The relationship between spreading rate, heat flow into the base of the lithosphere and total global heat lost is complex, but Bickle concludes that mid-ocean ridges similar to modern ridges (in other words, fed by *basaltic* liquids) would have to produce $18 \, km^3/yr$ at 2.8 Ga to explain the relatively cool late-Archaean continental metamorphic assemblages. This rate of plate production compares with about $3 \, km^3/yr$ today: in other words, the rate was six times faster in the late Archaean, and much faster than that in the early Archaean. The mean age of subducted oceanic crust today is about 60 Ma, when the oceanic lithosphere is about 70–80 km thick (Forsyth 1977); in the late Archaean, mean oceanic crust would have been around 20 Ma old, and 40 km thick if the ridges were similar to modern ridges.

Below the modern mid-ocean ridges, partial melting takes place to produce a relatively light crust of basalt (hydrated at its top), underlain by perhaps three to four times as much of rather denser residual depleted peridotite. In principle, what goes up must go down again, and cold material is denser than hot material. Thus, if the oceanic lithosphere is *in bulk* chemically and mineralogically equivalent to cold mantle, it will be heavier than the underlying asthenosphere and it will sink. But in the very early stages the lithosphere is not much thicker than the basalt fraction, which though cold is chemically fractionated and hydrated and thus lighter than the underlying asthenosphere. Away from the ridge, as the lithosphere thickens, its bulk chemical composition includes residual peridotite and more nearly approaches that of the mantle (and it is cooler than the mantle), so it becomes able to sink. Very young oceanic crust is subducted in some places, but in general modern oceanic lithosphere does not become unstable until it is about 40 Ma old. In this lies the paradox first considered by Green (1974) and in detail by Bickle (1978). In order to dissipate enough heat, the mid-ocean ridges must have created new plates very rapidly indeed in the Archaean. But if they did, the mean age of subducted oceanic plate would have been perhaps 20 Ma, and the plate would have been too young and too dominated by light crust to sink easily. *This* subduction could not have driven the plate system.

What is the explanation? Unless ridge push was once much greater, something must be wrong with the analysis... The analysis depends first on the metamorphic temperatures and pressures from Archaean cratons. The insecurity of analysis based on metamorphic geotherms has been discussed above. But those estimates would have to be very badly wrong to allow an escape from the paradox; and the evidence from the diamonds, stolen or not, is very hard indeed. More probably, something is wrong with the assumption that the heat was lost by plate creation in mid-ocean ridges which were *similar* to modern mid-ocean ridges; major plate creation must take place at spreading loci (random volcanism is not efficient, as it has a chaotic effect on subduction), but the Archaean mid-ocean ridges could have been quite different from modern mid-ocean ridges. One possible answer is that the parental liquid at the ridge was komatiite. A komatiitic ridge, fed by liquids at, say, 1750°C, would dissipate 30% more heat than a basaltic ridge with similar spreading rate. Moreover, komatiitic crust would be denser and allow more rapid subduction of cooled plate, allowing faster world-wide spreading rates. A less extreme position is taken by Bickle (1984b, 1986), who comments that either komatiite melting temperatures are not directly related to mantle temperatures, or our interpretation of geological processes in high-grade Archaean terrains is erroneous. Hargraves (1986) has also attempted to quantify the Archaean thermal budget, and has suggested that a possible alternative to faster spreading rates is that the ridge length was greater. If Archaean heat flow were three times that of the present, 27 times as much ridge would have been required to dissipate the heat. If so, then the model suggests that the Archaean Earth was covered by many small plates moving slowly. Of komatiites, more in the next chapter, and of Archaean plate tectonics, more later.

If plate tectonics did indeed operate, albeit in a modified form, then presumably the processes acting at the edges of the continents − rifting in some places, accretion or calc-alkaline volcanism along other margins − would be broadly similar to those acting today. Much discussion continues about the precise nature of Archaean crust formation (e.g. Kröner 1984): Weaver and Tarney (1984) point out that several critical geochemical features point to the importance of hydrous fluids during crustal generation, and like Campbell and Taylor (1983) they consider that subduction has been the dominant mechanism through which formation of continental crust has taken place.

Finally we return to the mountains of jelly, so summarily dismissed above. Subduction and plate collision implies the formation of mountains; Archaean sedimentary facies demand that mountains existed, and Archaean metamorphic geobarometers imply that thick crust and rapid erosion (and

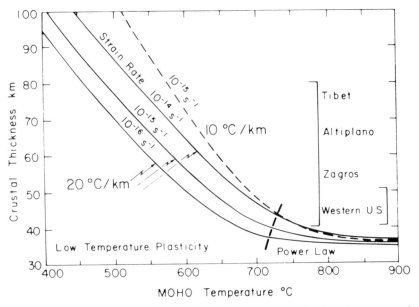

Figure 5.24 The crustal thickness supportable at a given compressional strain rate, assuming a range of Moho temperatures and temperature gradients of 20°C/km and 10°C/km. The range of crustal thicknesses for major elevated regions today is indicated on the right. In the Archaean, if Moho temperatures were high, crustal thickness would be severely limited. (From England & Bickle 1984.)

hence mountains) occurred. England and Bickle (1984) use a pseudo-plastic model of the continental lithosphere to model the height of Archaean mountains. The crustal thickness supportable at a given compressional strain rate is related to the temperature gradient in the crust and the Moho temperature (Fig. 5.24). A thick (e.g. 60 km) crust might survive some millions or tens of millions of years if it were formed by thrust duplication of crust (e.g. in a continental collision), but thick crust formed above a hot Moho (e.g. by magmatic accretion of sialic material) would rapidly creep and spread out. Erosion would also, of course, be vigorous, so metamorphic facies should record rapid decompression events, especially in crust formed by magmatic over- or underaccretion. England and Bickle (1984) used the geobarometric evidence for high pressures in granulite assemblages (Wells 1979) to estimate the size of the driving forces of Archaean tectonics: if undisturbed crust were 35 km thick and thickened crust 70 km, then the lateral force sustaining the thick crust (to allow erosion) would have been of the order of $6 \times 10^{12} \mathrm{Nm}^{-1}$, not greatly different from today.

... plastic stress
Sweeps through the dull dense world, compelling there
All new successions to the forms they wear;
Torturing th' unwilling dross that checks its flight
To its own likeness, as each mass may bear
And bursting in its beauty and its might
from trees and beasts and men into Heaven's light
The splendours of the firmament of time
May be eclipsed, but are extinguished not ...

Shelley, *Adonais*

6 Archaean volcanism

Yet is the stocke not lessened nor spent
But still remains in everlasting store
As it first created was of yore:
For in the wide wombe of the world there lyes
In hateful darkness and deepe horrore
An huge eternal Chaos, which supplyes
The substaunces of natures fruitful progenyes

Spenser: *Faerie Queen III*. vi.

Archaean volcanic rocks contain much of the available geological information about the early evolution of the Earth's mantle, about the thermal structure of the upper asthenosphere and lithosphere in Archaean time, and about the origins of the continents, oceans and atmosphere. Early life itself may have existed on the flanks of a volcano. Should we be able to understand what information to search for, how to draw it out and then how to digest it, we could learn much about how the Earth's surface took shape.

In Chapter 3 an outline was given of the type of information available. Volcanic rocks occur widely in greenstone belts; most have been altered either by syn-eruptional hydration or by later metamorphism, or both, but nevertheless original petrological characteristics have been deduced from them by enthusiastic geologists. Most Archaean volcanic rocks are (meta) basalts, but suites of komatiitic, calc-alkaline and even alkaline character do occur, and the Archaean diamonds known from the Witwatersrand imply that kimberlites too erupted. Most attention below is given to the komatiites, since they are lavas of specifically Archaean character, and are rare in younger strata.

6.1 Andesitic suites

Andesitic suites occur in many Archaean terrains, but they are not as common as basaltic sequences. In the Abitibi belt, for example, Goodwin (1979) found that about three-fifths of the volcanic rocks are basaltic, about a third andesitic, and the remainder are dacites and rhyolites. In specific areas andesites predominate, forming massive piles. The Zimbabwe craton is similar: most of the lavas there are basaltic, but in the west of the craton a major belt of andesites occurs as part of a well-developed calc-alkaline

198

sequence. Both petrographic and geochemical studies (Bickle *et al.* 1983) show that Archaean calc-alkaline sequences are closely similar to modern belts.

6.1.1 Examples: the Maliyami Formation

The Maliyami Formation is a 2.7-Ga old sequence of lavas and pyroclastic rocks on the western margin of the Zimbabwe craton, studied by Harrison (1968, 1970), from whose work the following is taken. The lavas are augite andesites in which clinopyroxene is typically fresh, although the ground-mass is usually altered. Associated with the lavas are agglomerates, with fragments ranging from a few millimetres to 30 cm long, and bedded tuffs. Felsites also occur in places, interbedded with the andesites.

The lavas display some pillow structures, but these are not common. Most lavas contain granules or laths of fresh augite, highly altered feldspar and minor pseudomorphs after orthopyroxene. In some lavas, rare ag-gregates of serpentine imply that olivine was present. Amydaloidal lavas are generally fine grained, with low-greenschist facies mineralogy and rare ground-mass pyroxene. Porphyritic lavas include examples with altered feldspar phenocrysts and also examples with chlorite pseudomorphs after orthopyroxene. Phenocrysts are typically 1–3 mm long. In some rocks, devitrified glass is present (glass is very rare in Archaean lavas; some also occurs in the Belingwe Belt).

Textures are best illustrated by Figure 6.1. Table 6.1 lists some typical analyses.

Pyroclastic rocks in the sequence have generally been highly altered, but often display well-developed welded textures. Rarely, small primary amphibole crystals occur, as hornblende andesite fragments in agglomerate. Generally, however, the andesites are pyroxene, not hornblende phyric.

Alteration in the rocks is very variable (Harrison 1970). Some rocks are almost totally altered to low greenschist facies assemblages, though in others some very fresh (by Archaean standards) material exists. Much of the alteration in the less metamorphosed rocks may have taken place during early but very variable hydrothermal activity in the pile.

It is interesting to note the close similarity between this volcanic pile and sequences rich in basaltic andesite and andesite above modern subduction zones: none of the volcanic rocks described from the Maliyami Formation would be out of place today. Furthermore, the Maliyami Formation is intruded and metamorphosed by the Sesombi Batholith, a tonalite contain-ing highly sericitised, zoned plagioclase, quartz, minor biotite and minor hornblende. Rb/Sr dating by Hawkesworth *et al.* (1975) showed that the batholith is isotopically indistinguishable from the Maliyami Formation within the limits of error of the technique: the parallels between this and

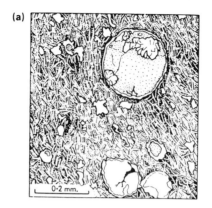

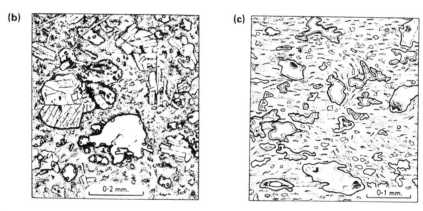

Figure 6.1 Textures in Archaean andesites, from Harrison (1970). (a) Amygdaloidal andesite, Maliyami Formation, Bulawayan Group. The large rounded amygdale is filled chiefly with chlorite and aggregates of prehnite. The rim is composed of an inner layer of pale green chlorite and an outer layer of chalcedonic silica. The two vesicles at the bottom of the field are filled with coarsely crystalline quartz mosaic, magnetite, and an outer rim of pale green chlorite. The small irregular vesicles are filled with green chlorite and chalcedonic silica. (b) Porphyritic andesite, Maliyami Formation, Bulawayan Group. The drawing shows the degree of alteration of the main minerals. The large aggregate on the left of the field consists of a number of unaltered augite phenocrysts showing cleavage, and pseudomorphs of hypersthene crystals replaced by fibrous chlorite, chalcedonic silica, prehnite and serpentine. The tabular stippled areas are sericitised plagioclase feldspars. The large irregular vesicle is filled with fibrous emerald green chlorite and small crystals of prehnite (heavy outline). (c) Welded Tuff, Maliyami Formation, Bulawayan Group. The drawing illustrates the shapes of the glassy shards which were deformed during deposition. The constituents have been chiefly replaced by carbonate and silica. The individual particles have either devitrified cores of silica or have been replaced by carbonate. The distinct rim is a glassy material with a fine granular texture. The groundmass of altered feldspar microlites, carbonate, and chlorite shows flow texture.

Table 6.1 Examples of Archaean lavas

	66/116*	66/119†	4‡	G79§	G56¶	NG 208‖	B4**
SiO_2	66.00	54.18	53.05	51.04	45.17	47.40	46.74
Al_2O_3	13.71	15.88	24.17	14.77	11.67	6.06	6.30
FeO	5.37	5.68	1.99	8.35	10.91	8.30	11.07
Fe_2O_3	1.52	2.40	1.80	0.56	0.43	2.31	1.24
MgO	1.13	5.54	0.81	9.71	17.92	29.57	27.93
CaO	4.04	8.64	2.29	8.95	7.42	5.42	6.32
Na_2O	3.06	2.85	4.18	1.75	1.27	0.11	0.75
K_2O	1.56	0.71	6.60	0.36	0.36	0.24	0.14
TiO_2	0.65	0.63	0.21	0.69	0.65	0.26	0.31
P_2O_5	0.23	0.16	0.16	0.73	0.18	0.14	0.03
MnO	0.06	0.12	0.11	0.12	0.16	0.18	0.18
H_2O	2.37	2.98	2.04	2.02	3.87	(4.8)	(4.74)
CO_2	0.01	0.04	3.07	0.40	nil	nd	nd
Total	99.71	99.81	100.48	99.70	100.06		

* Spherulitic andesite. Que Que (Kwekwe), Zimbabwe (from Harrison, 1970).

† Andesite, Que Que (Kwekwe), Zimbabwe (from Harrison 1970).

‡ Leucite phonolite, Kirkland Lake, Ontario (from Cooke and Moorhouse 1969).

§ Basalt, Belingwe Belt, Zimbabwe (from Keep 1929).

¶ Komatiitic basalt (almost a komatiite), Lonely Mine, Zimbabwe (from Macgregor 1928, recalculated to 100% anhydrous).

‖ Pillowed komatiite, Belingwe belt (from Bickle *et al.* 1975, recalculated to 100% anhydrous).

**Komatiite flow, Belingwe Belt (from Nisbet *et al.* 1977, recalculated to 100% anydrous, with FeO : Fe_2O_3 in atomic ratio 10 : 1, FeO in rock 8.29, total on analysis 100.49).

a young calc-alkaline belt of intrusives surrounded by lavas of similar age (as in the Sierras and Cascades) are very close.

6.1.2 The Pilbara

Bickle *et al.* (1983) and Barley *et al.* (1984) have identified and described a 3.5-Ga old calc-alkaline province in the East Pilbara Block. As outlined in Chapter 3, the terrain consists of an extensive greenstone sequence intruded by voluminous granodioritic plutonic rocks. The calc-alkaline province includes both lavas and plutonic rocks contemporaneous with them within the ± 50 Ma resolution of available geochronology.

The supracrustal sequence of the Warrawoona Group (Fig. 3.21) contains thick, locally developed sequences of mafic to intermediate calc-alkaline lavas and coarse pyroclastic rocks. Bickle *et al.* (1983) consider that such sequences south of Marble Bar and in the McPhee Dome are calc-alkaline volcanic centres. Barley (1981) described the evolution of volcanic centres in shallow-water environments, to sub-aerial rhyolite lava flows and domes associated with the emplacement of high-level intrusives. Sheets of volcanogenic sediments derived from this volcanism interfinger with tholeiitic and komatiitic lavas in other parts of the Warrawoona Group.

Lavas in the dominantly felsic volcanic formations range from basalt through andesite to dacite and rhyolite. Most are andesite or dacite. The most mafic lavas are plagioclase–phyric basalts containing clinopyroxene (now mostly altered). Andesites contain more abundant plagioclase, and dacites have phenocrystal quartz. Both the andesites and dacites have pseudomorphs after pyroxene and microphenocrysts of Fe–Ti oxides as the major mafic phases (this is characteristic of Archaean calc-alkaline sequences) though some andesites do contain pseudomorphs after amphibole.

The felsic volcanic sequences have been intruded by subvolcanic porphyries and high-level porphyritic granitoids. Typical phenocrystal phases in these rocks include quartz, plagioclase, amphibole and biotite. Interestingly, some intrusions have porphyry-style Fe–Cu–Mo sulphide mineralisation: porphyry copper deposits are very rare in Archaean strata, presumably not because they did not exist but because their high-level host strata have for the most part been eroded off.

The critical observation made by Bickle *et al.* (1983) is that the extrusive volcanic rocks and the intrusive granitoids are both part of the same suite, which is generally of calc-alkaline chemistry. Their interpretation is based on the available isotopic dates. Felsic volcanics of the Duffer Formation have been precisely dated by a U–Pb zircon age of 3452 ± 16 Ma (2σ errors) (Pidgeon 1978) which is supported by a Sm–Nd whole-rock isochron from mafic and felsic volcanics low in the succession which gives 3560 ± 32 Ma (Hamilton *et al.* 1979). Gneissic granitoid rocks give U–Pb zircon ages of 3417 ± 40 Ma and an ion microprobe U–Pb zircon age of 3485 ± 30 Ma. The three U–Pb ages are very close, and seven samples from less deformed plutonic rocks of the Northern Shaw Batholith give 3450 ± 57 Ma, or 3499 ± 22 Ma for a nine-sample isochron (Bickle *et al.* 1983).

In many Archaean terrains which include both plutonic and andesitic rocks there is strong controversy as to the age relationship between the intrusives and the extrusives. Bickle *et al.* (1983) show that within the error in dating, plutons and lavas in the Pilbara suite are contemporaneous. They consider that both the granodioritic intrusions and the felsic volcanics belong to the same event, sampled at different levels. Dimroth *et al.* (1982) came to similar conclusions in the Rouyn–Noranda area of the Abitibi Belt (Fig. 6.2). The tectonic and magmatic history of Archaean volcanic rocks is generally complex, and field relationships are frequently equivocal: Bickle *et al.* stress the point that geochemical surveys which do not pay close attention to the structural setting of sampled rocks are of little use. Only when there is careful structural control can sense be made of such complex terrains.

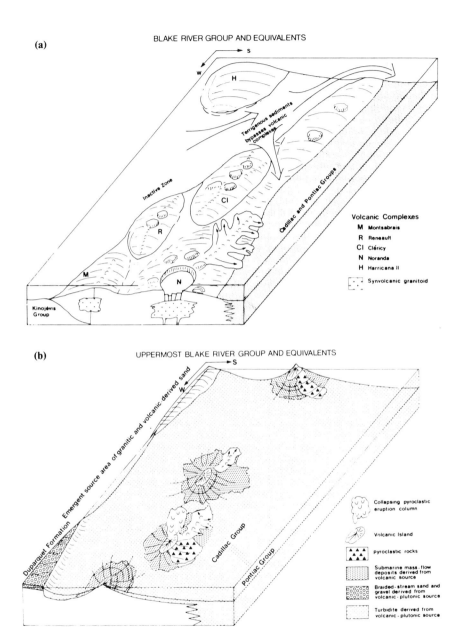

Figure 6.2 Reconstructions of the environmental setting of Archaean volcanic suites (from Dimroth *et al.* 1982). (a) Physiographic diagram of part of the Abitibi Belt during extrusion of the Blake River and Harricana groups. Area shown is about 150 km × 70 km. Note the identification of individual volcanic complexes, including caldera collapse features. (b) Schematic physiographic diagram at the stage of emergence of the Blake River volcanoes. Note the interfingering of volcanoclastic aprons and turbidites.

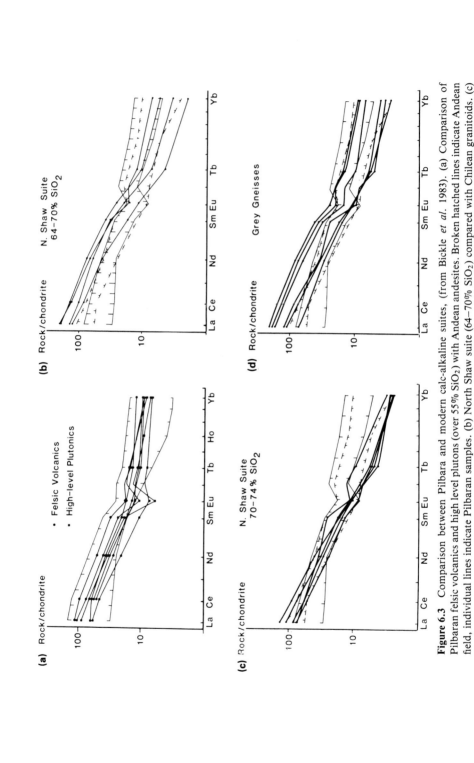

Figure 6.3 Comparison between Pilbara and modern calc-alkaline suites, (from Bickle *et al.* 1983). (a) Comparison of Pilbaran felsic volcanics and high level plutons (over 55% SiO_2) with Andean andesites. Broken hatched lines indicate Andean field, individual lines indicate Pilbaran samples. (b) North Shaw suite (64–70% SiO_2) compared with Chilean granitoids. (c) North Shaw suite (over 70% SiO_2) compared with Chilean granitoids. (d) Grey gneiss suite, again compared with Chilean granitoids.

As interpreted by Bickle *et al.*, the plutonic and magmatic suites in the Pilbara are closely related. Furthermore, high-strain grey gneisses in the west and south of the Shaw Batholith are chemically and isotopically similar to plutonic rocks of the North Shaw suite, and it is possible that the high-level calc-alkaline plutons and the deeper gneissic terrains share a common origin.

Geochemically, the plutons are closely similar to modern Andean granitoids (Fig. 6.3). However, the sedimentary–volcanic record preserved in the east Pilbara is not similar to that expected from a major Andean-type belt. Volcanism occurred in a quiet, shallow-water environment (Barley *et al.* 1979), with only individual felsic volcanic centres protruding. It is possible that the mafic lava suite is slightly different in age to the granite, and that the mafic lavas formed in a rifting environment, but the precision of dating is not yet adequate to resolve this. When seen over a 50-Ma timespan, modern calc-alkaline chains are very complex. Their history can include many episodes of triple-junction migration, with at times episodes of subduction, transform movement and rifting. For example, the young basin off Queen Charlotte Island of British Columbia (Yorath & Hyndman 1983) has seen both subsidence due to rifting and subsidence from flexure during episodes in the development of what is dominantly a calc-alkaline belt above a subduction zone on the western edge of North America.

Barley *et al.* (1984) concluded that the parent magmas for both the calc-alkaline and tholeiitic volcanics in the Pilbara were mantle-derived. This conclusion was supported by isotopic evidence from some of the least-altered rocks in the Duffer Formation andesites and dacites, which give an extremely low initial $^{87}Sr/^{86}Sr$ ratio of 0.6998 ± 0.0009 (Barley & deLaeter 1984). A spectrum of fractional crystallisation trends involving observed phenocryst phases appears to relate more evolved members to parent magmas. Although there are some differences, the close overall chemical similarity between the Pilbara calc-alkaline belt and modern parallels is striking. Either the physical conditions and major element chemistry of the magmatic source regions have not evolved much over 3.5 Ga, *or* (and more probably) the composition of crustal calc-alkaline rocks is buffered in such a way that the final compositions of upper crustal and extrusive magmas are relatively constant despite variations in source conditions. If the flux of water into the source region is the major control on melting and fractionation, then the nature of the high-level products may well have changed little with time.

6.2 Alkaline rocks

Alkaline rocks are apparently very rare in Archaean strata, although Ujike (1985) has pointed out that this rarity may be more apparent than real. In most greenstone belts they are absent, and only a small proportion of Archaean plutons is alkaline in character. It is possible that this rarity is a consequence of erosion (since many modern alkaline volcanoes tend to occur at high level), but it *is* tempting to think that the apparent rarity is real, and that there really were few alkaline volcanoes in the early part of the Earth's history. Such is the temptation, but there is as yet no clear evidence.

One of the best examples of an Archaean alkaline suite is in the Kirkland Lake area of north eastern Ontario, in the Timiskaming Group. The lavas of this group have been described in detail by Cooke and Moorhouse (1969). The Group mostly contains sedimentary rocks – conglomerates, lithic sandstones, greywackes and argillites, but with important intercalated andesites and trachytes. The lowest sequence of volcanics in the succession includes andesite and trachyte flows with minor basalt, and at higher

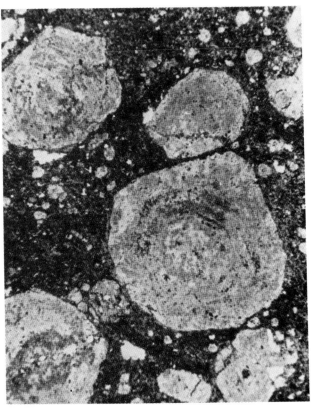

Figure 6.4 Archaean alkaline lava (from Cooke & Moorhouse 1969): leucite phonolite with polygonal pseudoleucites containing concentric zones of inclusions. Plain light.

stratigraphic levels early trachyte is followed by abundant 'leucitic' flows and pyroclasts. In order of abundance, the volcanics include trachyte, 'leucitic' trachyte, mafic trachyte, andesite and minor basalt and quartz trachyte. Hypabyssal syenite intrusions are associated with the extrusives.

The 'leucitic' rocks are perhaps the most interesting. Leucite is now entirely pseudomorphed by pseudoleucite, which ranges from 0.5 mm to 2 cm across and constitutes 5–90% of the rock (Fig. 6.4). 'Leucite' tephrite consists of soda sanidine and augite phenocrysts set in a ground mass of augite, plagioclase and pseudoleucite. Phonolite also occurs. Some pebbles of 'leucite' lava include melanite garnet.

An analysis of a selected lava is given in Table 6.1. Cooke and Moorhouse (1969) considered that differentiation of a parental calc-alkaline magma gave rise to alkaline trachytes and finally to potassic mafic trachytes and leucitic lavas. The setting may have been in an Archaean island arc: they also drew close comparison between the Timiskaming and modern lavas in western Italy. Ujike (1985) has shown that there is a close comparison between the Timiskaming samples and modern alkalic rocks in mature island arcs. This would imply strongly that the Timiskaming volcanism represents the last stage of a late Archaean island arc volcanism. Trace element systematics in the lavas are consistent with derivation of the parent magmas from a deep, enriched mantle source where garnet remained in the refractory residue of the partial melt.

6.3 Kimberlites: the case of the missing diamonds again

There were kimberlite pipes erupting on surface in the Archaean; the stolen diamonds from the University of Witwatersrand collection prove the matter – or would prove it, could they be found. Green diamonds of up to eight carats were found in Witwatersrand conglomerates on Klerksdorp Commonage in the 1890s. Until they are found again, not much more can be said....

6.4 Komatiites

Geologists are attracted to the Archaean by what is special and unusual: one of the most interesting of all aspects of the Archaean geology is the widespread occurrence of komatiites. These very magnesian lavas, discovered by Viljoen and Viljoen (1969) provide a route towards an understanding of the composition and temperature of the Archaean mantle. They are also of considerable economic value (see Ch. 7). Furthermore, each of the major Archaean problems – the nature and tectonics of the mantle, the origin of the continents, the history of the oceans, and not least, the early history of life – is closely intertwined with the early volcanic history of the Earth.

A komatiite is most simply defined as 'an ultramafic volcanic rock' (Arndt & Nisbet 1982). This is fundamentally a petrographic definition, which recognises that the rock is extrusive and has a mineralogy dominated by olivine, ± pyroxene (and glass). But all 'komatiites' are altered; most are merely assemblages of serpentine and chlorite, and even a fresh komatiite could be so dominated by glass (e.g. a pillow rim) that its ultramafic character would be difficult to recognise. Thus a chemical subdefinition is used to specify the rock as 'ultramafic'. Quite arbitrarily, the lower MgO content of the rock type is set at 18%. Lavas with MgO content greater than 18% are komatiites, and are *modally* ultramafic although their norm may include substantial feldspar (because of the composition of the glass). Finally, it should be recognised that almost all 'komatiites' are really meta-

Table 6.2 Diagnostic features of komatiite and metakomatiite (after Arndt & Nisbet 1982).

Features indicating volcanic origin include:
> chilled flow tops, polyhedral jointing, well-developed spinifex texture, pillows, fragmental structures (tuffs and breccias): rapid cooling textures, abundant glass (now typically altered).

Features indicating ultramafic nature:
> a predominance of olivine ± clinopyroxene, or pseudomorphs after them in a once glassy groundmass. MgO > 18% on an anhydrous basis: this value corresponds to the presence of modal olivine without modal feldspar; in the norm there is 15–30% olivine and circa two-thirds mafic minerals. Olivine compositions are generally Fo_{90-94} in cores of crystals.
> High $CaO:Al_2O_3$ (typically 0.8 or more), high Cr, Ni, low Ti and low incompatible minor elements when compared to basalts.

Characteristics of komatiitic basalt
General   Spatial association with komatiite common.

Features visible in field include:
> Pillows; flows with chilled tops; polyhedral jointing, etc.; fragmental textures; clinopyroxene spinifex, both random and columnar.

Petrographic features:
> Both olivine and clinopyroxene spinifex textures. Olivine spinifex occurs in more magnesian rocks; clinopyroxene spinifex is common in rocks with MgO bulk contents of 18–10%. Olivine microphenocrysts, circa Fo_{88}, pyroxenes typically augite to magnesian pigeonite. Groundmass after glass.

Chemical character:
> High Mg, Ni, Cr; low alkalis, Ti, Nb, Zr, Fe/Mg; high SiO_2 at given MgO; all in comparison to tholeiites. CaO/Al_2O_3 usually above 0.8.

Note: For a detailed discussion of the definition of komatiite, see Arndt and Nisbet (1982), Brooks and Hart (1972), and especially Viljoen and Viljoen (1969). For a discussion of komatiitic basalt see Cameron and Nisbet (1982), and references cited therein.

komatiites: devitrified glass is very rare though it does occur, and even fresh olivine is most uncommon. Igneous petrologists in their enthusiasm tend to elide the 'meta'; so shall I.

Magnesian basalts are often associated with komatiites and often have textures related to those of the more magnesian rocks. These basaltic rocks linked with komatiites are called 'komatiitic basalts' and typically have MgO contents in the range 10–18%. Table 6.2 shows the characteristic features of komatiites and komatiitic basalts.

6.4.1 Spinifex texture: shapes of olivine and pyroxene crystals in komatiitic rocks

Olivines and pyroxenes in komatiites display a wide variety of unusual textures. Examples are illustrated in Fig. 6.5. 'Hopper' olivines are equant to elongate crystals with hollow or embayed cores and euhedral to subhedral outlines (Donaldson 1982). 'Plate' olivine consists of tabular plates or blades stacked parallel or nearly parallel to one another, like a pack of cards. 'Branching' olivine shows a variety of branching textures, including, amongst other types, herringbone-like, harrisitic textures. 'Polyhedral' olivine consists of equant to tabular euhedral crystals with no embayments, and 'granular' olivines are equant, subspherical crystals. The shape of an olivine crystal varies according to its crystallisation history. Polyhedral olivine forms at slow cooling rates; equant 'hopper' olivines form at faster cooling rates and greater degrees of supercooling; with yet faster cooling and greater supercooling, 'hopper' olivines are elongate, and at very high cooling rates olivine crystallises as chains, lattices, or feathers. Branching and plate olivines form at fast cooling rates, in constrained growth (Donaldson 1982). Most of these forms of olivine can be seen in komatiites; often a single flow will display a wide variety of textures, depending on the cooling history of each part of the flow.

Spinifex is the name given to a texture characterised by large skeletal plate or lattice olivine grains, which may be randomly oriented but often are subparallel, and also to long acicular pyroxenes, which too may be random or subparallel. *Platy olivine spinifex* consists of complex book-like olivine plates, usually in subparallel orientation. The composite plates may be up to 1 m long, though only 0.5–2 mm thick. Trapped between the fronds of olivine is an interstitial assemblage of fine skeletal pyroxene, chromite (which may be cruciform or dendritic), and often devitrified glass. *Random olivine spinifex* texture is composed of smaller olivine plates, randomly oriented. *Pyroxene spinifex* texture contains long clinopyroxene needles in a matrix of fine augite and devitrified glass, or augite, plagioclase and devitrification products. Pyroxene needles may be oriented in long, parallel sheaves up to 1 m long, or as fans of radiating crystals. Typically the

209

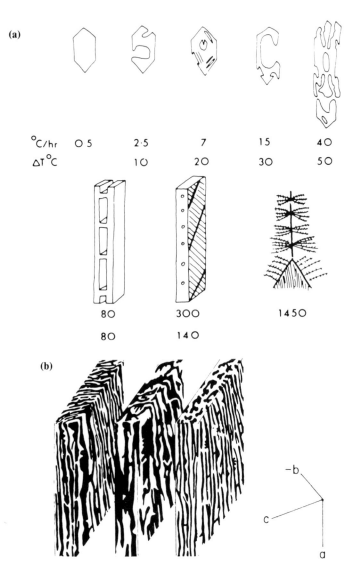

Figure 6.5 Shapes in olivine crystals in komatiites. (a) Variations in shapes of olivine crystals grown from mafic melts, as a function of cooling rate (°C per hour) and degree of supercooling (Δ*T*) at the time of crystallisation (from Donaldson 1982). Numbers refer to experiments on a lunar olivine basalt. (b) Sketches illustrating the form and orientation of linked parallel growth olivine (from Donaldson 1982). (c) Olivine crystals, now pseudomorphed by serpentine, set in a once-glassy groundmass. Some crystals (starwars space ship) are wholly skeletal, others are much more equant. Field of view 3 mm across. From a Belingwe komatiite pillow lava (from Nisbet *et al.* 1977). (d) 28% MgO komatiite from Belingwe. Note large, partly serpentinised olivine, skeletal, and hollow pyroxene needles, quench chromite cross and triangle, and once-glassy groundmass. Field of view 3 mm across. (From Nisbet *et al.* 1977.) (e) Equant olivines (partly serpentised), clinopyroxene laths, fine groundmass, from komatiite, Belingwe Belt. (f) Large plate pseudomorphs after spinifex olivine, Ruth Well, Western Australia. Note tufts of spinifex grass at corners of photo, after which the texture is named.

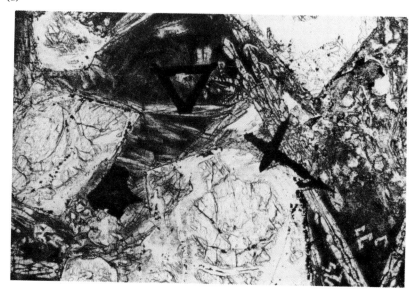

(e)

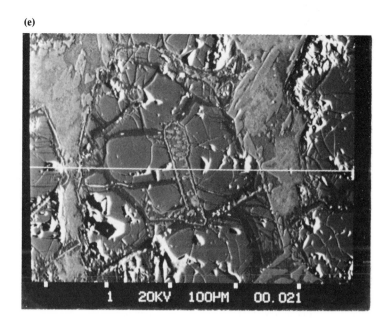

1   20KV   100μM   00.021

(f)

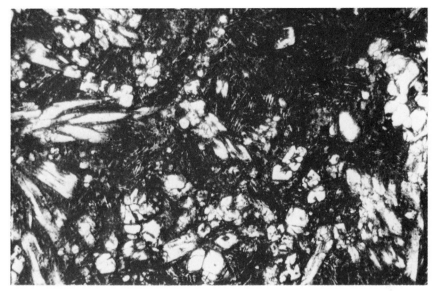

Figure 6.6 Textures in komatiitic basalts. Thin section of rock collected by J.L. Orpen from Belingwe Belt. Subequant olivine (Fo_{88}, to Fo_{83} in groundmass), acicular and interstitial augite, plagioclase microlites (An_{64} to An_{60}), titano–magnetite and minor glass.

pyroxenes are hollow, with devitrified glass or fine microlites in their axes (Fig. 6.6).

6.4.2 Field textures in komatiites and komatiitic basalts

Komatiite occurs as flows, pillow lavas or as pyroclastic rocks. A classic komatiite flow from Munro Township, Ontario is shown in Figure 6.7: in this Pyke *et al.* (1973) and Arndt *et al.* (1977) distinguished between the upper (A) zones of the flow and the lower, more olivine-rich B zones. At the top of the flow (A_1) is a unit of 150 mm of brecciated and altered material after glass containing blades of serpentine pseudomorphs after olivine. Beneath this (A_2) is a spinifex zone with an upper randomly oriented spinifex region and a thick lower region of plate spinifex. The lower region ranges up to several metres thick. The B zones are quite different. At the top (B_1) there may or may not be a thin layer of foliated skeletal elongate hopper olivine phenocrysts. Below this is medium to fine-grained peridotite made of *circa* 70% phenocrysts of mostly equant cumulus olivine crystals set in a matrix of skeletal subcalcic clinopyroxene, cruciform dendritic or euhedral chromite and devitrified glass. The base of the B unit passes to a thin zone of microspinifex texture and then a 0.3 mm glassy base.

213

(a)

(b)

Figure 6.7 Komatiite Flow, Munro Township, Ontario. (a) Division of flow: from left, base of overlying flow; A zone, B zone, Drs. Arndt and Viljoen. (b) Detail of contact between spinifex A zone and cumulate B zone. (c) Diagrammatic sections through three types of komatiite flow: left = a flow with an upper spinifex zone; middle = a flow with limited spinifex texture; right = a flow without spinifex texture (from Arndt *et al.* 1977).

The origins of this spectacular layering have been variously discussed, but especially interesting are Donaldson (1982), who also reviews earlier work, Huppert *et al.* (1984), Huppert and Sparks (1985a,b) and Turner *et al.* (1985). Komatiitic liquids had very low viscosity (Fig. 6.8), around 0.1–1 Pas or 1–10 poise, because of their highly magnesian composition and high temperatures. Consequently, the Reynolds number of komatiite flows, $Re = Q/\nu$ (where Q is flow discharge rate and ν the kinematic viscosity) would be very high, and greatly above the critical value for the onset of turbulent flow. Komatiitic magma thus would have flowed turbulently up fissures and then turbulently during flow over the ground (Nisbet 1982b, 1984c). The following analysis (illustrated in Fig. 6.9) follows Huppert *et al.* (1984), who described the sequence of events in a komatiitic eruption under water.

Within the komatiite magma, mixing by turbulence maintains a uniform temperature throughout the span of the flow, and greatly increases heat transfer to the surroundings. Thus at the head of the fissure and at the base of the flow, komatiite could melt and assimilate the underlying rock. At the top of the flow a thin crust would form in contact with water, insulating the interior. Near the source this crust would be less than 0.5 cm thick, increasing away from the source as the temperature in the magma decreases.

Below this crust would be turbulent liquid. For flow discharge rates of

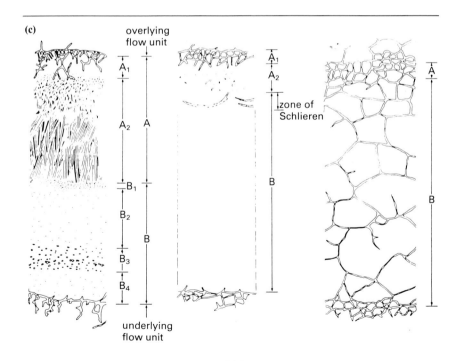

(a)

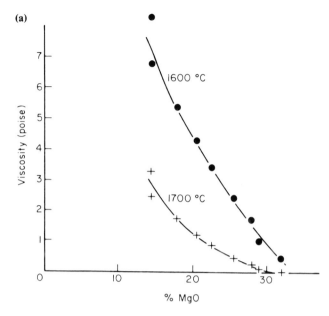

(b)

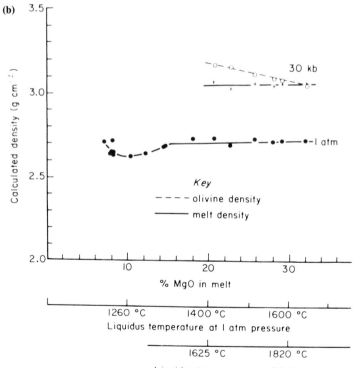

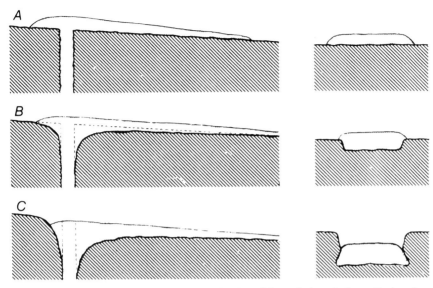

Figure 6.9 Longitudinal and cross-sectional sketches of the evolution of a komatiite lava flow (from Huppert *et al.* 1984). Early stage is shown in A; later the lava erodes the mouth of the fissure and the base of its channel (B), eventually to become incised (C).

$10 \, m^2 sec^{-1}$ the cooling rate is around $300 \,^{\circ}C$ per hour near the source, with steadily lower cooling rates away from the source. The base of the flow would melt and erode the country rock: near the source, after a week of flow the channel could be cut deeper than 20 m into the underlying ground for a flow of the same discharge rate as above. This erosion by melting of the ground beneath the flow could contaminate the lava by up to 10%.

Much of the textural detail seen in komatiite flows probably formed during the cooling of ponded lava which had drained into depressions after the magma supply had stopped. If the crust of the lava were thin (and field evidence suggests that this was often the case) the ponded lava would continue to convect and initial cooling rates would be tens to hundreds of degrees per hour. As temperature fell and the crust thickened, the turbulence would diminish and olivines would nucleate as latent heat was released. Since the viscosity of komatiitic liquid is so low (Fig. 6.8) these

---

Figure 6.8 (a) Calculated viscosity of selected Belingwe lavas at $1600 \,^{\circ}C$ and $1700 \,^{\circ}C$ (from Nisbet 1982b). (b) Calculated densities of selected Belingwe lavas at liquidus temperatures (from Nisbet 1982b). Lower line (dots) is at 1 atm pressure; upper line (crosses) at 30 kbar. Also shown (dashed line and open circles) are the densities of olivines in equilibrium with 30 kb melt. Melt densities at 30 kb were calculated using the Birch–Murnaghan equation and $K_o = 0.15 \, mb$, $K' + 6.5$: these values are only very approximate estimates. (See Fig. 8.5 for a different estimate, not assuming equilibration and with different values for K_o, K'.)

olivines would fall to the floor when turbulence decayed, producing the 'B' layer of peridotitic cumulates.

Huppert *et al.* modelled the growth of spinifex texture in the 'A' zone by using an analogous model of Na_2CO_3 solution cooled from above. Initially, during vigorous thermal convection, small dendrites of olivine nucleate under the top surface of the flow. At first these crystals would be randomly oriented, but with time the olivine crystals would become increasingly perpendicular to the roof, hanging down into the liquid and trapping stagnant, less dense residual liquid between the plates. Thus the 'A' zone of the flow grows downward into the cooling magma, eventually to meet the cumulate zone of equant olivine phenocrysts which have fallen to the floor. The high cooling rates indicated by Donaldson's experiments are achieved because of the convective heat transfer from the turbulent liquid.

Other textures seen in komatiites include pillow lavas (Fig. 6.10) and pyroclastic textures. Pillow lavas in Belingwe and Barberton are closely associated with flows (which may not display spinifex texture). It is likely that pillows formed as 'toes' in distal regions of unponded komatiite flows. Pillows are typically very small in comparison to mafic pillows (Nisbet *et al.* 1977, Bickle *et al.* 1975). Within the pillows a rim of altered material after glass can be distinguished (Fig. 6.11), surrounding an interior with textures ranging from what was once hyalocrystalline to a core containing pseudomorphs after hopper and equant olivines in a groundmass of

Figure 6.10 Komatiite pillow lava, from Reliance Formation, Belingwe Belt. (Photo A. Martin and M. J. Bickle.)

Figure 6.11 Pillow rim in komatiite, Reliance Formation, Belingwe Belt. Whole rock is altered, but original textural detail is faithfully preserved. (Photo M.J. Bickle.)

(a)

(b)

Figure 6.12   Field textures in komatiitic and magnesian basalt. (a) Pillow lava, Zeederbergs Formation, Belingwe, in magnesian basalt. Note abundant spherulites. (b) Columnar joints, Belingwe Belt. Each column is *circa* 30 cm across. (c) Ocelli in magnesian lava flow. (d) Folded columnar clinopyroxene spinifex, Reliance Formation, Belingwe. (e) Characteristic komatiitic basalt textures, drawn from field sketch. Heights in metres.

(c)

(d)

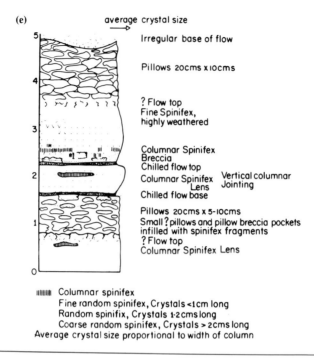

(e)

average crystal size

Irregular base of flow

Pillows 20cms x 10cms

? Flow top
Fine Spinifex,
highly weathered

Columnar Spinifex
Breccia
Chilled flow top
Columnar Spinifex   Vertical columnar
Lens   Jointing
Chilled flow base

Pillows 20cms x 5-10cms
Small ? pillows and pillow breccia pockets
infilled with spinifex fragments
? Flow top
Columnar Spinifex Lens

ıııııı   Columnar spinifex
Fine random spinifex, Crystals <1cm long
Random spinifix, Crystals 1-2cms long
Coarse random spinifex, Crystals > 2cms long
Average crystal size proportional to width of column

clinopyroxene, tremolite, chlorite and chromite. Clinopyroxenes are often pseudomorphed by tremolite, which preserves hollow spinifex habits and subradiate plumose bundles of microlites. Olivine spinifex is not found in pillows, presumably because cooling was by conduction, not during convection.

Pyroclastic komatiite rocks are not widely reported, but they do occur (Gélinas *et al.* 1977, Nisbet & Chinner 1981). Associated mafic and felsic rocks are often pyroclastic (Byerly & Lowe 1986).

Komatiitic basalts too have a family of very distinctive textures, which include spinifex clinopyroxene and spherical textures, or 'ocelli'. Figure 6.12 shows some examples: in these komatiitic basalts, the spinifex is magnesian clinopyroxene − typically in needles, not olivine. In contrast to komatiites, in which olivine is the dominant phase followed by clinopyroxene, in komatiitic basalts clinopyroxene dominates, including magnesian pigeonite and, more generally, augite. In komatiites, plagioclase only occurs rarely, at a very late stage in crystallisation; or, more generally, remains occluded in the glass: komatiitic basalts, on the other hand, may have early grains of equant olivine but are dominated by clinopyroxene and then plagioclase. The pyroxene forms a variety of textures, including fine random spinifex (small sheaves of radiating crystals up to 1 cm long), coarser random spinifex (sheaves up to 5−10 cm long) and lenses of parallel needles of clinopyroxene aligned perpendicular to the flow top. In some examples, these lenses include bands 1–2 m thick of parallel crystals (Fig. 6.13). In thin section the crystals have beautiful skeletal textures and are typically hollow; larger crystals create domains dominating the orientation of smaller, later crystals.

The 'ocelli' are spherical structures, 1–5 cm across, containing intergrown and often radial bundles of clinopyroxene (or pseudomorphs now made of tremolite–actinolite) and plagioclase set in a country rock of intergranular–intersertal texture.

The composition of minerals in komatiites varies greatly according to the composition of the parent magma and to the stage in the crystallisation

Figure 6.13 Lenses of parallel columnar spinifex clinopyroxene, with random spinifex clinopyroxene between. From outcrop of Figure 6.12(e).

history during which the mineral grew. In komatiite the olivines range from Fo_{93} in cores to Fo_{88} (though margins are invariably altered). Clinopyroxenes are typically aluminous augites or pigeonites, sometimes ranging towards clinoenstatite with $Mg/Mg + Fe$ generally varying to 60–70, reflecting their later stage of growth. In one very fresh 14% MgO komatiitic basalt (Fig. 6.6) Cameron and Nisbet (1982) report equant microphenocrysts of olivine (Fo_{88-89}), ground mass olivine (Fo_{83}), skeletal aluminous augite, magnesiochromite and plagioclase microlites (An_{60-64}).

On a larger scale, komatiitic basalts typically occur as pillow lavas and flows. Pillows range from 30 cm–15 m in long axis, and textures are similar to those found in less magnesian basalts, though concentric bands of ocelli are very common (as in some modern mid-ocean ridge lavas; see Walker *et al.* 1981). Flows range up to 30 m or more in thickness and extend over many kilometres. Often they display columnar jointing. Fragmental rocks include tuffs, agglomerates and pillow breccia.

6.5 Basalts

Komatiites and komatiitic basalts are characteristically Archaean rocks and therefore well known to Archaean geologists, but it is worth remembering that most mafic rocks in greenstone belts are 'normal' tholeiitic lavas. In the Belingwe Belt, for instance, 1 km of komatiitic lavas is succeeded by 5.5 km of basalt, including tholeiitic and komatiitic basalt. Tholeiitic basalt was probably the most common of Archaean lavas, and very extensive and thick sequences of basalt pillow lavas are widespread in most Archaean terrains. In the Abitibi Belt, Dimroth *et al.* (1985) have used systematic mapping of mafic eruptive sequences to investigate the palaeogeographic setting of Archaean basaltic lavas. They were able to identify both proximal and distal eruptive facies in flows, one of which could be mapped over an outcrop area of 30 × 20 km. In large flows, massive and gabbroic lava domains give way distally into pillows over a curved front; in smaller flows, lobate tongues or narrow channels of massive lava are found between pillows. Thick units of pillow breccia and associated pyroclastic rocks, together with upward increasing vesicularity may indicate shoaling. From their mapping, Dimroth *et al.* were able to identify two types of volcanic terrain: submarine lava plains and submarine central volcanic complexes. They concluded that a clear correlation exists between the location of ore deposits and palaeogeography. Cu–Zn sulphides appear to be located at synvolcanic faults and at the base of upward-shoaling sequences. Since these lavas in general are texturally similar to modern tholeiites, their field characteristics are not here further discussed; typical examples are described in Arndt *et al.* (1977) and Nisbet *et al.* (1977).

6.6   Ultramafic complexes

A striking feature of satellite photographs of the Zimbabwe craton is the presence of bright green scars on the landscape. Most of these are waste dumps from asbestos or chrome mines located in large Archaean mafic–ultramafic complexes. Examples of such complexes include the Mashaba and Shabani bodies (Ch. 7) and the complexes of the Barberton Mountain Land (Anhaeusser 1985). In North America the Stillwater Complex is very similar in age and petrography (Jackson 1961). It is discussed in detail in Section 7.4.2.

The Mashaba Complex is one of the most interesting (Wilson 1968a,b). It consists of a set of four layered units. Unit 4 (Fig. 6.14) ranges from basal serpentised dunite, through pyroxenite to gabbros which are quartz bearing

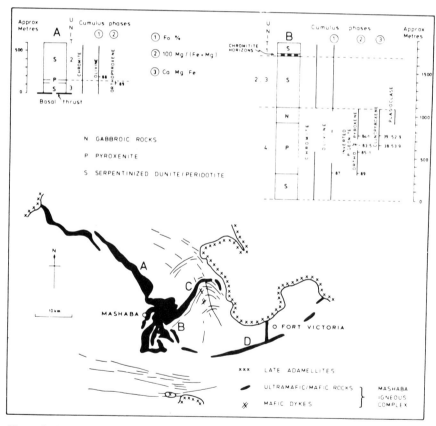

Figure 6.14   Sketch map of the Mashaba Igneous Complex, with associated radial ring dyke pattern: A = north-west arm; B = central sector; C = north-east arm; D = eastern arm (from Wilson 1981).

225

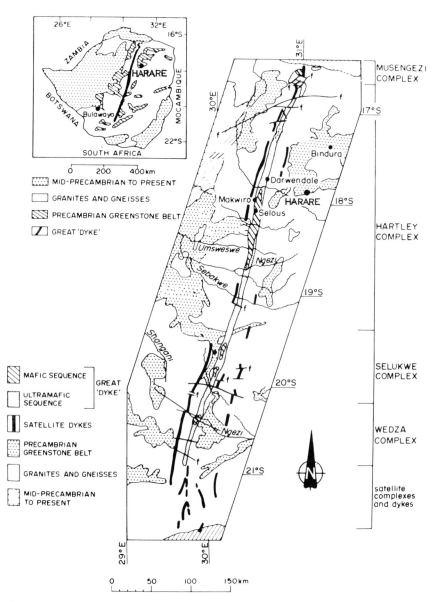

Figure 6.15 The Great Dyke of Zimbabwe, showing individual complexes, (from Wilson 1982).

at the top. The main sill (units 2 and 3) consists of dunite, harzburgite and some pyroxenite. Unit 1 (Fig. 6.14) may be much older than the other units (Wilson 1981). Though there is as yet little geochemical evidence on which to found such a hypothesis, it is tempting to speculate whether complexes such as the Mashaba body may be the residual products of large, crustal magma chambers fed from below by komatiitic liquid (Fig. 3.40). Such chambers would be doubly diffusive (Nisbet & Chinner 1981), and would have lower ultramafic cumulate and upper basaltic liquid: large volumes of mafic liquids would leave the top of the chambers to produce thick basalt piles on the surface. Eventually, when the supply of melt at the base ceased, a dominantly ultramafic complex would be left, with at its top residual fractionated mafic liquid. This latter trapped liquid would be basaltic and fractionate to silica-rich final differentiates.

The Great Dyke (Wilson & Wilson 1981, Wilson 1982) is perhaps the most spectacular of all Archaean plutonic bodies (Fig. 6.15). It is 2.5 Ga old, 480 km long and on average 8 km wide, and consists of four distinct complexes each with a lower ultramafic zone capped by gabbroic differentiates. These are discussed in Chapter 7 (Fig. 7.28).

Gravity studies across the dyke indicate that at depth the cross section is V-shaped, with the possibility of deep central dyke feeders (Podmore 1970, 1982). There has been much controversy over the composition of the parental liquid. The mineral compositions clearly indicate that the liquid was tholeiitic, but the preponderance of ultramafic rocks implies either that the parent liquid was highly magnesian or that extensive high-level mafic differentiates have been eroded. However, Wilson (1977) estimated that only 150 m have been eroded from the top of the Hartley Complex. Detailed geochemical modelling by Wilson (1982) leads to the conclusion that the parental magma contained about 15% MgO (a komatiitic basalt liquid), and was injected into a magma chamber about 1 km high. In one of the most thorough petrological studies ever published, Wilson (1982) described the operation of that chamber. It was probably stratified, and fractionation may have been controlled by doubly diffusive convection.

6.7 The composition of Archaean mafic and ultramafic lavas

In 1969 Viljoen and Viljoen first showed that there is conclusive evidence for the existence in the Archaean of ultramafic extrusive rocks. For many years previously there had been a 'magnificent argument', especially between Bowen (1938) and Hess (1938), about whether ultramafic liquids could exist. By 1960 the consensus was that they probably could not exist; certainly it was thought that no *extrusive* ultramafic rocks could occur. Thus the discovery of komatiites came as a surprise (Dickey 1972), even though ultramafic lavas had been well described and analysed previously (Macgregor 1928, Keep 1929). Since 1969, controversy about the interpretation of the geochemistry of komatiites has been strong (and remains so), but many very interesting facts have emerged.

First, there is the problem of alteration. There are *no* completely fresh komatiites, and only a small number of outcrops in which any primary mineralogy is preserved, especially in the Belingwe Belt where some rocks display only minor alteration of phenocrysts. One outcrop in the Belingwe Belt contains nearly fresh minerals and an optically isotropic but probably cryptocrystalline groundmass. A few komatiitic basalts are moderately fresh (some still with glass present), but most have been heavily altered. Thus in general it is necessary to reconstruct the original bulk chemistry of komatiitic liquids by an unsatisfactory process of assumptions based on the chemistry of an altered *mélange* of secondary minerals, by calculating the liquids in equilibrium with preserved fresh minerals and by a circuitous argument based on the textural and crystallisation history as recorded in pseudomorphs. The alteration itself is of great interest, though generally ignored in the scurry for original compositions.

Typically, in better-preserved komatiite sequences the degree of alteration is very variable, with apparently rapid spatial and temporal changes in temperatures and intensity of recrystallisation: often the initial alteration seems to have been produced by very early hydrothermal processes soon after eruption. Superimposed on this early alteration are varying degrees of regional metamorphism (e.g. Jolly 1982), ranging from a few rocks with no apparent post-burial recrystallisation to rocks in the upper amphibolite facies, beyond which recognition of metakomatiites becomes unconvincing.

Stable isotopes can help in deducing alteration histories. Figure 6.16 is a plot of δD vs. $\delta^{18}O$ for a set of serpentine samples from the Belingwe Belt. The serpentines can be roughly grouped into three sets: (*a*) a group with δD below about $-60‰$ (*b*) a sample with δD around $-40‰$, and (*c*) a group of intermediate δD, heavy in oxygen. Also plotted on the graph is the meteoric water line for modern water, and two pairs of curves representing waters in equilibrium with group (*a*) and (*b*). Each curve-pair shows equilibrium waters for water/rock ratios of infinity (upper curve) and 0.285 (low curve in curve-pair). The lower curve-pair, in equilibrium with group (*a*), crosses the meteoric water line at slightly over $30°C$. The simplest and most reasonable explanation of this serpentinisation is that it is modern, a consequence of tropical weathering. Indeed, modern serpentinisation in Zimbabwe can reach depths of 100 m, and road-cuts in ultramafic rock rapidly weather in hot, wet summers. In contrast, the group (*b*) sample may have been in equilibrium with oceanic water at rather over $100°C$. Archaean oceans most probably did not have isotopic compositions exactly as today, but nevertheless the data suggest hydrothermal alteration. Group (*c*)

228

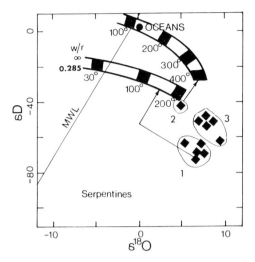

Figure 6.16 Plot of $\delta^{18}O$ vs δD for samples from the Belingwe greenstone belt. (See text for explanation).

samples may also represent equilibration with hot oceanic water, of shifted isotopic composition. Thus the evidence suggests both modern meteoric alteration (for which there is much field evidence) and an earlier, not well understood, hydrothermal event involving hot oceanic water. This early hydrothermal event may have been syn-eruptional, and may be a cause of the very variable metamorphic grade seen in many komatiite terrains, with intense and hot alteration near fluid channels and less pervasive, cooler alteration on the edges of the system where water/rock ratios were lower.

Various authors have attempted to see through the alteration history of the lavas to deduce the original composition of the magmas. A wide variety of ingenious but not entirely convincing arguments has been proposed (e.g. Nisbet *et al.* 1977) to show that some at least of the now-altered bulk composition of the magmas is original (Arndt *et al.* 1977, Smith & Erlank 1982). Bickle (1982) reviewed the matter and concluded that there is good evidence that liquids at least as magnesian as 24% were erupted. In Belingwe relatively 'fresh' rocks with 28% MgO occur; both there and in Barberton, phenocryst-poor but highly altered lavas range up to 33% MgO on an anhydrous basis (Green *et al.* 1975), and it is probable that at least some of these retain their original magnesium content although heavily hydrated.

Often a figure of 32% MgO is assumed for the composition of the most magnesian liquids erupted: nevertheless, it must be stressed that the foundation for this assumption is very circumstantial, despite the vast edifice of speculation (see below and Section 8.1.3) built upon it. 24% MgO liquids almost certainly existed (Elthon 1986, Bickle 1982), most probably 28%

MgO lavas were common, but 32% MgO liquids are not proven to have existed, though likely. The discussion that follows should be read with that caveat in mind. Discussions of trace element compositions are of even more doubtful authenticity (see below).

6.8 Possible relationships between komatiites and komatiitic basalts

Suites of komatiites and komatiitic basalt exist in close stratigraphic relationships in many areas. Does this close spatial and temporal proximity mean that the two lava types are related? In other areas, and in post-Archaean successions, komatiitic basalts often occur alone. Various authors (e.g. Cameron & Nisbet 1982, Arndt & Nesbitt 1982, Nisbet & Chinner 1981, and Arndt & Nesbitt 1984, amongst many others) have investigated this problem, and come to a variety of answers.

Nisbet and Chinner (1981) suggested that in certain circumstances (Fig. 6.17) parental komatiites (e.g. at 25–28% MgO) could fractionate at high level to produce komatiitic basalts of the compositions seen in some suites where komatiite and komatiitic basalt are intimately intermingled. The density of komatiitic liquids would have been high (Fig. 6.8b) in comparison to basaltic and felsic magmas, and it is possible, following Huppert and Sparks (1981) and Walker *et al.* (1981), that these very magnesian lavas could only erupt to the surface in special circumstances at an early stage in an extensional event when no crustal magma chamber was present (Nisbet & Chinner 1981, Nisbet 1984a). Later, when a chamber had developed (Fig. 5.6), doubly diffusive processes would control eruptive products, and only evolved magnesian basalt would reach the surface. This effect would thus enhance the probability of eruption of the minimum density fraction,

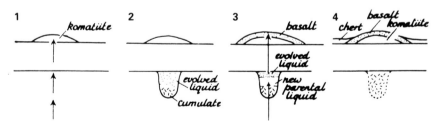

Figure 6.17 Model of the development of komatiitic basalt from parental komatiite liquid, by development of a doubly diffusive stratified magma chamber in the lithosphere. Evolved liquid (komatiitic basalt) is lighter and thus erupted in normal circumstances. (From Nisbet & Chinner 1981.) See also Figure 3.40. Note that in some other examples of associated komatiitic basalts and komatiites, this type of process has probably not occurred: the two suites appear to be petrogenetically distinct (Arndt & Nesbitt 1984).

around 8–10% MgO. The eruptive suite would include unfractionated parental melts and fractionated komatiitic basalt but little in between, and the relative proportions of the two components would depend on local tectonic factors – particularly whether or not the crust was in tension. In contrast, in Munro Township, Arndt and Nesbitt (1984) investigated a similar dichotomy between komatiite and komatiitic basalt. Here, too, the composition of the most commonly found basalts coincides with the density minimum. However, trace element ratios in the two magma types appear to rule out any hypothesis that the two magma suites are related by low-pressure fractionation, unless subtle contamination effects have occurred. Arndt and Nesbitt therefore conclude that either the magma suites were independently derived by melting of sources with different compositions (differing degrees of initial depletion), or they could have formed from the same depleted source, with some pyroxene being left as a residual phase or fractionating at high pressure during formation of the basalts. Some lavas could have formed by mixing of komatiite and komatiitic basalt liquids, to form a hybrid magma.

Huppert and Sparks (1985a,b) have modelled the ascent of ultramafic magmas through continental crust. When the ascent is turbulent, heat transfer to the surroundings can be rapid, and the wall rocks of the conduit can melt and be assimilated into the magma. Komatiites, being very hot liquids with low viscosity, are likely to be turbulent on ascent and can probably assimilate country rock very rapidly. Under suitable flow conditions, komatiites can be contaminated with up to 30% of crustal material, derived in the most part from the lower continental crust if the eruption is supracontinental. It is possible that some komatiitic basalts in greenstone belts were produced in this way as highly contaminated komatiite. Such lavas would have the trace element characteristics of the continental lower crust dominating over the low trace-element contents of the original parent liquid, and would not obviously be related to the parent. In a field area where both contaminated and uncontaminated lavas had erupted, simple geochemical modelling involving fractionation of olivine might suggest that the two lava suites came from quite distinct mantle source regions. From this would be drawn interesting but wholly erroneous conclusions about mantle heterogeneity in the source area.

Is contamination a common mechanism for generating komatiitic basalt? Little is yet known about this, but it may be that a very large number of komatiitic liquids did indeed suffer contamination in this way, scouring regions of the lower crust of their trace elements. The curious ocelli-like textures of many komatiitic basalts have been attributed to a variety of causes: it is possible that some represent the remains of miscible but incompletely mixed contaminating liquids rapidly erupted and frozen. Contamination may also have occurred on a grand scale; Campbell (1985) has suggested that the presence of Ca-poor pyroxene in many large Archaean layered intrusions and its crystallisation prior to Ca-rich pyroxene may also be a result of contamination of a mafic or ultramafic parent on ascent by assimilation of siliceous country rock.

The contamination problem is very complex: with some mathematical models it seems most improbable that any uncontaminated lavas at all managed to ascend and erupt. Are therefore all geochemical conclusions drawn from komatiites suspect? Perhaps so, but the low trace-element contents and chondritic inter-element ratios seen in many komatiites would suggest strongly that at least some magmas did erupt without much contamination. Furthermore, many conclusions drawn from the major element contents of the more magnesian lavas seem to be robust against the possibility of contamination. In particular, the MgO content of the liquids (and hence their implied temperature) would be reduced, not increased by contamination.

It is probable that many komatiites escaped contamination because they were erupted in rapid succession in a tensional setting (Fig. 5.5). In such a setting, a new parcel of magma ascending from depth into the elastic lithosphere would be likely to rise by propagating a crack through the weakest segment of the overlying plate, which would be the warm core of the last dyke to be injected if dyke injection were frequent. This dyke-splitting takes place at modern mid-ocean ridges, and has been observed in ophiolite complexes. If it took place in greenstone sequences laid down on continental crust, the komatiite liquid would ascend not through silicic country rock but through a wall rock of cool komatiite. In such circumstances contamination would be minimal. Perhaps many small packages of komatiitic melt ascended in this way, protected from contamination by their elder siblings.

6.9 Implications of the major element compositions of komatiites: the source region

If very magnesian liquids really did once exist, then several important points follow. Green et al. (1975) first showed that a 32% MgO liquid could only exist at very high temperature (Fig. 6.18). Thus, by implication, the source region in the mantle was very hot (Green 1975), much hotter than today (Mckenzie & Weiss 1980). Such high temperatures if widespread in the mantle, would mean that tectonic processes in the Archaean would have been radically different from today (Nisbet 1984b). Alternatively, it has been suggested that temperatures recorded in komatiites were not representative of the whole Archaean upper mantle; rather, they may represent the atypical products of hot plumes rising from great depth, such as the mantle/core boundary (Campbell & Jarvis 1984) (see Ch. 8).

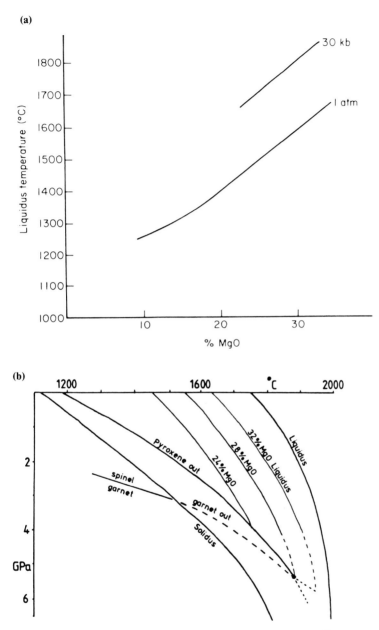

Figure 6.18 (a) Liquidus temperatures of magnesian basalts and komatiites at 1 atm and 30 kb (from Nisbet 1982b). At 1 atm, for komatiite liquids $T_{liquidus}$ is given approximately by $T_{liq} = 1400 + 20 \ (MgO\% - 20)°C$. (b) Phase relations for melting mantle-like compositions from experiments on komatiites (the intersection of the garnet melting curve with the pyroxene melting curve is hypothetical). (Personal communication from M. J. Bickle.)

Much argument has raged about the chemical and physical nature of the source region from which komatiites were derived. Green (1975) and Arndt *et al.* (1977) pointed out that in order to derive a 32% MgO lava from a peridotite source mantle there must either have been a very high degree of partial melt in the source region, or the source must have been very refractory. Both possibilities pose major problems. Crudely, in a closed system (MgO% in source) = [(1 − fraction of partial melt) × MgO% in residue (olivine)] + [(fraction of melt) × 32]. If the degree of melt were high (50–80%, say), how could such a melt accumulate? Surely such a low viscosity liquid would escape to higher level at a much earlier stage in melting, leaving a refractory residue? On the other hand, if the degree of melt were low, very high temperatures would be needed. Many ingenious lovely things have been devised to escape these horns. Arth *et al.* (1977) and Arndt (1977c) suggested a sequential melting process, while Bickle *et al.* (1977) pointed to evidence for polybaric assimilation of country rock into the rapidly rising magma. This latter evidence is closely connected to the strong evidence from mathematical models that many lavas suffered significant contamination at shallow level (Huppert *et al.* 1984). The artefact of comparatively small quantities of Si or Ti etc. added to the ascending melt could lead to very varied conclusions about the minerals controlling fractionation and melting. In particular, trace element compositions even of fresh komatiites probably reflect interaction with country rock on ascent and eruption, and may only be a very wayward guide to processes in the Archaean mangle (Nisbet 1984b, Bickle 1984a). Major element composition, although not necessarily substantially contaminated during eruption (Huppert *et al.* 1984) can reflect the melting in of country rock on ascent.

There has been much discussion about whether the variation seen in komatiite suites reflects control of the chemistry of the magma suites only by olivine, or by olivine and also orthopyroxene. For instance, the chemical variation seen in lavas of the Ngezi Group in the Belingwe Belt (Nisbet *et al.* 1977) seems to show a component of orthopyroxene control. This apparent role of orthopyroxene in the melting process could simply be an artefact of the rotation of geochemical trends by alteration, or it could be a consequence of contamination of ascending lavas by continental crust (perhaps unlikely, since trace incompatible-element contents are low and have near-chondritic ratios), or it could be real (see Section 8.1.3). Thus, quite apart from the problems of post-eruptive alteration, the interpretation of komatiite geochemistry is a piece of complex detective fiction, much more difficult than we once thought.

Some of the early work on the melting problem is illustrated in Figure 6.19. The figure is a simple geometric solution of the closed system problem, assuming that melt and residue = source, and that both residue and melt compositions evolve as melting proceeds. If however, the melt

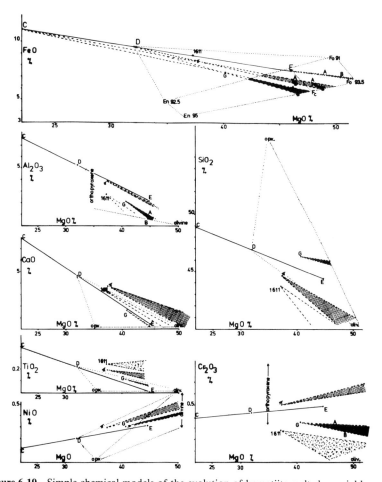

Figure 6.19 Simple chemical models of the evolution of komatiite melts by variable melting of batches of source. These models are generally invalid, since there is evidence for polybaric melting on ascent (Bickle *et al*. 1977) and for contamination on eruption (Huppert *et al*. 1984); nevertheless they are interesting. The line $C–D$ is the linear trend shown by komatiite lavas in the Reliance Formation, Belingwe. E is the point to which this trend projects for $TiO_2 = 0$. If the system is simple and batches of lava rise directly from a steadily melting source it can be modelled as follows: A represents residue in equilibrium with early liquid C, B represents residue in equilibrium with late liquid D. If C and D are derived from similar source materials at different stages, then $C–D–E$, $E–A–B$, C-source, A, and D-source–B are straight lines, and shaded areas denote possible residue compositions for each source. Possible source materials shown are π (pyrolite); G (average garnet herzolite) and 1611 (nodule 1611). Bounds on solid source compositions are set by olivine and orthopyroxene compositions.

Note that this simple model assumes a particular type of variable 'conveyor-belt' batch melting. Other physical models (e.g. a liquid source) lead to different conclusions, and contamination by Ti, Ca, etc. on ascent or eruption would invalidate point E.

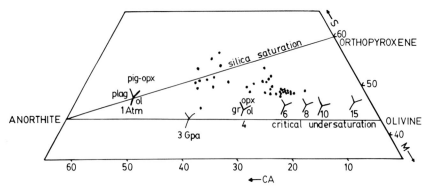

Figure 6.20 Simple CMAS approach to komatiite melting, showing apparent olivine or olivine orthopyroxene control. Projection in C–A–MS, after Herzberg and O'Hara (1985). Ascending melts would precipitate olivine. (Data from Nisbet *et al.* 1977.)

(a)

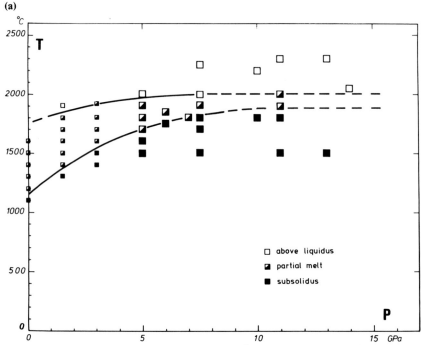

Figure 6.21 (a) Phase diagram for a natural lherozite sample (from Takahashi & Scarfe 1985). Results from 1 atm and piston cylinder work indicated by small squares. Solid squares, subsolidus; open squares, superliquidus; half-shaded squares, crystals plus liquid. (b) Schematic diagram showing some constraints on eruption of highly magnesian komatiite liquid. Arrows show adiabatic ascent path of 32% MgO liquid: liquidus and solidus curves estimated from recent results. Most ascent paths of liquid were probably non-adiabatic. Compare with Figure 6.18b.

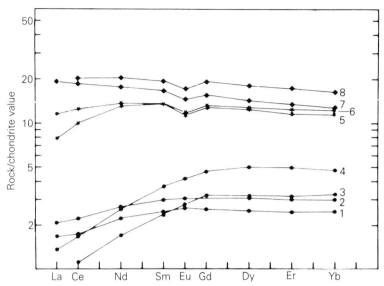

Figure 6.22 Selected rare earth patterns of depleted komatiite (solid dots), komatiitic basalt (stars), and tholeiite (diamonds) (from Weaver & Tarney 1979).

(b)

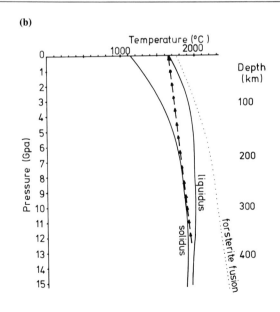

extracted is only a small proportion of the total mass of the source, then for many elements source and residue will lie close together. However, the model probably fails on the closed-system assumption. It is also possible that solitary waves of magma can ascend (Scott & Stevenson 1985): in this latter case, processes similar to zone-refining would drastically alter the trace element contents of the liquid.

Figure 6.20 shows a simple CMAS approach to the problem, after O'Hara (1968) and Herzberg and O'Hara (1985). At high pressures (over 30 kb) the melts formed from a refractory peridotite source are highly magnesian but above the plane of critical undersaturation; they could fractionate varying quantities of olivine on ascent to give a komatiitic to komatiitic basalt suite at the surface. Takahashi and Scarfe (1985) have determined the melting behaviour (Fig. 6.21) of samples of natural herzolite to 140 kbar (equivalent to over 400 km deep). They showed, as expected, that melts close to the peridotite solidus at 50–70 kbar are no longer basaltic but rather komatiitic in composition. Thus the major element compositions of komatiites are consistent with derivation as an early partial melt of a peridotitic mantle: if so, however, the trace element content of komatiites, which is often as low as roughly twice chondritic levels (Fig. 6.22), would imply that the parent peridotitic mantle must have been extremely depleted, at least in some places. More probably, komatiites represent high degrees of melt.

6.10 Through a glass darkly: the trace element and isotopic window to the Archaean mantle

Bickle *et al.* (1976) pointed out that komatiites (especially those with relict glass) do provide a window to the Archaean mantle: however obscured this window may be by crustal contamination it remains our most powerful way of insight into the early tectonic history of the Earth. Several problems stand out: the possibility of lateral heterogeneity in the Archaean mantle and its implications; the isotopic evolution of the mantle and evidence for vertical heterogeneity, and thus for a layered mantle; and the heat production of the early mantle. The general problem of the composition of the Archaean mantle has been carefully reviewed by Sun (1984).

Various authors have studied rare earth element abundances in komatiites (Bickle *et al.* 1976, Hawkesworth & O'Nions 1977, Arth *et al.* 1977, Arndt & Nesbitt 1982). Most such studies showed that the more magnesian komatiites have 2–3 times the rare earth contents of chondritic meteorites (which may provide an analogue of the composition of the bulk earth), though typically (but not always – Nesbitt & Sun 1979) the light rare earths in komatiites are rather closer to chondritic levels. This is generally interpreted as evidence for a degree of widespread but not general depletion of the source region in the asthenosphere, which presumably had earlier lost some light rare earths. Archaean komatiitic basalts and basalts, on the other hand, often have flat to light-enriched rare earth patterns (Fig. 6.22), and the upper crust (Fig. 5.13) is in general enriched in light rare earths compared to chondrites (Ch. 5; McLennan & Taylor 1982, Taylor & McLennan 1985). One possible interpretation of this disparate evidence is that there has been a continuous depletion of the mantle as continents grew through geological time. If so, in the Archaean the mantle would have been less depleted than today. On the other hand, it is equally possible to hold the opposite view that the mantle was highly depleted. These are general statements: more probably, the mantle may have been vertically or laterally heterogeneous (Nesbitt & Sun 1977): some komatiites, such as those from Barberton, show flat to heavy rare-earth enriched patterns, and differ in other significant major and trace elements from typical Munro Township and Belingwe examples. Nesbitt *et al* (1979) pointed out that two broad classes of komatiites can be distinguished – one class richer in Al (e.g. Munro Township, Belingwe) and those poorer in Al and thus with higher CaO/Al_2O_3 ratios (especially in Barberton). To summarise, the rare earth elements, together with more 'incompatible' major and trace elements are most simply interpreted as giving a picture of a heterogeneous Archaean mantle, which included regions rich in garnet and orthopyroxene. Komatiite magmas either originated in these regions or ascended through them, and were contaminated by assimilation of wall-rock.

Several problems arise: (a) is this model, which ascribes chemical variation in lavas to source variation, justified when we know so little about the mechanism of ascent and fractionation in lavas; (b) could the variation instead be recording contamination by melting of the ground or country rock during eruption (Huppert *et al.* 1984, Huppert & Sparks 1985a,b); and (c) could it simply reflect artefacts of post-eruptive alteration? These problems are discussed in the series of publications by Nesbitt, Sun *et al.*, Huppert *et al.*, and Claoue-Long *et al.* (1984) and to some extent surmounted; but how reliable is geochemical evidence from 'incompatible' elements, given the propensity of komatiites for eroding out country rock on eruption (Bickle 1984a,b, Nisbet 1984c)? In the Kambalda lavas, Western Australia, Chauvel *et al.* (1985) and Roddick (1984) have demonstrated the likelihood that the lavas were extensively contaminated in incompatible elements on ascent. Major elements, such as Al, would less easily be drastically altered by crustal contamination, though alteration could certainly occur. Cattell *et al.* (1984) have considered the possibility of contamination in komatiitic lavas from the Abitibi Belt. A Sm/Nd isochron from Newton Township gave 2826 ± 64 Ma, while U/Pb analysis of zircons gave 2697 ± 1.1 Ma. They concluded that, when only the Sm/Nd system is considered, a crustal contamination model is possible, but requires either that the age of the contaminant was little greater than that of the lavas, or that the contaminant had an unusually high ε_{Nd} to explain the ratios observed. The age of eruption is probably recorded by the U/Pb system. However, when heavy rare earth and other trace elements are considered, it is difficult to construct a self-consistent crustal contamination model. Crustal contamination may be significant in determining contents of elements such as Ca, Al, and minor and trace elements and isotopes. Nevertheless, much of the variation seen in rare earth elements and in isotopes in and between komatiite suites probably represents variation in subcrustal rocks, either because a variety of source mantle compositions existed, or because variation was imposed by reactions on ascent through mantle country rock (Bickle *et al.* 1977). There is evidence both for large-scale heterogeneity in geochemical differences between komatiite suites erupted in different places, and for small-scale heterogeneity in variation between samples taken from small areas (e.g. Arndt & Nesbitt 1982). Either this means that the mantle had considerable lateral variation, or that the mantle was heterogeneous vertically, with ascending liquids variously interacting with a chemically stratified country rock above the source region of melting; or that high-level processes are still poorly understood.

6.11 The evolution and stratification of the mantle

Certain key questions arise: how has the mantle evolved, and to what extent has it been stratified throughout geological time; from how much of the mantle was the continental crust and hydrosphere derived; what were the sources of heat in the Archaean, and how has heat production in the mantle varied? In large part these questions are as yet unanswerable (and beyond the scope of this discussion), yet they must be tackled if Archaean geology is to be understood.

Isotopic analysis offers a route to the mantle that is less tortuous than the trace and minor element path (but see O'Hara 1977). Zindler (1982) has reviewed Nd and Sr systematics in komatiites and related rocks. If it is assumed that the bulk earth contains chondritic relative abundances of rare earth elements, then a variety of elemental and isotopic ratios can be estimated. These estimates can be used to define bulk earth evolution models for Nd and Sr isotopes (Fig. 6.23). $^{143}Nd/^{144}Nd$ ratios from some Archaean rocks (Abitibi and Zimbabwe cratons) show that they may have been derived either from undifferentiated mantle segments or from mantle which was evolving towards the modern mid-ocean ridge basalt source. However, Sr isotopes in clinopyroxenes from Abitibi suggest that the host lavas do not represent ancient equivalents to mid-ocean ridge basalts. Rather, they are isotopically more closely comparable to modern island-arc products. In contrasts, $^{143}Nd/^{144}Nd$ ratios in lavas from the Onverwacht Formation, Barberton, plot significantly above a single-stage mantle evolution path. They may have been derived from a source which had previously been depleted in Nd relative to Sm. Possibly the mantle source for Isua and the Onverwacht Formation was depleted in light rare earths early in the Earth's history. If so, major continent-forming events could have taken place at a very early stage.

In more detail, what can be said about the state of the Archaean mantle? Was it depleted or enriched? Was it heterogeneous or homogeneous? Figure 6.24, from Hegner *et al.* (1984) who summarise the problem well, compares the results of Nd isotopic studies from a variety of Archaean rocks. Large negative deviations of $^{143}Nd/^{144}Nd$ from the chondritic evolution of Nd are seen in the Pongola and Usushwana suites, and in the Stillwater Complex (DePaolo & Wasserberg, 1979). DePaolo (1981) reports negative $\varepsilon_{Nd} = -2.8 \pm 0.2$ for Stillwater, which dated as 2701 $\pm$ 8 Ma. Crustal contamination was regarded as a plausible explanation of the low initial ε_{Nd}, but the uniform Nd distribution in all rocks would imply that contamination, if it took place, must have had a distinct mode. In contrast, there is the important evidence that the initial ε_{Nd} values from other Archaean mantle-derived rocks range from 0 to $+3$, implying that the mantle was chondritic or LREE-depleted. However, Hegner *et al.* recognise the possibility of mixing: in the case of the Ushushwana suite an array giving an apparent age of 3.1 Ga could be interpreted as mixing between 2.87 Ga old magma and older continental crust. Thus inferred initial ε_{Nd} values, even when they are positive, need not necessarily be representative of the source, and perhaps the Sm–Nd system is more liable to produce systematic errors in apparent initial isotopic ratios than the Rb–Sr system, because of the small radiogenic increment in ^{143}Nd in most suites. In general, Hegner *et al.* showed that magmatic rocks derived from magma reservoirs emplaced in lower continental crust are prone to contamination and are largely unsuitable for reconstruction of Archaean mantle geochemistry, a conclusion also reached long ago by Pb isotopic studies.

Komatiites offer further routes into this problem although not necessarily a way out. They can be contaminated, yet they undeniably sample the mantle. Dupré *et al.* (1984) considered that the mantle source region for lavas erupted in the Alexo region, Abitibi, was depleted (Fig. 6.25) long before eruption. The $^{147}Sm/^{144}Nd$ ratio of what they consider to be uncontaminated komatiite is 0.25, which reflects the depleted nature of its mantle source. The Th/U ratio of about 3.4 also probably represents depletion. The initial ε_{Nd} of ($+2.44 \pm 0.51$) indicates that mantle depletion took place long before magma formation. The source region may have separated from a chondritic mantle 400 Ma prior to eruption. To return to the problem of heterogeneity, comparisons between the Alexo and other Abitibi komatiites suggest that the source region was highly heterogeneous by 2.7 Ga. All the samples studied appear to have come from depleted material, but there were great varieties in the degree of depletion. In Newton Township, Abitibi, ε_{Nd} values range from $+1.5$ to $+4$ (Cattell *et al.* 1984). In Munro Township, if an age of 2.7 Ga is assumed, ε_{Nd} varies from $+1.0$ to $+2.5$ (Zindler 1982). Although all samples appear to have come from a depleted material, the source region may have been very heterogeneous (Dupré *et al.* 1984), or contamination very insidious.

Chauvel *et al.* (1985) have contrasted lead isotopic data with Nd isotope results from komatiites and basalts collected from the Kambalda area, in the Yilgarn Block, Australia. ε_{Nd} values ranged from -2 to $+4$, when

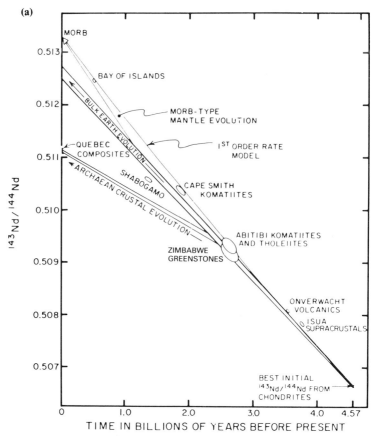

Figure 6.23 Bulk Earth evolution diagrams for Nd and Sr isotopes (from Zindler 1982). (a) $^{143}Nd/^{144}Nd$ evolution, showing bulk Earth trend and data from specific regions. Note the deviation of mid-ocean ridge source material (MORB-type evolution) and Archaean crustal evolution in the late Archaean. (b) $^{87}Sr/^{86}Sr$ diagram.

242

calculated for a 2.7-Ga model age, the highly positive results reflecting what must have been a strongly depleted mantle source. Negative results may either reflect continental contamination or a heterogeneous source. In contrast to Nd isotopes, initial ratios of Pb isotopes do not vary much, and are best explained by crustal contamination. Arndt and Jenner (1985) studied basalts from the same area and concluded that the trace element geochemistry was best explained as implying that komatiites and Mg basalts in the area were unrelated by simple fractionation or partial melting processes: possibly the basalts record an enriched mantle source which included a component of subducted sediment.

It is possible then to infer from the isotopic studies that below the Archaean cratons there were heterogeneous regions of the deep lithosphere which were either the komatiite sources or, more probably, through which komatiitic liquids passed and suffered contamination. The heterogeneity was probably sited in the cold lithosphere because only there would it not be smeared out by convection in the asthenosphere. In the asthenosphere, horizontal stratification may have developed, but lateral heterogeneity

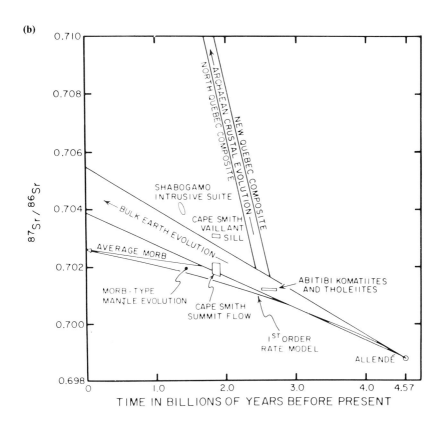

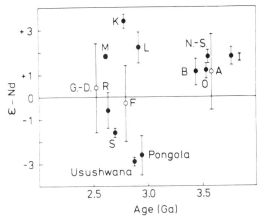

Figure 6.24 Comparison of initial ε_{Nd} values from a variety of Archaean rocks (from Hegner *et al.* 1984). $\circ$, ε_{nd} values from rocks of known age; solid symbols, ε_{nd} values from isochrons. I = Isua, Greenland; K = Kambalda, Australia; R = Belingwe, Zimbabwe; O = Onverwacht, South Africa; G-D = Great Dyke, Zimbabwe; F = Fiskenaesset, Greenland; A = Amitsoq, Greenland; M = Munro Township, Canada; S = Stillwater, USA; N-S = North Star, Western Australia; L = Lewisian, Scotland; B = Bimodal gneiss suite, Swaziland. (Data from Fletcher & Rosman 1982 and Hegner *et al.* 1984.)

would presumably be fairly short-lived (of the order of a few hundred million years) because of the high temperature and low viscosity of the rock. In this context it is worth remembering that a lithosphere *circa*. 150 km thick existed in southern Africa 3 Ga ago (see Ch. 5). A long-lived deep lithospheric heterogeneity is thus not improbable in an old craton, even as far back as 2.7 Ga.

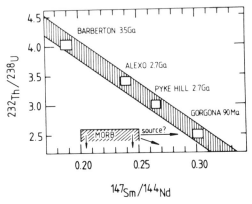

Figure 6.25 Th/U vs. Sm/Nd plot (from Dupré *et al.* 1984). Komatiites of different ages define a rough negative trend, suggesting that U/Th and Sm/Nd ratios were fractionated together during depletion.

Stable isotopic data appear to support the conclusions inferred from Sm/Nd and Rb/Sr systems. Oxygen isotopes in fresh minerals are especially interesting, since the maximum contamination which could be introduced during thermal erosion of the country rock would not be great enough to reset significantly such a major component of the lava as oxygen. Figure 6.26 shows the variation in $\delta^{18}O$ for fresh olivines from komatiites from the Belingwe Belt (Reliance Formation), compared with modern tholeiites and alkalic lavas, as well as young highly magnesian lavas from Gorgona Island. The great spread in the Belingwe olivines is obvious, as well as the overall heavy isotope ratios. Part of this pattern may be a consequence of the temperatures of crystallisation in the komatiites, which were high and varying; the fractionation of oxygen isotopes between lava and olivine is temperature dependent and thus the olivine data may represent liquids with $\delta^{18}O$ from about $+5$ to $+7.5$. Nevertheless, it seems that the spread in oxygen isotopes represents a varied set of parental magmas derived either from differing regions of the mantle, or at differing temperatures, or with a differing fractionation history. The overall 'heavy' pattern would suggest either derivation from a refractory source, or from a source region close to something analogous to a modern subduction zone (compare with Zindler's (1982) suggestion that Abitibi clinopyroxenes reflect an island-arc setting, though Abitibi olivines, by way of contrast, have 'light' oxygen isotope ratios). Although the evidence is not conclusive and the arguments subtle, the simplest explanation of the oxygen isotope data is that an essentially modern water cycle was in operation, with water being incorporated into subducted ocean floor, separated from that crust in the subduction zone, and playing a major role in controlling the temperature and chemistry of the melt regime above the subduction zone.

Studies of isotopic ratios in lavas can be used in general terms to model

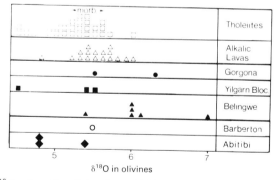

Figure 6.26 $\delta^{18}O$ values for olivine from Abitibi, Barberton, Belingwe, the Yilgarn, and Gorgona Is. komatiites, compared with modern lavas. (From Kyser & Nisbet, unpublished data.)

mantle evolution, in a way that is complementary to the use of isotopes in determining the history of the sedimentary mass (Section 5.6). O'Nions *et al.* (1979), Jacobson and Wasserburg (1979) and Allègre *et al.* (1983), amongst others, attempted to use geochemical models of isotope and trace element distributions in the mantle and crust to find out how and when the continents grew, and whether all of the mantle was depleted to produce the continents, or whether the continents are derived just from the upper part of the mantle. O'Nions *et al.* concluded that a model which only involved half the mantle in the production of the continental crust could produce a residual modern upper mantle with isotopic ratios similar to the source material of mid-ocean ridge basalts. Jacobson and Wasserburg similarly concluded that only the upper third of the mantle was depleted to form the continents; by implication, whole mantle convection is unlikely. Thus it is possible that for most of the earth's history the mantle has been divided into chemically discrete upper and lower layers. More recently, however, Allègre *et al.* (1983) have dissented. They attempted to invert Nd and Sr isotopic data to constrain crust and mantle evolution, and concluded that only very wide limits (30–90%) could be set to the fraction of the total mantle which has been depleted. In general, the data are at present not adequate to allow us to discriminate between the various models of continental growth: more thought is needed. They felt too that better data are needed before it is possible to use isotopic evolution models to tell whether or not the continents were extracted from the upper mantle only.

6.12 The rates of growth of the continents and depletion of the mantle

Much of the discussion in Chapters 5 and 6 has circled around the problem of when the continents grew, and how the mantle became depleted. Figures 2.7–2.12 show the complementary nature of the upper mantle and continental crust (Section 2.8); how did the separation take place?

Allègre (1985) and Taylor and McLennan (1985) have reviewed the various arguments on crustal and mantle evolution. Hurley *et al.* (1962), Hurley (1968) and Hurley and Rand (1969) proposed models of continental growth over time at a steady or even accelerating rate (Fig. 6.27). Moorbath (1977) and Moorbath and Taylor (1981) discuss in detail the mechanisms by which the continental crust is created from the mantle via calc-alkaline magmatism, with the appearance of the first true continental crust *circa* 3700 Ma ago. They consider that there is only minor recycling of the continental crust through the mantle.

In contrast, Armstrong (1968), Fyfe (1978) and Armstrong (1981) consider models in which very extensive volumes of continental crust appeared

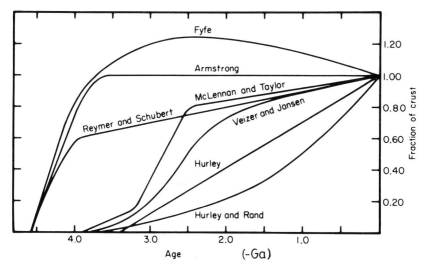

Figure 6.27   Various crustal growth models (from Taylor & McLennan 1985). Models include those of Fyfe (1978), Armstrong (1981), Reymer and Schubert (1984), McLennan and Taylor (1982), Veizer and Jansen (1979), Hurley (1968), and Hurley and Rand (1969).

very early on in the history of the Earth and have since been maintained. In Armstrong's models, the volume of continent is being continuously recycled, destroyed and regenerated. In this type of model, continents are eroded, returned into the mantle in sediments and in altered sea floor, while simultaneously material is extracted from the mantle in calc-alkaline belts. If destruction and construction of crust are equal, the process is steady-state.

The evidence in this debate is complex. There is stratigraphic evidence in the apparent lack of old crust (but crust is recycled and reworked in most models) and in the extraordinary abundance of 2700-Ma greenstone belts (Moorbath once commented, in the early 1970s, that most Archaean Rb–Sr data then available would fit on the same isochron, implying a massive late-Archaean event). There is isostatic evidence, difficult to interpret but implying from the supposed constancy of continental freeboard and oceanic volume (a matter of debate) that continents have grown steadily (Raymer & Schubert 1984; but see also Abbott 1984). Most powerfully, there is isotopic evidence, but the isotopic evidence is especially complex and controversial. There is fairly general consensus that the atmosphere and core segregated very early on, and in particular that at least the noble gas component has been in the atmosphere since prior to 4.4 Ga. However, the evidence for continental differentiation is less clear, though Allègre *et al.* (1983) would suggest a mean age for the continents of somewhat over 2 Ga, which corresponds interestingly with the mean age of the sedimentary mass at about 1.9 Ga (Section 5.6). Veizer and Jansen (1985) suggest that by about 2.5 Ga ago the global sedimentary mass was nearly the same size as today, and that since then recycling has been the dominant feature of sediment evolution. If so, sedimentation now is *circa* 90% cannibalistic. Galer and O'Nions (1985) have used Th, U and Pb isotopes to argue strongly that recycling of incompatible trace elements from the upper continental crust into the mantle can only have limited importance, and that the upper and lower mantle convect as separate layers with steady entrainment of lower mantle material over time (amounting to roughly half the upper mantle mass over 4.5 Ga). But the upward partitioning of highly incompatible elements did not necessarily coincide with the segregation of the major elements of the continental crust – possibly the beginning of the fractionation history of Th/U and U/Pb predates the formation of continents.

As yet, there remains no consensus on continental growth. The most popular models (Fig. 6.27) are mixing models, somewhere between the extremes of continuous continental growth and continuous recycling, in which continental crust is considered to be a mixture of recycled component originating from ancient crust and a newly extracted component added either steadily or in pulses from the mantle. In this type of model the mass of the continents increases over time, as does the mass of the recycled component, while the proportion of newly added mantle component steadily declines.

7 Mineral deposits in Archaean rocks

There stood a hill not far, whose grisly top
Belched fire and rolling smoke; the rest entire
Shone with a glossy scurf – undoubted sign
That in his womb was hid metallic ore,
the work of sulphur, Thither, winged with speed
A numerous brigade hastened...Mammon led them on.

Milton, *Paradise Lost*, I. 670

Some years ago, C. J. Allègre pointed out that many of the world's Archaean terrains had once belonged to Queen Victoria: although most such regions were added to her estate by the pilotage and later the scientific enterprise of Captain Cook, not to mention other accidents of discovery, fits of absence of mind and most significantly the distribution of beaver habitats, a powerful motive (other than desire to get to Fashoda first and forestall the French) was the search for economic minerals. Today, in all Archaean shields, mining plays a very important or even dominant role in the local economy.

Gold is the mineral most closely associated with the Archaean, but Archaean rocks are also valuable sources of minerals formed in mafic–ultramafic bodies (nickel, chrome, platinum-group elements, asbestos). An enormous variety of other minerals also occurs in Archaean rocks – iron, copper, lead, zinc, lithium, tungsten, tin, beryl, semi-precious stones and industrial minerals. In the following descriptions, the deposits associated with aqueous transporting fluids, both on the surface and in hydrothermal systems, are discussed first, then deposits associated with mafic and ultramafic magmas and cumulates in magma chambers, and then other deposits.

7.1 Gold deposits

The world's gold deposits can be grouped into two classes: the Witwatersrand and the rest. More genetically, the deposits can be classified as *palaeoplacer* (sedimentary) and *lode* (hydrothermal) deposits. In Archaean terrains both varieties occur, including the Witwatersrand palaeoplacer and many important lode deposits. A characteristic feature of the deposits is their 'gold only' nature, though with subordinate silver in lode deposits. In the palaeoplacers possible primary uranium occurs, which is associated with, but in detail is spatially separate from, the gold. Gold also occurs as a co-product of Archaean Cu–Zn massive sulphide deposits (e.g. Noranda, in the Superior Province, Canada).

In general, a variety of classification schemes can be set up to distinguish Archaean gold deposits, each scheme depending on some aspect of the host rock's mineralogy, the mineralogy of the ore deposit, the timing of formation of the deposit and the prejudice of the person setting up the classification. Since this work is not specifically on Archaean economic geology (an enormous topic), interested readers are referred to special volumes on Archaean gold deposits published by the Geological Society of Zimbabwe (Foster 1984), the Ontario Geological Survey (Colvine 1983) and the Canadian Institute of Mining and Metallurgy (Hodder & Petruk 1982).

In general terms, the presence of widespread Archaean gold deposits raises the questions: (a) What was the original source of the gold? (b) How was it concentrated? and (c) Was the Archaean different in some way from later aeons, so that gold deposits were more common then than now? In the discussion that follows, chemical processes responsible for the primary concentration of gold are outlined, and then a variety of gold deposits is described, with the purpose of illustrating these three problems.

7.1.2 The transport of gold in fluids within rock

The concentration of gold is a multistage process involving the liberation of gold from source rock by a leaching fluid of some sort; the transport of the gold in the fluid, then precipitation of the gold at another site; then perhaps one or more repetitions of the process; followed in some cases by erosion and sedimentary reconcentration of the eroded and transported gold.

Initially, gold must be extracted from a source rock, which is typically country rock around a heat source: for example, a lava pile around a sub-volcanic pluton or intrusive, or a terrain of older intrusions around a new intrusion, or a region in proximity to material undergoing metamorphism. Very large volumes of fluid have been involved in forming deposits: Fyfe and Kerrich (1984) calculate that the gold deposits of the Timmins area, Canada, where about 100 million ounces have been produced to date, may have been concentrated by leaching of up to $5000\,km^3$ of rock by anything up to $750\,km^3$ of fluid.

Most hydrothermal, or *lode*, gold deposits appear to have formed in the temperature range 175–450°C: Archaean gold–quartz veins typically formed toward the upper end of this range, at 320–480°C (Fyfe & Kerrich 1984). Ambient conditions in modern hydrothermal systems to depths of

4–5 km appear to approach those for a column of water at boiling point throughout its length. Thus at 2.3 km, pure water would boil at 350°C, while a 10% NaCl solution would boil at 350°C at a depth of 1.8 km (Seaward 1984). Evidence from Archaean lode gold deposits, however, suggests that pressures were at lithostatic, not hydrostatic levels even at depths of 4–8 km. In active modern hydrothermal systems, the oxidation potential of fluids is rather low, and hydrogen partial pressures are around 0.1 b. The active Broadlands system (New Zealand) in which gold, silver, tungsten and mercury minerals are at present being deposited, has a pH of 6.2 at 260°C, while Salton Sea geothermal brines have a pH of 4.15 at 320°C.

Seward (1984) and Fyfe and Kerrich (1984) have outlined the chemistry of gold transport. Gold occurs in two oxidation states, Au^+ and Au^{3+}, in aqueous systems, and under 'hydrothermal' conditions (e.g. 250–400°C, pH = 4) the activity of Au^{3+} is negligible compared to Au^+. Au^+ forms moderately stable complexes with soft Lewis base-type ligands such as CN^- and HS^-. Examples of complexes include $Au(CN)_2^-$, AuS^-, $Au(HS)_2^-$, $Au(SO_3)_2^{3-}$. Other harder ligands form less stable complexes such as $AuCl_2^-$. In general, stability of gold in fluid solutions increases markedly with temperature. If gold is transported in solutions as a hydrosulphide complex, decrease in temperature of an ascending fluid will precipitate gold: this will be most marked in sub-aqueous settings where fluids approach the point of debouchment into the ocean and interact with cool high-level or oceanic water. The complexes can also be precipitated by any process which causes a decrease in the activity of reduced sulphur, such as dilution or oxidation. Similarly, precipitation from chloride complexes, which may be important in high temperature, high-f_{O_2} transport of gold, can be brought on by decrease in temperature or dilution by high-level water (Seward 1984).

Groves et al. (1985) have argued that gold may precipitate in response to sulphidation of Fe-silicates in wall-rocks to veins, and accordingly suggest that aqueous transport was via a gold–sulphur ligand. Gold may also precipitate in response to carbonatisation of wall-rocks, implicating a CO or COS ligand (Fyfe & Kerrich 1984). There are probably several gold-transporting molecules and several mechanisms which may mediate its precipitation from hydrothermal solution.

Some of the gold-carrying species may be supplied, ultimately, by biological activity around water intake areas. For example

$$FeS_2 + CH_4 + 2H_2O \rightarrow FeS + H_2S + 3H_2 + CO_2$$

$$2FeS_2 + C° + 2H_2O \rightarrow 2FeS + 2H_2S + CO_2$$

involve methane (probably organically supplied) and organic carbon in kerogen ($C°$ in the lower equation). Carbon isotope values as low as $\delta^{13}C$ of $-9.5‰$ have been obtained from Fe-dolomite which is often associated with gold, and may imply that depleted (organic) carbon was present in the source region as an important carbon donor. More generally, biological activity is very important in controlling the general chemistry and oxidation state of sea water (see Section 8.4.1). Some fluids probably came from sea water; in other cases, prograde metamorphism may have driven hydrous fluids off from a heating rock pile along grain boundaries. In this latter environment, highly efficient extraction of some elements can occur. Fyfe and Kerrich (1984) estimate that across a major prograde metamorphic facies boundary $10\,km^3$ of rock will lose about $0.5\,km^3$ of fluid, which will be rich in H_2O and also contain much CO_2 and minor Cl^-. In many ore deposits, carbonate gangue may be formed via reaction with wall-rocks from CO_2 carried in solution or from magmatic fluids.

7.1.2 Types of Archaean gold deposits, in greenstone terrains: Zimbabwe, Australia, Canada, South Africa

Archaean granite–greenstone terrains contain abundant gold deposits (Anhaeusser 1976). The Zimbabwe craton (Fig. 7.1) is a classic example, with a history of mining reaching back to the Middle Ages, and a political history often dominated by the search for gold. The gold deposits (Foster & Wilson 1984, Foster 1982, Wiles 1957) include both a variety of strata-bound bodies in banded ironstones and volcaniclastic rocks, and an assortment of deposits in veins and 'shears' (note that in mining parlance a 'shear' is simply a 'zone of intense fracture' (Lindgren 1928), and has not necessarily undergone any simple or pure shear).

Kerrich (personal communication) has pointed out that an intriguing and largely unexplained feature of the hydrothermal deposits is the conjunction of extreme enrichments of crustally rare metals (Au, Ag) with low concentration or depletion of the abundant and generally mobile base metals (Cu, Pb, Zn). If this were not the case, conventional recovery of gold by cyanidation would not be economically feasible, given the heavy cyanide consumption by Zn (Kerrich & Hodder 1982).

Strata-bound deposits have accounted for about a fifth of total gold production in Zimbabwe. Most strata-bound ores occur in ironstones, either closely associated with stratiform concentrations of iron sulphides and iron carbonates, or in zones of fracturing and brecciation (Foster & Wilson 1984). There appears to be a bias in age, in that the older (3.5 Ga) ironstones are richer in gold than younger (2.7 Ga) ironstones. Older rocks tend more often to be associated with ultramafic rocks. Some strata-bound ores are also found in felsic tuffs and agglomerates.

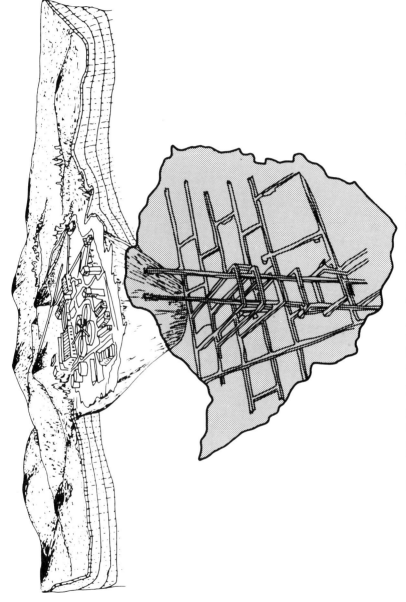

Figure 7.1 Gold mining in Zimbabwe (by permission, Zimbabwe Science News).

Most of Zimbabwe's gold comes from what are thought to be non-strata-bound deposits, and most of these are in veins (which host three-fifths of all gold ore bodies in Zimbabwe). Auriferous veins are very varied: they range from a few centimetres to 20 m thick, and can be followed along strike for distances of a few metres to several kilometres. The rock mineralogy is predominantly of quartz, often with minor carbonate minerals. Typically, veins have had complex histories, with several cross-cutting remobilisation events. Sulphide minerals are often disseminated in the veins; gold occurs as masses, as fine-grained disseminations or in microfractures, or as inclusions or solid solutions in sulphide minerals such as pyrite, arsenopyrite, chalcopyrite and galena (Foster & Wilson 1984). The wall-rocks are often intensely altered close to the veins; mafic rocks show propylitic alteration to chlorite–sericite–carbonate assemblages, while granitic country rocks show an altered envelope of quartz and sericite. Ultramafic rocks show well-developed extensive regions from a few centimetres to many tens of metres across of talc-carbonate–actinolite mineralogy, often preserving original igneous textures even in rock which is now wholly carbonate.

Other non-strata-bound deposits occur in mineralised shear zones, which typically consist of veinlets of quartz and carbonate in a core of 'sheared' rock. Sulphide minerals and gold occur both in the veinlets and also in slivers of altered country rock between veinlets.

Similarly, in Western Australia, most gold production comes from quartz veins, or from vein-related alteration zones, but in Australia many such deposits have been perceived as being essentially of strata-bound nature despite their vein character (Groves *et al.* 1984). Over half the production is from Kalgoorlie; in this and in the majority of other camps, the host rocks are tholeiitic metabasalts or metadolerites. Some deposits associated with ironstones or felsic volcanics do occur, but as in Zimbabwe, these are of minor significance in terms of total gold output.

Groves *et al.* (1984) consider the main vein type of mineralisation to be typically discordant but strata-bound, in that the vein distribution is controlled by local faults and shear zones, which are themselves controlled by variation in the competence of local stratigraphic units. Faults and shear zones may have acted as channelways which directed fluid flow and focused hydraulic fracture in susceptible stratigraphic units. Thus many vein deposits may be strata-bound but nevertheless 'epigenetic' (formed at a time later than the formation of the host country rock). Ho *et al.* (1985) used fluid inclusion studies to examine vein quartz associated with some Western Australian gold deposits. They found that gold deposition was from low salinity, H_2O-CO_2-rich fluids with about 20–30 mol% CO_2 and with H_2S and N_2 present. These fluids were alkaline to near-neutral pH and had densities of 0.7–0.8 g cm^{-3}. Vein quartz was deposited over a temperature range of 250–400°C and at pressures of 1–2 kbar; gold mineralisation may have taken place at slightly higher pressures and temperatures. Ho *et al.* considered that the fluids were most probably of metamorphic origin.

Groves *et al.* (1985) reviewed gold mineralisation in general in Western Australia, and concluded that a metamorphic–replacement model best explained most deposits. In this model, ore fluid and ore components were derived by devolatilisation of dominantly volcanic sequences during the metamorphism of the base of a greenstone pile. Gold was transported as a reduced sulphur complex (e.g. $H Au(HS)_2$), by fluids which passed via faults and shear zones.

In Canada the controversy of whether gold deposits are strata-bound has also developed. More generally, the argument can be phrased in rather different and not necessarily equivalent terms: 'are most deposits *syngenetic* (in other words, contemporary or penecontemporaneous with the formation of the host rock) or *epigenetic* (later than the host rock)?' Strata-bound ores are not necessarily syngenetic, and non-strata-bound ores are not necessarily epigenetic (except in the most restrictive sense), in that they may have formed in the later stages of a continuous event such as the eruption of a volcanic pile.

Many of the important Canadian gold mines are in lodes or, to use Lindgren's (1928) terminology, 'large fracture zones, filled with ore and partially replaced country rock'. However, many of these vein deposits appear to be limited to specific stratigraphic horizons (Karvinen 1982). The matter is further complicated by the association of many gold mining districts with very long linear or curvilinear zones of intensely deformed schistose or altered rocks, such as the Kirkland Lake/Larder Lake Break (e.g. Hodgson & MacGeehan 1982). These 'breaks' may have originated as faults active at the time of deposition of the volcanic and sedimentary rocks hosting the gold deposits: indeed, there are often major facies changes across the breaks. However, each mine and each mine camp (a camp is a district including a group of similar mines) is different from the next in the details of its geological setting. Figure 7.2 shows the typical stratigraphic settings of some major gold camps in the Superior Province, and Figure 7.3 gives examples of local settings of specific mine camps. Mining camps typically occur in rocks of low to middle greenschist facies, in terrains composed predominantly of mafic and ultramafic rock with minor felsic volcanics and variable proportions of clastic sediments. Most mines are associated with mafic rocks but, interestingly, in contrast to the regional setting, most mines contain felsic volcanics within the mine workings (Hodgson & MacGeehan 1982). In the mines themselves, felsic rocks, major zones of carbonate alteration, and units of carbonate, sulphide and sometimes oxide facies ironstones are more common, and ultramafic rocks less common, than in the surrounding strata in the mining camps. Stratiform ore zones, which

255

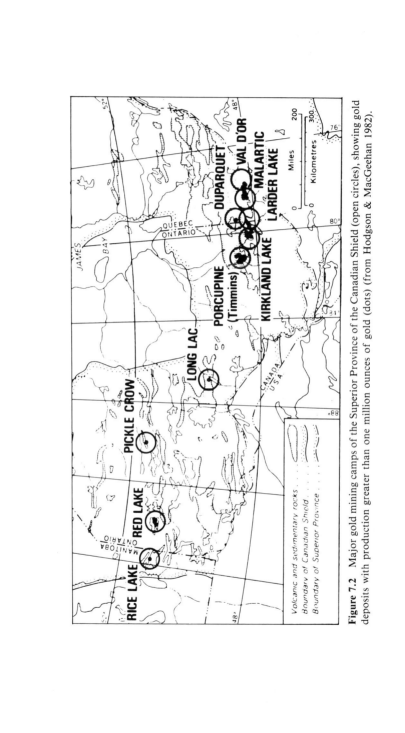

Figure 7.2 Major gold mining camps of the Superior Province of the Canadian Shield (open circles), showing gold deposits with production greater than one million ounces of gold (dots) (from Hodgson & MacGeehan 1982).

may (or may not) have been of exhalative origin, often occur in deposits in which volcanic rocks occur rather than in deposits where only epizonal felsic intrusions are present. Extensive zones of carbonate-rich altered rock (which are often roughly concordant with the regional stratigraphy) or carbonate-rich sedimentary rocks are associated with many deposits, especially when the deposits are associated with quartz-bearing felsic volcanic rocks (Hodgson & MacGeehan 1982).

A good example of this is in the Timmins/Kirkland Lake districts where there is a common association between ore bodies and carbonate-bearing rocks. Karvinen (1982) considered these carbonate-bearing zones to be strata-bound, and that the history of the ore zones of the Timmins area is closely connected with the history of the carbonate mineralogy. Similarly, in the Barberton Mountain Land, South Africa, Pearton (1984) and Viljoen (1984) have emphasised the importance of carbonate-bearing rocks in gold mineralisation. Often the carbonate-rich material has been produced by the alteration of ultramafic flows or tuffs. In some cases (e.g. in Barberton, in various places in the Abitibi Belt, and in komatiitic rocks in Western Australia), perfect textural preservation of characteristic komatiitic textures occurs, such as the pseudomorphic replacement of spinifex-textured olivine by carbonate.

In summary, it is clear from field and petrographic relations that both primary exhalative and structurally controlled carbonate horizons exist. The degree of gold concentration into the primary horizons and the extent of remobilisation from them remains unresolved.

7.1.3 The source and concentration of gold in greenstone belts: syngenetic or epigenetic, synthermal or epithermal?

Gold is where you find it – the major deposits in Archaean greenstone belts occur in a bewildering variety of settings, though most are in veins of some sort. Keays (1984), Saager et al. (1982) and Saager and Meyer (1984) have considered the problem of how the gold was originally brought to the upper crust. The delivery vehicle must either have been mafic or ultramafic magma, rising from the mantle; or tonalitic melts of mantle parentage; or

Figure 7.3 Stratigraphy and stratigraphic setting of gold mineralisation in nine major gold mining camps of the Superior Province (from Hodgson & MacGeehan 1982). Hodgson (1986, personal communication) notes that while the geometrical relationships of the rock units shown on these diagrams do correspond broadly to the field relationships, their interpretation as of "stratigraphic" origin is questionable. In probably all cases, felsic intrusives post-date the initial phase of deformation of the stratiform rocks, and so are not syn-volcanic. Many contacts in the stratiform units are faulted. Hodgson also notes that the "iron formations" of the Porcupine camp are almost certainly stratiform carbonate alteration zones formed relatively late in the geological development of the area, not exhalatives.

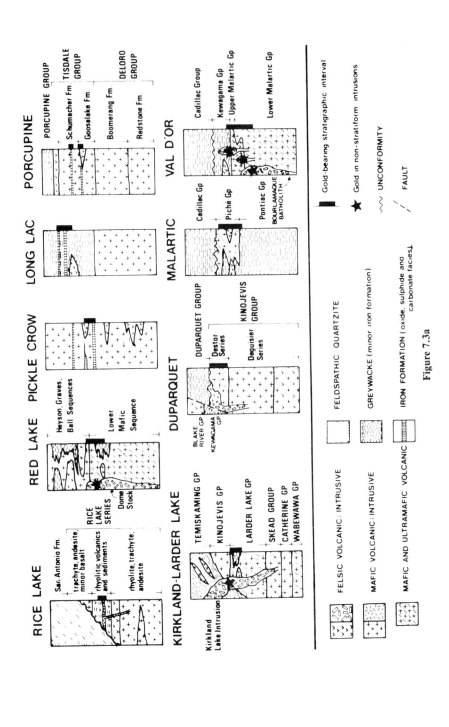

Figure 7.3a

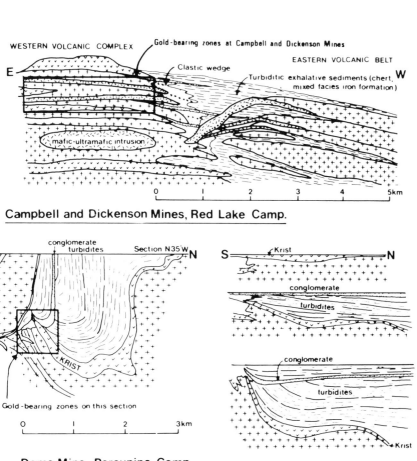

WESTERN VOLCANIC COMPLEX
Gold-bearing zones at Campbell and Dickenson Mines
EASTERN VOLCANIC BELT
Clastic wedge
Turbiditic exhalative sediments (chert, mixed facies iron formation)
mafic-ultramafic intrusion

0 1 2 3 4 5km

Campbell and Dickenson Mines, Red Lake Camp.

conglomerate
turbidites
Section N35°W
S N
Gold-bearing zones on this section
KRIST

0 1 2 3km

Krist
conglomerate
turbidites
conglomerate
turbidites
Krist

Dome Mine, Porcupine Camp.

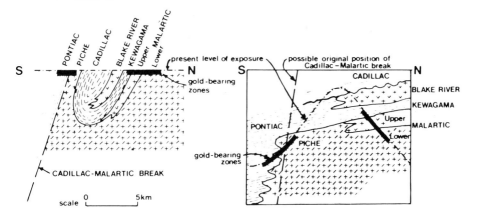

PONTIAC PICHE CADILLAC BLAKE RIVER KEWAGAMA Upper MALARTIC Lower
present level of exposure
S N
gold-bearing zones
CADILLAC-MALARTIC BREAK
scale 0 5km

possible original position of Cadillac-Malartic break
S N
CADILLAC
BLAKE RIVER
KEWAGAMA
Upper MALARTIC
Lower
PONTIAC
PICHE
gold-bearing zones

Section and Interpreted Stratigraphy, Malartic Camp

Figure 7.3b

granitic melts derived by partial melting of the lower crust, which scoured the deep continental crust of elements such as gold; or, perhaps improbably, the gold has resided in the upper crust since some primordial differentiation of the Earth, and has simply been redistributed since.

Saager and Meyer (1984) studied both granitoid and volcanic rocks in Southern Africa. They showed that granitoid bodies typically have *circa* 1 ppb Au, generally contained in erratically disturbed accessory pyrite. The rock-forming minerals are generally very poor in Au, and there is no obvious relationship between Au content and differentiation trends in the granitoids. In contrast, volcanic rocks show varied but often high Au contents (0.1–400 ppb), and usually contain more abundant and more varied sulphide minerals. Keays (1984) pointed out that mafic or ultramafic rocks could be the primary means of bringing Au to the upper crust from the asthenosphere. He also showed that in many rocks, Au is effectively inaccessible to concentration processes. For instance, in mid-ocean ridge basalts the Au content of crystallised cores of pillow lavas, typically 0.2–0.8 ppb, is most probably contained within silicate and oxide phases, and is effectively locked into the rock except under extreme conditions of weathering and alteration. The Au which *is* accessible is typically in glassy margins of pillows, and may leave the basalts at a very early stage; unless the Au deposit forms simultaneously with eruption, the accessible Au is lost. Similarly, Keays demonstrated that many sedimentary rocks are also poor source rocks for Au in epigenetic ore bodies.

However, in contrast to modern basalts, gold may remain accessible in highly magnesian lavas. These lavas, including komatiites, komatiitic basalts and picrites, have comparatively high platinum-group element content, and were probably rich in Au relative to other rocks in greenstone belts. Keays (1984) pointed out that most magmas become saturated in sulphur at an early stage, and thus immiscible sulphide droplets separate out and are left behind in deep-level magma chambers. In contrast, magnesian lavas only become saturated in sulphur at high level, just prior to eruption, because they are so much hotter than basalts. Thus the sulphur, Au, Ni, Cu and platinum group elements are carried much higher, and may even be carried to extrusion. This is especially true of the more magnesian komatiites, which may suffer very little fractionation during rapid ascent. On eruption, massive exchange with sea water takes place, either immediately or during metamorphism of the rocks by fluids in hydrothermal circulation through the developing hot volcanic pile (Seward 1984), around conduits in that pile. Such exchange may produce strata-bound syngenetic or epigenetic deposits, depending on the time of major hydrothermal movement and redeposition of gold. Later, metamorphic fluids may reconcentrate the gold (Fyfe & Kerrich 1984). Many deposits have probably been through at least two thermally driven stages of concentration, an early

260

volcanic stage and a later metamorphic stage often followed by a tectonic event.

Viljoen (1984) has explored the association of gold deposits with komatiites. Although the komatiites themselves may now be altered, metamorphosed and poor in gold, they may have been a principal midwife for delivering the Au from the mantle to the general environment of what is now a mining camp (e.g. Barberton, Timmins). Groves *et al.* (1984) comment that although concentration factors from source to deposit are so high that small differences in absolute Au content of the source may not be significant, a source enriched in gold is obviously helpful. Viljoen suggested that as a first stage in the concentration of the gold disseminated in komatiites, deposition took place in hydrothermal systems around active eruption centres, removing gold from bulk country rock and concentrating it in veins and at rock-water interfaces. Such deposits would be common on stratal horizons, in vein stockworks and in fault zones, and would be broadly confined to the stratigraphic level of rocks in and surrounding the eruption centre. Deposits would often be closely associated with inter-calated cherty sediments, ironstones, carbonates and tuffs laid down at the sediment/water interface. Figure 7.4 shows some possible settings of komatiite-related gold deposits in Southern Africa. Note that later epigenetic processes, such as the intrusion of a granite or the reconcentration of mineralisation along a shear zone or a fault, could enhance and redistribute the mineralisation.

An alternative view, proposed by Kerrich and Fyfe (1981), is that komatiites may be preferential sinks for gold rather than sources, given their high bivalent metal inventory for carbonisation. This emphasises the danger of simplistic genetic links where spatial associations exist. Ultramafic rocks may variously act as preferred sources or preferred sinks.

Barberton is one of the most interesting of the auriferous African greenstone belts. Both quartz-rich vein-type ores, generally transgressive to bedding, and also stratiform ores occur (Maiden 1984). The ores have undergone metamorphism, deformation and recrystallisation, and initially stratiform mineralisation appears to have been mobilised in places by ductile flow of sulphides and elsewhere via a fluid phase during metamorphism. Movement of this metamorphic fluid through permeability channelways resulted in the formation of some structurally controlled ores (Maiden 1984).

More specifically, Karvinen (1982) and Fyon and Crocket (1982) have identified local settings of mineralisation in the Timmins district. Karvinen (1982) considered that both concordant and discordant carbonate-rich rocks formed during periods of submarine exhalative activity as hydrothermal fluids circulated around several major explosive felsic vents. Figure 7.5 illustrates this concept. Circulating brine transferred and redeposited the

261

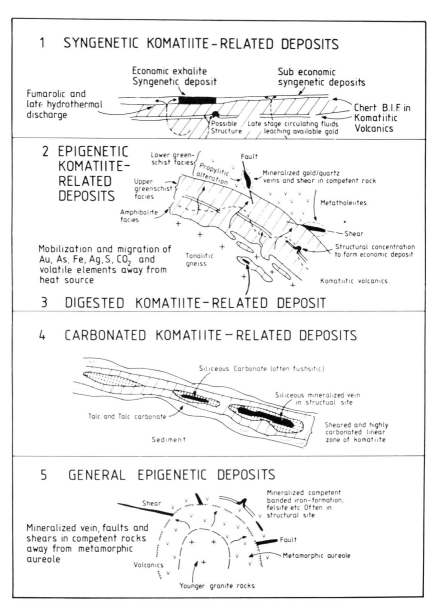

Figure 7.4 General model for Archaean komatiite-related gold deposits of Southern Africa (from Viljoen 1984).

Figure 7.5 Postulated history of the Timmins area (from Karvinen 1982). (a) Possible environments of primary gold deposition. (b) Evolution of stratigraphy with continued exhalative activity. (c) Development of metamorphogenic veins with folding and regional metamorphism.

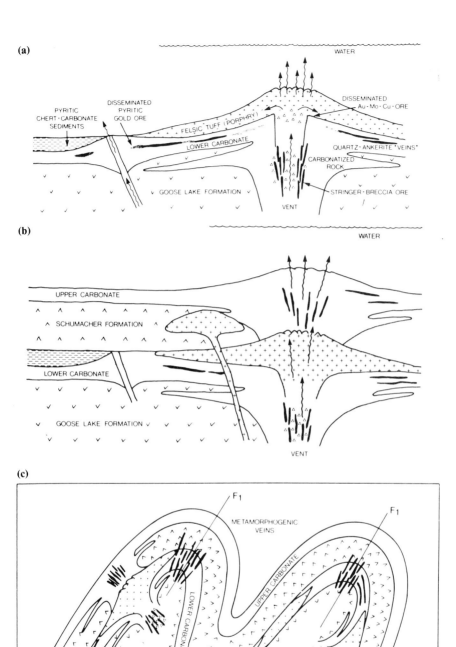

(a)

WATER

PYRITIC CHERT-CARBONATE SEDIMENTS

DISSEMINATED PYRITIC GOLD ORE

DISSEMINATED Au·Mo·Cu·ORE

FELSIC TUFF ('PORPHRY')

LOWER CARBONATE

QUARTZ·ANKERITE 'VEINS'

CARBONATIZED ROCK

STRINGER·BRECCIA ORE

GOOSE LAKE FORMATION

VENT

(b)

WATER

UPPER CARBONATE

SCHUMACHER FORMATION

LOWER CARBONATE

GOOSE LAKE FORMATION

VENT

(c)

F₁

METAMORPHOGENIC VEINS

F₁

UPPER CARBONATE

LOWER CARBONATE

gold on stratal surfaces, in cross-cutting conduits and in vent breccias. Some of the components of these deposits were ore bodies remobilised later during metamorphism to produce epigenetic but essentially strata-bound deposits.

An interesting aspect of these interpretations is that the main initial concentrating process took place in hydrothermal systems, often close to felsic volcanic centres overlying mafic or komatiitic lavas. Hydrothermal systems penetrating magnesian lavas would, potentially, be able to scour gold from a fertile source region and transport it upward, to redeposit the metal at a point where the temperature dropped rapidly, such as the surface vent, or at the sediment/rock boundary on the sea floor. However, komatiitic and basaltic eruptions were probably – with notable exceptions – not violently explosive, and comparatively short-lived. In contrast, felsic vents were probably long-lived in one place, and for the most part subject to periodic explosions. Thus hydrothermal systems around them would be able to penetrate fractured rock and hot breccia, and would be long-lived or frequently reactivated in one place. Fyon and Crocket (1982) showed that one variety of pervasive carbonate alteration was associated with a sea-floor hydrothermal event and predated later metamorphism. Kerrich and Hodder (1982) commented that auriferous sediments may have originated where fluids debouched onto the sea floor, although the fluids were not of seawater origin, while vein deposits formed at $320-480°C$ in fractures through which hydrothermal fluids moved. Possibly the gold was transported as a carbonate or carbonyl-related complex. Most interesting, perhaps, is the presence of extensive carbonate or even carbon (Pearton 1982, 1984), and field evidence possibly implies that the carbon was on occasion reduced from carbonate (in comparison, for a discussion of the oxidation state of carbon in modern mid-ocean ridge, see Welhan & Craig 1983). 'Graphite' is common in gold mines, but the term is generally a field term for a dirty, dark grey–black, carbon-rich material, not necessarily graphite. Downes *et al.* (1984) have investigated some of this material associated with the Hoyle Pond gold deposit in Ontario. In one auriferous vein, carbon formed 0.3% of the rock over a 6-m wide mineralised zone. More than 20% of the carbon appeared to be of organic origin, probably aromatic polymers. The association raises the broader question of whether much of the original synthermal gold concentration was organically mediated. It is also possible evidence for the pervasive existence of life in late Archaean hydrothermal systems, since if life occupied one such system it would presumably occupy all such systems (see Ch. 4).

There is a strong and fascinating controversy about the significance of metamorphism in producing the final concentration of gold. One widely held view (Williams 1986) is that many of the more important Archaean gold-quartz vein systems were deposited from metamorphic fluids (Fyfe &

Kerrich 1984) expelled during the dehydration of supracrustal (i.e. wet) rocks during metamorphism, and there is substantial evidence in favour of this view in many ore deposits. However, some or many quartz vein systems may have been formed directly by magmatic fluids originating from nearby intrusions. Burrows *et al.* (1986) have suggested this type of model for the Hollinger–McIntyre vein system, Timmins, Ontario, and for the Golden Mile system, Kalgoorlie, Western Australia. They conclude that the stable carbon isotope ratios in carbonate associated with the systems probably reflect a magmatic, not metamorphic origin of the H_2O-CO_2 fluid which deposited the mineralisation. Their model is interesting and powerful; so are the metamorphic and hydrothermal models, and each is probably valid in specific instances.

7.1.4 The Shamva and Hemlo gold deposits: the potential for gold in metasediments

Some very interesting gold deposits occur in metasedimentary rocks. Foster *et al.* (1985) have described the Shamva deposit, in northern Zimbabwe. The deposit is located in a 2.7-Ga succession of aquagene pyroclastic and epiclastic sediments and minor flows of rhyodacitic composition, which were intruded soon after deposition by plagioclase porphyry stocks. Pyrite occurs as disseminations in a mixed, probably resedimented volcaniclastic–epiclastic sequence and also as a fracture-controlled mineralisation. Gold occurs in the pyrite and also in microfractures in the metasediments.

Foster *et al.* consider that there was a complex history of hydrothermal events in the pile, beginning with what may have been synsedimentary deposition of pyrite and minor base metal sulphides in response to the high-level emplacement of a porphyry stock. This was followed by intense potassic alteration of the mineralised sediments and remobilisation of the ore elements. The final hydrothermal event appears to have been an event of CO_2 metasomatism, possibly linked with regional upper greenschist metamorphism. The deposit is now in metasediments which exhibit high As, Au, K_2O, Rb/Sr and CO_2 levels, in a porphyry and shear-related setting: such rocks should be good targets for exploration.

There is an interesting comparison between the Shamva deposit and the Macassa lode gold deposit in the Kirkland Lake area (Kerrich & Watson 1984). Here gold is produced from faults, veins and breccias in a country rock of Timiskaming metasediments and syenitic intrusive rocks, the whole cut through by the fault system of the Kirkland Lake break. Kerrich and Watson consider that the ore was precipitated from hydrothermal fluids at 350–460°C, the fluids being derived from dehydration of volcanic and sedimentary country rock, or from a magmatic source.

In 1982–3 an important new gold deposit was proven in the Hemlo area, north of Lake Superior, Canada. By 1984, press reports indicated that major ore reserves existed, sufficient to generate a minor gold rush in the area. The area had been investigated for gold deposits since 1869; by 1979 the area was still described as being of future potential (Muir 1982), but no major discovery had been made. Since the discovery, much interest has been directed towards previously neglected Archaean metasediments. In view of Hemlo's importance in changing exploration thinking, it is briefly described here.

The regional geology of the area has been described by Muir (1982, 1983). The area is part of a small greenstone belt in the Superior Province. In the belt, two supracrustal sequences occur. The Heron Bay Sequence includes mafic flows of tholeiitic lava, associated with mostly dacitic calc-alkaline rocks (including rhyolites) and closely related metasediments. The other sequence is mainly mafic flows. In the metasedimentary rocks both argillites and arkosic wackes occur, consisting of low-grade, low-temperature assemblages for the most part, but locally sillimanite-bearing assemblages occur near to granitic intrusions.

The Hemlo deposit occurs at a contact (Fig. 7.6) between crystal tuffs and metasediments (Patterson 1984). The metasediments include graded siltstones, pelites, reworked tuffs, and calc-silicates, while the crystal tuffs consist of altered rocks with sericite, tourmaline, green mica, barite and haematite. Ore is hosted by altered tuffs, siliceous metasediments and fragmental rocks (Patterson 1984). The ore mineralogy includes pyrite, molybdenite, native gold, stibnite and cinnabar. One interesting but perhaps misleading point is the association of barite with the ore zone, a characteristic feature of modern Kuroko deposits. Barite also formed elsewhere in the Archaean: perhaps the best known Archaean barite deposit is the North Pole deposit in the Pilbara (see Ch. 3), which has been identified as a former evaporite (Buick et al. 1981).

The Hemlo deposits are large, with reserves of 76 million tons at 0.24 ounces of gold per ton (8.2 g/t). Most workers have suggested that the deposit is penecontemporaneous with volcanism, either syngenetic or epithermal (Patterson 1984). Hydrothermal fluids of moderately high fo_2 which contain sulphate and permitted isotopic fractionation between oxidized and reduced S species, may have favoured the dissolution, transport and precipitation of gold (Cameron & Hattori 1985). A possible model is shown in Figure 7.7; however, it is also possible that the gold is associated with a hydrothermal alteration assemblage that overprints the regional amphibolite facies metamorphism, such that the mineralising event was epigenetic. One important feature of the Hemlo discovery is that it has stimulated a wave of exploration into metasedimentary Archaean terrains, in the hope of finding other similar deposits.

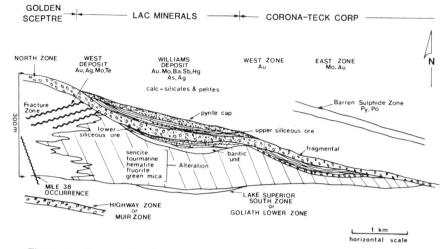

Figure 7.6 Stratigraphic relationships at the Hemlo deposit (from Patterson 1984).

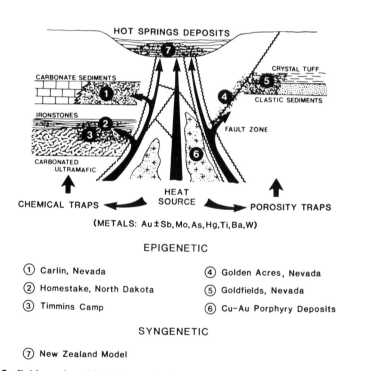

Figure 7.7 Epithermal model of the genesis of gold deposits, with examples (from Patterson 1984).

7.1.5 The Witwatersrand gold deposits

Over half of all gold ever mined (though production is now declining) and much uranium has come from the Witwatersrand succession in South Africa (Pretorius 1975). This succession is somewhere between 2.3 and 2.7 Ga old. Underlying granites have been dated as 3.1–2.64 Ga old (van Niekerk & Burger 1978, Allsopp 1964), while lavas from the upper part of the sequence have given U–Pb zircon ages between 2.3–6.4 Ga (van Niekerk & Burger 1978). The interpretation of these radiometric ages is controversial. As discussed in Chapter 1, many authors regard the Archaean/Proterozoic boundary as being diachronous, representing the age of 'cratonisation' (presumably, thickening of the lithosphere) in specific areas: on this reasoning the Witwatersrand succession, laid down on relatively stable basement, is characteristic of Proterozoic successions, and (by way of contrast) the granite–volcanic terrain of parts of the Californian Sierras would be Archaean since in places the terrain overlies a very thin modern lithosphere and has many similarities to greenstone-granitoid areas of Archaean age. If, however, the inter-aeon boundary is regarded simply as an orthodox chronological boundary, then the Witwatersrand succession is probably of latest Archaean or earliest Proterozoic age, depending on how the controversial radiometric results are interpreted. A rather similar controversy surrounds the Fortescue Group in Australia (Blake 1984a,b).

Several hundred tons of gold are produced each year from the Witwatersrand reefs. These reefs are fossil gold placers, laid down typically by shallow, braided streams in proximal to distal settings (Tankard *et al.* 1982), and close analogies can be drawn between rocks associated with specific placers and the facies models established by Miall (1978); the Scott, Donjek, South Saskatchewan and Platte models are all represented. In some cases where extensive palaeoslopes are preserved, the full range of facies models is developed (Tankard *et al.* 1982). In addition, some diamictites in the West Rand Group may be of glacial origin, deposited by submarine debris flows, but with striated pebbles (Strijdom, communication to Tankard *et al.* 1982, p. 124; Hambrey & Harland 1982).

The stratigraphy of the succession is outlined in Chapter 5 (Table 5.1). Figure 7.8 shows the sites of major fluvial influx in the Central Rand Group: a set of sedimentary packages can be recognised, separated by unconformities. In each package, pebble lag or gravel bar deposits are overlain by sandstones; the deposits probably grew both laterally and by downstream accretion in shallow, braided streams (Tankard *et al.* 1982). Depositional surfaces were relatively flat, and sediment dispersal was unconfined. Placers often developed on the unconformity surfaces where degradation prevailed initially. Regionally, the distribution of gold and uranium in the Witwatersrand placers appears to be related to alluvial fan development and degrada-

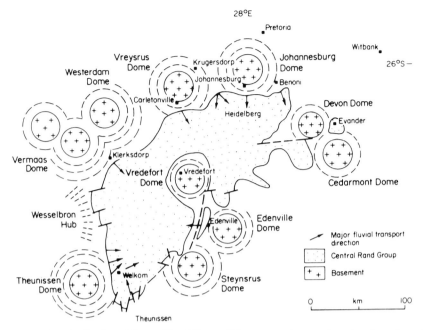

Figure 7.8 Distribution of Central Rand Group, Witwatersrand succession, showing adjacent granite domes and sites of major fluvial influx (from Tankard *et al.* 1982).

tion (Minter 1978, Buck & Minter 1985). Figures 7.8, 7.9 and 7.10 illustrate this. Each sedimentary package may represent a basin response to tectonically controlled erosion and aggradation (Tankard *et al.* 1982).

The mineralogy of the deposits is very diverse, including many minerals recognised as detrital (Feather & Koen 1975), and also some formed *in situ* during burial and metamorphism. Important minerals include pyrite, uraninite, brannerite and gold. Conglomerate reefs typically consist of well-rounded pebbles (70% of rock) up to 50 mm across, of vein quartz, minor chert, jasper, quartzite, quartz porphyry and assorted metamorphic and other fragments. The matrix (30% of rock) is mostly quartz and fine-grained phyllosilicates: sericite (dominant), with pyrophyllite, muscovite, chlorite and chloritoid. Ore minerals include early detrital gold, pyrite, uraninite and carbon, secondary pyrite and later minerals formed during gold remobilisation and sulphide mineralisation (Feather and Koen 1975). Pyrite predominates, often exceeding 90% of ore minerals. Of the detrital minerals, Viljoen *et al.* (1970) suggested that the primary source was in the greenstone belts of the Kaapvaal and Zimbabwe cratons (possibly in part from the crust which has been removed from above the Limpopo Belt), a proposal supported by isotopic work of Koeppel and Saager (1974). However, the identification of gold provenance is complicated by the effects

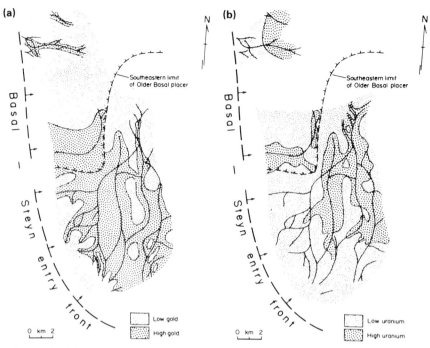

Figure 7.9 Subcrop maps of the Steyn placer palaeosurface, Welkom goldfield, South Africa, showing distribution of detrital gold (a) and uranium (b) in relation to fan geometry. Uranium is preferentially concentrated in finer-grained distal facies (from Minter 1978, modified by Tankard *et al.* 1982).

of remobilisation of ore minerals during burial and regional metamorphism to greenschist facies (Feather & Koen 1975). Saager *et al.* (1982) considered that metamorphism was essential to the development of most greenstone belt gold lodes. However, in the Witwatersrand placers it has caused extensive overprinting of the mineralogy. Alternatively, the gold may be derived from epithermal precursors in granitoids.

Despite the metamorphism, some of the material in the placers is very well preserved. In particular, carbon-rich seams are characteristically associated with some placer-deposits, and some appear to represent the remains of organisms living on unconformity surfaces. Possibly these organisms played a role in the concentration of gold. Zumberge *et al.* (1978) analysed the kerogen of some carbon-rich seams and found a variety of alkyl-substituted aromatic hydrocarbons, low molecular weight aliphatic hydrocarbons, aromatic sulphur and aliphatic oxygen compounds, apparently derived from the polymerisation of biochemicals from decayed micro-organisms produced by burial and metamorphism and by irradiation by uranium in the ores. They suggested that some of the gold was initially

270

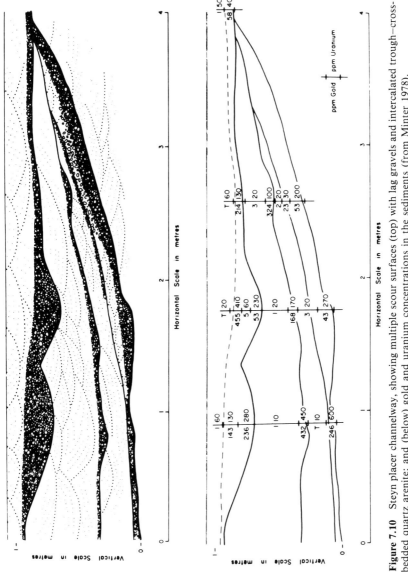

Figure 7.10 Steyn placer channelway, showing multiple scour surfaces (top) with lag gravels and intercalated trough–cross-bedded quartz arenite; and (below) gold and uranium concentrations in the sediments (from Minter 1978).

trapped in gold–organic complexes in organic mats. Mossman and Dyer (1985) have suggested that the erosion, transport and deposition of gold were extensively controlled by procaryotes. Their model involves the weathering of gold from its Archaean source rock under anaerobic conditions, probably in the presence of sulphur-cycling microbial organisms, followed by transport as a solution or colloid to the braided alluvial plains. There, in the presence of extensive procaryote microbial mats, which now are represented as kerogen, the gold was precipitated.

7.2 Base metal deposits

With some notable exceptions, most base metal production is from relatively young rocks. Porphyry copper deposits, for instance, are characteristically found associated with high-level calc-alkaline intrusions, and most commonly in modern mountain chains such as the Andes. Their expectation of preservation from erosion is low, and most are presumably washed rapidly away to sea. Only in rare cases do circumstances conspire to preserve such deposits, and Archaean porphyry copper deposits are rare, though they do exist. Nevertheless, Archaean andesites, dacites and rhyolites are common; presumably they were erupted close to or below sea level, and thus they are potential hosts of massive sulphide deposits comparable to modern Kuroko, Besshi and Cyprus deposits. In particular, deposits analogous to Kuroko-type bodies, set in felsic volcanics, are common.

Three mines are chosen for case studies.

7.2.1 Kidd Creek

The Kidd Creek ores, near Timmins, Ontario, Canada are stratiform, massive base-metal sulphides associated with felsic volcanic rocks. The deposit was found by airborne electromagnetic survey in 1959, and proved, by drilling in 1963, to be a very large zinc–copper–tin–silver prospect. The geology of the mine has been described in detail by Walker and Mannard (1974) and Walker *et al.* (1975). Altered felsic metavolcanics associated with the deposit have been dated by a Sm–Nd isochon at 2674 ± 40 Ma by Maas *et al.* (1986).

The regional geology of the area is similar to that around Timmins: the mine is in the Abitibi Belt, on the northern edge of the Porcupine mining camp, in a steeply dipping overturned rhyolitic volcaniclastic pile (Fig. 7.11) containing fragments ranging up to a metre across, with little matrix in much of the rock. The fragments are very heterogeneous, both lithologically and texturally. Most abundant are felsitic clasts, but locally fragments

272

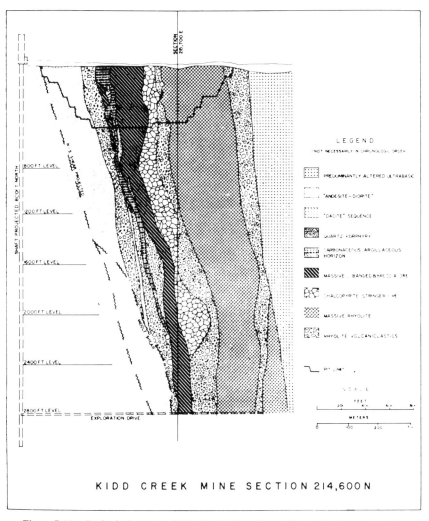

Figure 7.11 Geological section, Kidd Creek Mine (from Walker & Mannard 1974).

of pyrite, sphalerite, and other sulphide minerals occur. In some horizons dacitic clasts are a significant minor component.

The ore bodies occur in the upper levels of the rhyolite volcaniclastic unit, partly in association with a carbonaceous horizon (Walker & Mannard 1974). This latter horizon contains up to 10% carbon-rich material, as well as rocks which range from carbonaceous argillite or slate to carbonaceous chert, and also includes assorted volcaniclastic fragments in a dolomitic and carbonaceous matrix.

273

Massive rhyolite also occurs as irregular to broadly conformable bodies within the rhyolite volcaniclastics, and in places appears to be intrusive into the fragmental rocks. Above the rhyolitic volcaniclastics is a quartz–feldspar porphyritic rhyolite ('quartz porphyry'), and above that a sequence of basaltic or andesitic volcanics. Intrusive mafic rock ('andesite–diorite') also occurs in the immediate vicinity of the ore body. One very interesting feature of the geology is that altered ultramafic rocks adjoin the felsic pile (see Fig. 7.11). These appear to be komatiites, with relict spinifex texture. Regional metamorphism of the whole pile has taken place, to greenschist facies assemblages, and the area has been strongly and inhomogeneously deformed.

The ore bodies include several types of ore. *Stringer* ore consists of irregular chalcopyrite stringers in a rhyolite host. *Massive, banded* and *bedded* ores of pyrite, sphalerite, chalcopyrite, galena and pyrrhotite occur in rhyolitic rocks, agglomerate and carbonaceous hosts. Good examples of sedimentary bedded sulphides occur in the carbonaceous strata. *Fragmental* ore is also associated with the carbonaceous horizon, and fragments of sulphide may be up to several metres across. Walker and Mannard (1974) suggested that some massive ores may originally have been fragmental.

In discussing the ore body, Walker and Mannard draw comparison with the Kuroko deposits of Miocene age in Japan. The stringer ores may represent mineralisation in pipe-like alteration zones marking the location of fumarole feeders through the volcanics to the sea floor. The massive ores may have formed by precipitation on, or as replacement near, the sea floor. Breccia zones probably represent shattering by major phreatic explosions. In general, the local volcanic and ore facies closely resemble the complexity to be expected around an active sub-aqueous volcano with active hydrothermal circulation.

7.2.2 Noranda

The ore deposits of the Noranda region, Quebec, are also associated with rhyolites. The deposits occur in the thick andesites and rhyolites of the upper part of the Blake River Group, in the Abitibi Belt. The flows and domes were extruded sub-aqueously, and form extensive stratigraphic sheets. Five distinct episodes of rhyolitic activity can be identified (Spence & de Rosen-Spence 1975). The metamorphic grade is generally low.

Ore deposits typically occur at or near the top of rhyolitic units, and are commonly associated with lava domes and explosion breccias. Simmons *et al.* (1973), in describing the Millenbach massive sulphide deposit, recognised the presence of the dome of porphyritic rhyolite as the most significant factor in formation of the sulphide body. Knuckey *et al.* (1982) related these rhyolite domes in the Millenbach area to fifteen massive sulphide

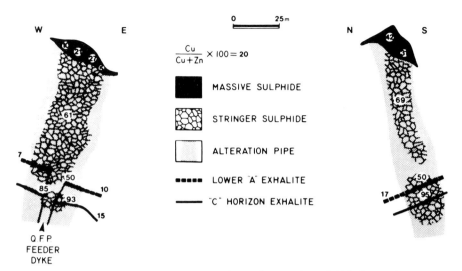

Figure 7.12 North–south and east–west sections of a massive sulphide lens, Millenbach deposit, showing metal ratios (from Knuckey *et al.* 1982).

lenses. Each lens is a characteristic, steep-sided conical cap of massive sulphide overlying a pipe-like zone of stringer and disseminated sulphides (Fig. 7.12). Ore bodies range up to tens of millions of tons. The positions of the lenses appear to be controlled by synvolcanic faults, and the largest lens occurs at the intersection of two fracture systems and developed during a period of domal formation. Knuckey *et al.* (1982) concluded that the massive sulphides formed during an active volcanic period on top of submarine lava flows before, during and after the extrusion of the quartz–feldspar porphyry rhyolite domes. The sulphides appear to have been deposited as hard, encrusting sinters, forming bodies up to 50 m thick above individual hydrothermal vents. Later metamorphism has not been a major factor in redistributing the ores.

7.2.3 Geco

Many classic Archaean base-metal deposits occur in low-grade volcanic strata, where it is often relatively uncontroversial to infer a synvolcanic origin for the deposit. However, some base metal deposits do occur in high grade terrains – enough to emphasise that such terrains should not be left unexplored.

The Geco Cu–Zn–Ag deposit (Langford 1955, Friesen *et al.* 1982) lies in a highly deformed sequence of Archaean metasedimentary and metavolcanic rocks, somewhat to the north of the Hemlo area in Ontario. The regional grade of metamorphism is high, with mineral assemblages including sillimanite, anthophyllite, garnet and cordierite. Several phases of folding have deformed the rocks. Mineralisation includes: disseminated chalcopyrite–pyrrhotite–pyrite; massive pyrite–pyrrhotite–sphalerite–chalcopyrite; and disseminated pyrite–sphalerite.

Despite the grade of metamorphism, the complexity of structure and the obscurity of primary features of the deposit, Friesen *et al.* (1982) infer that the general stratigraphy, wall-rock alteration and metal-zoning of the deposit can be recognised. They considered that these features are clearly similar to those seen in other Archaean massive sulphide bodies of volcanogenic origin, and thus Geco is thought to be a volcanogenic deposit, later intensely metamorphosed and deformed. Its significance lies, together with the Renco gold mine which is sited in high-grade metamorphic terrain in Zimbabwe, in demonstrating that important ore bodies do occur in high-grade terrain.

7.2.4 *General synopsis of Archaean sulphide deposits*

Hutchinson (1982) has reviewed what is known about the genesis of Canadian massive sulphide deposits in Archaean and Proterozoic strata. He concluded that most of the metalliferous hydrothermal fluids which formed the ores were syn- or only slightly post-depositional. The hydrothermal fluid was typically generated by deep convective circulation of marine or meteoric water, not by magmatic differentiation. Important massive base-metal sulphide deposits may have formed by sea-floor discharge of fluids from hydrothermal systems. Figures 7.13 and 7.14 detail Hutchinson's model. Lowe (1985) has suggested that the sedimentary environment surrounding hydrothermal vents may have been a very important control on the later preservation of the deposits. Sub-aerial or shallow volcanic activity could produce ores, but they would be likely to be eroded. Distal units, on the other hand, may be good exploration targets. More generally, Groves and Batt (1984) suggested that there is a link between type of mineral deposit and the tectonic setting in which it is found. They distinguished between 'platform'-phase greenstone belts and 'rift'-phase greenstone belts. In Western Australia, older 'platform'-phase belts formed in shallow water are poorly mineralised. They host barite, small Pb- and sulphate-rich volcanogenic massive sulphides and porphyry-style Mo–Cu deposits. Younger 'platform'-phase belts formed in deeper water and host widespread gold deposits, and banded-ironstone hosted deposits are common. In contrast, 'rift'-phase greenstones host diverse and important deposits, including komatiite-associated Ni–Cu deposits (see below) and many large gold deposits. Models of this sort are very interesting and often extremely influential, but all grand generalisations suffer from the basic weakness that our understanding of the tectonic setting of greenstone belts

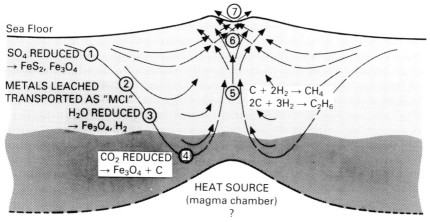

Figure 7.13 Diagrammatic illustration of syn-sedimentary, subseafloor hydrothermal convective system (from Hutchinson 1982): (1) Shallow level. (2) Leaching of metals from ferrous and other silicate structures. (3) Deeper level. (4) Production of strongly reduced fluid. (5) Production of hydrocarbon-rich saline fluid. (6) Vent system, stringer sulphide. (7) Massive sulphides precipitated at surface.

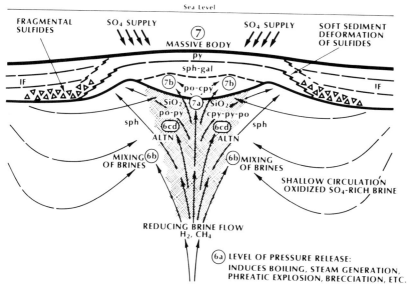

Figure 7.14 Detail of exhalative vent in Figure 7.13 (from Hutchinson 1982). 6. (a) Pressure-release boiling, explosions and brecciation. (b) Mixing of shallow oxidised brine with deep reduced brine. (c) Precipitation of sulphides in fractures (d) Rock alteration, stringer disseminated ore. (7) (a) Exhalation. (b) Sulphide precipitation.

is still very limited. One man's 'rift' may be another's 'trench–arc system' (see Section 3.6.4): great caution is needed.

7.3 Archaean nickel deposits

The deposits above are thought, for the most part, to have been formed by aqueous fluids. Mafic and ultramafic magmas also contain sulphide deposits, especially nickel sulphides, and these can be of major economic value. The topic has been reviewed in Buchanan and Jones (1984).

Most nickel production come from rocks younger than the Archaean – especially from the Proterozoic Sudbury Irruptive and from mines in Phanerozoic fold belts in the USSR. Nevertheless, Archaean rocks do produce significant amounts of nickel, and the deposits are of great geological interest, both for their scientific value and for their ability to set off feverish economic activity amongst the spinifex clumps, disturbing the kangaroos and sending share prices in London rocketing moments after the slightest utterance by an inebriated student geologist in a Yilgarnian pub. Such romantic days in Western Australia, along with the descent of Skylab and the collapse (with misses) of the Miss Universe stage in 1979, unfortunately are now nostalgia (until the next time), but there is a continuing interest in the close association between nickel sulphide deposits and ultramafic rocks, especially komatiites.

Most Archaean nickel deposits occur in strata thought to have been formed or metamorphosed around 2.7 Ga, although in some areas the interpretation of radiometric dates is controversial. In Western Australia the majority of Archaean deposits are either associated with intrusive dunite or with komatiites. A few gabbro-associated deposits also occur, and one deposit is hosted by ironstone. In Canada most Archaean deposits are komatiitic, as are most Zimbabwean deposits. Indeed, after the initial work by Viljoen and Viljoen (1969), most early research on komatiites was done as a result of discoveries made during exploration for nickel.

There are several excellent summaries and volumes devoted to Archaean nickel deposits. Amongst these are Groves *et al.* (1981), Coad (1979) and Naldrett (1979), and a brief summary of komatiite-hosted nickel deposits is given by Naldrett and Campbell (1982).

7.3.1 Partitioning, transport and deposition of nickel

Komatiite liquids are rich in nickel, which partitions into the liquid during partial melting and is retained on ascent, depending on how much olivine is crystallised out and at what temperature. Figure 7.15 shows the variation with temperature of the distribution coefficient for nickel between olivine

278

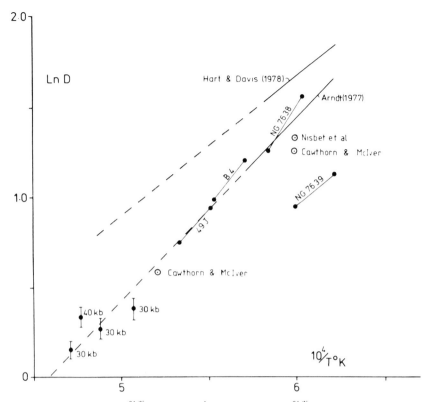

Figure 7.15 Plot of $\text{LnD}_{Ni}^{Ol/liq}$ against $(10^4/T)$ in K, where $D_{Ni}^{Ol/liq}$ = (wt % Ni in olivine) ÷ (wt % Ni in liquid), showing data from various experiments (solid lines), extrapolations (dotted lines) and assorted other samples. (For sources, see Bickle (1982), from whom this diagram is taken.)

and liquid. At very high temperatures and pressures, nickel partitions almost equally between olivine and liquid. Thus in a source region for komatiitic melts, the nickel contents of olivine and liquid would be comparable. At lower temperature, nickel partitions strongly into the olivine; in consequence, a liquid precipitating olivine in a magma chamber would rapidly be depleted in nickel. Thus basaltic liquids tend to be much poorer in nickel than komatiitic liquid. In the case of basaltic partial melts, less nickel probably partitioned into the basaltic liquid during partial melting, and proportionately more would have been removed at higher level by equal amounts of precipitation, when compared to komatiites.

Intrinsically, then, a komatiitic liquid which as ascended rapidly to the surface and has precipitated little olivine, or has precipitated that olivine at high temperature, would tend to be rich in nickel. Typically, a 30% MgO komatiite may have up to 1500 ppm nickel in the silicate host. However, even 1500 ppm nickel in a silicate host is not an economic concentration. A further process is required to produce an ore body.

Keays (1982), Naldrett and Cabri (1976) and Naldrett and Turner (1977), amongst others, have investigated the sulphide content of komatiite magma. Keays (1982) suggested that komatiite liquids at depth are under-saturated in sulphur. As they ascend, they eventually attain sulphur-saturation, probably at a late stage. The sulphur separates into an immisc-ible sulphide melt, which scavenges nickel from the silicate melt since nickel preferentially partitions strongly into the sulphide melt. Komatiites are thought to have arrived at the surface charged with droplets of an immisc-ible, nickel-rich sulphide melt. Sometimes, the erupting conduit may pass through sulphur-rich strata (e.g. a sulphide facies ironstone or sulphate-bearing evaporites) and stope out sulphur which is added to the immiscible melt, and thermal erosion on ascent or at the base of the erupting lava (Huppert *et al.* 1984) may also contribute sulphur.

Duke and Naldrett (1978) studied the scavenging process whereby nickel can be partitioned into immiscible sulphide melt. They found that the

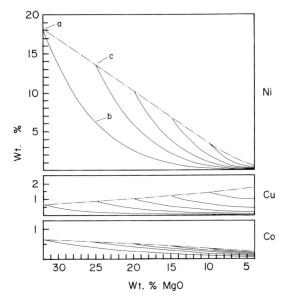

Figure 7.16 Compositions of initial sulphide melt to form from silicate liquids which become sulphide-saturated at given MgO concentrations (dash–dot line). For example, 32% MgO, 1600 ppm Ni parent liquid initially exsolves a sulphide with 18.2% Ni (point a). As fractiona-tion of olivine and molten sulphide proceeds, when the parent liquid has reached 25% MgO, the increment of sulphide forming has 6.1% Ni (point b). In contrast, a silicate liquid which first reaches sulphide saturation when MgO is 25% gives an initial sulphide increment of 13.6% Ni (point c). (From Duke & Naldrett, 1978).

distribution ($D^{S/L}$) of nickel between sulphide melt S and silicate liquid L was given by:

$$D^{S/L}{}_{Ni} = \exp(6.74 - 0.649 \ln(W^L_{MgO}))$$

where W^L_{MgO} is the weight percent of MgO in the host silicate liquid.

Thus the distribution coefficient changes with the MgO content of the komatiite. At 32% MgO, $D^{S/L}{}_{Ni}$ is about 90; at 20% MgO, $D^{S/L}{}_{Ni}$ is 120. Figure 7.16 illustrates the composition of the initial sulphide melt forming from a silicate liquid which becomes sulphide-saturated at a given MgO, and the compositions of subsequent sulphide melts. The Ni/Cu ratio also changes as MgO evolves. In this way, high concentrations of nickel can be produced in a sulphide matrix, which is then economically accessible. Fleet (1986), summarising earlier work, has discussed the problems of Ni/Fe exchange reactions and partitioning into sulphide liquid. The matter is extremely controversial and it may be some years before a consensus emerges.

7.3.2 Nickel sulphide deposits

A. Western Australia The nickel sulphide deposits of Western Australia have been reviewed by Marston *et al.* (1981). Most deposits are either associated with intrusive dunite bodies or with komatiite flows. Figure 7.17 shows a schematic cross section which summarises the settings in which deposits are known to occur.

(1) *Dunitic bodies.* Deposits associated with dunites typically occur in subconcordant lenses of dunite ranging from 500–10 000 m long and 50–1100 m thick. The rock is very magnesian (often 50% MgO), and occasional relict olivine cores range from Fo_{87-95}. There is evidence for the early existence of magmatic sulphides in the dunitic lenses, although regional metamorphism and alteration have played an important role in controlling the final nature of the sulphide mineralisation (Marston *et al.* 1981): in low metamorphic grade settings, lenses may be barren of sulphide; in medium grade lenses, disseminated mineralisation occurs; and in high grade and highly strained rocks massive, matrix and disseminated sulphides can occur. In some areas, metamorphism has been extremely important in redistributing sulphide (Porter & Mackay 1981); in other cases, magmatic factors still predominate. Many lenses have clastic sediments or felsic volcanic rocks stratigraphically beneath them, and mafic or ultramafic rocks above (Marston *et al.* 1981).

The sulphide shoots in dunitic bodies include massive, matrix (with

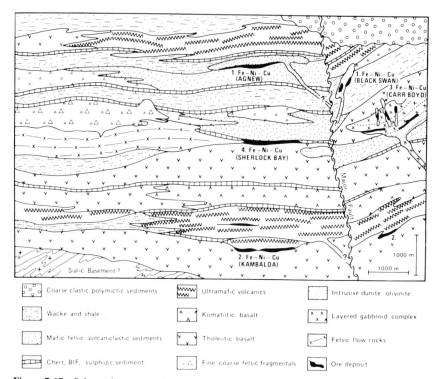

Figure 7.17 Schematic cross section showing the geological setting of nickel sulphide deposits in Western Australia (from Marston *et al*. 1981).

interstitial silicate) and disseminated ores near margins of lenses, and disseminated ores in the cores and above. In massive sulphide, nickel contents range up to 6–9%, with disseminated bodies up to 4% Ni. Naldrett and Turner (1977) studied sulphide mineralisation in a dunitic body at Yakabindie, and suggested that the deposit was formed by fractional crystallisation of a liquid containing over 33% MgO. Thus the original source of the nickel-rich sulphide liquid was probably a komatiitic liquid at high level, although there was also textural and chemical evidence that metals and sulphides had been distributed during metamorphism or alteration of the host rock (Naldrett & Turner 1977). However, Marston *et al*. (1981) pointed out that some dunitic rocks probably crystallised from less MgO-rich melts, quoting unpublished work by R. Hill to suggest maximum MgO contents of 23%.

(2) *Volcanic-associated bodies.* Much of the high grade, economically viable, Western Australian nickel is in deposits associated with ultramafic volcanic rocks, particularly in the Kambalda area. These

282

deposits are often smaller than deposits in dunitic bodies, but often have much higher grades of ore. Nickel sulphides are typically located at the base of formations of komatiitic volcanics. The geology of the Kambalda field has been described in detail by Gresham and Loftus-Hills (1981). Most of the ores occur in the lower part of the komatiite sequence, and 80% of the ore is contact ore occurring at the base of the lowermost ultramafic flow and occupying elongate troughs in the foot-wall basalt/ultramafic contact. These troughs are thought by Gresham and Loftus-Hills to be original depressions in the volcanic topography. The troughs are narrow, elongate structures, with very variable length, width and depth. Some are up to 2.3 km long, but usually they are only 150–250 m wide, and often less. The depths of the troughs range from a few metres to 100 m. Fig. 7.18 shows the basal contact at Lunnon Shoot and a reconstruction of the Lunnon Trough, in the Kambalda area.

Groves *et al.* (1986) have examined in detail the textures of the komatiitic host rocks of the Kambalda nickel deposits (Fig. 7.18b). They demonstrated that interspinifex Fe–Ni–Cu sulphide ores, which underlie some hanging wall sulphide ores, formed through thermal erosion of the underlying komatiite flows and possibly also of sediments. However, in general, thermal erosion by komatiites may have been rare, and erosion may have been most vigorous where basal concentrations of sulphide liquid (which has high thermal conductivity) were present in localised lava channels.

Massive ores occur commonly in contact ore bodies, ranging up to 5 m thick but usually less than 1 m. These contain over 80% sulphide minerals (predominantly pyrrhotite, pentlandite and pyrite). This ore is often banded, with alternating pyrrhotite and pentlandite-rich bands, the banding usually being parallel to wall-rock contacts and probably resulting from recrystallisation (Gresham & Loftus-Hills 1981). Matrix ores occur both in contact and hanging-wall ore bodies. These latter, hanging-wall bodies, usually occur within 100 m of the ultramafic/basalt contact and show a close spatial relationship to contact ores. Matrix ore bodies also are usually less than 5 m thick and average 1 m, with 40–80% sulphides, associated with interstitial silicates of moderately to highly magnesian composition. Usually contacts between this and massive ore are very sharp. Disseminated ore (10–40% sulphides) also occurs in contact and hanging-wall bodies, interstitial in an ultramafic host. Contacts with matrix ores are moderately sharp, but not as sharp as contacts between massive and matrix ore.

B.   Canada   In Canada, similar but economically less important deposits

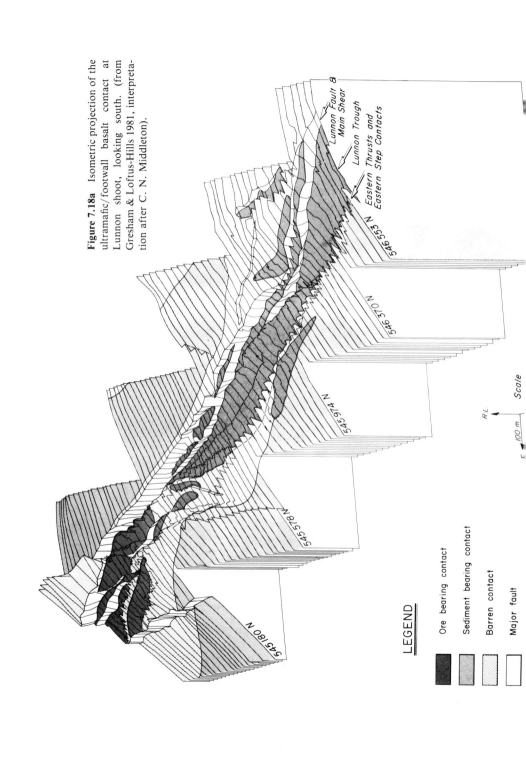

Figure 7.18a Isometric projection of the ultramafic/footwall basalt contact at Lunnon shoot, looking south. (from Gresham & Loftus-Hills 1981, interpretation after C. N. Middleton).

Lunnon Fault &
Main Shear

Lunnon Trough

Eastern Thrusts and
Eastern Step Contacts

546 553 N

546 310 N

545 974 N

545 578 N

545 180 N

RL

Scale

100 m

LEGEND

Ore bearing contact

Sediment bearing contact

Barren contact

Major fault

are widespread in the Abitibi belt (Coad 1979), especially around Timmins. Most of the deposits are related in some way to komatiitic volcanism. An example is the Langmuir deposit (Coad 1979, Green & Naldrett 1981). Figure 7.19 shows a pair of simplified cross sections of the Langmuir 2 deposit. Mineralisation occurs at the base of a spinifex textured komatiitic flow, with massive ore at the bottom, overlain by 'net-textured' ore forming a 'net' around silicate crystals, then by cumulate peridotite, then by spinifex-textured rock of the upper part of the flow. Figure 7.20 shows a three-dimensional reconstruction of the Langmuir 2 deposit, showing how the massive ore is distributed in relation to irregularities in the surrounding strata. The south end of the main ore zone is underlain by andesite, while

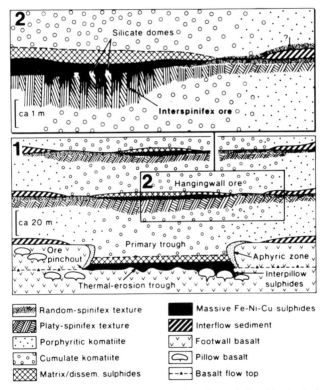

Figure 7.18b Schematic representation, not to scale, of (1) relationships in the lower part of the Kambalda komatiite pile emphasizing trough structures and showing hangingwall ores; and (2) relationships between massive ores, interspinifex ores and komatiite flow-tops at Lunnon shoot (from Groves *et al.* 1986).

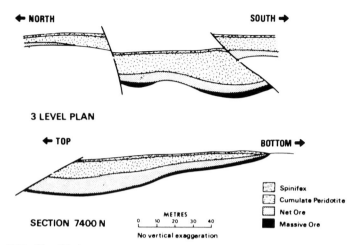

Figure 7.19 Simplified cross sections, at right angles to one another, of Langmuir 2 nickel deposit. (From Green & Naldrett 1981.)

the north end is underlain by ultramafic rocks, interpreted to be a near-surface magma chamber or lava pool feeding the overlying flows and grading laterally into flows. Coad (1979) interpreted the palaeogeography more conservatively, pointing to the probability that later folding has obscured relationships. The deposit produced 1.25 million metric tons at 1.45% Ni between 1973 and 1975.

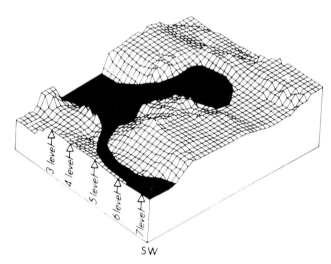

Figure 7.20 Three-dimensional view of the Langmuir 2 deposit, showing distribution of massive ore (black). (From Green & Naldrett 1981.)

286

Also near Timmins is the Texmast deposit (Coad 1979), located in spinifex-textured komatiites, and lying on a foot-wall of intermediate to felsic volcanogenic sedimentary rocks and tuff. The sulphides occur in the ultramafic pile as lenses which may be associated with a later gabbro dyke. Possibly the lenses were once associated with a feeder pipe, and the dyke subsequently intruded in the region of the feeder pipe. Nickel reserves in the deposit total at least 3.8 million tons at 1% Ni.

C. Zimbabwe Several Archaean nickel deposits, mostly associated with komatiites, have been found in the Zimbabwe craton. Most are associated with extrusive ultramafics which are stratigraphically equivalent to the Bulawayan komatiites of the Belingwe greenstone belt. Detailed descriptions of the deposits are given by Viljoen and Bernasconi (1979), Anderson *et al.* (1979), Moubray *et al.* (1979) and Williams (1979). There are many close parallels between deposits such as those at Shangani–Damba, Epoch and Perseverance and the Canadian and Australian deposits described above, though Zimbabwean deposits tend to be of rather lower grade (in part reflecting different cut-off grades and lower operating costs in Africa in the 1970s). The Madziwa ore body (Stagman 1978) contains sulphide segregations in differentiated gabbroic rocks intruded into granitic gneisses, and the Empress deposit occurs in amphibolite derived from gabbro intruded into a thick andesitic pile (Stagman 1978). Not all nickel deposits are komatiitic!

7.3.3 Models

Many models have been proposed to account for the genesis of Archaean nickel deposits, each deposit being different and each deposit generating almost as many models as visiting geologists. Green and Naldrett (1981) have summarised the more popular models as follows: (a) magmatic sulphide accumulation, with the sulphur either being mantle-derived or crustally derived, (b) volcanic-exhalative activity and (c) metamorphism, deformation or alteration models (Fig. 7.21). The exhalative models are similar to those developed for other Archaean massive sulphide deposits, and demand a heat source to drive circulating aqueous fluids, a supply of reduced sulphur and a hydrothermal system capable of carrying nickel from source rocks to deposit. They fail in many cases to explain the apparently magmatic textures of the ore bodies.

The metamorphic models have application in many nickel deposits, especially in Western Australia, where post-magmatic processes have certainly redistributed and in some cases probably upgraded pre-existing nickel deposits. In many nickel deposits, early sulphide minerals appear to have been remobilised either by late magmatic heat (as a lava pile cools) or by metamorphic heat and fluids.

287

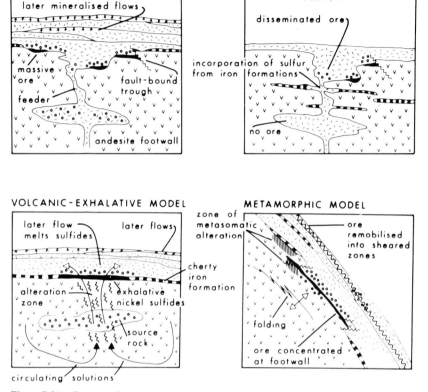

Figure 7.21 Cartoons illustrating modes of formation proposed for nickel sulphide deposits of the Langmuir type (from Green & Naldrett 1981).

Nonetheless, most komatiitic and dunitic ore bodies seem to be of mainly magmatic character. The essential feature (Fig. 7.22) of most models is that a sulphur-saturated komatiitic magma, either at shallow depth or during extrusion, precipitated an immiscible sulphide liquid rich in nickel at the base of the magma (Usselman *et al.* 1979). There is much controversy about the source of the sulphur; in some cases, undersaturated komatiitic magmas may have stoped sulphur out of crustal rocks such as sulphide facies ironstones.

To generalise, many deposits may form when erupting komatiite liquid rises and becomes saturated in sulphur (Keays 1982). It may thermally erode its conduit and on eruption erode a trough into the underlying rock (Huppert *et al.* 1984, Huppert & Sparks 1985a,b). As the eruption proceeds, lava flows in a trough. At the base of the flow, and after eruption ceases, lava pools build up in the lowest topographic region, and sulphide

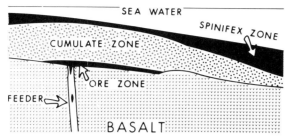

Figure 7.22 Diagrammatic longitudinal section through an ore-bearing komatiite flow (from Usselmann *et al.* 1979).

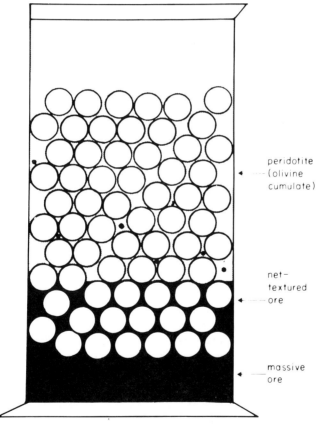

Figure 7.23 The billiard-ball model (from Naldrett & Campbell 1982): billiard balls lie in a beaker filled with water, and mercury is poured in. At the base, a layer of mercury (massive ore); above, some balls are forced into mercury by the overlying weight of other balls (net-textured ore). Above, a few drops of mercury may be trapped between balls (disseminated low-grade ore).

liquid precipitates out, collecting in topographic depressions such as the base of the lava channel. This precipitation will build up pools of sulphide liquid below the silicates, at the base of the olivine cumulates in the cooling komatiite flow (Fig. 7.22). Naldrett and Campbell (1982) have reviewed the mechanism of separation of sulphide from silicate liquids, drawing comparisons with the Naldrett billiard-ball model (Fig. 7.23), which explains the distinction between massive, net-textured and disseminated ore. The sulphide liquid is heavily enriched in nickel because of the preferential partitioning of nickel into it. Research continues; for fifteen years, both Archaean nickel exploration and academic research into the early history of the Earth have profited from a mutual, almost symbiotic fascination with komatiites.

7.4 Platinum group elements

Most platinum and associated elements (Pd, Pt, Rh, Ir, Os, Ru) are mined from the Bushveld Complex, a vast Proterozoic mafic igneous complex in South Africa. However, many analogous igneous complexes of Archaean age are known, and there is great potential for finding platinum in rocks older than 2500 Ma. In particular, large deposits of platinum are known to exist in the Great Dyke and in the Stillwater Complex, Montana. There is also considerable scientific interest in the platinum group element contents of komatiitic liquids: understanding komatiites may help us to understand more about the evolution of the mantle, and may also help in searching for new deposits of platinum and nickel.

7.4.1 Platinum in Archaean plutonic bodies

The six platinum-group elements all exhibit strong siderophile and chalcophile tendencies. In any sulphide or metallic minerals crystallising from mafic or ultramafic magmas, they are very strongly enriched. The principal source of platinum group elements in the Western world is the Merensky Reef, in the Proterozoic Bushveld Complex. This reef is a thin sheet of coarse pyroxenite containing platinum and gold minerals and sulphides. Exploration for platinum group elements in Archaean mafic–ultramafic plutonic bodies has often concentrated on finding analogous zones to the Merensky Reef (Mennell & Frost 1926), and such exploration has been highly successful in the Stillwater Complex of Montana. Since the Stillwater Complex is both economically valuable and classic petrological ground, it is worth considering in some detail. The Great Dyke too contains an extensive platinoid horizon, which has also been compared to the Merensky Reef.

7.4.2 Stillwater Complex

The Archaean Stillwater Complex, of southern Montana, has been studied by Hess (1960, and various papers quoted therein), Jackson (1961) and Page (1977), amongst others: it is one of the most celebrated of all mafic igneous bodies. In 1962 an exploration program was initiated, because of the similarity of the complex to the Bushveld complex, the known presence of platinoids and the occurrence of sulphides in the Stillwater Complex (Conn 1979). Figure 7.24 is a geological map of the complex showing the position of the mineralised horizon. The age of the complex is still debated, but is probably close to 2.7 Ga.

The complex has been classified into a set of distinct zones: a Basal Zone of medium-grained noritic rocks and bronzite cumulates (60 m); an Ultramafic Zone consisting of a lower harzburgite member (1000 m) of harzburgite, dunite, bronzitite, and chromitite, and an upper Bronzitite Member; a Banded Zone (4000 m) of anorthosite, norite and gabbro, marked by the presence of plagioclase as a cumulus mineral, including an upper division of anorthosite, gabbro and troctolite, with olivine appearing in cumulates (Jones *et al.* 1960, Jackson 1961, Page 1977). Todd *et al.* (1982) and Irvine *et al.* (1983) have reclassified the stratigraphic subdivision of the complex, as illustrated in Figure 7.25.

Todd *et al.* pointed out that the complex is the product of two parent liquids, one with ultramafic characteristics and the second anorthositic.

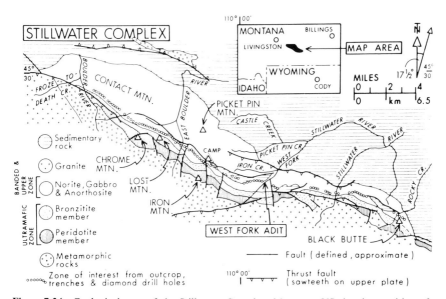

Figure 7.24 Geological map of the Stillwater Complex, Montana, US showing position of mineralised horizon (from Conn 1979).

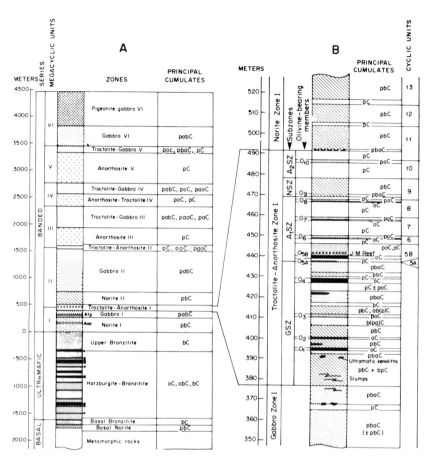

Figure 7.25 Stratigraphic subdivision of the Stillwater Complex (from Irvine *et al.* 1983). A = Major divisions; B = Subdivision of Troctolite-Anorthosite zone 1. Note J.M. Reef. Abbreviations: p = plagioclase; o = olivine; b = bronzite; a = augite; C = cumulate; O_1–O_9 = olivine bearing members; Aaa = all American anorthosite; Afp = Frog Pond anorthosite; GSZ = gabbro subzone; A_1SZ, A_2SZ = anorthosite subzones; NSZ = Norite subzone. Small solid bands in Harzburgite bronzite zone in A denote chromitite layers.

Through the whole complex, two principal sequences of crystallisation could be seen in the cumulus silicate minerals: the earlier order of crystallisation, in the ultramafic series and lower banded series, is olivine, bronzite, plagioclase, augite; the later order, in the upper banded series, is plagioclase, olivine, augite, bronzite or hypersthene. Todd *et al.* identified both orders through cumulate successions thousands of metres thick, and concluded that two parental magmas were responsible. They suggested that the Pt and Pd in the main J-M reef were derived from the first parent, and the S from the second. The two liquids may have differed sufficiently in density to form separate layers in the magma chamber, and their crystallisation and mixing may have been controlled by doubly diffusive convection (Irvine *et al.* 1983). This is illustrated in Figure 7.26.

The J-M reef, thought to have been produced in this process, is generally 1–3 m thick and has been traced for 40 km, which is the maximum possible length within the outcrop area of the intrusion. It contains small concentrations (0.5–1.0%) of chalcopyrite, pyrrhotite and pentlandite, in which are included minute grains of platinum group minerals. Grades range up to 22.3 g of Pt and Pd per ton, with a Pt/Pd ratio of 1/3.5 (Todd *et al.* 1982). Barnes (1982) and Barnes and Naldrett (1985) suggested that the Pt-rich sulphide liquid equilibrated with a large volume of magma, perhaps a column at least 1 km thick, and that scavenging of Pt from the magma column could have been a consequence of the injection of a buoyant plume of primitive magma into the chamber (Fig. 7.27). How distinct the injected magma was from the liquid in the chamber remains a matter of debate – were they simply parent and daughter liquids, or more different? Fleet (1986) has strongly challenged the interpretation by Barnes and Naldrett on both textural and geochemical grounds, and has suggested that post-magmatic effects may be important in the sulphide chemistry: the controversy is fascinating and demonstrates the present lack of consensus about sulphide geochemistry.

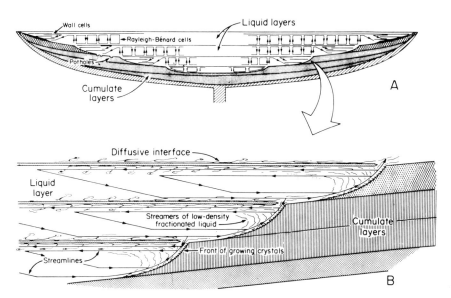

Figure 7.26 Cartoon showing solidification of a layered intrusion by lateral growth of cumulate layer from magmatic liquids stratified by density and undergoing double-diffusive convection. See also Figure 3.40. (From Irvine *et al.* 1983.)

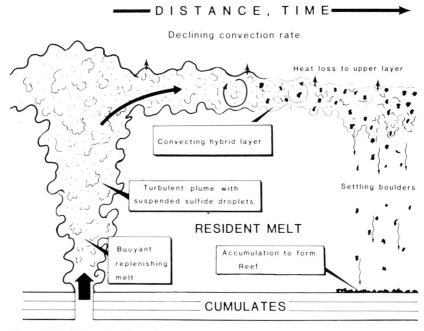

Figure 7.27 Schematic illustration of sequence of events following injection of a pulse of buoyant replenishing melt into the Stillwater magma chamber (frrom Barnes & Naldrett 1985).

7.4.3 The Great Dyke

Platinoids have been known since 1925 in the Great Dyke, Zimbabwe (Mennell & Frost 1926); the initial discovery was made as a result of an article by a senior government geologist in a local newspaper drawing analogies with known deposits and predicting 'where to find it'. The platiniferous horizon occurs in the Dyke a short distance below the base of the gabbroic rocks, and is of great extent. In the Selukwe Complex, Mennell and Frost (1926) described a platinum zone 1–2 m thick, occurring in a 30–50-m 'pyroxenite–norite' band, about 10 m below the overlying norite layer. Mennell and Frost drew parallels between the Great Dyke platinum reef and the Merensky Reef of the Bushveld Complex: as with the Stillwater Reef, discovery was preceded by good geological intuition. In the platinum horizon or so-called 'potato-reef', (named for its tendency to weather into nodules), platinum is present in association with copper and nickel, the platinoids being finely disseminated in base metal sulphides. Ore grades are between 3 to 5 g/ton of combined platinum and palladium, and reserves are very large.

Most probably, other large Archaean ultramafic bodies, such as the

Mashaba Complex, also contain significant platinum reserves (although not, perhaps, equal to the Proterozoic Bushveld Complex).

7.5 Chrome

Archaean rocks, particularly in Zimbabwe, contain roughly a quarter of the world's chrome reserves. Most significant are the chrome deposits of the Great Dyke (2.5 Ga) and of the Selukwe Complex (3.5 Ga), both of which are mined on a large scale.

7.5.1 Great Dyke

The Great Dyke has been described briefly in Chapter 6 (see Fig. 6.15). Chromite seams occur at the base of macro-units (Fig. 7.28), each of which comprises a lower chromitite, overlain by dunite (or harzburgite), which in turn passes gradationally through olivine bronzitite to bronzitite. The chromitites are usually coarse grained (1–3 mm grain size) with seams ranging from 2 cm to 12 cm thick (Wilson 1982).

Wilson (1982) studied the ultramafic sequence in the Hartley Complex of the Great Dyke, a 250-km long body with a lower ultramafic zone capped by gabbroic rocks, and with a saucer or boat-like structure (Mennell and Frost 1926, Worst (1960). Crystallisation of cumulus phases occurred at or near the floor of the magma chamber, and the mineral chemistry indicates that the volume of magma from which each unit crystallised was significantly less than that represented by the whole thickness of the body. The chamber was probably around 1200 m high, varying from 600 m initially to 1000 m under the gabbro. Most probably the chamber was an open system, stratified and with its chemical evolution controlled by doubly diffusive convection (Wilson 1982). Wilson inferred the parental liquid to contain approximately 15% MgO: equivalent to a komatiitic basalt. He suggested that the chromite compositions are strongly related to textural and mineralogical environments: seams of chromite probably precipitated in response to periodic influxes of magma into the magma chamber, which changed oxygen fugacity in the melt and returned the liquid to a less evolved state. After precipitation, as the crystals cooled, extensive subsolidus re-equilibration probably took place. This may not have much modified the compositions of coarse-grained chromites, but the compositions of associated silicates and smaller chromites included in silicates may have been substantially modified.

The chrome reserves of the Great Dyke are vast. Stagman (1978) estimated ore reserves as 10 000 million tons with chromic oxide content ranging from 60% to 47% and chromium/iron ratios of between 2.2 and 4 to 1.

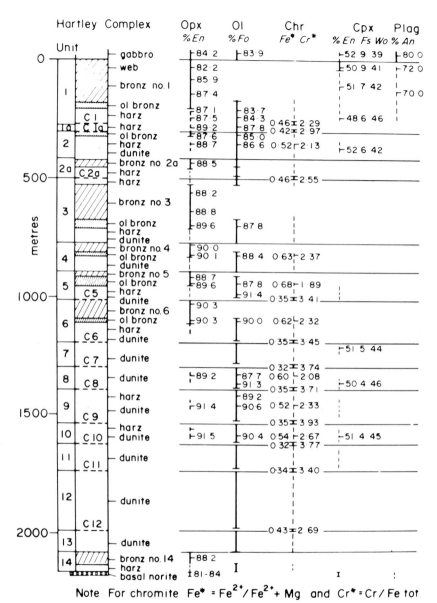

Figure 7.28 Stratigraphic succession of the ultramafic zone of the Hartley Complex, Great Dyke, showing chromite seams (C1–C12). Open hatching = bronzitites (bronz); close hatching = olivine bronzitites (ol bronz). Unhatched areas = poikilitic harzburgite (harz) and dunite. Cumulus phases = solid lines; Post-cumulus phases = dashed lines. (From Wilson 1982.)

7.5.2 Selukwe

Close to the Great Dyke but 3.5 Ga old and quite different in setting are the chromitite deposits of the Selukwe area around the town of Shurugwe (Sections 3.4.3, 3.7.2). These deposits are podiform, occur in early Archaean ultramafics, and have produced over 11 million tons of chrome (far more than the dyke). The local stratigraphy is outlined in Table 7.1.

The older rocks of the area lie upside down, in the eroded remains of a major early Archaean nappe which was emplaced prior to 3420 Ma (Cotterill 1979). Chromitite occurs in the Selukwe Ultramafic Formation, as extremely elongate, ribbon shaped, lenticular pods. Primary sedimentation structures similar to slump and flame structures, load casts, minor unconformities and grading have been reported (Cotterill 1969). The lenticular shape of the ore bodies seems to be an essentially primary feature produced by sedimentation processes in the magma chamber, probably by convection currents. Since deposition, deformation has complicated the shape of the bodies, but they were originally stratiform. Chromitite horizons are restricted to rocks which were originally olivine cumulates, at or near to their contact with pyroxenitic cumulates. Cr_2O_3 contents of the ore are around 60%, with Cr/Fe ratios of 3.5 or 4 to 1.

Table 7.1 Archaean geological succession in the Selukwe area (from Cotterill 1979).

Age (Ma)	Geological units	Events, comments
2500	Great Dyke	
2600–2900	Chilimanzi and Selukwe granites	contact metamorphism, metasomatism
3400–3600	Tonalite and granodiorite intrusions and biotite gneisses	tectonic emplacement of a pyroxenite/dunite body metasomatism
Nappe Emplacement		emplacement of major nappe over Selukwe area, inversion of sequence.
	Wanderer Formation, comprising: tholeiitic basalts (over 1000 m) iron Formation (0–600 m) basal beds (silts, sands, conglomerate or basal unconformity)	
Wanderer Erosion Surface		unconformity
	Selukwe Ultramafic Formation: metapyroxenite and metadunite with chromitite	tectonic emplacement
	Selukwe Greenstone: magnesian basalts, greywacke with ultramafic detritus	

Immediately above the ultramafic formation is the Wanderer unconformity surface, representing a major erosional event. During this erosion the No. 11 ore body at the Selukwe Peak mine projected above the unconformity surface, shedding talc-carbonate rock and chromitite into the conglomerate on the shore around it.

7.6 Asbestos

Chrysotile asbestos has become most unpopular in the past decade in the western world, partly because of its somewhat unfair verbal association with blue asbestos, and partly because of its own nasty properties. It is extraordinarily useful in fighting and controlling the spread of fire and in stopping automobiles; yet the lives it has saved must be put against those it may have cost. In the Third World, cheap and thermally efficient asbestos roofing and efficient asbestos space heaters provide a much appreciated improvement in living standards: something very valuable, if properly and safely done. It is against this background that asbestos mines must calculate their ore reserves – no simple unquestioned use such as greed, vanity and mistrust of government paper (Au), metals, armaments and money (Ni), automobiles and stainless steel (Cr), or bombs.

A significant proportion of the world's asbestos comes from Archaean ultramafic complexes in Zimbabwe, competing with younger ophiolite-associated bodies. Over three million tons of fibre have been produced, mainly from the Shabani and Mashaba ultramafic bodies. The Shabanie Mine (Laubscher 1963) exploits the largest occurrence of chrysotile fibre in Southern Africa (Fig. 7.29). The ore bodies occur in the central foot-wall dunite of the Shabani Complex (Ch. 3). The main fibre development appears to be around extensive fractures, through which hydrothermal solutions moved. Short fibres up to 3 mm long appear to replace olivine, while longer fibres (25–40 mm) seem to have grown in stress-controlled dilation seams.

The Mashaba mines, in the Mashaba ultramafic complex (Chs. 3, 6, and Fig. 6.14) are almost entirely of cross-fibre chrysotile (fibres lying at a high angle to the sides of veins). Fibre bodies lie close to channelways for hydrothermal solutions, and may be in part related to the intrusion of later granites (Wilson 1968b).

7.7 Iron ore

Banded ironstones contain much of the world's presently economic iron ore, having successfully put many older iron mines on Mesozoic ironstones

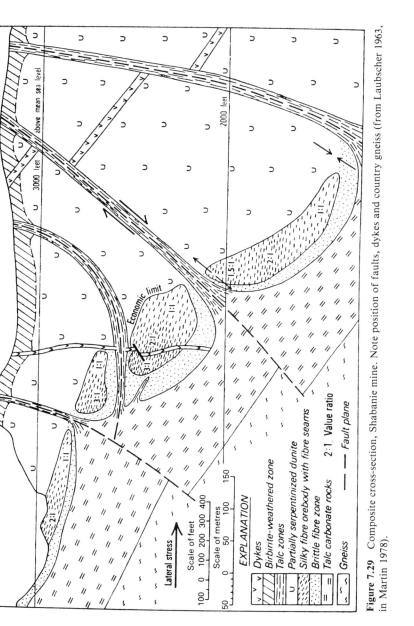

Figure 7.29 Composite cross-section, Shabanie mine. Note position of faults, dykes and country gneiss (from Laubscher 1963, in Martin 1978).

EXPLANATION

⌄ ⌄	Dykes
	Birbirite-weathered zone
∪	Talc zones
	Partially serpentinized dunite
	Silky fibre orebody with fibre seams
	Brittle fibre zone
= =	Talc carbonate rocks
∫ ∫	Gneiss

2:1 Value ratio
— — Fault plane

Lateral stress

Scale of feet
100   0   100 200 300 400
Scale of metres
50   0   50   100   150

3000 feet above mean sea level

2000 feet

Economic limit

out of business. Phanerozoic ironstones are typically higher in Al and P than Precambrian banded ironstones, and often are not amenable to beneficiation. Major European steel producers have generally chosen to use imported Precambrian ores in preference to local 'minette' ores, with considerable social consequences, including unemployment, strikes and riots.

The best-known Precambrian ironstones are from the Archaean/Proterozoic boundary, but some are truly Archaean. In general, Archaean banded ironstones are neither as thick nor as extensive as the later deposits, which were laid down on large basins in stable continental crust (Ch. 5). Nevertheless, several major mid-Archaean iron ore deposits have been mined. Two good examples are the Steep Rock deposits, Canada (Ch. 4), and the Buchwa ore body in Zimbabwe.

7.7.1 Steep Rock Lake

The Steep Rock iron ore deposits occur close to the base of the Steep Rock group, which was unconformably deposited on top of older granitoid basement (Wilks & Nisbet 1985). The basal unconformity is well exposed in several places. Figure 7.30 illustrates a section through part of the stratigraphy. The ore zone lies above the band of carbonates which includes the stromatolites described in Chapter 4. In summary, the stratigraphy includes: (a) older granitoid basement; (b) carbonates, mostly of organic origin; (c) a manganese mineral-rich band (the 'Paint Rock') with minor iron ore; (d) the main ore body, mostly goethite; (e) 'Ashrock', overlying pyroclastics and lavas, some of altered but apparently very magnesian (komatiitic basalt) composition; and (f) assorted mafic lavas, intruded by later granites.

There has been much discussion about the origin of the ores. The deposits are mainly goethite with haematite and minor quartz and clay. Some bauxite occurs, of unknown but possibly (and most interestingly) Archaean age. The ore zones were extensive and deep, and production in the late 1960s was around 3 million tons per year. Production has now ceased, but extensive ore reserves still remain, possibly up to 500 million tons.

Ores show a variety of brecciated, vuggy and colloform structures, and various authors have suggested that they were produced by the replacement of original banded ironstone or limonite by either (a) hydrothermal solutions circulating from the nearby younger granitic intrusions, or (b) solutions circulating around the overlying volcanic vents of the Ashrock, which includes proximal pyroclastics, or (c) downward-percolating meteoric water. Each of these hypotheses has been proposed and disposed of by succeeding authors, including Bartley (1940), Jolliffe (1955), and Shklanka (1972).

300

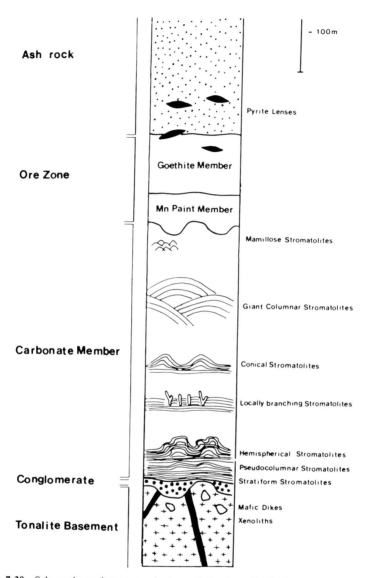

Figure 7.30 Schematic section across the base of the Steep Rock Group, Steep Rock Iron Mine, Ontario (From Wilks & Nisbet 1985).

7.7.2 Buchwa

The Buchwa deposit, though smaller, is also very interesting. Worst (1962) described major haematite iron ore deposits, found in jaspilite in the Buchwa syncline in southern Zimbabwe, east of Belingwe. Surrounding

301

strata in the syncline include ultramafic lavas, phyllites and quartzite. The host rock to the ore deposits is jaspilite, which is resistant to modern weathering and forms a 900-m high mountain peak, standing out above the surrounding granitic terrain. The ore bodies occur near the top of the mountain, facilitating mining operations to some extent, but also causing the incidental complications that the mountain is both regarded as a place of departed spirits (now further departed), and also supports forests of outstanding and rare beauty, now partially destroyed.

Worst (1962) concluded that the ore bodies were most probably formed by the replacement of silica by iron oxide, either by circulating solutions during metamorphism, or else by a supergene process involving ground-water moving down below an earlier erosion surface. Although the ore bodies are associated with komatiites, movement of the solutions appears to have been much later than the original deposition of the ironstones. Nearby, in the Belingwe Belt (Ch. 3), thick ironstones associated with komatiites are not known to be mineralised, although extensive desilicified zones do exist locally.

7.7.3 The Hamersley Group

Some of the most important iron resources in the world occur in the Hamersley Group of Western Australia which lies unconformably on top of the Pilbara greenstones. The rocks of the Hamersley Group (Trendall 1983) are very close to 2500 Ma old, and their time of deposition probably straddled the Archaean/Proterozoic boundary. Zircon from an ash-fall tuff within the group has been dated at 2490 ± 20 Ma (Compston et al. 1981). The Hamersley deposits mark the end of the Archaean, and are closely comparable to the Transvaal succession (Button 1976). Indeed, there is a close comparison between the Witwatersrand and Transvaal suites in Southern Africa and the Fortescue and Hamersley suites in Western Australia. Both mark the beginning of the Proterozoic record characterised by the existence of large, stable cratons.

The Hamersley Group outcrops over an area of $60\,000\,\mathrm{km}^2$. It is up to 2600 m thick and contains eight formations, which show very great lateral continuity although their thickness does vary. The succession is conformable throughout, and shows a broad alternation between shale (or shale and dolomite) and banded ironstone. In the upper part of the group there is a thick sequence of acid volcanics including rhyolite and dacite.

The Brockman Iron Formation forms about a quarter of the total stratigraphic succession. It is around 600 m thick and hosts most of the economic mineral deposits in the group. The basal unit of the formation is the Dales Gorge Member (180 m thick). This member contains chert–iron oxide and carbonate–silicate–chert bands. Above it is a shale member, and then the Joffre member (335 m thick) of banded ironstone with some carbonate–silicate–chert bands, followed by more shales.

Banding in the ironstone (Fig. 7.31) is remarkable for its lateral continuity: in all, 33 macrobands have been identified in the Dales Gorge Member. These bands, each a few metres thick, can be correlated across the whole 60 000 km^2 of outcrop area (Trendall 1983) and decimetre and centimetre scale bands in some units of the formation can be correlated tentatively across 400 km (McConchie 1984).

Trendall (1983) concludes that only seasonally controlled annual deposition could have produced the fine bands (or 'aftbands') in the ironstone, and only a chemical precipitation process could have produced the degree of regional continuity seen. It is possible that precipitation of iron was a

Figure 7.31 Banding in ironstone, Hamersley Group, Western Australia.

303

consequence of biological control on the iron oxidation state in the water: indeed, many authors favour some set of biological control (e.g. seasonal microbial blooms) on the formation of banded ironstones, although inorganic explanations have also been proposed (Cloud 1983b, Cairns-Smith 1978). Deposition of the Hamersley ironstones probably took place in a mid- to outer-shelf setting (McConchie 1984), perhaps in an environment which was in some way isolated from any source of clastic material (e.g. on a submarine platform) in water 150–250 m deep. Contemporaneous distant volcanism occurred, possibly some hundreds of kilometres away (McConchie 1984). Several authors have discussed the degree of oxidation of the ambient water: McConchie (1984) favoured the view that an atmosphere with an O_2 partial pressure around 10^{-6} atmospheres could have produced the deposits. The debate about the oxidation state of the late Archaean atmosphere has ranged widely, from oxic to anoxic, but it seems that the common presence of sulphates even in early Precambrian rocks would imply that the atmosphere has been at least mildly oxidising for a considerable period.

The ironstones typically run from 20–35% Fe, while in ore bodies this has been enriched by supergene processes to 60–65% Fe. Ores range from martite–goethite ores without significant secondary haematite to more mature martite–haematite–goethite ores with more haematite, to the most mature ores, such as those at Tom Price and Whaleback, which are martite–haematite deposits (Morris 1980, 1983). Reserves are enormous, with some bodies containing over 10^9 tonnes of ore.

The Hamersley Group also contains significant deposits of blue asbestos, or crocidolite, which is cross-fibre riebeckite. This type of asbestos is one of the least desirable of the world's mineral products as it is a very serious health risk, and is fortunately no longer mined.

To summarise: Archaean banded ironstones can act as progenitors of very large iron ore deposits if circumstances promote active circulation of fluids capable of replacing the silicate bands. In comparison with the Hamersley and later deposits, early Archaean iron ore bodies are relatively minor. Possibly this reflects the greater development of large sedimentary basins in the period 1.5–2.5 Ga, which may be a consequence of the development of more extensive regions of thick, stable continental lithosphere.

7.8 Other minerals

A vast assortment of minor minerals is produced from Archaean terrains, including precious stones (e.g. emeralds in Zimbabwe); minerals such as corundum, kyanite, mica, beryl; industrial minerals used for such disparate purposes as road metal, building stone, and toothpaste (corundum is a most effective ingredient for white, shiny but unfortunately short-lasting teeth); to assorted sources of minor but important elements (e.g. tungsten, tantalum, niobium, lithium). A good example of the last class of deposits is the Bikita Tinfield (Martin 1964), which is a major source of lithium. The ore is in large pegmatites, with border zones of mica, quartz and albite passing to wall zones of albite–oligoclase, quartz, mica and beryl, to zones rich in albite, petalite, spodumene and pollucite, to a massive lepidolite core. Only energy is lacking: pollution from Archaean uranium being generally regarded as more dangerous than the emphysema, radon liberated by combustion, and acid rain produced by coal and oil.

8 Models of the early Earth

Then the Lord answered Job out of the whirlwind and said
...'where were you when I laid the foundation of the earth?
Tell me if you have understanding.
Who determined its measurement − if you know!
Or who stretched the line upon it?
On what were its bases sunk, or who laid its cornerstone
When the morning stars sang together
and all the sons of God shouted for joy?
Or who shut in the sea with doors when it burst forth from the womb
When I made clouds its garment and thick darkness its swaddling band
and prescribed bounds for it and set bars and doors
and said: Thus far shall you come, and no farther
and here shall your proud waves be stayed?...
Have you commanded the morning since your days began
and caused the dawn to know its place...?
Have the gates of death been revealed to you,
or have you seen the gates of deep darkness?
Have you comprehended the expanse of the earth?

Declare, if you know all this.'   Job 38

Earth is at once the most improbable and most beautiful of planets. Its surface is infinite variety, its history complex and its future uncertain. We judge it beautiful since it is we who behold it: the presence of observers is the most extraordinary of all Earth's features, and the anthropic principle amongst the most powerful of guides to comprehending its history. To harbour its life it alone possesses oceans of water on its surface, set amongst with continents. What took place in the bowels of the Earth to allow this? How did the surface develop? When and where did life begin, and what role did it play in maintaining its home?

The search that follows attempts to examine the Earth *de profundis ad astra*, from the depths of the mantle upwards to the surface and atmosphere.

8.1 The bowels of the Earth

There has been much discussion about the thermal evolution of the Earth, especially with reference to the heat budget of the mantle and crust (Elder 1976, McKenzie & Weiss 1975, Sleep 1979, Davies 1980, Langan & Sleep 1982, Spohn & Schubert 1982, Turcotte 1980, Bickle 1978, McKenzie &

Richter 1981, *inter alia*). Bullard (1950) demonstrated that convective motion could occur in the mantle with vertical velocities of about 3 cm yr^{-1}, and that the resulting convective heat transport would dominate the heat flux and heat budget of the Earth. Convective models of plate evolution clearly show how important convective heat transport is to the modern Earth, over length scales as small as 100 km and times of 60 Ma. The rate of heat loss is controlled by the vertical extent of convection. In a convecting system appropriate to the Earth, temperature gradients are close to adiabatic: above the convecting region, the lithosphere loses heat by conduction. McKenzie and Weiss (1975) pointed out that the temperature of a vigorously convecting mantle varies little except within the top and bottom boundaries of the convecting system, and thus models can be constructed where the heat loss by conduction through the boundary layers can be expressed in terms of physical parameters of the fluid and its mean temperature. In this way they were able to estimate the variations of convective velocity and mean temperature with time, as the mantle aged.

Much depends on the scale of mantle convection. McKenzie and Richter (1981) compare the standard mantle convection models – one in which the whole mantle convects, and another in which the mantle is divided into two separately convecting upper and lower shells – with the familiar household double and triple glazing in cold climates (such as Saskatoon's). The layering introduces barriers to heat transport. In a well-made window, heat must be conducted into the glass across a thermal boundary layer of air, is then conducted through the glass, and then must pass through an outer thermal boundary layer of air before reaching the convecting exterior. The reduction in heat loss caused by the thermal boundary layers of air is the principal factor in making the window a good window, not the insulating property of glass, which is a much better conductor than air. Double glazing introduces four such thermal boundary layers, triple glazing introduces six, for a much better window. Similarly, a layered mantle will lose heat much more slowly than an unlayered mantle, since the heat must cross from the lower mantle into the upper mantle rather as if it crossed a pane of glass with attendant boundary layers. Thus if the Earth's mantle has been stratified throughout its history, it will have lost heat much more slowly than if whole-mantle convection has taken place. McKenzie and Richter (1981) concluded that if whole-mantle convection occurs, the surface heat flux is only about 50% greater than the rate of heat generation in the Earth, but if upper- and lower-mantle convection occurs in two separate shells, as seismological and geochemical arguments strongly suggest, then the ratio of present heat generation to present heat loss (the Urey ratio) is about 0.5. If so, the present-day surface heat flux is strongly controlled by the thermal structure of the Earth in its earliest days. Earth is a spendthrift, living on its inherited capital of primaeval heat, not on its radiogenic modern income.

8.1.1 Models of mantle convection

One of the most important variables in constructing models of convection is viscosity. Most geophysical models assume that the relevant viscosity is related in some way to the interior temperature of the mantle. Richter (1984) uses, as an approximation to the more realistic exponential temperature dependence

$$\frac{\nu_T}{\nu_o} = \left(\frac{T}{T_o}\right)^{-m} \tag{8.1}$$

where ν_T is viscosity at temperature T, and ν_o, T_o are present-day reference values. Glacial rebound calculations give $\nu_o = 3 \times 10^{17}\, m^2 s^{-1}$. The parental liquid at mid-ocean ridges is originally probably *circa* 1350°C, and 1350°C is also required if the 400 km seismic discontinuity is to be explained as an olivine–spinel transformation: thus $T_o = 1350°C$ approximately. If $m = 0$, then viscosity is temperature independent, while $m = 30$ gives an order of magnitude change in viscosity for a temperature change of 100°C, approximately what is observed in simple experiments on small (and not necessarily representative) samples of mantle materials. The horizontally averaged temperature of the Earth in actively convecting regions is adiabatic, and thus T should be interpreted as the temperature on the adiabat at the base of the convective thermal boundary layer (Richter 1984). Most probably, in the past, closer to the time of the early Earth and with a higher rate of radioactive heat generation, the heat flux out of the mantle would have been larger. How much hotter would the interior temperature have been to allow the larger rate of heat loss? Richter (1984) showed that the answer depends strongly on viscosity, or on m in Equation 8.1. The temperature dependence of viscosity is thus one of the main physical properties controlling the secular cooling of the Earth. This applies to simple, petrologically uniform models of the mantle: any vertical petrological heterogeneity in mantle or upper mantle composition would obviously greatly complicate and compromise the model.

Richter (1984) further developed his model by regionalising it into oceanic and continental sectors (Fig. 8.1). Both regions share a common interior temperature. Under the oceans, the asthenospheric flow penetrates to the surface at mid-ocean ridges and the aspect ratio (length L of the convective motion : depth d of the flow), L/d, is larger than one. The continents, in contrast, impose a conducting lid over an isoviscous convection zone below, with the temperature at the base of the conducting lid being determined by rheology as the temperature below which earth materials become too cold and undeformable for effective heat transport by convection. For modern continents, this temperature is modelled as 1157°C, above a con-

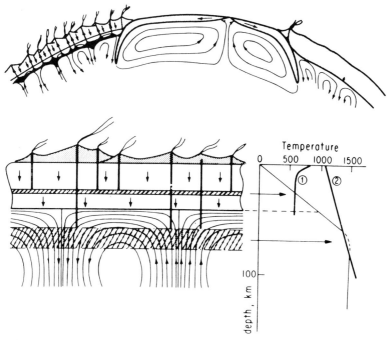

Figure 8.1 Schematic diagram of the regional styles assumed in the calculations of Richter (1985). On the top left is a lithosphere whose base is chemically defined with a fixed cut-off temperature (1150°C) at a time when there is widespread melting of the mantle below it and volcanic eruption onto the surface. The lower diagram shows this regime in detail. Melts derived from dry melting upper mantle are erupted onto the surface, become hydrated and subside under the weight of over-accreted later lavas. Basal subsiding lithosphere is heated above 1150°C and entrained back into the mantle circulation. Middle part of sketch shows familiar plate-tectonics scheme involving oceanic lithosphere. Right of sketch shows a thick continental lithosphere, locally in the diamond stability field. (From Richter 1985.)

vective mantle at 1350°C. The temperature at the base of the lid is purely determined by rheology and independent of heat flux into the continent.

Some results of this regionalised model, and its evolution through time, are given in Figures 8.2a, 8.2b and 8.3. Figure 8.2a shows the calculated interior temperature of the Earth, radiogenic heat production per unit surface area and heat flux through continental and oceanic regions, for a model which assumes mantle-wide convection and a viscosity ratio exponent, $m = 30$ in Equation 8.1. Note that *circa* 4 Ga ago the interior temperature was below 1700°C in this model. Figure 8.2b shows similar results for a model in which the mantle has been layered and $m = 15$. In this case, the mantle temperature prior to 3.5 Ga is close to 1700°C, and only about half as much heat production is needed to satisfy the modern heat flux from the Earth. The discrepancy between heat production and heat flux

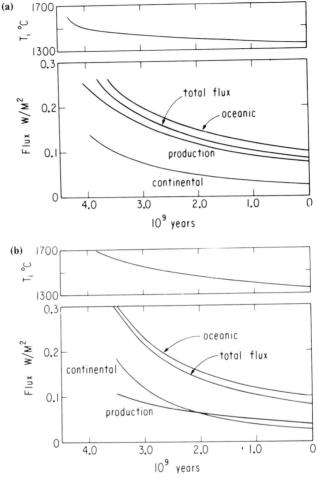

Figure 8.2 (a) Interior temperature of the mantle (top diagram), radiogenic heat production per unit surface area, and regionalised heat flux as a function of time, assuming mantle-wide convection in the Earth, with a viscosity exponent, $m = 30$ (eqn 8.1). (From Richter 1984.) (b) Same as Figure 8.2a but in with a layered mantle, and $m = 15$.

represents the contribution to surface heat loss by very old or possibly primordial heat.

Both models in Figure 8.2 (though especially the layered case) demand high subcontinental heat flow in earliest Archaean times: a subcontinental heat flow of 0.2 Wm^{-2} would give conductive gradients of the order of 100°C/km. In such circumstances very extensive partial melting would have taken place at the base of the continents, and heat would be transferred upwards by voluminous tonalitic melts, leaving behind a refractory granulitic

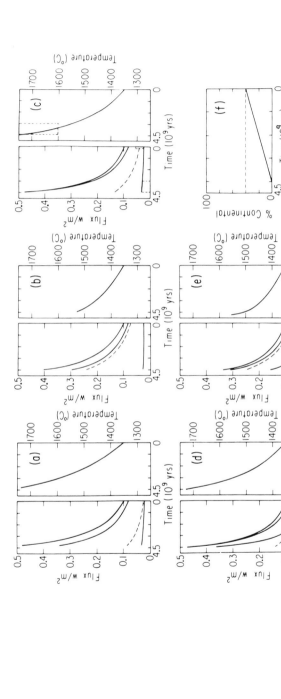

Figure 8.3 Evolution with time of the heat production, heat flux and interior mantle temperature, from Richter (1985). Dashed curve is heat production per unit surface area. Left-hand set of panels shows: top-heat flux curve for oceanic regions; middle curve = average total flux; bottom curve = reduced heat flux into base of the continental lithosphere. Right-hand set of panels shows interior temperature. Top left panel (a) is for a layered mantle, $m = 15$, continental lithosphere is 175 km thick; centre top panel (b), for mantle wide convection, $m = 30$ and 175 km thick continental lithosphere; top right panel (c) for a layered mantle, $m = 15$, 175 km thick continental lithosphere and continents growing as in diagram (f); bottom left panel (d) is for a layered mantle $m = 15$, and the base of the continental, lithosphere fixed at $T = 1157°C$; bottom centre panel (e) is for mantle-wide convection, $m = 30$, base of continental lithosphere at $1157°C$.

lower crust and depleted upper mantle. By this type of mechanism a chemically stabilised depleted lithosphere could also develop below the crust. Some constraint on this is available from the observation that 3.2–3.3-Ga old Archaean diamonds existed, presumably at depths of 150 km below the continents and at 900–1300°C (Richardson *et al.* 1984, Ch. 6). Temperatures of, say, 1300°C in the basal lithosphere would imply interior temperatures in the mantle higher by ΔT, where, following Richter (1984),

$$\Delta T = \pi^{3/8}(K\nu/g\alpha k^3)^{1/4} F_R^{3/4} \tag{8.2}$$

and K = thermal diffusivity, ν = kinematic viscosity, g = gravity, α = thermal expansion coefficient, k = thermal conductivity and F_R is the heat flux into the base of the continent. This would give, using values from Richter, ΔT = approximately 550°C if the heat flux into the base of the continental Archaean lithosphere were 0.1 Wm^{-2}, compared to ΔT of approximately 200°C today. If such a large heat flux could be accommodated by local partial melting, a mantle at approximately 1850°C would underly the early Archaean lithosphere. An extreme model, perhaps, but illustrative.

Figure 8.3 shows the results of a variety of models of mantle interior temperature as a function of time, from Richter's (1985) models. Each model assumes a different initial temperature and style of mantle convection. Most would suggest Archaean mantle temperatures of 1500–1700°C. These temperatures are not inconsistent with those inferred from komatiites, since an average interior temperature of, say, 1550°C would imply that in local areas of convective upwelling, maximum temperatures about 200°C hotter would exist, hot enough (at 1750°C) to produce komatiites. As the Earth cooled, this local maximum would also decline, and production of komatiite would cease. Today, with an average interior temperature around 1350°C, maxima around 1500°C may locally occur. Gorgona Island, where young komatiites occur, may have been above such a maximum.

Christensen (1984a,b,c, 1985a) took a rather different approach to the problem. The viscosity of mantle rock is a strong function of temperature, pressure and stress. Most models of mantle viscosity are based on extrapolations from measurements of bulk modern mantle behaviour (e.g. post-glacial rebound), or on extrapolations from experiments on single crystals of mantle minerals such as olivine, or on small rock samples. All these extrapolations are to some extent suspect. In the Archaean mantle, the mineralogy and geochemistry may have been substantially different from the modern Earth; and secondly, extrapolated data from small samples may not well represent large-scale conditions at very different pressures and temperatures. Christensen attempted to tackle part of this problem by investigating models where viscosity varies exponentially with pressure and temperature. His results show that viscosity models of this sort can revise substantially the results obtained from models where viscosity does not vary spatially inside convection cells.

The thermal behaviour of the Earth is usually expressed in terms of numbers such as the Nusselt number Nu which measures the efficiency of heat transport, and the Rayleigh number, Ra, which is a measure of how vigorous convection is. For constant viscosity convection, an exponential relationship,

$$Nu = (Ra)^\beta \qquad (8.3)$$

is found, with β of the order of $\frac{1}{3}$. On a cooling planet, however, the value of β may be smaller, and thus the Nusselt number becomes only weakly dependent or virtually independent of the internal temperature or internal viscosity. Furthermore, the surface velocity no longer depends on the Rayleigh number in the convecting zone: the stagnant surface layer becomes the bottleneck for the heat transport.

These results would imply that the heat loss of the planet might not be strongly coupled to the internal temperature of the mantle, contrary to traditional assumptions. Models based on the weak dependence of the Nusselt number on the Rayleigh number suggest that the Archaean heat flow and plate velocities were not substantially different from their present values, although the mantle temperature was about 300°C higher (Christensen 1985b). Christensen suggests that the present day Urey ratio, or the ratio between radioactive heat production and heat loss, may be only about 0.5 or less.

8.1.2 Komatiites and diamonds

Geophysical models of the behaviour of the early Earth are very powerful, but necessarily based on a variety of simplifying assumptions. In contrast, the geological evidence for the state of the Earth's interior is imprecise, yet can occasionally offer valuable insight into a very difficult problem. Most geologists have at one time or another experienced the devastation of having their simple-minded, rock-bound evidence destroyed (not necessarily correctly) by a powerful body of geophysical theory: nevertheless, there still are contributions which field-based study can make in constraining the basic assumptions of mantle models.

In studying the early mantle, two geological facts stand out: the presence of komatiites (Ch. 6) and the presence of diamonds (Ch. 5). The komatiites erupted at temperatures up to 1650°C (Green et al. 1975). If they ascended

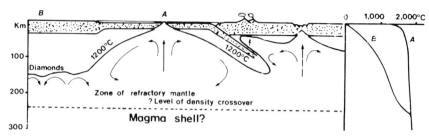

Figure 8.4 Cartoon illustrating some of the more speculative ideas about Archaean tectonics, from Nisbet (1985a). Geotherms at right are for locations A (below mid-ocean ridges) and B (below old cratons), and are 'conservative': actual conditions under ridges may have been rather hotter.

adiabatically the adiabatic gradient in liquid ultramafic lava of about $1°C/km$ (Nisbet 1982b) would imply a mantle at *circa* $1700°C$ at 50 km depth, or $1800°C$ at 150 km depth. A non-adiabatic ascent would imply a hotter mantle yet. Experimental results would suggest temperatures of, say, $1900°C$ at *circa* 50 kb. In contrast, the diamond evidence (Ch. 5), implies temperatures of $900-1200°C$ at 150–200 km (Boyd *et al.* 1985). How can this disparity be accommodated, and how does it influence the geophysical models discussed above?

One possible answer lies in the type of model that Richter (1984, 1985) proposed, with a regionalised thermal structure. Under the continents a thick, cool, chemically stabilised and depleted keel may have developed as the cratons froze downwards; in contrast, under the oceanic regions, much hotter conditions may have prevailed (Fig. 8.4). Furthermore, if Christensen's models are good approximations to reality, a fairly hot mantle need not necessarily have led to substantially higher heat flow through the crust, nor even to faster plate velocities: thus it is possible to accommodate the metamorphic evidence (Ch. 5) which appears to be saying that the continents were not much hotter than today, even at 150 km, while yet retaining a hot mantle capable of producing komatiites.

8.1.3 The possibility of a magma ocean

> The One l-lama, he's a priest
> The two l-llama, he's a beast
> And I will bet a silk pajama
> That there ain't no three l-lllama.
>
> Ogden Nash, *The Lama*

Komatiites have generated an extraordinary array of outlandish speculations about the nature of the Archaean mantle, ever since the problem was first discussed in detail by Green (1975). Nisbet and Walker (1982) raised

314

the possibility that a massive buried magma ocean had existed in the Archaean mantle, overlain by a floating layer of depleted olivine-rich peridotite. They pointed out that at depth in the Archaean mantle, it is possible that olivine was less dense than melt. Various authors have developed the suggestion that a magma ocean, or Large Laterally Linked Archaean Magma Anomalies (LLLAMAS) existed.

Nisbet and Walker's model has been refined somewhat by the calculations and measurements of Herzberg (1983), Rigden *et al.* (1984) and Ohtani (1984, 1985), and strongly supported by recent experimental work by Agee and Walker (1986). Much depends on the assumptions made about the composition (especially the maximum MgO content) of komatiite liquid erupted on the Archaean surface and the composition of olivine in equilibrium with it, and on the temperature and pressure path followed by the ascending liquid. Densities of the liquids are estimated by a third-order Birch–Murnaghan equation of state, after Stolper *et al.* (1981). Some estimates suggest that at a pressure around 80 kbar, olivine becomes less dense than co-existing ultramafic liquid (Fig. 8.5), and orthopyroxene and clinopyroxene too show a density cross-over, which is mainly a result of the fractionation of iron into the liquid and the relative incompressibility of SiO_2 in olivine compared to liquid. However, Herzberg (1985) has vigorously disputed these estimates, considering that olivine cannot float in natural anhydrous liquid at any pressure. If the density cross-over *did* exist in the Archaean mantle, it is possible that a magma shell surrounded the Earth, overlain by a layer of floating olivine (in other words, a depleted dunitic layer), and possibly floored by the olivine to γ-spinel phase change or by an orthopyroxene-garnet solid solution mineral. Various authors (e.g.

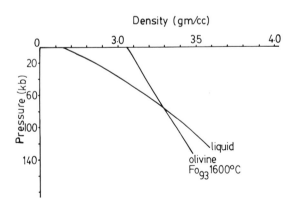

Figure 8.5 Variation of estimated densities of komatiitic liquid and Fo_{93} olivine at 1600°C. Reality is, of course, much more complex, since the temperature of the liquid would be higher deeper in the earth, and the Mg content of the olivine would vary sympathetically with liquid temperature.

Hofmeister 1983) have suggested that the very early Earth had a substantial magma ocean: by perhaps 4 Ga ago this may have contracted to the magma shell of Figure 8.4. Nisbet and Walker (1982), in pointing out that the magma ocean may have been floored by a phase change, raised the entertaining possibility that the modern division between upper and lower mantle is a chemical fossil of this phase change.

Takahashi and Scarfe (1985), Herzberg (1983), Walker and Herzberg (1985) and O'Hara and Herzberg (1985) have investigated the shape of the mantle's melting curves. It has long been known that the mantle's solidus and liquidus converge with increasing pressure, but it is not obvious whether they become subparallel (as assumed by Nisbet & Walker 1982) or whether they intersect (Herzberg 1983). Walker (1986) has pointed out that if Herzberg's prediction is correct, and that the curves do indeed converge to a singular point where the mantle could transform directly to a melt of its own composition, the consequences are very remarkable indeed. For an arbitrary selection of mantle components which fall in from space, no convergence should be expected. If there really is a singular point where solidus and liquidus converge, or even a close approach to one, then most probably the mantle is itself some sort of special composition, such as that of a solidified liquid of eutectoid character. Walker considers that theories of mantle origin by accretionary accumulation or as a crystalline residue from melting are not compatible with this conclusion. On the other hand, magma ocean theories, or theories of melting over a protracted interval as proposed by Herzberg, are compatible with a liquidus/solidus convergence. However, it must not be forgotten that the mantle is a very complex body with a long history – perhaps all these models are much too simplistic.

O'Hara *et al.* (1975) previewed the whole controversy; as a sequel, Herzbeg and O'Hara (1985) have studied the major element geochemistry of 83 mantle peridotites and 61 komatiites. When plotted in CMAS co-ordinates, it is apparent that these samples define a trend which is not primarily due to an olivine-control process (but see also Fig. 6.20). Herzberg and O'Hara suggest that perhaps the trend represents the pressure-induced compositional trace of eutectic liquids in equilibrium with mantle assemblages from 40–150 kbar. They raise the possibility that the upper mantle formed out of the whole mantle as an ultrabasic partial melt, with the transition zone and lower mantle being the complementary eclogite and pyroxenite residua.

The solidus and liquidus curves illustrated in Fig. 6.21, if they are correct (which is a matter of controversy), place an interesting constraint on the maximum MgO content of erupted liquid. At pressures of *circa* 100 kbar (10 GPa) and greater, partial melts must have been at *circa* $1900-2000°C$: it is improbable that any substantial part of the mantle was at a greatly super-liquidus temperature in the mid- or late Archaean. Any liquid ascending from this region could either rise adiabatically (to arrive at the surface at about 1700°C) or cool on slower ascent (to arrive at a lower temperature). Thus 1700°C is roughly the maximum temperature of eruption, though this figure does depend on assumptions about the slope of the adiabat in ultramafic liquid – see Nisbet (1982b). The liquidus temperature of komatiite at 1 atmosphere pressure is linearly related to MgO content (Section 6.9), and at 1700°C no melt could exist which was more magnesian than 35% MgO. In fact, field evidence suggests that the most magnesian lavas erupted were about 32% MgO (Section 6.7), which would imply eruption at or above 1650°C. This is not far different from the implications of Figure 6.21.

Much of this debate hinges on the supposed mantle solidus and liquidus, derived from experiments on nodules recovered from kimberlites. The more fertile of the nodules may represent the source mantle from which komatiites were derived. However, it is also possible that the nodules originally were trapped liquids (Nisbet 1986a) which became frozen into the base of the Archaean continental lithosphere (Fig. 8.6) or they may be the relics of Archaean subduction zones. Though they may since have been heavily reprocessed by trace element metasomatism, their major element composition may still roughly approximate that of liquids rising in the mid-Archaean mantle. If this is so, they are not necessarily a good guide to the composition of the uppermost Archaean mantle, and conclusions about solidus and liquidus convergence must be treated with care.

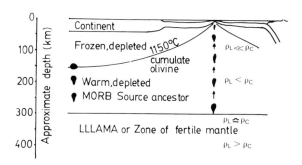

Figure 8.6 Possible model for upper mantle structure in mid-Archaean. Liquid shell exists at depth (top arbitrarily put at 300 km), overlain by a lighter depleted layer. Rising liquids may become frozen and trapped at base of continental lithosphere (later sampled as nodules in kimberlite), or may erupt at surface as komatiite. It is also possible that the nodules may be residual material derived from Archaean subduction zones. (From Nisbet 1986a).

8.1.4 Consequences for models of the Archaean Earth

Did the LLLAMA exist? As yet, the matter is unresolved. Nevertheless, the debate, whatever its resolution, has profound consequences for geophysical and isotopic models of mantle evolution. The mantle is not and was not a homogeneous uniform medium: rather, it was and is a complex, stratified and dynamic body. Isotopic evidence (Ch. 6) clearly indicates even in the Archaean it was heterogeneous in some way, either vertically or laterally; the contrast between komatiites and diamonds shows that major horizontal temperature differences existed. Perhaps the isotopic heterogeneity of Archaean lavas simply records variable sampling of the base of the lithosphere, in which frozen-in heterogeneity could accumulate.

Little consensus emerges from all this. One possible answer is that the Archaean mantle did have a magma ocean, did have a very variable viscosity structure, and was capped by a lithosphere which acted as a good thermal barrier. In this case, Archaean surface heat loss may not have been very substantially greater than today, but the interior temperature of the asthenosphere may have been 300–400°C hotter than now.

There are of course many more conservative models. One favourite idea is that komatiites were derived from deep plumes, which may have risen from as low as the core/mantle boundary (Green 1975, Campbell & Jarvis 1984, Takahashi & Scarfe 1985). Such models would not demand a very hot mantle – Campbell and Jarvis suggest mantle temperatures only 100°C hotter than today at 3.8–2.5 Ga – but seemingly fail to accommodate the apparent abundance of komatiite in the Archaean record. In contrast, the magma ocean models postulate a series of thermal boundaries through which any plumes from deep level would have to penetrate. Processes at these thermal boundaries would have been very interesting indeed (Christensen 1984c). Possibly some komatiites were derived from the boundary postulated at the top of the LLLAMA, as plumes rising upwards to the surface. A LLLAMA, if it existed, would convect vigorously; above it would be a refractory layer of harzburgite or dunite which too would convect in the solid state; above that would be the lithosphere. The regionalisation of this lithosphere, into thick depleted continental keels and thin cooling oceanic plate, would affect the underlying convection (Richter 1985). Beneath the continents, the thermal boundary at the top of the LLLAMA would allow the lithosphere to grow downwards into the physically and chemically stabilised cap, in some places reaching 150 km by 3.2 Ga, as shown by the diamond data (Richardson *et al.* 1984). Thus the stabilisation of the lithosphere would be fundamentally controlled by physico-chemical factors such as density and melt segregation, not by the purely physical thermal constraints upon which simple convection models are based.

8.2 Plate tectonics

Did plate tectonics operate on the Archaean Earth? Bickle (1978) showed that the thermal constraints demand that if it did not exist, some other

318

process must have been involved in order to dissipate heat. If so, what? Modern plate tectonics involves large stable areas of lithosphere, which interact at mutual boundaries, being produced, moved or consumed. In that large stable areas obviously existed at least in the end of Archaean (e.g. Western Australia), some type of surface 'plate' did exist, at least in continental regions. But did similar large areas of oceanic lithosphere exist? What was the length-to-depth scale of the motions, especially in oceanic areas? How representative of lithospheric thickness are the few preserved fragments?

Richter (1984) showed that today, if the return flow in plate tectonics is restricted to the upper mantle, and the interior temperature of the upper mantle is about $1350°C$, simple oceanic plate systems should have length-to-depth ratios (L/d) of about 15.5. Most whole-mantle convection models (but with exceptions) seem to demand plates which move too fast and are too large. In the Archaean, if L/d were significantly smaller (i.e. smaller plates), a greater concentration of heat-producing elements would be needed. Other authors have suggested that Archaean plates were small and fast moving, above an essentially chaotic mantle convecting at high Rayleigh number. All convective models of course depend very heavily on assumptions about the viscosity structure of the mantle, and are thus very subjective in that they are only as good as their mantle models.

Geological evidence offers a complementary perspective on the problem. The existence of calc-alkaline suites (Ch. 6) strongly implies that some process analogous to subduction took place; the interpretation of some greenstone belts as extensional basins strongly suggests that, in other places, extension went to infinity to produce something comparable to a mid-ocean ridge. Finally, there is strong evidence for the existence of massive 'stable' cratonic areas by 2.5 Ga in Australia, Southern Africa, parts of Asia and the Americas, with Archaean diamonds demonstrating, in Southern Africa at least as well as in Arkansas, that the lithosphere locally extended to a depth of 150 km. This implies that 'plates', or large rigid areas of mechanically strong lithosphere with no significant internal deformation, *did* exist. They may have been local slabs above a chaotic mantle, but large rigid areas were certainly able to survive.

8.2.1   Were mid-ocean ridges komatiitic?

Much geological nonsense and perhaps some geophysical nonsense too has been written about Archaean plate tectonics. Amongst the contributions to this ever-expanding industry, Nisbet and Fowler (1983) and Arndt (1983) independently suggested that if Archaean plate tectonics did indeed occur, it would have been a form of plate tectonics involving an oceanic crust which was, in bulk, komatiitic, and fed from komatiitic liquids. They both suggested that Archaean mid-ocean ridges were komatiitic. A simple modern model of plate tectonics (e.g. Richter & McKenzie 1978) assumes that the lithosphere is essentially cold asthenosphere. As such it is denser than asthenosphere, and will eventually fall back into it. Today, this approximation is nearly valid, since the basaltic crust (which is light, and hydrated) is a relatively minor component of old lithosphere: essentially, the negative buoyancy of the cold surface plate becomes so great that the slab falls. Arndt pointed out that a komatiitic Archaean oceanic crust would have been much more dense than modern basaltic crust. Like modern crust, komatiitic oceanic crust would eventually fall back to the asthenosphere as it cooled. In contrast, an Archaean oceanic crust of basalt (very thick because of extensive partial melting) would not become negatively buoyant until a very long time after creation; perhaps too long to accommodate plate tectonics on this planet. Nisbet and Fowler (1983) came to similar conclusions, though they assumed from isostatic and fractionation evidence a thicker oceanic crust than in Arndt's model. Figure 8.7 shows a model for komatiitic Archaean oceanic crust, based on the assumption that the crust was about 15 km thick. It should be stressed that this thickness is based on a series of weak assumptions: constraints are very

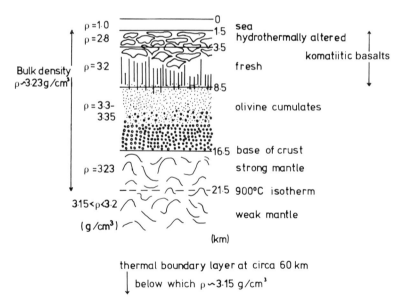

thermal boundary layer at circa 60 km
below which $\rho \sim 3.15$ g/cm^3

Figure 8.7 Petrological model of Archaean oceanic lithosphere assuming crust approximately 15 km thick and an asthenosphere temperature of 1700°C. Bulk composition of crust is komatiitic, and komatiite parental melts differentiate in doubly diffusive magma chambers to produce a komatiitic basalt upper crust (dykes and pillow lavas), with olivine cumulates in the lower crust. (After Nisbet & Fowler 1983): see Fig. 8.8 for temperature constraints.)

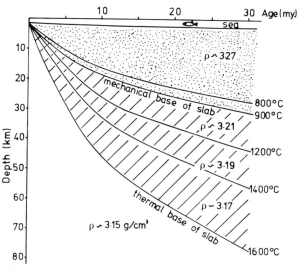

Figure 8.8 Cooling model of Archaean oceanic lithosphere, based on the simple assumption that lithosphere is cooled mantle (from Richter & McKenzie 1978). Density of forsteritic asthenosphere taken as $3.15\,gm/cm^3$ at $1700°C$, and densities of regions of lithosphere calculated assuming the linear coefficient of thermal expansion, $\alpha = 3 \times 10^{-5}\,K^{-1}$. Mechanical base of slab arbitrarily set at $900°C$ for refractory mantle. (After Nisbet & Fowler 1983).

poor. The crust, if fed by komatiite liquid, would stratify into an upper komatiitic basalt layer and a lower cumulate layer. The model can be extended, by using the Richter–McKenzie assumption that lithosphere is cooled mantle (Fig. 8.8) fed at the ridge by a lava at $1700°C$. This model overstates the density of the lithosphere somewhat, but petrological arguments show that a lithosphere that is slightly negatively buoyant soon develops, with a cool, dense komatiitic crust and mantle overlying a hot, comparatively light, depleted olivine-rich mantle. Figure 8.9 is a cartoon showing how Archaean oceanic plates may have developed. In contrast to modern plates, Archaean komatiitic plates may have been hotter at given depth, and probably were subducted into a weaker, much less viscous mantle. Forces involved in Archaean plate tectonics may have been half an order to an order of magnitude less than today, because of the low viscosity.

This model makes many gross assumptions and oversimplifications; nevertheless it demonstrates that some form of Archaean plate tectonics could have occurred, and if so, it may have involved a komatiitic parent melt at the mid-ocean ridge. Other models, such as those which invoke chaotic motion at high Rayleigh number and thus small L/d can also be constructed, though it is not immediately apparent how such models could produce calc-alkaline suites of essentially modern aspect as seen in the Pilbara.

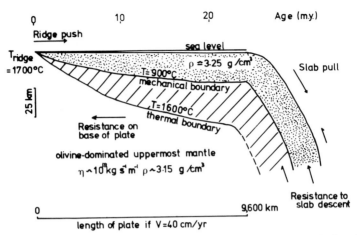

Figure 8.9 Cartoon of Archaean oceanic plate and the main forces acting on it (from Nisbet & Fowler 1983).

8.2.2 Models for Archaean subduction zones

If plate tectonics did occur, and if mid-ocean ridges were sub-aqueous (Ch. 5), then the oceanic crust would have been hydrated. If so, a model of Archaean subduction zones can be constructed. Figure 8.10 shows a possible model of an Archaean subduction zone at a continental margin. In this model, the subducted lithosphere is much thinner than today, with a hydrated komatiitic crust. The subduction zone provides volatiles to the overlying continental wedge: the descending slab would liberate these volatiles rather closer to the trench than today, because it was thinner and in a hotter setting. Abundant volatiles would promote melting: in the Archaean this would produce very extensive rising liquids in the subcontinental mantle, fractionation at the base of the continental crust, and partial melting in the basal continental crust, to give a calc-alkaline suite on the surface, residual granulites in the basal crust, and a refractory mantle wedge (presumably replenished by convection in the asthenosphere). Crustal melts would be hot and tonalitic. Because the setting was so hot compared to today, melts would be comparatively dry. More water from the slab would give more melt, not wetter melt, to give voluminous tonalites and pyroxene andesites in the calc-alkaline suite. Eventually, the local tectonic environment would change, and subduction in the area would cease, allowing the continental crust and the lithosphere below it to cool slowly and thicken: the diamond data imply that some areas had cooled enough, for long enough, to give a 150-km thick lithosphere by *circa*. 3.3 Ga in parts of Southern Africa. These regions may have been stable for several hundred million years prior to 3.3 Ga, as protected interiors of continents

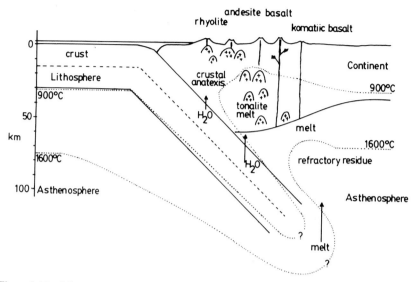

Figure 8.10 Schematic cartoon of an Archaean subduction zone. Note that in this model both the suboceanic and subcontinental lithosphere are on average considerably thinner today. Oceanic crust is assumed to be hydrated (see text). Thickness of oceanic crust is poorly constrained. Initially, subducted crust loses water and CO_2, which promotes partial melting below and within leading edge of continent, producing upward redistribution in the crust of the early melting fraction and radiogenic elements. At intermediate depth, very extensive partial melting takes place in subcontinental mantle. This would produce magnesian melts of densities around 3–3.1 g/cm³ (for density estimates, see Nisbet & Walker 1982). Such melts would be trapped at the base of the crust and would fractionate there: light fraction would be added to crust, heavy fraction would produce refractory residual mantle. Volatiles would stream through crust. Extensive tonalitic melt at high temperatures would rise to surface. More volatiles would produce more melting: in this very hot environment, steady-state volatile concentrations would not be high. Deep crustal granulites (density 3.0 g/cm³) would be formed, as would amphibolites from regional metamorphism at higher level. The crust would be both underaccreted and overaccreted rapidly until it reached a thickness controlled by dry melting of deep crustal material. At greater depth, magnesian melt would rise from the descending slab. If the force balance were extensional, back-arc spreading could take place in the continental lithosphere, allowing eruption of komatiite and komatiitic basalt in subsiding stretched supracontinental basins. This may be the origin of many greenstone belts. The overthickened continental crust above the subduction zone would rapidly be eroded once subduction had stopped. Where the continent was thickest, very rapid decompression would take place, bringing 5–10 kbar (500–1000 MPa) metamorphic assemblages to high levels. Elsewhere, decompression would be slower, and isotopic clocks would not be set until much later. The availability of CO_2 is an interesting problem. It is improbable that thick pelagic carbonate sediments existed, but it is possible that carbonate was an important component of hydrothermally altered komatiitic oceanic crust. Thus the slab would be a donor of CO_2 as well as H_2O to the crust. The subcontinental asthenosphere was probably also a major source of CO_2, which would stream up through the base of the crust from the fractionating subcrustal melt. (From Nisbet 1984d).

(Fig. 5.23). Schulze (1986) has suggested that diamonds may have originated in subducted metaserpentinite, or carried-down Archaean ocean floor. This proposal has many attractions, and is not inconsistent with stable isotope results from diamonds and their host rocks. It is also possible that a subduction zone may have caused the variation in oxygen fugacity needed (Haggerty 1986) to promote diamond growth. Perhaps subducted metaserpentinite, hosting diamonds, was buoyant and thus plated onto the base of the lithosphere. Figure 8.11 shows a schematic and very speculative model of the top of the mantle and the lithosphere in the late Archaean.

This model (Fig. 8.11) is richly speculative, but something of the sort must have taken place. Possibly a more chaotic, less-ordered tectonics was responsible for Archaean calc-alkaline zones, introducing water to the subcontinental asthenosphere by a recycling process with small L/d. For example, in the Zimbabwe craton, Wilson (in Nisbet *et al.* 1981) sketched

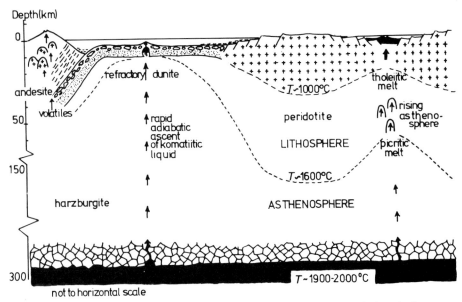

Figure 8.11 Schematic model for the uppermost mantle and lithosphere in late Archaean time. Oceanic crust includes hydrated upper pillow lavas and lower cumulate layers with komatiitic composition in bulk. The thickness of the Archaean oceanic crust is a matter of prejudice: this diagram follows the opinion of Arndt (1983). Continental thickness varies. In old, stable areas it was probably similar to today's thickness, but less in stretched regions and more above subduction zones; similarly, lithosphere thickness varies, depending roughly on $\sqrt{t}$, where t is time since last major disturbance. Zone of very extensive partial melt may exist at depth in asthenosphere. (From Nisbet 1984d.)

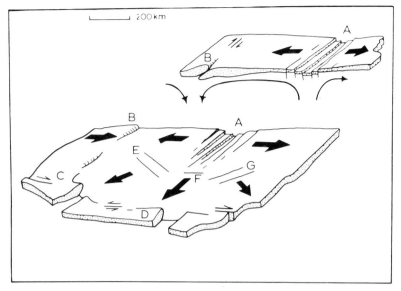

Figure 8.12 Three-dimensional diagram to illustrate, as an alternative to classical plate notions, possible continental crustal response to small-scale convective motions in the mantle, (from Wilson, in Nisbet *et al.* 1981). This type of tectonics could only occur in regions of thin lithosphere above vigorously convecting asthenosphere. At A and perhaps to a lesser extent at E, F, and G, the deposition of thin basal sediments is likely as a first stage, followed by ultramafic to mafic volcanism. A widespread continuous volcanic cover could result, thick in the basins and thinner elsewhere. In the areas above down-wellings, underthrusting of crustal slabs could occur (B, C, D). Some transcurrent motion could be seen where there is opposing or different motion in the underlying convective system (e.g. near C, D).

out examples of possible crustal response to small-scale convective motions in the mantle (Fig. 8.12). This type of model could account for the observed volcanic facies seen in the Zimbabwe late Archaean quite as well as a sub-duction model presupposing large plates. The geological record cannot, in geophysical parlance, be uniquely inverted.

8.3 Continents and water

He had brought a large map representing the sea
Without the least vestige of land
And the crew were much pleased when they found it to be
A map they could all understand.

Lewis Carrol, *The Hunting of the Snark*

Continents greatly complicate model-making: indeed, some geophysical models dispense with them entirely. But they are unfortunately necessary to the Archaean geologist, who would not exist without them. They are a critical component of the Earth's fabric.

Of what are the continents made? Why are there continents, and how old are they? To answer these questions, we can only look to the geological record, and then perhaps try to extrapolate backwards. The record goes back to about 4.3 Ga (Compston & Pidgeon 1986): from that time onwards we can reasonably assume, and from 3.5–3.6 Ga we can certainly assume, that the dichotomy between continents and oceanic basins has existed. On other inner planetary bodies, in contrast, an Earth-like dichotomy does not exist; or if a hypsographic bimodality is present, the proportions are quite different. Mercury and the Moon, for instance, are essentially covered by basalt or basaltic differentiates or detritus; Venus appears to have a unimodal hypsometric curve (Phillips *et al.* 1981, Phillips and Malin 1983, Kaula 1984), with few distinct continental and oceanic surfaces and only Ishtar Terra may be a true continental region. This comparison is most interesting since Venus is so closely similar in size to the Earth, and it is possible that its initial geochemical inventories were roughly the same (though this point can be strongly debated). Why then is Venus so different from Earth, though both planets remain tectonically active?

Campbell and Taylor (1983) suggested that the critical factor distinguishing the surface evolution of the two planets is the presence of water on Earth and not on Venus. Water may constitute roughly 0.1% of the mantle on Earth, but it is also in the original sense of the word, the Earth's outer mantle: 'and round it has cast, like a mantle, the sea' (Psalm 104, in Grant's paraphrase). Campbell and Taylor pointed out that without the presence of water in hydrated oceanic crust, subduction zones would not generate calc-alkaline liquids. The deep crust and upper mantle of a continent above a subduction zone are essentially 'saturated' with water, in the sense that addition of more water from below provokes more melting. Sialic crust would not be concentrated separately from simatic crust on a dry Earth: instead, basaltic fractionates would probably be more randomly spread over a non-regionalised surface. Furthermore, the topography of high areas would not be controlled by erosion: on a dry planet some wind erosion might occur, but lithospheric creep would probably dictate relief (England & Bickle 1984). It is possible that some primaeval dichotomy between continental and oceanic regions may have been produced by a heterogeneous late bombardment, but most geologists would consider that on Earth the continents as we know them today were assembled by the tectonic and magmatic aggregation of granitoid material (in the widest sense), including the assortment of rocks that was able to collect on top of the granitic raft, or to be produced by deformation, metamorphism or partial melting of the granites. Some hidden part of the continental material may indeed be reworked primaeval scum which collected at the top of the earliest Earth, but its survival in the continents depends on the maintenance of the granitic raft. To quote Campbell and Taylor, 'no water, no granites' and, more broadly, 'no oceans, no continents'. 'Subduction' is the word originally used in our language to describe the process by which Adam lost his spare rib (Milton, *Paradise Lost* VIII. 536): its geological adaptation suggests the analogy that the continents have been created from the mantle reservoir by subduction of the oceanic slab. Perhaps, when one considers the original meaning, it is not surprising that Venus did not choose to allow subduction of her anatomy.

Quite separate from the problem of the crustal dichotomy between continents and oceans is the problem of crustal volume. D. Walker (1983) pointed out that whereas the lunar crust is about 10% of the volume of the Moon, the terrestrial crust is only about 1% of the volume of the Earth's mantle. More generally, smaller planets probably have volumetrically more important crusts. If there were no crustal recycling by subduction, but only generation of crust, the total terrestrial production of crust would approach a lunar proportion, but this would be on the assumption that now, 4.5 Ga into the planet's history, crust production is complete. Walker (1983) prefers to look elsewhere for an explanation of the difference between the two bodies, by investigating the effects of an early terrestrial magma shell sequestered at depths greater than 150 km in Archaean time. Possibly the Archaean crust and the underlying olivine-rich mantle were complementary above a foetid magma ocean, with a mafic to komatiitic early oceanic crust overlying a depleted residual harzburgitic layer, which in turn capped the magma ocean. As the magma ocean froze over, a heterogeneous mantle would result. Simultaneously, serial accretion, aggregation and, at times, destruction of continental granitoids would occur. The oceanic crust today on an essentially solid mantle has a thickness governed by the temperature of the rising mantle and the solidus of the slightly wet modern mantle.

To conclude: the continents appear to be a serially collected amalgam of innumerable granitoid melts generated above subduction zones, and depend for their creation and maintenance on the presence of deep oceans. Continental crust may include a nucleus of light, primaeval liquid of low melting temperature fractionated from mafic or ultramafic melts, but over all geologically recorded time the continents have been essentially composed of granitoid rafts. These rafts have been remelted, to give residual granulitic assemblages and derived granitic liquids; they have been eroded, to give the modern inventory of sediment; and they have in part been transported back to the mantle. In all, the role of water is apparent. The surface geology of the Earth in almost every aspect reflects the presence, on this planet alone, of free and liquid water.

8.4 The degassing of the planet

Water, then, is crucial to the workings of the Earth. But where did the water come from, and when?

Models of the growth of the asthenosphere and hydrosphere have been almost as varied as models of continental growth. Most work accepts the notion that the bulk of the atmosphere is of secondary origin, in that it has been degassed from the interior of the Earth. The primary accretionary atmosphere appears to have been lost either during the activities of accretion or blown away in the young solar system. Our present atmosphere is the much altered remnant of the gases which were lost from the young Earth's mantle: these gases included carbon gases and water, as well as a wide variety of other components. Today, the oceans and the carbonates trapped in the sedimentary column are the largest component of degassed volatiles left on the surface.

How fast was the degassing? Did the atmosphere form rapidly, or has it grown slowly over the history of the Earth? Degassing obviously occurs today, since volcanoes exude all manner of exhalations, and noble gases from the mantle can be detected in the water above mid-ocean ridges.

Noble gas evidence strongly suggests that there was an early catastrophic phase of degassing. Most probably, there was an initial catastrophe, possibly impact induced, followed by a long period of continuous degassing of the sort seen today. Various models of the degassing process can be constructed to test how soon the catastrophe occurred, and how much of the mantle was affected (Ozima & Podosek 1984). The strongest evidence comes from helium, argon and xenon isotopes. Sarda *et al.* (1985) used the systematics of ^{40}Ar and ^{129}Xe in mid-ocean ridge basalts to conclude that there was a very early and extensive burst of degassing with a time constant of about 4 Ma, followed by a slower process more similar to modern degassing over about 0.5 Ga. They determined the mean age of the atmosphere to be around 4.4 Ga. Ozima and Podosek (1984) concluded that if this basic picture is correct, then presumably the dominant source of the present atmosphere is the depleted mantle; the contribution from undepleted mantle is evidently small since it is inferred not to be extensively differentiated and degassed. O'Nions and Oxburgh (1983) used calculations of the Earth's helium flux to deduce that the upper mantle loses its small amount of radiogenic heat and helium efficiently, but is isolated from a lower-mantle reservoir from which 90% of the heat lost through ocean basins is derived.

328

Many samples of mantle-derived material appear to contain a component of ^{129}Xe in excess of what would be expected if the xenon in rock had the same history as the atmosphere. Excess ^{129}Xe seems to exist in some CO_2-rich gas from deep wells, and also in some samples of mid-ocean ridge basalts and mantle xenoliths (Ozima *et al.* 1985) but not in granites. The existence of this excess ^{129}Xe indicates that some part of the Earth incorporated an amount of short-lived ^{129}I (half-life 17 Ma) on accretion. This ^{129}I decayed into ^{129}Xe, and thus the existence of excess ^{129}Xe indicates that some part of the Earth has not undergone extensive exchange with the atmosphere, or the source of the atmosphere, since a few tens of millions of years after accretion. Ozima *et al.* (1985) argue that an early established ^{129}Xe excess in the upper mantle is unlikely to have survived the processes of plate tectonics. This is because Xe is likely to be carried down into the mantle in subducted sediments, and thus atmospheric and upper-mantle xenon are likely to have been well mixed by the processes of mid-ocean ridge eruption and subduction. More likely then is the supposition that the excess ^{129}Xe did not originate in the degassed upper mantle but was transported there from some other region which has been isolated from the upper mantle–atmosphere system for almost the whole history of the Earth (Ozima *et al.* 1985).

Summarising all this, there appears to be strong evidence that the upper mantle degassed rapidly to produce the forerunner of the modern atmosphere 4.4 Ga ago or earlier. Since then, a continuous slow degassing process has been in operation, similar to modern degassing at mid-ocean ridges. There also appears to be considerable evidence that a deeper reservoir exists which has been for the most part separate from the plate tectonic cycling system of the upper mantle for nearly all of the Earth's history: from this deeper reservoir there is a slow leak upwards of rare gases and, presumably, other chemical species. But most of the modern atmosphere is descended from the atmosphere that degassed very early in the Earth's history.

Returning then to water, the implication is that if the rare gases escaped from the mantle to the atmosphere so early in the planet's history, so too probably did water and carbon gases. This conclusion is not rigorous, since water is chemically essential to the Earth's style of tectonic activity and is massively cycled, while the rare gases are in comparison marvellously uncomplicated. But nevertheless, it is likely that substantial oceans have indeed existed on the surface of the Earth since 4.4 Ga.

8.4.1 The depth and maintenance of Archaean oceans

Till all the seas gang dry, my dear
And the rocks melt with the sun
                                    Burns

The Archaean oceans played a critical role in dictating the later geological evolution of the planet. They provided a reservoir deep enough to allow the hydration of the oceanic crust at the mid-ocean ridge and hence to generate the continents; they also supplied a home for early life. In Chapter 5 the various isostatic controls on oceanic depth and continental relief were explored: Archaean oceans were obviously present, but were they simply puddles (Towe 1983), or were they deep enough to cover the mid-ocean ridges? The evidence was outlined in Chapter 5. It is not strong, but suggests that the ridge crests were indeed covered. It is worth returning to the matter here in further detail.

First, there is the necessity of hydrating oceanic crust to make granitoids (Campbell & Taylor 1983). It is possible to hydrate basaltic crust by meteoric water, as on Iceland today (Kristmansdottir 1982), but, arguably, pervasive and deep alteration, which is nowadays sufficient to introduce water even to ultramafic rocks (Stakes et al. 1984) can only occur when water is introduced in large quantities at the ridge axis. If the ridge crest were exposed sub-aerially for, say, 1 Ma, the $100°C$ isotherm would be at a depth of about 1 km in the plate when it submerged. If so, hydration would occur in newly created crust by meteoric circulation, but the nature of the massive chemical exchange between sea water and rock would progressively change as water/rock ratios changed (Kristmansdottir 1982). Circulation systems would retain water for much longer than in a sub-aqueous setting (Spooner & Fyfe 1973), and most probably oceans with exposed ridges would have more available Na and Mg and less Ca and Si than today. The modern aspect of Archaean evaporite sediments (J.G.C. Walker 1983a, Fig. 8) and the presence of Archaean granites would suggest that the ridges were indeed covered.

Secondly, volumetric arguments also suggest that mid-ocean ridges were covered in the Archaean. Ito et al. (1983) concluded that modern oceans appear to be suffering a steady net loss of water to the mantle. Not all subducted water is recovered through eruption in andesitic volcanoes. Abbott and Lyle (1984) attempted to calculate the fate of subducted water, and concluded that a thickly sedimented plate will return H_2O to the asthenosphere above it if the subducting plate is older than 11 Ma, and CO_2 if the plate is older than 25 Ma. They further suggested that since Archaean plates were probably subducted at much younger ages than today, the amount of volatile recycling would have been much lower than at present, despite the greater total consumption rate. Return of water to the surface would depend on its fate in the subcontinental asthenosphere, and the solubility of water in a convectively active region; on the solubility of water in rising mid-ocean ridge komatiitic melts (in contrast to modern basaltic melts); and also on the volume of melt (which would be controlled by availability of water and the temperature): in short, it seems likely that the late Archaean oceans were more voluminous than today. Third, there are the isostatic arguments outlined in Chapter 5. Archaean continental crust was probably as thick as or thicker than today – thus the oceans would have been as deep as today.

All these arguments, taken together with the isostatic and facies arguments outlined in Chapter 5, would point to deep late Archaean oceans. Most likely, rapid early degassing produced deep oceans as early as 4.4 Ga ago. Since then, the oceanic level may have fluctuated, probably dropping slowly in post-Archaean time, but the ridge crest has remained covered. Should further loss of water to the asthenosphere via subduction zones mean that water level eventually fell to about 500–1000 m above the ridge crest, a weak buffer would help stabilise sea level, as basaltic lavas would then become water saturated and would degas directly into the sea: if water level fell substantially below the crest, subduction loss would be eventually slowed and, finally, would almost cease. But nothing in the geological record suggests this ever happened in the past.

In contrast, the planet Venus seems originally to have had substantial quantities of water, but now has lost virtually all. Watson *et al.* (1984), Kasting *et al.* (1984) and Hartle and Taylor (1983) examined the implications of earlier work (Donahue *et al.* 1982) that deduced from the high deuterium/hydrogen ratio of the Venus atmosphere the conclusion that substantial free water existed once on the planet. Kasting *et al.* conclude that the evidence is most easily explained if oceans of liquid water were initially present. Hostetler (1981) interpreted the rare gas concentrations of the two planets to imply that Venus degassed about one-seventh of the volatiles that Earth has outgassed: such calculations are subject to many assumptions, but most probably substantial water, possibly in oceans in the order of a kilometre deep, did exist on Venus. The general chemical and physical similarity between the two planets would also suggest kilometre deep oceans on the young Venus.

Venus has lost its water: Earth has not. On Venus, early surface temperatures were probably at least 80–100°C, and may have been much higher. These high temperatures may have allowed water vapour to become a major constituent of the atmosphere at all altitudes (on Earth, water is trapped in the lower atmosphere) and solar EUV radiation (in the ultraviolet part of the spectrum), which was probably high in the early history of the solar system, would have removed hydrogen from the abundant water vapour in the upper atmosphere. Kasting *et al.* suggest that something equivalent to a terrestrial ocean of water could in this way be eliminated in only 600 Ma. Such an atmosphere is a 'moist greenhouse': it has liquid water, but rapidly loses it because water is efficiently mixed into the upper atmosphere. Alternatively, Watson *et al.* (1984) have suggested ways in which a 'runaway greenhouse' may have developed. In either case, loss of hydrogen must have left residual oxygen, which presumably reacted with surface lavas, and eventually was returned to the mantle by subduction or some similar process. A third possibility has been proposed by Matsui and Abe (1986) who suggested that early impact-generated H_2O atmospheres of very similar masses formed on both Venus and Earth, but whereas on Earth the H_2O could condense to form an initially hot (600 K) ocean (in other words, a moist greenhouse), such condensation probably did not occur on Venus which experienced much more solar radiation. Venus would then rapidly lose its uncondensed H_2O.

Earth avoided catastrophic dehydration: we exist. Indeed, it has been suggested that the early Earth may have been in severe danger of encountering not greenhouse conditions, but a runaway glaciation, which would have so changed the planet's albedo that permanent glaciation might have ensued. Even as the solar luminosity increased with time, if a glaciated Earth had once developed, it would have reflected so much radiation that liquid oceans would never have formed. Some models suggest that the initial temperature on Venus may have been around 350–370 K (Kasting *et al.* 1984, Henderson-Sellers 1983), while on Earth the effective temperature (i.e. the temperature without any atmospheric greenhouse increment) today is 235 K (Lewis & Prinn 1984). On the modern Earth, an atmospheric greenhouse effect sustains pleasant temperatures. The Archaean Earth, in the light of a fainter sun, presumably enjoyed a substantially stronger atmospheric greenhouse, which slowly weakened as the sun grew warmer. Owen *et al.* (1979) proposed that surface temperatures in the field of liquid water were maintained on the early Earth by a CO_2-rich atmosphere, and Henderson-Sellers and Cogley (1982) suggested that the early hydrosphere was stabilised by about 1650 ppmv of CO_2 (5 × present atmospheric level), or more. In this way, 'habitable' temperatures were maintained on Earth; but since the temperatures were comparatively low, a moist or runaway greenhouse was not sustained on Earth for long enough to dehydrate the planet. Perhaps moist greenhouse conditions may have occurred for a short period, with early high CO_2 levels (Section 8.4.2), but for most of the Earth's history the surface temperature must have been within perhaps $20°C$ of its present value (Fig. 8.13), low enough to ensure that water remained trapped in the lower atmosphere (Kasting *et al.* 1984), and thus low enough to avoid massive loss of hydrogen to space and consequent planetary dehydration.

Hart (1979) drew attention to the dangers of 'thermal runaway' in the atmosphere. The Earth appears to have been extremely fortunate in its situation in the solar system, close enough to the sun to maintain liquid oceans with a modest greenhouse increment, yet not so close that eventual catastrophe became unavoidable. Mars is eternally glaciated, its original small surface water inventory possibly 100 m deep (Squyres 1984,

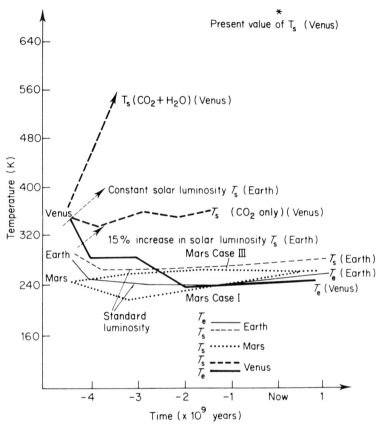

Figure 8.13 Evolution of the early atmosphere. Calculated evolutionary histories of the temperature of the atmospheres of the Earth (fine lines), Venus (heavy lines) and Mars (dotted lines). T_e is effective temperature (without greenhouse increment), T_s the surface temperature. For Earth, temperatures have been calculated for different percentage changes in incident solar radiation; for Venus the effective temperature decreases as planetary albedo increases and the surface temperature is strongly controlled by atmospheric composition. Mars Case III is for early degassing and Case I for later degassing. (From Henderson-Sellers 1983.)

Rossbacher & Judson 1981) now permafrost or ice cap, while the early Perelandrian conditions on Venus inevitably led to the present inferno. On Earth, since life exists, the greenhouse increment has been managed over the last 4 Ga to maintain the surface temperature within the region of probably 0–40°C (the optimum range for life). The continual presence of life implies that the controls on CO_2 level may have been very sensitive to changes in solar luminosity, with sufficient feedback to sustain the surface environment within a narrow temperature range. This constancy of the Earth's temperature, which goes together with the maintenance of liquid oceans over longer than 4 Ga, is at once both one of the most astonishing and one of the most natural features of the planet. Water is at the centre of our existence: yet we accept rainfall not as a continuing miracle but rather as a commonplace presence, an everyday nuisance in England and an expected blessing elsewhere.

8.4.2 Controls on hydrospheric and atmospheric composition

Xenoliths from the upper mantle and lavas erupted from modern volcanoes which are not at plate boundaries and which appear to tap deep mantle sources, such as Kilauea and also MORB glasses, contain considerable amounts of CO_2. Andersen *et al.* (1984) showed from a study of mantle xenoliths from Victoria, Australia, that the subcontinental upper mantle probably contains large reservoirs of free fluids rich in CO_2. Gerlach and Graeber (1985) have estimated that parental liquids to Kilauea carry *circa* 0.3% H_2O and 0.65% CO_2 by weight, as well as 0.13% S and many minor components. Over 27 years, approximately 18×10^{12} g of H_2O and 38×10^{12} g of CO_2 were supplied by parental magma: most of the CO_2 separated as a vented chamber gas, while much of the H_2O was stored as reservoir equilibrated melt, to be vented from lavas or to remain in the lava. Kilauea taps a deep-mantle source; although the composition of the source is a consequence of a 4.5-Ga history of mantle evolution, these data and other studies of mid-ocean ridge basalt inclusions, andesites (Garcia *et al.* 1979) and basalts (Muenow *et al.* 1979) do suggest strongly that the mantle has, in places, CO_2/H_2O ratios of 1 or higher. Perhaps the early Earth may have degassed at least as much of the carbon gases as H_2O especially as the carbon gases are chemically much more easily lost from magma to the exosphere. Why then does the Earth have an atmosphere–hydrosphere of *circa* 365 bars H_2O but virtually no CO_2? If the CO_2 inventory in calcareous sediments were to be added to the atmosphere total, the CO_2 pressure would be *circa* 70 bars (Hendersen-Sellers 1983), almost the same as the present Venus atmosphere, and in about the same ratio to H_2O as found in fluids in old deep subcontinental mantle (Eggler 1983). This would suggest a cumulative primaeval atmosphere of at least 365 bars H_2O, 70 bars CO_2. More likely, if the oceans have sustained water loss for some eons (Ito *et al.* 1983), the cumulative primaeval H_2O pressure would be of the order of at least *circa* 500 bars; if Venus has degassed only a seventh as extensively as Earth (Hostetler 1981), the cumulative CO_2 pressure implied by this on Earth would also be *circa* 500 bars. Since a massive H_2O atmosphere has existed from the beginning of the geological record, it is geologically reasonable also to expect an early massive carbon gas atmosphere. In a controversial calculation, Javoy *et al.* (1982) suggested that the very early exogenous reservoir of carbon was about five times larger *circa* 4.4 Ga ago than at present (i.e. a primaeval exosphere with 350 bars CO_2): this calculation has been disputed (Walker 1983b, Javoy *et al.* 1983), but it may be that an early massive H_2O and massive carbon gas atmosphere was degassed, the carbon being very rapidly returned to the mantle.

The process of removal of carbon from the atmosphere may indeed have kept in step with degassing, so that although the 'cumulative' degassing may have been massive, a massive actual CO_2 atmosphere either never built up or, more likely, was very short-lived. Veizer *et al.* (1982) have shown that the early oceans (and also, to a lesser extent, the modern oceans) were buffered by the mantle. CO_2 would rapidly be removed as $CaCO_3$, $MgCO_3$ or as alkali carbonates. The kinetics of this process would be controlled by the availability of rock for weathering, either on the ocean floor, on the continental surface (if it existed), and most particularly by large-scale hydrothermal pumping of sea water through komatiitic mid-ocean ridges. All these factors depend on the rate of plate movement, but it appears that by 3.8 Ga, the CO_2 had been reduced to an important but trace component of the atmosphere, enough to produce a modest and managed greenhouse increment.

The probability that large quantities of carbon gases were degassed by the early Earth raises the question of why a moist greenhouse did not dehydrate the planet. As discussed above, a catastrophic greenhouse developed on Venus, which was closer to the Sun. Hydrogen was lost rapidly, and within a few hundred million years the planet's surface, and presumably its mantle too, were substantially dehydrated as the oceans disappeared. It is possible that a very similar process began on Earth, with an initial moist greenhouse and hydrogen loss to space (Fig. 8.14). However, oxidation of carbon gases in the atmosphere and precipitation of carbonate in mid-ocean ridge hydrothermal systems may have returned carbon rapidly to the mantle. If this happened rapidly enough, the moist greenhouse may have disappeared before loss of the oceans: on Venus, closer to the Sun, the oceans may have been lost first. The legacy on Earth would be an oxidised mantle (Eggler 1983, Mattioli & Wood 1986), and a D-rich system.

Since at least 3.8 Ga (Schidlowski *et al.* 1983), and most probably since *circa* 4.0–4.2 Ga or even earlier, a more subtle control has operated on the CO_2 level of the atmosphere. Today, and throughout the geological record, the CO_2 level is set by life, which may impose an extremely finely controlled homeostasis on CO_2, CH_4, NH_3 and thereby on the greenhouse increment to the surface temperature (Lovelock & Margulis 1974, 1984). It is this homeostasis which may have protected the oceans, and hence allowed the growth and maintenance of the continents. Schidlowski (1980) has summarised the evidence for this inference that organic control on carbon was the same 3.8 Ga ago as today. Carbon in mantle-derived lavas has an average $\delta^{13}C$ value of circa $-5‰$, or possibly more for komatiitic liquids.

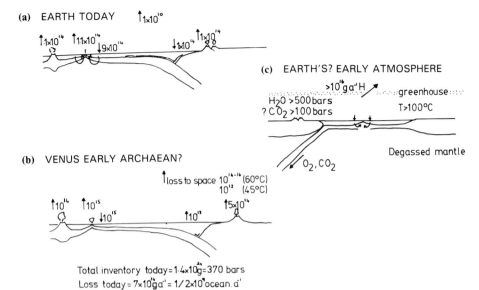

Figure 8.14 Speculations on mass balance in the early atmosphere. (a) EARTH. Top cartoon shows modern flux of water, from estimates by Ito *et al.* 1983. If Ito *et al.* are correct there is a steady loss of water to the mantle. (b) VENUS. Archaean cartoon shows a possible much greater loss to space, depending on surface temperature (calculated from Kasting *et al.* 1984). Other fluxes are guesses from models of Figures 8.4–8.9. (c) Third cartoon shows the possible situation in the early atmosphere, if carbon gases degassed with H_2O and were not preferentially retained in the mantle. Early greenhouse conditions would have developed, with substantial loss of hydrogen to space, oxidation of carbon gases to CO_2 and return of carbonate and oxidised species to the mantle. This process may have occurred in the first 10^8 years of the Earth's history, until CO_2 was preferentially removed from the exosphere and replaced in the mantle by the plate tectonic process, moderating the greenhouse and reducing the loss of hydrogen to space. Water inventory is for modern Earth.

On the modern Earth, loss from the mantle is approximately 10^{13} g at ocean islands, 10^{14} g at mid-ocean ridges. Return to mantle is close to 10^{15} g through hydrothermal alteration of new oceanic crust and subduction of wet sediment, partially compensated by loss of 10^{14} g by calc-alkaline volcanoes venting water to atmosphere. Loss of hydrogen to space is trivial. Net loss of water to mantle today is roughly 7×10^{14} ga^{-1}, which would dehydrate the oceans in about 2 Ga (Ito *et al.*). Note that the uncertainty in these figures is exceedingly great, but nevertheless, it does appear that the oceans are slowly being returned to the mantle. Cartoon (b) shows possible flux on early Archaean Venus. Mid-ocean ridge magmatism was probably komatiitic, delivering very much more water to the atmosphere. However, hydration of new oceanic crust probably removed only 2–5 times the modern terrestrial flux of water, depending on the rate of sea-floor spreading (see Bickle 1978, Nisbet & Fowler 1983). Deposition of sediment would be minimal, and calc-alkaline volcanism dependent on the rate of sea-floor spreading. Total flux may have been such that degassing matched or exceeded return to the mantle. If Ito *et al.* (1983) are correct, Earth's Archaean ocean would have been *circa* 7.5 km deep, implying a continental crust over 50 km thick (Fig. 5.1). A very significant dehydration of the planet could have taken place in the earliest Archaean if surface temperature was enhanced by a CO_2 greenhouse effect. Possibly the Earth began with a deep ocean which was partially removed in a greenhouse atmosphere by loss of hydrogen to space, leaving a legacy of oxidation in the atmosphere and mantle. Eventual removal of CO_2 by plate tectonics may have stabilised the oceans.

Much of that carbon is reprecipitated in carbonates in hydrothermally altered igneous rock, with $\delta^{13}C$ also around $-5‰$ to $-6‰$ (Cocker *et al.* 1982). Carbon which inhabits the exosphere partitions (see Ch. 4) into carbonate deposited in sediments by sea water ($\delta^{13}C$ of 0‰) and by organisms ($\delta^{13}C$ of $-25 \pm 5‰$). Since the degassed and hydrothermally precipitated carbon are comparable isotopically (the precipitated carbon returns to the mantle), then, crudely, $\delta^{13}C_{lava} = R\delta^{13}C_{organic} + (1 - R)\,\delta^{13}C_{carbonate}$, where R is the ratio of organic carbon to total sedimentary carbon. Schidlowski (1980) showed that R has always been about 20% throughout the geological record: indeed, if $\delta^{13}C_{lava}$ has varied slightly as komatiitic ridges gave way to basaltic ridges, R may have been larger in the past. Organisms may have been very important in controlling the Archaean carbon cycle, and hence CO_2 levels.

8.5 Gaia

We shall not cease from exploration
And the end of our exploring
Will be to arrive where we started
And know the place for the first time
Through the unknown remembered gate
When the last of Earth left to discover
Is that which was the beginning.

T. S. Eliot, *Little Gidding* (Four Quartets)

The discussion thus crosses from water to life. Lovelock and Margulis (1974), Margulis and Lovelock (1981) and Lovelock (1979) have pointed out that the modern atmosphere is completely out of chemical equilibrium. The atmosphere is managed by a biological control system, which acts in concert with inorganic chemical processes such as the hydrothermal reactions at the mid-ocean ridge crest and the weathering of the continents. This biological control system, they assert, is a network of intricate feedbacks which act cybernetically to maintain a very fine level of stability on the Earth's environment. Earth's present environment is chemically infinitely improbable: the system is driven in thermodynamic improbability as was the 'Heart of Gold' in the *Hitch-hiker's guide to the galaxy*. If it is so controlled today, it is a sound uniformitarian argument to suggest that biological control has maintained the planet's surface environment ever since life began, possibly prior to 4 Ga ago, since life very rapidly occupies all available niches and the major biochemical reactions were established very early on.

How can this assertion be justified, in practical models? Consider Watson and Lovelock's (1983) example of a planet covered in black and white daisies. In the early history of the planet, with a low solar luminosity, black daisies would thrive, absorbing the available heat and lowering the reflectivity of the planetary surface. As the sun warmed up, all other things being equal, natural selection would operate, more white daisies would be favoured and, eventually, with a hot Sun, the planet would be entirely covered in white daisies, reflecting much of the incident radiation. A planet without life would slowly warm as the sun warmed; in contrast (Fig. 8.15), the daisy planet would initially be black and have a surface warmer than the effective inorganic temperature, and would then gradually turn white, first at the equator, then towards the poles, to maintain a constant surface temperature eventually lower than the effective surface temperature. Finally, the control would fail, the environment would become too hot, the daisies would die and a thermal catastrophe would occur, to return the planet to the inorganic effective surface temperature.

This is a simple model, but it illustrates how biological organisms, by a fine control of the greenhouse gases in the atmosphere may have maintained a nearly constant surface temperature over 4 Ga. If conditions become hotter, life flourishes and CO_2 is consumed; if conditions become colder, biological productivity declines and CO_2 builds up again. Lovelock (1979) makes the case that this control is really exceedingly complex, involving every component of the exosphere and directly controlling all aspects of the atmosphere, hydrosphere, sedimentation and albedo of the Earth.

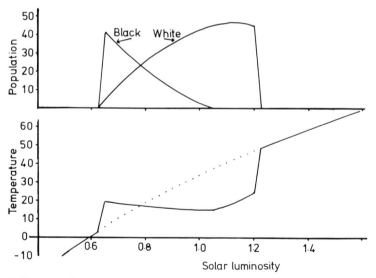

Figure 8.15 The daisy planet model of Watson and Lovelock (1983). Top diagram shows change in relative abundance of black and white daisies with solar luminosity (which increases with time). Bottom diagram shows surface temperature variation with time (solar luminosity increase). Solid line = daisy planet; dotted line = dead planet.

In terms of the control on CO_2 and greenhouse increment, the initial terrestrial conditions must have been such that inorganic buffers (Walker *et al.* 1981) allowed free water on the planet, at probably near-neutral pH. Most probably, the early 'effective' temperature (i.e. the temperature in the absence of a greenhouse effect) of the surface was slightly below $0°C$, and supplemented by a inorganically controlled greenhouse increment chiefly from carbon gases and water. In the very early history of the planet (4.4 Ga) the initial massive degassing of the hydrosphere might have produced a danger of thermal runaway (see above), but as water passed through new lava, probably at mid-ocean ridge hydrothermal systems, Ca^{++} and Mg^{++} must have removed most of the CO_2 as carbonate in hydrated crust, and as sedimented carbonate, leaving perhaps 0.01–10 bars of CO_2. Since life began, the carbonate exchange at mid-ocean ridges must have been supplemented by the carbon directly precipitated as organic residues of organisms living near hydrothermal systems and in shallow water. Much of this material would have been immediately returned via subduction zones to the mantle if plate tectonics operated.

The early Earth probably degassed carbon gases at a very substantially higher rate than today, and a massive continental inventory of weathered cations may not have been available to fix CO_2. In this context, the role of mid-ocean ridge processes was obviously critical in removing CO_2 and also in maintaining oceanic pH. Organic control on the chemistry of mid-ocean ridge hydrothermal systems is very important today (Edmonds & von Damm 1983); could it have been important in the past? Possibly, it was (see below), and the consequent thermal regulation of the surface temperature of the planet preserved the oceans from the fate of dehydration through an eventual moist greenhouse and a quite different atmosphere. The subtle managing of atmospheric composition and maintenance of the thermal stability of the oceans may have extended what, in the absence of life, would have been a rather short time interval (of the order of $10^8–10^9$ yr) of free surface water and neutral pH to give, instead, a sustained and extraordinary habitable environment. Alternatively, it can be argued that on an inorganic Earth, the time interval allowing free surface water would actually have been fairly long (Hendersen-Sellers 1983). Perhaps the Earth was just lucky. However, once life began, it began to change the air. Co-evolution is a demanding process, and the organisms sustain an atmosphere rich in oxygen and inimical to the anaerobic organisms which may have flourished early on. But life adapts: the thermal stasis was continued, though the players have changed over time.

If life did maintain the subtle control that allowed water to persist on the surface not for hundreds but for thousands of millions of years, then it could be argued, as Lovelock (1979) does, that life is in a sense the architect of our planet. The continents need water (to produce calc-alkaline magmas) for their growth and maintenance (Campbell & Taylor 1983); the sediments exist because they are transported by water; perhaps even plate tectonics itself is allowed on Earth but restricted on Venus (Phillips & Malin 1983) because water is present here. It has even been suggested that part of the difference between the core and the magnetic field of Venus and Earth may be a result of the difference in the surface temperature of the two planets (Stevenson *et al.* 1983).

All this is rich speculation and to be treated as such, but it raises many questions worth following. Most specifically, is there any evidence that early life could have maintained an ecosystem at the mid-ocean ridges? What environments did early life occupy? What, indeed, is life?

8.6   Life

> Like as the waves make towards the pebbled shore
> So do our minutes hasten to their end
> Each changing place with that which goes before
> In sequent toil all forwards do contend.
> ...
> And nothing 'gainst Time's scythe can make defense
> Save breed, to brave him when he takes thee hence.

Shakespeare, Sonnets XL, XII

Even more than water, life is the feature most strange and most anomalous on a strange and wonderful planet. Yet we cannot properly define it. What is life? Engels defined life as the mode of action of albuminous substances. Not a very precise definition, especially when one considers the essentially democratic, lively but definitely not living action of throwing an egg at a politician. Bernal (1967) proposed the lengthier but somewhat unenlightening definition that life is a self-realisation of the potentialities of atomic electron states. Perhaps one could define an organism as being alive if it can reproduce itself. But such a definition places all the emphasis on one function of life – is not a eunuch alive? Alternatively, a living organism can be defined as an organism which builds up an ever-increasing degree of local order at the thermodynamic expanse of its surroundings, and which is capable in certain circumstances of participating in self-replication. But this too is unsatisfactory. It is a mechanical definition, which reduces life to something not much different from the growth of a salt crystal in solution, except that it is more complex.

Cardinal Newman (1880) had it better. He, following Thomas Scott, lived by the parable 'Growth, the only evidence of life'. By its deeds it is known: life is disequilibrium. More than that, it is sustained disequilibrium, and living communities represent ever-increasing disequilibrium. Not only does life exist by kinetically maintaining itself in disequilibrium, but it propagates that disequilibrium and, if Lovelock (1979) is correct, it alters its environment to sustain that too in disequilibrium. The thermodynamic consequence is profound: life can only exist in time, because only in time can kinetics be exploited to sustain disequilibrium. In time, reproduction and growth inevitably lead to competition and natural selection, and it is natural selection that sustains and increases the disequilibrium: indeed, the degree of advancement of a life form can be measured by the extent to which it is capable of existing out of equilibrium with its external setting, from the simplest procaryote which can maintain an internal pH very different from its host fluid, to a man standing on the moon. All life is subject to natural selection, and it is natural selection that has shaped the diversity of the genomes and moulded Gaia. Of all living organisms only we, on rare occasions, can transcend natural selection: rarely do we choose to do so; more commonly, in the social perversion of Darwinism (Trevor-Roper 1985), we enshrine competition, in contradiction to the biblical ethic of loving one's neighbour.

Thus we cannot properly define life, but we can identify it as sustained disequilibrium, existing in time, reproducing, and therefore subject (excepting ourselves if we so choose) to natural selection. Whether there is purpose to life is not a matter for natural sciences; Kant's third antinomy shows that natural science can never prove or disprove the existence of God. I believe, others do not: faith is the only proof possible. A believer accepts in predestination a duality reminiscent of the dualities of modern physics: from the point of view of the scientific observer, the history of life is chance in time; from the point of view of the theologian the creator is outside time, created time, and is aware of chance. The two views are not in conflict. The body is machine, essential but bound in time, and we are close to unravelling its secrets; the mind must have evolved by the same pattern of chance, whether predetermined or not. It is also machine, though not so deterministic; and its structure may take centuries to unravel. The soul, the third member of this trinity, is beyond the realm of empirical natural science. Crick (1981) doubts the existence of a creator; others adopt the Pelagian or British heresy, that life can through its own efforts attain immortality; in contrast, the orthodox believer follows Augustine (398) in his essentially modern views, accepting time as a created dimension in which life develops. Only in time can disequilibrium be sustained. Incidentally – and it is an important point in modern North America – both Augustine's discussion of time and that in the letter to the Hebrews (4.7–10) rapidly demolish the 'creationist' heresy that the world was put together in six solar days. 'What was God doing before He created the Earth? – creating Hell for those who ask silly questions' (Augustine).

8.7 The origin of life

Life began, but how? An enormous variety of unlikely ideas has been advanced. Most popular is the idea that it began in an organic soup, a pre-biotic bouillon of assorted amino acids. However, for such a soup to exist in the open ocean, production of organic molecules by ultraviolet radiation, lightning, and the like would have to be faster than destruction of the soup by similar processes and also by 'cracking' as the sea water cycled through hydrothermal systems at the mid-ocean ridge: a volume equal to the total volume of the oceans would have passed through a hot primaeval komatiitic ridge system in the order of a million years or so. Most probably, the 'soup' would be a tenuous consommé of floating molecules, something interesting but not life-nourishing. Perhaps something else is needed.

Crick (1981) pointed out that to the 'honest man...the origin of life appears...to be almost a miracle, so many are the conditions which would have had to be satisfied to get it going.' The fundamentals of the genetic replicating mechanism must have been established early on: the choice of the four bases each in RNA and (perhaps later) in DNA; the choice of the 20 amino acids and the lettering of the genetic code shared by virtually all life today. All this is a matter for the molecular biologist; the geologist can only helpfully point out that the prebiotic fluid would almost certainly have contained abundant C, S (from sub-aqueous volcanism and volcanic gases) and P (in hydrothermal fluids, although continental alkaline volcanism was rare). NH_3 is a major problem, as is CH_4. In a letter, Darwin once imagined a warm ammoniacal little pond in which the magic recipe was put together, but ammonia photodissociates very readily and has a very short atmospheric residence time. Similarly for methane: Welhan and Craig (1983) showed that with methane in the oceans the residence time of gas injected from mid-ocean ridges is about 30 years. One possible source of ammonia in the early atmosphere is the catalytic photochemical reduction of atmospheric nitrogen by TiO_2 in desert sands (Hendersen-Sellers & Schwartz 1980), but in general the atmosphere probably had a very low ammonia partial pressure – around 10^{-8} atmospheres or less (Wigley & Brimblecombe 1981). Thus the primordial soup appears an improbable host for life: even if it existed, and was not pyrolysed by reactions at the mid-ocean ridges and around volcanoes, it would be poor in NH_3 and CH_4.

Crick and Orgel (1973) adopted an ingenious way out of the problem, by proposing quite simply that it did happen once, but not here. This is an old idea, dating back to Anaxagoras and, more recently, Arrhenius and Haldane. 'Directed Panspermia', their hypothesis, expanded by Crick (1981), is the idea that the Earth was seeded by an altruistic life form, which had itself evolved billions of years earlier. There is something very appealing in this hypothesis, for it implies that the galaxy is now inhabited by innumerable DNA-based life forms: but there is no evidence whatever for or against it. In 1970 the final Natural Science Tripos Essay paper in Cambridge (an examination unique to that university and of extraordinary value in stimulating interest into the frontiers of the sciences) posed the topic 'Crick for God'. Panspermia suffers from exactly this weakness: having denied the deity it invents a substitute.

If we deny panspermia, and yet accept Crick's powerful analysis of the minute probability of life's beginning, we return to the solitude of Earth. That any planet was habitable at all is extraordinarily unlikely (Hart 1979); that life managed to begin multiplies the physical improbability by extreme organic improbability. Perhaps we are indeed alone.

The problem of creating a self-replicating machine is of extraordinary difficulty. We could, today, construct a computer society which was able to mine its own raw materials by robot miners, then process the materials in factories and turn them into replacement robots and directing computers. But those who were lucky enough to read Dan Dare 30 years ago will remember the story of one such self-sufficient computer, Orak, and its catastrophic collapse when faced with a non-programmed bug in the shape of Colonel Dare. Natural selection, too, is a non-programmed set of challenges. Too complex a machine will fail, if because of its complexity it reproduces too slowly to meet natural challenges.

A more sophisticated version of Orak is the ideal von Neumann (1966) machine, able to reproduce itself by following instructions and to place a copy of that list of instructions in the new machine. Mutations can spring up in the copy: most changes will be fatal, but on rare but crucial occasions they will help and natural selection can operate. The simplest cell is a perfect von Neumann machine, with a list of instructions, a body, and an extraordinary ability to breed.

Yet the cell is still too complex, it seems, to be the first machine; in this case, the objection is that chance could not have put together such perfection. If it were assembled by chance (and we do not know that), the first such self-replicating machine must have been dominantly 'list' material, not body components. But how can a list – Schrödinger's (1944) 'aperiodic crystal' – reproduce itself by itself in the beginning? A crystal can repeat its formula, but how can it detach a part of itself to become a new crystal? How can an organic polymer do what salt cannot?

Life is improbable, and it may be unique to this planet, but nevertheless it did begin, and it is thus our task to discover how the miracle happened. For much of this century the debate has centred on the problems of how a self-replicating system could be assembled by some chance event. To recapitulate, most living organisms today store their genetic information in DNA, transfer that information via RNA, and express it in proteins to construct a body. Both RNA and DNA are 'lists': it seems intuitively reasonable that the earliest organic life used the less complex RNA, not DNA, as its store of information. This simplifies things somewhat, but nevertheless there remains the problem of simultaneously creating, by supposedly random chance, both the RNA and the protein enzymes needed as catalysts to help the RNA to replicate itself. To create one complex organic molecule is unlikely enough, but to create two different types of molecule together is unbelievable. Thus, if the information-containing molecule (RNA?) needed a catalyst to replicate, we are perhaps justified in turning to an extraordinary beginning such as directed panspermia.

However, the situation is not as bad as it appears. After all, we *did* begin. Work by Zaug and Cech (1986) and by Guerrier-Takada and Altman (1984) has demonstrated that in certain ways RNA can act in a remarkable fashion to catalyse the synthesis of itself. RNA molecules may be able to act not only as information-carriers, but also as enzymes able to help in the assembly of themselves (Westheimer 1986). This is conceptually possible because RNA molecules can contain self-splicing introns, which are RNA lengths which can splice themselves out of the RNA molecule and then act as enzymes to catalyse reactions involving the parent molecule, and presumably would be capable of aiding in the synthesis of a new RNA molecule (Fig. 8.16). In other words, if it is possible to put together the right RNA molecules by inorganically assembling some nucleotides, then perhaps the molecules can do the job of replication by themselves, unaided by proteins; natural selection immediately assists, and the von Neumann machine eventually becomes a human being. In this process only one type of molecule needs to be formed at the beginning, not two. The chance of life changes from impossible to merely wildly unlikely.

Gilbert (1986) has envisioned an RNA world in which the first self-replicating molecules existed. In this model, the first organic stage of evolution proceeds by RNA molecules performing the catalytic activities needed to assemble themselves from some source of nucleotides. Once self-replication is successfully accomplished, the force of natural selection will produce the evolution of more sophisticated self-replicating patterns and probably a wide range of RNA-based enzymic activities. The self-splicing introns which RNA molecules can contain (Westheimer 1986) can in theory both remove themselves from the replicating RNA molecules and also reinsert themselves. Gilbert argued that two such introns, separated by an exon, could remove both themselves and the intervening exon from one RNA molecule and insert themselves into another RNA molecule. In this way genetic information could be transferred from one molecule to another in an RNA-based equivalent of sex. Transfer of genetic information in this way would allow rapid and coherent genetic change in populations of RNA molecules. Thus, early evolution need not necessarily have relied only on the slight chance of a mutation in a single molecule having a fitness advant-

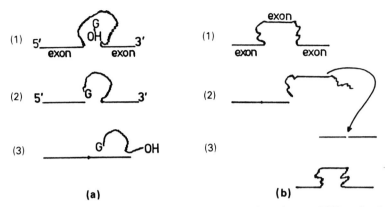

Figure 8.16 RNA and the beginning of life. Diagram (a) shows how an RNA molecule can detach an intervening sequence (after Westheimer 1986). Initially (1) the RNA consists of two sequences bearing information (exons), separated by the sequence to be detached. Under attack by guanosine the intervening sequence is cut out (2) and the two remaining exons are spliced together (3). Numbers 5′ and 3′ refer to the two ends of the RNA sequence, defining carbon atoms in the ribose sugar to which phosphates are attached. The detached intervening sequence can then act as an enzymic catalyst. Diagram (b) shows how information could be exchanged in an RNA world (Gilbert 1986). In (1) an RNA molecule contains three information-bearing sequences, or exons, with intervening sequences or introns which have properties similar to those illustrated in (a). These intervening introns, and the exon between them, could be detached and the parent molecule spliced together (2). The detached introns, carrying between them an exon, could then cleave another RNA molecule (see arrow) and insert themselves into it (3), thereby transmitting genetic information from one RNA molecule to another.

age, but instead could have acted, via this infectious transmission of advantageous genetic elements, to change whole populations of molecules (Fig. 8.16).

At a later stage, RNA molecules may have learnt to synthesise proteins, first by developing RNA molecules able to bind amino acids (Gilbert 1986), and then later by arranging them according to an RNA template. Such proteins would be able to carry out the catalytic functions of an enzyme more effectively than RNA-catalysts, and would come to dominate the system.

Eventually, instead of single-stranded RNA, reverse transcription may have produced double-stranded DNA. DNA, being double-stranded, is a much more reliable store of information than RNA because an error on one strand can be corrected by reference to the other. RNA would then continue to act as the mechanism for transfer of information from the basic DNA store to synthesise proteins: the central dogma of DNA $\rightleftharpoons$ RNA $\rightarrow$ protein would have been created. Gilbert suggested that the intron/exon structure of eucaryotic and some archaebacterial genes may remain as a fossil of this history, a reminder of the initial RNA world.

345

We have thus a systematic and coherent model of how life could have begun, given one (and only one) basic event, which is the creation of an RNA molecule in an environment which offered a supply of nucleotides and, presumably, some sort of containment so that daughter molecules did not travel too far away too soon.

8.8   The home of life

I have made it my rule not to read this literature on prebiotic evolution until someone else comes up with a recipe that says 'do this and do that, and in three months, things will crawl in there'.

Max Delbrück, *Mind over matter*

To turn now to the setting in which the first living organisms were created, can we deduce anything? This, perhaps, is the proper contribution of geologists to the search for our origins. There are several possible locations in which life may have begun: in the open ocean; in the shallow margins of oceans; in the hydrothermal systems around volcanoes or mid-ocean ridges; or in some extraordinary place, such as an obscure puddle hit by a meteorite, or a volcano under an ice-cap (Schwartz & Henderson-Sellers 1984).

These extraordinary localities are quite possible, considering the improbability of the whole event, but it is worth investigating the major habitats in detail (Fig. 8.17). Modern life depends either on the sun or on hydrothermal circulation for its basic source of energy. Thus it is reasonable to suppose either that the earliest life was photosynthetic or chemoautotrophic.

Corliss *et al.* (1981) pointed out that Archaean mid-ocean ridges probably sustained a flourishing community of anaerobic chemoautotrophs. They suggested that the earliest life may have existed in this setting (Fig. 8.18), a suggestion supported somewhat by the apparent antiquity of the archaebacterial line, many of which bacteria inhabit such settings (Woese 1981, Kaine *et al.* 1983). If the first life were chemoautotrophic, where would it have begun? Nisbet (1985b) considered the most probable sites to be in the exit chimneys of the hydrothermal systems, at the sediment/water interface above the intake regions of such systems, or in vesicles in the rock (Fig. 8.18) through which large quantities of fluid passed. All three of these sites are in the hydrothermal system, not the ocean. Corliss *et al.* suggested that amino acids could be synthesised and preserved in exit vents: simultaneously, organic molecules in the water would be trapped by filtration through the intake regions, to build up deposits of abiologically synthesised organic compounds.

346

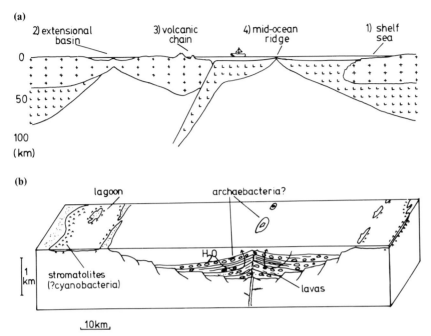

Figure 8.17 (a) Cartoon illustrating possible habitats of Archaean life. Shallow-shelf seas (1) could support photosynthetic life; in extensional basins (2), both shallow sea floor and hydrothermally-bound life could have existed; above subduction zones in volcanic chains (3), hydrothermal systems would have been common, often in shallow waters which might also support photosynthetic life; at mid-ocean ridges (4), hydrothermal systems could have supported flourishing communities. Pelagic life may also have existed in the photic zone (from Nisbet 1985b). (b) Detail of Figure 8.17, in an extensional basin. In localities protected from clastic debris as at Belingwe, stromatolites would have grown photosynthetically. In the centre of the basin, the volcanic axis would have acted as host to vigorous hydrothermal systems which may have combined chemoautotrophic bacteria. (From Nisbet 1985b.)

How did things begin? For life to begin in open water, a self-replicating molecule, such as a short string of tRNA perhaps 100 nucleotides long would have to be assembled and remain assembled for long enough to replicate itself. To replicate itself, the RNA molecule would have needed help from specific RNA-dependent enzymes, or ribozymes, made or accidentally encountered by the RNA molecule. These enzymes would somehow have to be kept next to the RNA molecule, or replication would cease as they drifted away. In other words, a package is needed to keep the RNA molecule and its helpers together. More than that, the daughter RNA molecules would somehow have to be equipped either with the detachable enzymes, with a package to hold in any enzymes they made and the means to make the enzymes, or with the means to make a package and the enzymes. Thus not only is a replicating molecule needed *ab initio*, with its

347

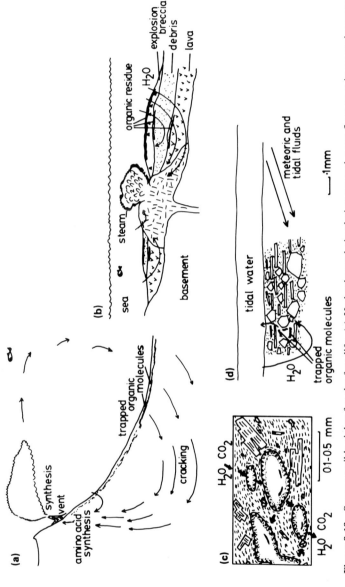

Figure 8.18 Some possible sights for the first life. (a) Hydrothermal circulation around a sea-floor vent in an underwater setting (e.g. see Corliss *et al*. 1981). (b) Silicic volcanism on sea floor. Note explosion debris. (c) Fluid movement through vesicular or brecciated rock. Longer organic molecules could possibly be trapped in open spaces. (d) Water circulation through soft sediment in shallow or intertidal setting. (From Nisbet 1985b.)

constituent ribozyme, but also a bag, presumably made of lipids (a 'soap-bubble'), in which to keep the whole assemblage. All this is extraordinarily unlikely: to return to the probability paradox, life thus not only appeared in an improbable solar system on an unusual planet in (perhaps) the relatively short time in which it was habitable, not only assembled a widely unlikely molecule, but also managed to build itself a home at the same time. Having done so, if Lovelock (1979) is correct, it managed to reproduce itself and to tailor the environment to its liking. The monkey, having invented the typewriter and banged out the complete Shakespeare without error, then proceeded to become pregnant, to set up a theatre and with descendants as actors, to perform the plays in a critically comfortable atmosphere.

Cairns-Smith (1982) has suggested an escape from this lonely line of argument. He pointed out the similarity between crystal growth and simple life. In a well-argued book he demonstrated the implausibility of the suggestion that nucleic acid was assembled abiotically. Bernal (1967) argued that clay minerals may have played an important catalytic role in assembling life. Cairns-Smith suggested that replication itself began through crystallisation: life may have originally been based on clay minerals. Only later did organic molecules become involved and eventually take over the business of replication. This argument quite avoids the objections to the direct birth of an organic replicating system. Clays and related minerals are commonest in soft sediments and in altered volcanic piles as found in the hydrothermal systems which circulate through mid-ocean ridges. Cairns-Smith's hypothesis is extraordinarily interesting and powerful; nevertheless it still calls on extremely improbable events.

Another alternative is also a development of Bernal's argument. All altered lavas and all soft sedimentary rocks are assemblages of crystals, matrix, and innumerable small to submicroscopic vesicles or cavities. Fluids circulating through the body of a rock travel from hole to hole, as if through a fine filter. Possibly, life could have begun in such a cavity (Nisbet 1985b): such a cavity in a hydrothermal system or in soft sediment, would be in a steady flux of CO_2, H_2O, perhaps H_2S or SO_4^{2-} species and perhaps, short chain organic molecules (Fig. 8.18) as well as phosphates and cations dissolved in the brine. If long chains of nucleotides could be assembled with the help of catalysis by some mineral phase, such as a clay mineral, or an iron oxide mineral (Holm 1985, Holm et al. 1983) or a zeolite, then possibly the minerals lining a cavity could have assembled a long chain molecule from the components in circulating brine. Should a molecule of this sort form, it would be trapped within the cavity by its size (Fig. 8.18). Any daughter enzymes might similarly be trapped by their size. Should a self-replicating RNA form, it would thus maintain access to its long daughter molecules during replication, in contrast to the situation in the open ocean. Periodically, in an active volcano or spreading centre, the very frequent small earth-

349

quakes would open inter-pore spaces and gaps: a self-replicating system born in a rock vesicle could colonise a large region around its birthplace, within the 10–100 000 year lifespan of a local volcanic heat source or depositional environment. In such a setting, the mineral catalysis which initially helped to construct the replicating nucleic acid would later become a capricious nuisance: a system which could surround itself with a bag of lipids to isolate itself from the cavity wall would be strongly favoured by natural selection. If it did so, it would immediately also be pre-adapted to life in the open sea, once the next earthquake released it. A similar story can be constructed for a soft-sediment scenario: once replication begins, natural selection is capable of driving the organism across the gap between the first cell and ourselves.

Max Delbrück (1986) complained that he found the various models for the origin of life unconvincing, since they lacked experimental verification. Delbrück was one of the founders of molecular biology, who revolutionised the study of life by applying to biology the rigorous approach of his mentor, Niels Bohr and Rutherford. His complaint is valid: can we specify a series of experimental steps which will produce, at the end, a self-replicating system, and were these steps possible in nature in the early Archaean? If we can answer Delbrück's complaint we will at least have a plausible explanation of how life began, though not necessarily the true explanation. What follows is one geologically reasonable set of experimental steps to answer the complaint. Many other pathways could be proposed: the path proposed here is simply a personal preference.

The *first* step is to find the right ambient conditions, with abundant H_2O, CH_4, NH_3, phosphate, a mildly alkaline pH, a temperature around 40°C and an ample supply of energy. Such conditions do exist in nature, in the cooler parts of some hydrothermal systems. Mid-ocean ridge systems, such as those at the Galapagos Spreading Centre, produce hot fluids with low pH of 3–4 (von Damm *et al.* 1985), but in the cooler regions of such hydrothermal systems and where a sedimentary cover overlies the hydrothermal system the pH is higher, around 6–7 (Bowers *et al.* 1985). On Iceland, which is an exposed mid-ocean ridge, the hydrothermal systems contain meteoric water and have a pH of 7.5–9 or higher, depending on temperature (Arnórsson *et al.* 1982, 1983a,b; Arnórsson 1985). It is these Icelandic geothermal systems that are most interesting: they contain regions where pH is 7.5–8.5, temperature is around 40°C, and there are significant partial pressures of CO_2, CH_4, NH_3, H_2S and a wide variety of species in solution (Figs 7.13, 7.14), including Mg. In general, in hydrothermal systems, phosphates are rapidly mobilised from the rock. Minerals such as galena are common precipitates in regions where fluids cool. By inference, cooler regions of Archaean hydrothermal systems, especially those analogous to modern Icelandic systems, could have had a temperature around $40°C$, pH fluctuating around 7.5–8.5, abundant and variable CO_2, CO, H_2, CH_4, NH_3, H_2S, phosphates, sulphides and Mg^{++}. Probably nowhere else on the Archaean Earth (Abelson 1966) could such conditions have existed. So the first step would be to make a model hydrothermal system.

The *second* step is to construct the basic chemical materials. Fox and Dose (1977) have summarised the ways in which this can be done – the territory is fairly well explored. Formaldehyde, if it formed in relatively low concentrations from $CO + H_2$, would condense to sugars; ribose is a possible end product. Purines and pyrimidines can be formed by heating cyanide (a possible if unlikely species in the volcano-hydrothermal environment) in aqueous ammonia. Phosphates would be present in the hydrothermal fluids. Thus the second step would be to vary the model hydrothermal system to produce all three: ribose, bases and phosphates.

The *third* step is to assemble a polynucleotide. The critical factor here is the presence of a catalyst. Bernal (1951) outlined the idea that clay minerals may have provided the suitable catalytic surface, and the hypothesis has been explored in detail, by Odom *et al.* (1979a,b) and Rao *et al.* (1980). Odom *et al.* (1979a) showed that clays in fluctuating environments could have helped to promote nucleotide oligomerisation. Cycling of clay in combination with cyanamide promoted high levels of condensation of nucleotides to a mixture of oligonucleotides and dinucleotide pyrophosphate. Thus clay mineral catalysis may have been very significant in assembling a polynucleotide, and clay minerals are ubiquitous in the cooler parts of hydrothermal systems. Galena, another mineral typical of hydrothermal systems, may also have been an important catalyst (Sleeper & Orgel 1979).

It is also possible that iron oxide (Holm 1985, Holm *et al.* 1983) and zeolite catalysis may have been critical in assembling a polynucleotide. Zeolites, which are characteristic of hydrothermal systems, approach enzymes in their ability to act as exquisitely specific catalysts (Wright *et al.* 1986). In relatively dry environments (possible in some gas-dominated parts of subaerial volcanic fumarole systems), organic molecules could be held in the channels of more open natural zeolites: in the microenvironments of a zeolite mineral it is not impossible that an RNA chain could be constructed. Zeolites can also act as molecular sieves, which could trap large organic molecules but allow small organic molecules to pass through to supply the components from which the large molecules could be constructed. In general, a subaerial fumarole system, which would contain fluctuating mineral–fluid, mineral–gas and fluid–gas interfaces with varying pH and temperature plus abundant and powerful catalysts, provides the most attractive site for this critical first synthesis. Thus the third step would be to construct an RNA chain from the basic materials provided in the second step and with the help of clay or iron oxide minerals characteristic of hydrothermal systems, or perhaps with zeolite minerals in fluctuating, sometimes dry, conditions found in gas fumarole systems.

The *fourth* step is to find the right RNA molecule, capable of initiating the RNA world imagined by Gilbert (1986). Here the experimental guide is the work of Zaug and Cech (1986) and Guerrier-Takada and Altman (1984). An RNA molecule capable of initiating the RNA world must be able to detach a ribozyme able to assist in the rapid, non-random assembly of copies of the original RNA molecule. The best conditions for this process appear to be $T = 40°C$, pH fluctuating from 7.5–8.5, the presence of Mg^{++}, a confined environment such as would be found in a large zeolite cage or a small vesicle, where daughter ribozymes would not be lost. All of these are the typical conditions of the cooler regions of an Icelandic hydrothermal system.

The *final* step would be to duplicate in the laboratory the mechanisms by which the RNA world discovered a reliable energy pathway, constructed a cell membrane and managed to bind proteins. We know something of how this is done in modern life: it may be possible to show if naked, virus-like RNA could learn these tricks. If life *did* begin with RNA, then those critical accessory molecules which are based on nucleotides, such as ATP and co-enzyme A, would almost certainly have been present too from the very beginning. Any replicating RNA molecule which learned the trick of using ATP as the basis of a primitive energy chain would gain some independence from the vagaries of a fluctuating hydrothermal system and would thus be strongly favoured by natural selection. Somehow, too, the first life learned to surround itself with a bag made of a phospholipid bilayer. Again, selection would strongly favour such a development, but can it be duplicated in the laboratory? The critical role of phosphates both in the utilisation of energy and in the cell membrane is interesting and can be interpreted as eloquent testimony for a hydrothermal origin. On the Archaean planet, perhaps only in such a setting would a non-negligible supply of phosphates be reliably present. Proteins too must have come in here somehow. Amino acids have been synthesised inorganically in systems which are analogous to hydrothermal systems, and perhaps it may be possible to show in the laboratory how the RNA world managed to bind them as proteins, exploiting the hydrothermal fluids which would have a very small but significant component of amino acids available to be trapped by the RNA molecule. This final step would thus have to show how a replicating RNA molecule inhabiting the RNA-world could construct proteins and a cell membrane. Perhaps it can be done experimentally: if so, Delbrück's complaint will be answered.

The sequence of steps outlined above is not the only sequence which can be imagined, but it has few great leaps of assumption. Most of the steps have been tried, and we have an idea that each step can be surmounted. Since we have no evidence that life has begun anywhere else, or at any other time than on this planet 4 Ga years ago, the steps may be most improbable both individually and collectively, but they are perhaps not wholly impossible (Nisbet 1986b). Darwin (1959) in a letter published long after his death once asked why, if life began once, it does not do so all the time, making a constant supply of new forms. There are two answers to this: perhaps new life is occasionally born in modern hydrothermal systems but the product would be an RNA-based cell with little chance of survival against highly specialised modern bacteria: more plausibly, the creation of life was something that was so improbable that it only happened once, by an extraordinary accident on an extremely special planet.

If Delbrück's complaint is answered, and life *is* created by a series of experimental steps (which would, of course, have to be designed so as to amplify a low probability of success), what would the consequences be? Most probably, the experiments would serve to emphasize the division in society between those who believe that the universe and its inhabitants are an accident of pure chance, and those who see the hand of the deity. Cosmologists can imagine a model of an accidental, inflationary universe created by a fluctuation in nothingness: added to this would be a model of the chance evolution of life in a cosmos devoid of purpose. Yet faith is the substance of things hoped for, the evidence of things not seen, and faith is essential to the believer. To *prove* the hand of the deity would be to disallow faith and to make a mockery of Biblical teaching in which we are told that we cannot prove God: we can only live in faith: 'Through faith we understand that the worlds were formed by the word of God, so that things which are seen were not made of things which do appear' (Hebrews 11.3).

The stages that followed the first replication were complex and demanding, but essentially controlled by chance and natural selection. DNA, not RNA, may have taken over as the key molecule or, if Cairns-Smith is right, it displaced an earlier clay-based information carrier. From the ancestor, life colonised hydrothermal systems as chemoautotrophs, and the floor of shallow seas as photosynthetic organisms. Possibly the streamlined eubacterial genome is a result of modifications introduced to counter the higher risk of genetic error in shallow settings irradiated by ultraviolet light. Molecular tinkering began (Jacob 1983). The eucaryotic chimaera was created from fragments of the available parent lines; life diversified. The invention of sexual reproduction capitalised on the structure of the DNA ('important biological objects come in pairs'); by accepting a reduction in rate of reproduction because only one sex can have children, sexual organisms gain a new method of shuffling the genome in the co-evolutionary competition. With sex, presumably, came at some stage the invention of programmed death, since it is advantageous in the genome-shuffling race to remove the preceding generation: fish, flesh and fowl and man accept this strategy, tortoises choose rather to remain monuments of unageing intellect. But that is a post-Archaean story: sex seems to be a Proterozoic invention, as far as we can tell.

Geology has once only, through Darwin, managed to influence the development of society as a whole, to alter the lives of humanity. The results were ugly in early 20th-century Europe. The political misuse of Darwin's hypothesis produced a supposedly 'scientific' cloak for racism and totalitarianism. In contrast, the Gaia hypothesis, should it be proven, stresses the common heritage and common responsibility of life. We are Gaia, and it is now our responsibility to manage the planet and its atmosphere, together. If the hypothesis is proven, its impact on the human condition may be equal to that of Darwin. The modern revolution in geology, plate tectonics, has had no such massive impact; rather, it is an interesting matter for the media wisely to discuss and mangle each time an earthquake or volcano reminds us of our fragility. Only in the Archaean, in the question of the origin and actions of life, and in the debate about the Gaia hypothesis, does geology remain an explosive science capable of discovering something able to shake the foundations. In this, to return to the beginning of the book, is the attraction and the problem of the Archaean.

Glossary of geological terms for non-geologists

Geological terms, like those of all quantitative sciences, are carefully defined and carry precise meaning. The brief explanations given here are *not* precise, but are given in the hope that they will make the book somewhat more intelligible to non-geologists. For more rigorous definitions, standard glossaries, such as the American Geological Institute's *Glossary of geology*, edited by R. L. Bates and J. A. Jackson, should be consulted. In particular, most rock types are more strictly defined than is given here. Biological terms are explained for geologists in Table 4.1.

a   Abbreviation for year.

adamellite   (Quartz monzonite) granitoid rock, with quartz (10–50%) and plagioclase/ total feldspar ratio of 0.35–0.65.

adiabat   *PT* path followed by body which is expanded or compressed without giving or receiving heat.

aeon (also **eon**)   Longest geological time division. Also sometimes used to represent 10^9 years.

agglomerate   Chaotic coarse assemblage of angular pyroclastic fragments.

albedo   Reflectivity: ratio of reflected to incident energy.

amphibole   Chain silicate minerals of wide variety, e.g. tremolite, $Ca_2Mg_5Si_8O_{22}(OH)_2$. Other amphiboles include actinolite, hornblende, riebeckite.

amphibolite   Intermediate grade metamorphic rock or facies, *circa* $> 450°C$. Characterised by presence of amphiboles such as hornblende.

andesite   Extrusive igneous rock, usually containing plagioclase (e.g. andesine) and mafic phase(s); *circa* 55% SiO_2.

Archaean (also **Archean, Archaeozoic**)   Division of time prior to 2500 million years ago. The initial accretionary time of the Earth's history is often called 'Hadean'.

arenite   Sedimentary rock of sand-sized fragments.

arkose   Feldspar-rich sandstone, close to granitoids in composition.

asthenosphere   Literally, 'sick' or weak sphere of Earth. Region where deformation is dominantly plastic, and heat transfer is mainly by convection rather than conduction. Usually applied to region of mantle below the lithosphere.

banded ironstone (also **banded iron formation**)   Sedimentary rock with bands of iron-rich minerals and silica.

basalt   Mafic igneous rock, usually with calcic plagioclase and clinopyroxene plus assorted other minerals: *circa* 49–50% SiO_2.

basement   Rocks, continental crust, which provide substrate for later deposition.

basin   Depository for sedimentary material: term is not precisely used in most Archaean literature.

batholith   Large plutonic body.

355

Bouma sequence   Specific set of textures in a sediment; diagnostic of deposition by a turbidite.

calc-alkaline series   Suite of igneous rocks including basalts, andesites, dacites and rhyolites, usually produced above subduction zones.

charnockite   High-grade metamorphic rock − see section 3.8.

chert   Cryptocrystalline silica which often forms sedimentary rock.

chondrite   Type of stony meteorite thought to approximate in composition to the material which made the Earth.

CHUR   Chondritic uniform reservoir − see section 2.5.1.

clastic sediment   Made of rock or organic fragments, e.g. as opposed to a chemical precipitate.

clinopyroxene   Mineral $X(i - p)Y(i + p)Z_2O_6$, where X may be Ca,Na; Y includes Mg,Fe,Al,Ti; Z is Si,Al. Augite includes $(Ca,Mg,Fe^{+2},Al,Ti)_2(SiAl)_2O_6$.

concordia   See section 2.6.

conglomerate   Coarse clastic rock, usually with pebbles to boulders set in a sandy or silty matrix.

core   Iron-rich centre of the Earth, 2885−6370 km below the surface.

cover   Sedimentary deposits laid down on earlier basement.

craton   Large stable region of the Earth's crust.

crust   Surface layer of the Earth, about 35 km thick in continental regions and of sialic character, including granitoids, metamorphic rocks and sediments; and about 8 km thick in oceanic regions, where it is composed of basalts, gabbros and cumulate rocks, overlain by sediment.

cumulate   Term applied to rocks formed by the accumulation (e.g. by precipitation) of crystals.

δ   Notation used in describing variation in stable isotope ratio in parts per thousand from a standard − see section 4.1.9.

dacite   Igneous rock, extrusive equivalent of granodiorite; more quartz-rich than andesite.

detrital   Fragmental, e.g. sand; usually refers to material transported from its origin as fragments and then deposited.

diagenesis   Changes undergone by sediment after its initial deposition: grades into metamorphism.

diapir   Body of plastic, relatively light material (e.g. salt, magma) which pierces upwards into overlying strata.

differentiate   Rock formed as a result of magmatic differentiation, e.g. by crystal precipitation.

discordia   See section 2.6.

distal   With a source a long way away.

DM   Depleted mantle − see section 2.5.1.

dolomite   Carbonate rock with over 50% of mineral dolomite $(CaMg(CO_3)_2)$.

dunite   Rock dominantly composed of olivine.

dyke (dike)   Tabular cross-cutting igneous intrusion; also sedimentary cross-cutting structure.

ε Notation used in describing variation in radiogenic isotope ratio in parts per thousand from a given evolution curve – see Chapter 2.

effective temperature   Temperature of planetary surface in absence of a greenstone increment.

errorchron   Not quite an isochron, out of experimental error.

exosphere   Portion of Earth participating directly in atmosphere, ocean and recycling of sedimentary mass.

extrusion (ive)   Eruption of magma.

facies   Character of a rock including, depending on need and use, its appearance, composition and its environment of origin.

fan   Fan-shaped mass of sediment deposited at a change in gradient.

feldspar   Mineral family, $(MAl)(AlSi)_3O_8$, with $M = K$, Na, Ca, etc. Includes plagioclase feldspars (Na–Ca) and alkali feldspars (Na–K).

felsic   Rock rich in light-coloured minerals, e.g. feldspar.

fenestra   Window-like space in rock, either a pore or a region infilled with later material.

fluvial   Laid down by a river.

foliation   Planar fabric in rock, e.g. aligned flat minerals.

formation   Identifiable body of rock: basic unit of rock nomenclature.

fractionation   Separation of chemistry of a magma, e.g. by precipitation of crystals.

freeboard   Average height of continents above water level.

Ga 10^9 years (giga-annum).

gabbro   Coarse-grained equivalent of basalt; composed of calcic plagioclase, clinopyroxene with or without olivine and orthopyroxene.

garnet   Mineral of formula $A_3B_2(SiO_4)_3$, where $A = Ca$, Mg, Fe^{+2}, Mn^{+2}; $B = Al$, Fe^{+3}, Mn^{+3}, Cr, etc.

geotherm   Temperature–depth curve in Earth.

gneiss   Foliated metamorphic rock rich in feldspar and quartz: can be derived from meta-igneous or meta-sedimentary rock.

GPa   gigapascal, 1 GPa = 10 kbar.

granite   Strictly, a specific type of plutonic rock, with quartz plus a plagioclase feldspar/total feldspar ratio of 0.1–0.65.

granitoid   Family of granite-like rocks.

granodiorite   Granitoid rock, with quartz and plagioclase/total feldspar ratio of 0.65–0.90.

granulite   High-grade usually anhydrous metamorphic rock; T circa $> 700°C$ and P usually several kbar.

greenschist   Low-grade metamorphic rock or facies, T circa $> 300°C$. Characterised by presence of green minerals.

greenstone belt   Belt of rocks, usually including volcanic rocks and sediments at low to moderate metamorphic grade, often surrounded by granite or gneiss.

greywacke   Dark, sandy rock, often laid down by turbidity currents.

group   Set of related formations.

357

hammer Impact-activated user-friendly bear-unfriendly geognostical probe.

harzburgite Peridotite composed of olivine and orthopyroxene.

heat-producing elements U, Th, K, on modern Earth, also ^{26}Al, Pu etc. in early solar system.

homeostasis Maintenance of stable temperature in an organism despite wide external variations.

HREE Heavy rare earth element.

hydrothermal Associated with hot water or aqueous solutions, e.g. in circulation system around hot igneous body or volcano.

hypabyssal High level in crust.

hypsographic curve Cumulative frequency curve of proportion of surface area of Earth vs. elevation.

incompatible element Element which partitions into melt during partial melting, e.g. Ti.

intrusion (ive) Emplacement of magma into country rock.

inventory of sediments Accumulated mass of sediments on Earth.

island arc Chain of islands, e.g. Aleutians, usually volcanic and above a subduction zone.

isochron Straight-line plot (within experimental error) of isotope ratio from a suite of samples which gives the age of the isotopic closure of the suite.

isostasy Way in which units of lithosphere 'float' on asthenosphere.

isotherm Line or surface of constant temperature.

jaspilite Iron-rich siliceous rock; type of banded ironstone.

kb, kbar kilobar; 0.1 gigapascal; roughly $1000 \times$ atmospheric pressure.

kerogen Insoluble organic material.

kimberlite Type of peridotite erupted in pipe from great depth and hosting diamonds (rarely!).

komatiite Highly magnesian lava – see Table 6.2.

komatiitic basalt Magnesian lava – see Table 6.2.

λ Radioactive decay constant – see eqn. 2.1.

lamina Flat layer, usually *circa* 1 mm or less thick in rocks.

lapilli Small pyroclastic fragments, usually round.

lherzolite Peridotite composed of olivine, orthopyroxene and clinopyroxene.

liquidus Surface (e.g. in *PT* space) above which system is wholly liquid.

lithophile element Element usually found in silicate minerals.

lithosphere Strong cold surface layer of the Earth, including crust and uppermost mantle. Base of lithosphere can either be defined mechanically by strength, or thermally, as the level above which heat transfer is dominantly by conduction. Base is usually defined as an isotherm, e.g. $800°C$.

LLLAMA Large laterally linked Archaean magma anomaly, magma ocean, mythical beast seen only by Nisbet and Walker.

LREE Light rare earth element.

Ma Million years.

mafic rock Dark rock rich in magnesium (ma) and iron (fic) rich minerals.

magma Mobile igneous rocks including liquid and suspended crystals.

mantle Zone of the Earth below the crust and above the core, divided into the upper mantle (*circa* (8–35)–670 km deep) and lower mantle (670–2885 km deep).

metamorphic grade Recorded temperature or rank of metamorphism.

metamorphism Process of change in a rock, from an original state to a new state: usually occurs through changes in temperature or pressure.

metapelite Metamorphosed fine-grained aluminous sediment, such as a shale or mudstone.

meteoric water Rain, derived from atmosphere.

mgal milligal: one gal $= 1 \, \text{cm} \, \text{s}^{-2}$.

migmatite Rock in which segregated low-temperature melting liquid fraction is associated with high-grade metamorphic material.

Moho Base of crust, as defined by change in seismic velocity.

nappe Sheet-like transported rock unit, which may have moved many km.

olivine Mineral $(Mg,Fe)_2SiO_4$: forsterite (Fo) refers to the Mg end-member, and fayalite (Fa) to the iron.

ophiolite Fragment of crust and upper mantle, analogous to ocean floor.

orogen Region or belt of rocks which have been folded and deformed together at a particular time.

orthopyroxene Mineral $(Mg,Fe)_2Si_2O_6$: enstatite (En) refers to the Mg end-member, and ferrosilite (Fs) to the iron.

palaeoregolith Ancient soil or detritus horizon.

pelagian British heresy opposed by St. David and St. Augustine.

pelagic Oceanic, rather than near-shore.

peridotite Rock with over 90% mafic minerals, usually dominated by olivine.

Phanerozoic Division of time since the beginning of the Cambrian about 570 million years ago.

phenocryst Large conspicuous crystal, e.g. in a lava.

phreatoplinian event Type of violent volcanic explosion involving magmatic gases and steam. In memoriam Pliny the elder AD 79.

pillow lava Lava which shows pillow-like features, erupted underwater.

placer Surface mineral deposit formed by mechanical concentration.

plagioclase feldspar Group of feldspars with formula $(NaCa)Al(SiAl)Si_2O_8$. In fresh basalts, plagioclase is calcic.

plate tectonics Tectonic system of the modern Earth, involving the movement of large lithospheric plates, as spherical caps across the planet's surface. Deformation and igneous activity mostly occurs at junctions between plates, not within plates.

pluton Igneous intrusion, usually at deep level.

polybaric Many pressures.

Proterozoic Division of time from 2500 million years ago until about 570 million years ago.

provenance Place of origin.

proximal With a nearby source.

pyroclast Rock fragment ejected during a volcanic eruption.

pyroxenite Rock with over 90% mafic minerals, mainly composed of pyroxene.

quartz Mineral SiO_2.

REE Rare earth element. La, Hf are not REE but are often loosely included. (La), Ce, Pr, Nd, Pm, Sm, Eu, Gd, Tb, Dy, Ho, Er, Tm, Yb, Lu (Hf).

rhyolite Silicic igneous rock, extrusive equivalent of granite.

rift Region of separation of crust; usually marked by a rift valley.

σ Standard deviation.

serpentinisation Alteration (usually of olivine) to serpentine, by adding water.

sial Si, Al rich, e.g. granitoid.

siderophile Element typically found in metallic phase of a meteorite, and probably in the core.

sima Si, Mg rich, e.g. peridotite.

solidus Surface (e.g. in PT space) below which system is wholly solid.

solvus Surface separating field of solid solution from field of two or more phases.

spinifex Texture in olivine and clinopyroxene − see section 6.4.

strata Rock layers or, in Archaean usage, identifiable rock units.

stratabound Within a specific stratigraphic horizon.

stratigraphy (a) Study of rock strata; (b) position and order of strata.

stringer Long thin unit of rock.

stromatolite Organosedimentary structure − see Chapter 4.

subduction zone Region in which one lithospheric plate descends beneath another.

supergroup Set of related groups.

supracrustal Deposited or erupted on surface of the crust.

syntectonic Occurring during a period of tectonic activity such as deformation.

tectonics Workings of the Earth (including architecture and deformation of rock units on a broad scale).

terrain (terrane) Region of the Earth's surface with a characteristic geological style, e.g. Archaean terrain. Some workers distinguish between terrain and terrane, but this is ridiculous.

tholeiitic Family name of silica-saturated basalts.

tonalite Granitoid rock, with quartz and plagioclase/total feldspar ratio over 0.90.

tuff Pyroclastic rock.

turbidite Sedimentary rock laid down by a turbidity current.

ultramafic rock Rock very rich in magnesium and iron-rich minerals, such as olivine and pyroxenes.

unconformity Major break or gap in geological record, usually marked by different orientations of overlying and underlying rocks.

References

Abbott, D. H. 1984. Archaean plate tectonics revisited, 2. Palaeo-sea level changes, continental area, oceanic heat loss and the area–age distribution of the ocean basins. *Tectonics* **3**, 709–22.

Abbott, D. and M. Lyle 1984. Age of oceanic plates at subduction and volatile recycling. *Geophysical Research Letters* **11**, 951–4.

Abell, P. I., J. McClory, A. Martin and E. G. Nisbet 1985. Archaean stromatolites from the Ngesi Group, Belingwe greenstone belt, Zimbabwe; preservation and stable isotopes – preliminary results. *Precambrian Research* **27**, 357–83.

Abell, P. I., J. McClory, A. Martin, E. G. Nisbet and T. K. Kyser 1985. Petrography and stable isotope ratios from Archaean stromatolites, Mushandike Formation, Zimbabwe. *Precambrian Research* **27**, 385–98.

Abelson, P. H. 1966. Chemical events on the primitive Earth. *Proceedings of the National Academy of Sciences* **55**, 1365–72.

Agee, C. and D. Walker 1986. Experimental static compression and olivine flotation in ultrabasic silicate liquids. *EOS* **67**, 409.

Albarède, F. and M. Juteau 1984. Unscrambling the lead model ages. *Geochimica et Cosmochimica Acta* **48**, 207–12.

Allègre, C. J. 1985. The evolving Earth system. *Terra Cognita* **5**, 5–14.

Allègre, C. J. and D. Rousseau 1984. The growth of the continent through time studied by Nd isotopic analyses of shales. *Earth and Planetary Science Letters* **67**, 19–34.

Allègre, C. J., D. Ben-Othman, M. Polve and P. Richard 1979. The Nd–Sr isotopic correlation in mantle materials and geodynamic consequences. *Physics of the Earth and Planetary Interiors* **19**, 293–306.

Allègre, C. J., T. Staudacher, P. Sarda and M. Kurz 1983. Constraints on evolution of Earth's mantle from rare gas systematics. *Nature* **303**, 762–6.

Allsopp, H. L. 1964. Rubidium–strontium ages from the western Transvaal, *Nature* **204**, 361–3.

Anderson, D. L. and A. M. Dziewonski 1984. Seismic tomography. *Scientific American* **251** (October), 60–83.

Anderson, L. G., B. J. Varndell and G. J. Westner 1979. Some geological aspects of the Perseverance nickel deposit, Rhodesia. In *A symposium on mineral deposits and the transportation and deposition of metals*, C. R. Anhaeusser, R. P. Foster and T. Stratten (eds.) 67–98. Special Publication 5, Geological Society of South Africa.

Anderson, T., J. Y. O'Reilly and W. L. Griffin 1984. The trapped fluid phase in upper mantle xenoliths from Victoria, Australia: implications for mantle metasomatism. *Contributions to Mineralogy and Petrology* **88**, 72–85.

Anhaeusser, C. R. 1969. *The stratigraphy, structure and gold mineralization of the Jamestown and Sheba Hills areas of the Barberton Mountain Land.* PhD thesis, University of the Witwatersrand, Johannesburg.

Anhaeusser, C. R. 1976. Archaean metallogeny in Southern Africa. *Economic Geology* **71**, 16–43.

Anhaeusser, C. R. 1981a. The geological evolution of the primitive Earth – evidence from the Barberton Mountain Land. In *Evolution of the Earth's crust.* D. H. Tarling (ed.), 71–108. London: Academic Press.

Anhaeusser, C. R. 1981b. South Africa: the gneiss terrane. In *Precambrian of the Southern Hemisphere*, D. R. Hunter (ed.), 424–53. Amsterdam: Elsevier.

REFERENCES

Anhaeusser, C. R. 1984. Structural elements of Archaean granite–greenstone terrains as exemplified by the Barberton Mountain Land, Southern Africa. *Precambrian tectonics illustrated.* In A. Kröner and R. Greiling (eds.), 57–78. Stuttgart: Schweizerbart.

Anhaeusser, C. R. 1985. Archaean layered ultramafic complexes in the Barberton Mountain Land, South Africa. In *Evolution of Archaean supracrustal sequences,* L. D. Ayres, P. C. Thurston, K. D. Card and W. Weber, (eds), 281–301. Geological Association of Canada, Special paper 28.

Anhaeusser, C. R. and L. J. Robb 1981. Magmatic cycles and the evolution of the Archaean granitic crust in the Eastern Transvaal and Swaziland. In *Archaean geology,* J. E. Glover and D. I. Groves (eds.) 457–67. Special Publication 7, Geological Society of Australia.

Archibald, N. J., L. F. Bettenay, M. J. Bickle and D. I. Groves 1981. Evolution of Archaean crust in the Eastern Goldfields Province of the Yilgarn Block, Western Australia. In *Archaean Geology,* J. E. Glover and D. I. Groves (eds.), 491–504. Special Publication 7, Geological Society of Australia.

Arima, M. and R. L. Barnett 1984. Sapphirine-bearing granulites from the Sipiweak Lake area of the late Archaean Pikwitonei granulite terrain, Manitoba, Canada. *Contributions to Mineralogy and Petrology* **88**, 102–12.

Armstrong, R. L. 1968. A model for the evolution of strontium and lead isotopes in a dynamic Earth. *Reviews of Geophysics* **6**, 176–99.

Armstrong, R. L. 1981. Radiogenic isotopes: the case for crustal recycling on a near-steady state no-continent-growth Earth. *Philosophical Transactions of the Royal Society,* London, series A, **301**, 443–72.

Arndt, N. T. 1977a. Thick, layered peridotite–gabbro lava flows in Munro Township. *Canadian Journal of Earth Science* **14**, 2620–37.

Arndt, N. T. 1977b. Mineralogical and chemical variation in two thick, layered komatiitic lava flows, *Carnegie Institution of Washington Yearbook* **76**, 494–501.

Arndt, N. T. 1977c. Ultrabasic magmas and high degree melting of the mantle. *Contributions to Mineralogy and Petrology* **64**, 205–21.

Arndt, N. T. 1983. Role of a thin, komatiite-rich oceanic crust in the Archaean plate-tectonic process, *Geology* **4**, 372–5.

Arndt, N. T. and G. A. Jenner 1985. Kambalda komatiites and basalts: evidence for subduction sediments in the Archaean mantle, *Terra Cognita* **5**, 206.

Arndt, N. T. and R. W. Nesbitt 1982. Geochemistry of Munro Township basalts. In *Komatiites,* N. T. Arndt and E. G. Nisbet (eds.), 309–30. London: Allen & Unwin.

Arndt, N. T. and R. W. Nesbitt 1984. Magma mixing in komatiitic lavas from Munro Township, Ontario, In *Archaean geochemistry,* A. Kröner, G. N. Hanson and A. M. Goodwin (eds.) 99–114. Berlin: Springer.

Arndt, N. T. and E. G. Nisbet 1982. What is a komatiite? In *Komatiites,* N. T. Arndt and E. G. Nisbet (eds.), 19–27. London: Allen & Unwin.

Arndt, N. T., A. Naldrett and D. R. Pyke 1977. Komatiitic and iron-rich tholeiitic lavas of Munro Township, northeast Ontario. *Journal of Petrology,* **18**, 319–69.

Arnórsson, S. 1985. Gas pressures in geothermal systems. *Chemical Geology,* **49**, 319–28.

Arnórsson, S., S. Sigurdsson and H. Svavasson 1982. The chemistry of geothermal waters in Iceland I. Calculation of aqueous speciation from 0 to 370°C. *Geochimica et Cosmochimica Acta* **46**, 1513–32.

Arnórsson, S., E. Gunnlaugsson and H. Svavasson 1983. The chemistry of geothermal waters in Iceland II. Mineral equilibria and independent variables controlling water compositions. *Geochimica et Cosmochimica Acta* **47**, 547–66.

Arnórsson, S., E. Gunnlaugsson and H. Svavasson 1983. The chemistry of geothermal waters in Iceland III. Chemical geothermometry in geothermal investigations. *Geochimica et Cosmochimica Acta* **47**, 567–77.

REFERENCES

Arth, J. G., N. T. Arndt, and A. J. Naldrett 1977. Genesis of Archaean komatiites: trace element evidence from Munro Township, Ontario. *Geology* 5, 590–4.
Augustine of Hippo, St. 398. Confessions: Commentary on Genesis.
Awramik, S. M., J. W. Schopf and M. R. Walter 1983. Filamentous fossil bacteria from the Archaean of western Australia. *Precambrian Research* 20, 357–74.
Ayres, L. D. and P. C. Thurston 1985. Archaean supracrustal sequences in the Canadian Shield: an overview. In *Evolution of Archaean supracrustal sequences*, L. D. Ayres, P. C. Thurston, K. D. Card and W. Weber (eds.), 343–80. Geological Association of Canada, Special Paper 28.

Barghoorn, E. S. 1971, reprinted 1978. The oldest fossils. *Scientific American* (May 1971); reprinted in *Life: origin and evolution*, C. E. Folsome (ed.), 66–78. New York: W. H. Freeman.
Barley, M. E. 1981. Relations between volcanic rocks in the Warrawoona Group: continuous or cyclic evolution? In *Archaean geology*, J. E. Glover and D. I. Groves (eds.), 263–73. Special Publication 7, Geological Society of Australia.
Barley, M. E. and M. J. Bickle 1982. Komatiites in the Pilbara Block, Western Australia. In *Komatiites*, N. T. Arndt and E. G. Nisbet, (eds.), 105–16. London: Allen & Unwin.
Barley, M. E. and J. R. de Laeter 1984. Disturbed Rb–Sr systems of the Archaean Duffer Formation, Eastern Pilbara Block, Western Australia. *Journal of the Royal Society of Western Australia* 66, 129–34.
Barley, M. E., J. S. R. Dunlop, J. E. Glover and D. I. Groves 1979. Sedimentary evidence for an Archaean shallow-water volcanic-sedimentary facies, eastern Pilbara Block, Western Australia. *Earth and Planetary Science Letters* 43, 74–84.
Barley, M. E., G. C. Sylvester, D. I. Groves, G. D. Barley and N. Rogers 1984. Archaean calc-alkaline volcanism in the Pilbara Block, Australia. *Precambrian Research* 24, 285–321.
Barnes, S. J. 1982. Investigations of the Stillwater Pt/Pd horizon. Minneapolis adit area: stratigraphic relations, geochemistry and genesis. In *Workshop on magmatic processes of early planetary crusts: magma oceans and stratiform layered intrusions*, D. Walker and I. S. McCallum (eds.), 45–8. Lunar and Planetary Institute Technical Report, 82-01.
Barnes, S. J. and A. J. Naldrett 1985. Geochemistry of the J-M (Howland) Reef of the Stillwater Complex, Minneapolis Adit area: 1. Sulphide chemistry and sulphide-olivine equilibria. *Economic Geology* 80, 627–45.
Bartley, M. W. 1940. Iron deposits of the Steep Rock Lake area. *Ontario Department of Mines* 48, 35–47.
Barton, J. M. 1981. The pattern of Archaean crustal evolution in southern Africa as deduced from the evolution of the Limpopo Mobile Belt and the Barberton granite–greenstone terrain. In *Archaean geology*, J. E. Glover and D. I. Groves (eds.), 21–32. Special Publication 7, Geological Society of Australia.
Barton, J. M. and R. M. Key 1981. The tectonic development of the Limpopo Mobile Belt and the evolution of the Archaean cratons of southern Africa. In *Precambrian plate tectonics*, A. Kröner (ed.), 185–212. Amsterdam: Elsevier.
Beaty, D. W. and H. P. Taylor Jr. 1982. The oxygen isotope geochemistry of komatiites: evidence for water–rock interaction. In *Komatiites*, N. T. Arndt and E. G. Nisbet (eds.) 267–80. London: Allen & Unwin.
Belay, N., R. Sparling and L. Daniels 1984. Dinitrogen fixation by a thermophilic methanogenic bacterium. *Nature* 312, 286–8.
Ben-Othman, D., M. Polve and C. J. Allègre 1984. Nd–Sr isotopic composition of granulites and constraints on the evolution of the lower continental crust. *Nature*, 307, 510–15.
Bernal, J. D. 1951. *The physical basis of life*. London: Routledge and Kegan Paul.
Bernal, J. D. 1967. *The origin of life*, London: Weidenfeld & Nicolson.

Bernasconi, A. 1983. The Archaean terrains of central eastern Brazil: a review. *Precambrian Research* **23**, 107–32.

Berry, W. B. N. and P. Wilde 1983. Evolutionary and geologic consequences of organic carbon fixing in the primitive anoxic ocean. *Geology* **11**, 141–5.

Bettenay, L. F., M. J. Bickle, C. A. Boulter, D. I. Groves, P. Morant, T. S. Blake and B. A. James 1981. Evolution of the Shaw Batholith – an Archaean granitoid–gneiss dome in the eastern Pilbara, Western Australia. In *Archaean geology*, J. E. Glover and D. I. Groves (eds.), 361–72. Special Publication 7, Geological Society of Australia.

Bickle, M. J. 1978. Heat loss from the earth: a constraint on Archaean tectonics from the relation between geothermal gradients and the rate of plate production. *Earth and Planetary Science Letters* **40**, 301–15.

Bickle, M. J. 1982. The magnesium contents of komatiitic liquids. In *Komatiites*, N. T. Arndt and E. G. Nisbet (eds.), 479–94. London: Allen & Unwin.

Bickle, M. J. 1984a. Suspect Sm–Nd whole-rock ages. *Nature* **312**, 702–3.

Bickle, M. J. 1984b. Growth of the continental crust and lithosphere through early Earth history. *Terra Cognita* **4**, 80.

Bickle, M. J. 1986. Global thermal histories. *Nature* **319**, 13–14.

Bickle, M. J. and N. J. Archibald 1984. Chloritoid and staurolite stability: implications for metamorphism in the Archaean Yilgarn Block, Western Australia. *Journal of Metamorphic Geology* **2**, 179–203.

Bickle, M. J. and K. Eriksson 1982. Evolution and subsidence of early Precambrian sedimentary basins. *Philosophical Transactions of the Royal Society, London* Series A, **305**, 225–47.

Bickle, M. J., C. E. Ford and E. G. Nisbet 1977. The petrogenesis of peridotite komatiites: evidence from high-pressure melting experiments. *Earth and Planetary Science Letters* **37**, 97–106.

Bickle, M. J., A. Martin and E. G. Nisbet 1975. Basaltic and peridotitic komatiites, stromatolites and a basal unconformity in the Belingwe greenstone belt, Rhodesia. *Earth and Planetary Science Letters* **27**, 155–62.

Bickle, M. J., L. F. Bettenay, M. E. Barley, H. J. Chapman, D. I. Groves, I. H. Campbell and J. R. DeLaeter 1983. A 3500-Ma plutonic and volcanic calc-alkaline province in the Archaean East Pilbara Block. *Contributions to Mineralogy and Petrology* **84**, 25–35.

Bickle, M. J., L. F. Bettenay, C. A. Boulter, D. I. Groves and P. Morant 1980. Horizontal tectonic interactions of an Archaean gneiss belt and greenstones, Pilbara Block, Western Australia. *Geology* **8**, 525–9.

Bickle, M. J., C. J. Hawkesworth, A. Martin, E. G. Nisbet and R. K. O'Nions 1976. Mantle composition derived from the chemistry of ultramafic lavas. *Nature* **263**, 577–80.

Bickle, M. J., P. Morant, L. F. Bettenay, C. F. Boulter, T. S. Blake and D. I. Groves 1985. Archaean tectonics of the Shaw Batholith, Pilbara Block, Western Australia: structural and metamorphic tests of the batholith concept. In *Evolution of Archaean supracrustal sequences* L. D. Ayres, P. C. Thurston, K. D. Card and W. Weber (eds.), 325–41. Geological Association of Canada, Special Paper 28.

Bisschoff, A. A. 1972. Tholeiitic intrusion in the Vredefort dome. *Transactions of the Geological Society of South Africa* **75**, 23–34.

Bisschoff, A. A. 1982. Thermal metamorphism of the Vredefort dome. *Transactions of the Geological Society of South Africa* **85**, 43–59.

Black, L. P., I. S. Williams and W. Compston 1986. Four zircon ages from one rock: the history of a 3930 Ma old granulite from mt. Sones, Enderby Land, Antarctica. *Contributions to Mineralogy and Petrology*, **94**, 427–37.

Black, P. R. and L. W. Braile 1982. P_n velocity and cooling of the continental lithosphere. *Journal of Geophysical Research* **87**, 10557–69.

Blake, T. S. 1984a. The Lower Fortescue Group of the Northern Pilbara craton: stratigraphy and palaeogeography. In *Archaean and Proterozoic basins of the Pilbara, Western Australia*, J. R. Muhling, D. I. Groves and T. S. Blake (eds.) 123–43. University of Western Australia, Geology Department and University Extension, Publication 9.

Blake, T. S. 1984b. Evidence for stabilization of the Pilbara Block, Australia, *Nature* **307**, 721–3.

Blake, T. S. and N. J. McNaughton 1984. A geochronological framework for the Pilbara region. In *Archaean and Proterozoic basins of the Pilbara, Western Australia*, J. R. Muhling, D. I. Groves and T. S. Blake (eds.), 1–22. University of Western Australia, Geology Department and University Extension, Publication 9.

Boak, J. L. and R. F. Dymek 1982. Metamorphism of the *ca.* 3800-Ma supracrustal rocks at Isua, West Greenland: implications for early Archaean crustal evolution. *Earth and Planetary Science Letters* **59**, 155–76.

Bodmer, W. F. 1983. Gene clusters and genome evolution. In *Evolution from molecules to men*, D. S. Bendall (ed.), 197–208. Cambridge: Cambridge University Press.

Bowen, N. L. 1938. Mente et Malleo atque catino. *American Mineralogist* **23**, 128–30.

Bowers, T. S., K. L. von Damm and J. M. Edmond 1985. Chemical evolution of mid-ocean ridge hot springs. *Geochimica et Cosmochimica Acta* **49**, 2239–52.

Boyd, F. R., J. J. Gurney and S. H. Richardson 1985. Evidence for a 150–200-km thick Archaean lithosphere from diamond inclusion thermobarometry. *Nature* **315**, 387–9.

Bridgwater, D. and K. D. Collerson 1977. On the origin of early Archaean gneisses: a reply. *Contributions to Mineralogy and Petrology* **62**, 179–91.

Bridgwater, D., K. D. Collerson and J. S. Meyers 1978. The development of the Archaean gneiss complex of the North Atlantic region. In *Evolution of the Earth's crust*, D. H. Tarling (ed.), 19–70. London: Academic Press.

Bridgwater, D., J. H. Allaart, J. W. Schopf, C. Klein, M. R. Walter, E. S. Barghoorn, P. Strother, A. H. Knoll and B. E. Gorman 1981. Microfossil-like objects from the Archaean of Greenland: a cautionary note. *Nature* **289**, 51–3.

Broderick, T. J. 1979. *Explanation of the geological map of the country south of Nuanetsi, Nuanetsi and Beitbridge districts*. Rhodesia Geological Survey Short Report No. 46.

Brooks, C. and S. R. Hart 1974. On the significance of komatiite. *Geology* **2**, 107–10.

Brown, M., C. R. L. Friend, V. R. McGregor and W. T. Perkins 1981. The late Archaean Qôrqut granite complex of southern west Greenland. *Journal of Geophysical Research* **86**, 10617–52.

Bruce, E. L. 1926. *Geology of McArthur, Bartlett, Douglas and Geikie Townships (Redstone River area), District of Timiskaming*. Ontario Dept. Mines, Annual Report 35 (6), 37–56.

Buchanan, D. L. and M. J. Jones 1984. *Sulphide deposits in mafic and ultramafic rocks. Proceedings of IGCP Projects 161 and 91*, Institute of Mining and Metallurgy, London.

Buck, S. G. and W. E. L. Minter 1985. Placer formation by fluvial degradation of an alluvial fan sequence: the Proterozoic Carbon Leader placer, Witwatersrand Supergroup, South Africa. *Journal of the Geological Society* **142**, 757–64.

Buick, R. 1984. Carbonaceous filaments from North Pole, Western Australia: are they fossil bacteria in Archaean stromatolites? *Precambrian Research* **24**, 157–72.

Buick, R. and K. R. Barnes 1984. Cherts in the Warrawoona Group: Early Archaean silicified sediments deposited in shallow water environments. In *Archaean and Proterozoic basins of the Pilbara, Western Australia*, J. R. Muhling, D. I. Groves and T. S. Blake (eds.), 37–53. University of Western Australia, Geology Department and University Extension, Publication 9.

Buick, R., J. S. R. Dunlop and D. I. Groves 1981. Stromatolite recognition in ancient rocks: an appraisal of irregularly laminated structures in an early Archaean chert–barite unit from North Pole, Western Australia. *Alcheringa* **5**, 161–81.

Bullard, Sir. E. Crisp 1950. The transfer of heat from the core of the Earth. *Monthly Notices of the Royal Astronomical Society, Geophysical Supplement* **6**, 36.

Burrows, D. R., P. C. Wood and E. T. C. Spooner 1986. Carbon isotope evidence for a magmatic origin for Archaean gold-quartz vein ore deposits. *Nature* **321**, 851–4.

Button, A. 1976. Transvaal and Hamersley basins – review of basin development and mineral deposits. *Minerals, Science and Engineering* **8**, 262–93.

Button, A. 1981. The Pongola Group. In *Precambrian of the Southern Hemisphere*, D. R. Hunter (ed.), 501–10. Amsterdam: Elsevier.

Button, A., D. A. Pretorius, H. Jansen, V. Stockmayer, D. R. Hunter, J. T. Wilson, A. H. Wilson, C. F. Vermark, C. A. Lee and J. G. Stagman 1981. The cratonic environment. In *Precambrian of the Southern Hemisphere*, D. R. Hunter (ed.), 501–639. Amsterdam: Elsevier.

Byerly, G. R. and D. R. Lowe 1986. Barberton greenstone belt volcanism: succession, style and petrogenesis. Abstracts, *workshop on the tectonic evolution of greenstone belts*. 14–16. Houston: Lunar and Planetary Institute.

Byerly, G. R., D. R. Lowe and M. M. Walsh 1986. Stromatolites from the 3300–3500 Myr Swaziland Supergroup, Barberton Mountain Land, South Africa. *Nature*, **319**, 489–491.

Cairns-Smith, A. G. 1978. Precambrian solution geochemistry, inverse segregation and banded iron formations. *Nature* **148**, 27–35.

Cairns-Smith, A. G. 1982. *Genetic takeover and the mineral origins of life*. Cambridge: Cambridge University Press.

Cameron, E. M. and K. Hattori 1985. The Hemlo gold deposit, Onatrio: a geochemical and isotopic study. *Geochimica et Cosmochimica Acta* **49**, 2041–50.

Cameron, W. E. and E. G. Nisbet 1982. Phanerozic analogues of komatiitic basalts. In *Komatiites*, N. T. Arndt and E. G. Nisbet (eds.), 29–50. London: George Allen & Unwin.

Campbell, I. H. 1985. The difference between oceanic and continental tholeiites: a fluid dynamics explanation. *Contributions to Mineralogy and Petrology* **91**, 37–43.

Campbell, I. H. and G. T. Jarvis 1984. Mantle convection and early crustal evolution. *Precambrian Research* **26**, 15–56.

Campbell, I. H. and S. R. Taylor 1983. No water, no granites – no oceans, no continents. *Geophysical Research Letters* **10**, 1061–4.

Cann, R. L., M. Stoneking and A. C. Wilson 1987. Mitochondrial DNA and human evolution. Nature **325**, 31–6.

Carslaw, H. S. and J. C. Jaeger 1959. *Conduction of heat in solids*, 2nd edn. Oxford: Clarendon Press.

Cattell, A., T. E. Krogh and N. T. Arndt 1984. Conflicting Sm–Nd whole rock and U–Pb zircon ages for Archaean lavas from Newton Township, Abitibi Belt, Ontario. *Earth and Planetary Science Letters* **70**, 280–90.

Chase, C. G. and E. C. Perry 1972. The oceans: growth and oxygen isotope evolution. *Science* **177**, 992–4.

Chauvel, C., B. Dupré, N. T. Arndt and G. A. Jenner 1985. Isotopic heterogeneities in Archaean Greenstone belts. *Terra Cognita* **5**, 206.

Chauvel, C., B. Dupré, W. Todt, N. T. Arndt and A. W. Hoffman 1983. Pb and Nd isotopic correlation in Archaean and Proterozoic Greenstone Belts. *EOS* **64**, 330.

Chinner, G. A. and T. R. Sweatman 1968. A former association of enstatite and kyanite. *Mineralogical Magazine* **36**, 1052–60.

Christensen, U. R. 1984a. Heat transport by variable viscosity convection and implications for the Earth's thermal evolution. *Physics of the Earth and Planetary Interiors* **35**, 264–82.

Christensen, U. R. 1984b. Convection with pressure and temperature dependent non-Newtonian rheology. *Geophysical Journal of the Royal Astronomical Society* **77**, 343–84.

366

REFERENCES

Christensen, U. R. 1984c. Instability of a hot boundary layer and initiation of thermo-chemical plumes. *Annales Geophysicae* **2**, 311–20.

Christensen, U. R. 1985a. Heat transport by variable viscosity convection. II: Pressure influence, non-Newtonian rheology and decaying heat sources. *Physics of the Earth and Planetary Interiors* **37**, 183–205.

Christensen, U. R. 1985b. Evolution models based on variable viscosity convection. *Terra Cognita* **5**, 203–4.

Claoue-Long, J. C., M. F. Thirlwall and R. W. Nesbitt 1984. Revised Sm–Nd systematics of Kambalda greenstones, Western Australia. *Nature* **307**, 697–701.

Cloud, P. C. 1942. Notes on stromatolites. *American Journal of Science* **240**, 363–79.

Cloud, P. C., Jr. 1983. The biosphere. *Scientific American* **249**(3), 176–89.

Cloud, P. C. 1983b. Banded iron formation – a gradualist's dilemma. In *Iron formation: facts and problems*, A. F. Trendall and R. C. Morris (eds.), 401–16. Amsterdam: Elsevier.

Cloud, P. C. Jr. and K. Morrison 1979. On microbial contaminants, micropseudofossils, and the oldest records of life. *Precambrian Research* **9**, 81–91.

Coad, P. R. 1979. Nickel sulphide deposits associated with ultramafic rocks of the Abitibi belt and economic potential of mafic–ultramafic intrusions. *Ontario Geological Survey Study* **20**.

Cocker, J. D., B. J. Griffin and K. Muehlenbachs 1982. Oxygen and carbon isotope evidence for seawater–hydrothermal alteration of the Macquarie Island ophiolite. *Earth and Planetary Science Letters* **61**, 112–22.

Colvine, A. C. (ed.) 1983. The geology of gold in Ontario. *Ontario Geological Survey Miscellaneous Paper* 110.

Compston, W. and R. T. Pidgeon 1986. Jack Hills, evidence of more very old detrital zircons in Western Australia. *Nature* **321**, 766–9.

Compston, W., I. S. Williams, M. T. McCulloch, J. J. Foster, P. A. Arriens and A. F. Trendall 1981. A revised age for the Hamersley Group. *Geological Society of Australia Abstracts* **3**, 40.

Condie, K. C. 1981. *Archaean greenstone belts*. Amsterdam: Elsevier.

Conn, H. K. 1979. The Johns–Mannville platinum-palladium prospect, Stillwater Complex, Montana, USA. *Canadian Mineralogist* **17**, 463–8.

Cook, F. A. 1985. Geometry of the Kapuskasing structure from a Lithoprobe pilot reflection survey. *Geology* **13**, 368–71.

Cooke, D. L. and W. W. Moorhouse 1969. Timiskaming volcanism in the Kirkland Lake area, Ontario, Canada. *Canadian Journal of Earth Sciences* **6**, 117–32.

Corliss, J. B., J. A. Baross and S. E. Hoffman 1981. An hypothesis concerning the relationship between submarine hot springs and the origin of life on Earth. *Oceanologica Acta*, No. S.P. Proceedings of the 26th International Geological Congress, Paris, 1980, 59–69.

Cotterill, P. 1969. The chromitite deposits of Selukwe, Rhodesia. *Economic Geology Monograph* **4**, 154–86.

Cotterill, P. 1976. *The geology of the chromitite deposits, Selukwe, Rhodesia*. PhD thesis, University of London.

Cotterill, P. 1979. The Selukwe schist belt and its chromitite deposits. In *A symposium on mineral deposits and the transportation and deposition of metals*, C. R. Anhaeusser, R. P. Foster and T. Stratten (eds.). 229–46. Special Publication 5, Geological Society of South Africa.

Coward, M. P. 1984. Major shear zones in the Precambrian crust; examples from N. W. Scotland and Southern Africa and their significance. In *Precambrian tectonics illustrated*, A. Kröner and R. Greiling (eds.), 207–35. Stuttgart: Schweizerbart.

Coward, M. P. and M. C. Daly 1984. Crustal lineaments and shear zones in Africa: their relationship to plate movements. *Precambrian Research* **24**, 27–45.

Coward, M. P. and J. P. Fairhead 1980. Gravity and structural evidence for the deep structure of the Limpopo Belt, Southern Africa. *Tectonophysics* **68**, 31–43.

Coward, M. P., P. R. James and L. Wright 1976. Northern margin of the Limpopo mobile belt, Southern Africa. *Bulletin of the Geological Society of America* **87**, 601–11.

Crick, F. H. C. 1958. On protein synthesis. *Symposium of the Society for Experimental Biology (1957)* **12**, 138–63.

Crick, F. H. C. 1981. *Life itself: its origin and nature*. New York: Simon and Schuster, Touchstone.

Crick, F. H. C. and L. E. Orgel 1973. Directed panspermia. *Icarus* **19**, 341–6.

Dahlen, F. A. 1981. Isostasy and the ambient state of stress in the oceanic lithosphere. *Journal of Geophysical Research* **86**, 7801–7.

Darnell, J. E., Jr. 1983. The processing of RNA. *Scientific American* 249(4), 90–101.

Darwin, C., 1959. Some unpublished letters (1871) ed. Sir Gavin de Beer, Notes and Records of the Royal Society, London, 14, 1.

Davies, G. F. 1980. Thermal histories of convective earth models and constraints on radiogenic heat production in the earth. *Journal of Geophysical Research* **85**, 2517–30.

Davis, D. W. and G. R. Edwards 1982. Zircon U–Pb ages from the Kakagi Lake area, Wabigoon Subprovince, northwest Ontario. *Canadian Journal of Earth Sciences* **19**, 1235–45.

Dayhoff, M. O. 1983. Evolutionary connections of biological kingdoms based on protein and nucleic acid sequence evidence. In *Developments and interactions of the Precambrian atmosphere, lithosphere and biosphere*, B. Nagy, R. Weber, J. C. Guerrero and M. Schidlowski (eds.), 191–210. Amsterdam: Elsevier. (Reprinted from *Precambrian Research* **20**, 299–318.)

Delbrück, M. 1986. *Mind over matter*. Oxford: Blackwell.

DePaolo, D. J. 1981. Nd isotopic studies: some new perspectives on Earth structure and evolution. *EOS* **62**, 137–40.

DePaolo, D. J. 1983. The mean life of continents: estimates of continent recycling rates from Nd and Hf isotopic data and implications for mantle structure. *Geophysical Research Letters* **10**, 705–708.

DePaolo, D. J. and G. J. Wasserburg 1976. Nd isotopic variations and petrogenetic models. *Geophysical Research Letters* **3**, 249–52.

DePaolo, D. J. and G. J. Wasserburg 1979. Sm–Nd age of the Stillwater Complex and the mantle evolution curve for neodymium. *Geochimica et Cosmochimica Acta* **43**, 999–1008.

de Wit, M. J. 1982. Sliding and overthurst nappe tectonics in the Barberton greenstone belt. *Journal of Structural Geology* **4**, 117–36.

de Wit, M. J. 1983. *Notes on a preliminary 1 : 25,000 geological map of the southern part of the Barberton Greenstone Belt*. Special Publication of the Geological Society of South Africa **9**, 185–7.

de Wit, M. J., R. E. P. Fripp and I. G. Stanistreet 1983. *Tectonic and stratigraphic implications of new field observations along the southern part of the Barberton Greenstone Belt*. Special Publication of the Geological Society of South Africa **9**, 21–9.

de Wit, M. J., and R. Hart 1986. A mid-Archaean ophiolite complex, Barberton Mountain Land. Abstracts, *Workshop on the tectonic evolution of greenstone belts*, Lunar and Planetary Science Institute, Houston, 27–9.

de Wit, M. J., R. Hart and R. Hart, A. Martin and P. Abbott 1982. Archaean abiogenic and probable biogenic structures associated with mineralized hydrothermal vent systems and regional metasomatism, with implications for greenstone belt studies. *Economic Geology* **77**, 1783–802.

de Wit, M. J., R. Hart, C. Stern and C. M. Barton 1980. Metallogenesis related to seawater interaction with 3.5 by oceanic crust. *EOS* **61**, 386.

des Marais, D. J. 1980. The organic geochemical record in ancient sediments and the early evolution of Life – a short summary. In *The origins of life and evolution*, H. O. Halvorson and K. E. van Holde (eds.), 19–30. New York: Alan R. Liss.

Dickey, J. S. 1972. A primary peridotite magma revisited: olivine quench crystals in a peridotite lava. *Geological Society of America Memoir* **132**, 289–97.

Dimroth, E., L. Imreh, M. Rocheleau and N. Goulet 1982. Evolution of the south central part of the Archaean Abitibi Belt, Quebec. Part 1: Stratigraphy and palaeogeographic model. *Canadian Journal of Earth Sciences* **19**, 1729–59.

Dimroth, E., L. Imreh, P. Cousineau, M. Leduc and Y. Sanschagrin, 1985. Palaeogeographic analysis of mafic submarine flows and its use in the exploration for massive sulphide deposits. In *Evolution of Archaean supracrustal sequences*, L. D. Ayres, P. C. Thurston, K. D. Card and W. Weber (eds.), 203–22. Geological Association of Canada, Special Paper 28.

Dodson, M. A. 1973. Closure temperature in cooling geochronological and petrological systems. *Contributions to Mineralogical Petrology* **40**, 259–74.

Donahue, T. M., J. H. Hoffman, R. R. Hodges, Jr. and A. J. Watson 1982. Venus was wet: a measurement of the ratio of deuterium to hydrogen. *Science* **216**, 630–3.

Donaldson, C. H. 1982. Spinifex-textured komatiites: a review of textures, mineral compositions and layering. In *Komatiites*, N. T. Arndt and E. G. Nisbet (eds.), 213–44. London: Allen & Unwin.

Downes, M. J., D. J. Hodges and J. Derweduwen 1984. A free carbon and carbonate-bearing alteration zone association with the Hoyle Pond gold occurence, Ontario, Canada. In *Gold '82*, R. P. Foster (ed.), 435–48. Geological Society of Zimbabwe, Special Publication 1, Rotterdam: Balkema.

Drury, S. A., N. B. W. Harris, R. W. Holt, G. J. Reeves-Smith and R. T. Wightman 1984. Precambrian tectonics and crustal evolution in South India. *The Journal of Geology* **92**, 3–20.

Duke, J. M. and A. J. Naldrett 1978. A numerical model of the fractionation of olivine and molten sulfide from komatiitic magma. *Earth and Planetary Science Letters* **39**, 255–66.

Dunlop, J. S. R. and R. Buick 1981. Archaean epiclastic sediments derived, from mafic volcanoes, North Pole, Pilbara Block, Western Australia. In *Archaean geology*, J. E. Glover and D. I. Groves (eds.), 225–34. Special Publication 7, Geological Society of Australia.

Dupré, B., C. Chauvel and N. T. Arndt 1984. Pb and Nd isotopic study of two Archaean komatiitic lava flows from Alexo, Ontario. *Geochimica et Cosmochimica Acta* **48**, 1965–72.

Easton, R. M. 1985. The nature and significance of pre-Yellowknife Supergroup rocks in the Point Lake area, Slave Structural Province, Canada. In *Evolution of Archaean supracrustal sequences*, L. D. Ayres, P. C. Thurston, K. D. Card and W. Weber (eds.), pp. 153–67. Geological Association of Canada, Special Paper 28.

Edmonds, J. M. and K. von Damm 1983. Hot springs on the ocean floor. *Scientific American* **248** (4), 78–93.

Eggler, D. H. 1983. Upper mantle oxidation state: evidence from olivine–orthopyroxene–ilmenite assemblages. *Geophysical Research Letters* **10**, 365–8.

Elder, J. 1976. *The bowels of the Earth*. London: Oxford University Press.

Ellis, D. J. 1980. Osumilite–sapphirine–quartz granulites from Enderby Land, Antarctica: P–T conditions of metamorphism, implications of garnet–cordierite equilibria and the evolution of the deep crust. *Contributions to Mineralogy and Petrology* **72**, 123–43.

Ellis, D. J. and D. H. Green 1985. Garnet-forming reactions in mafic granulites from Enderby

369

Land, Antarctica – implication for geothermometry and geobarometry. *Journal of Petrology* **26**, 633–62.

Elthon, D. 1986. Komatiite genesis in the Archaean mantle, with implications for the tectonics of Archaean greenstone belts. In *The tectonic evolution of greenstone belts*, Lunar and Planetary Institute, Houston Workshop, 36–8.

England, P. C. and M. J. Bickle 1984. Continental thermal and tectonic regimes during the Archaean. *Journal of Geology* **92**, 353–68.

England, P. C. and S. W. Richardson 1977. The influence of erosion upon the mineral facies of rocks from different metamorphic environments. *Journal of the Geological Society of London* **134**, 201–13.

Eriksson, K. A. 1981. Archaean platform-to-trough sedimentation, East Pilbara Block. Australia. In *Archaean Geology*, J. E. Glover and D. I. Groves (eds.), 235–244. Special Publication 7, Geological Society of Australia.

Faure, G. 1977. *Principles of isotope geology*. New York: Wiley.

Feather, C. E. and G. M. Koen 1975. The mineralogy of the Witwatersrand reefs. *Minerals, Science and Engineering* **7**, 189–224.

Fleet, M. E. 1986. Geochemistry of the J-M (Howland) reef of the Stillwater Complex, Minneapolis adit area. 1: Sulfide chemistry and sulfide–olivine equilibrium – a discussion. *Economic Geology* **81**, 199–203 (and reply by S. J. Barnes and A. J. Naldrett 203–6.

Fletcher, I. R., K. J. R. Rosman, I. R. Williams, A. H. Hickman and J. L. Baxter 1984. Sm–Nd geochronology of greenstone belts in the Yilgarn block, Western Australia. *Precambrian Research* **26**, 333–62.

Fletcher, I. R. and K. J. R. Rosman 1982. Precise determination of initial ε_{Nd} from Sm–Nd isochron data. *Geochimica et Cosmochimica Acta* **46**, 1983–7.

Forsyth, D. W. 1977. The evolution of the upper mantle beneath mid-ocean ridges. *Tectonophysics* **38**, 89–118.

Foster, R. P. 1982. Gold in Zimbabwe. *Zimbabwe Science News* **16**, 151–5.

Foster, R. P. (ed.) 1984. *Gold '82: the geology, geochemistry and genesis of gold deposits*. Geological Society of Zimbabwe, Special Publication 1. Rotterdam: Balkema.

Foster, R. P. and J. F. Wilson 1982. Geological setting of Archaean gold deposits in Zimbabwe. In *Gold '82*, R. P. Foster (ed.), 521–52. Geological Society of Zimbabwe, Special Publication 1. Rotterdam: Balkema.

Foster, R. P., F. M. W. Farber, J. M. Gilligan and D. Green 1986. Shamva gold mine, Zimbabwe, A product of calc-alkaline-linked exhalative, volcaniclastic, and epiclastic sedimentation in the late Archaean. In *Turbidite-hosted gold deposits*, J. D. Keppie, R. W. Boyle and S. J. Haynes (eds.), Geological Association of Canada Special Paper.

Fowler, C. M. R. and E. G. Nisbet 1982. The thermal background to metamorphism – II: simple two-dimensional models. *Geoscience Canada* **9**, 208–14.

Fowler, C. M. R. and E. G. Nisbet 1985. The subsidence of the Williston basin. *Canadian Journal of Earth Sciences* **22**, 408–15.

Fox, G. E. 1985. Insights into the phylogenetic positions of photosynthetic bacteria derived from 5S rRNA and 16S rRNA sequence data. In *The global sulfur cycle*, D. Sagan (ed.), 30–39. Washington, DC: NASA Technical Memorandum 87570.

Fox, G. E., E. Stackebrandt, R. B. Hespell, J. Gibson, J. Maniloff, T. A. Dyer, R. S. Wolfe, W. E. Balch, R. S. Tanner, L. J. Magrum, L. B. Zablen, R. Blakemoore, R. Gupta, L. Bonen, B. J. Lewis, D. A. Stahl, K. R. Luehrsen, K. N. Chen, U. T. Cobley and C. R. Woese 1980. The phylogeny of prokaryotes. *Science* **209**, 457–63.

Fox, S. W. and K. Dose 1977. *Molecular evolution and the origin of life*. New York: Dekker.

Friedman, I. and J. R. O'Neil 1977. Compilation of stable isotope fractionation factors of

370

geochemical interest. In *Data of geochemistry*, M. Fleischer (ed.), Geological Survey Paper 440KK. Washington DC: US Government Printing Office, 6th edn.

Friesen, R. G., G. A. Pierce and R. M. Weeks 1982. Geology of the Geco base metal deposit. In *Precambrian sulphide deposits*, R. W. Hutchinson, C. D. Spence and J. M. Franklin (eds.), 343–64. Geological Association of Canada, Special Paper 25.

Froude, D. O., T. R. Ireland, P. D. Kinny, I. S. Williams, W. Compston, I. R. Williams and J. S. Myers 1983. Ion microprobe identification of 4100–4200 Myr-old terrestrial zircons. *Nature* **304**, 616–8.

Fyfe, W. S. 1978. Evolution of the Earth's crust: modern plate tectonics to ancient hot spot tectonics? *Chemical Geology* **23**, 89–114.

Fyfe, W. S. and R. Kerrich 1984. Gold: natural concentration processes. In *Gold '82*, R. P. Foster (ed.), 99–127. Geological Society of Zimbabwe, Special Publication 1. Rotterdam: Balkema.

Fyon, J. A. and J. H. Crocket 1982. Gold exploration in the Timmins district using field and lithogeochemical characteristics of carbonate zones. In *Geology of Canadian gold deposits*, R. W. Hodder and W. Petruk (eds.), 113–29. Canadian Institute of Mining and Metallurgy, Special Volume 24.

Galer, S. J. G. and R. K. O'Nions 1985. Residence time of thorium, uranium and lead in the mantle with implications for mantle convection. *Nature* **316**, 778–82.

Gane, P. G., A. R. Atkins, J. P. F. Sellschop and P. Seligman 1956. Crustal Structure of the Transvaal. *Bulletin of the Seismological Society of America* **46**, 293–316.

Garcia, M. O., N. W. K. Lin and D. W. Muenow 1979. Volatiles in submarine volcanic rocks from the Mariana Island arc and trough. *Geochimica et Cosmochimica Acta* **43**, 305–12.

Gariépy, C., C. J. Allègre and J. Lajoie 1984. U–Pb systematics in single zircons from the Pontiac sediments, Abitibi greenstone belt. *Canadian Journal of Earth Sciences* **21**, 1296–304.

Garrett, R. A. 1985. The uniqueness of archaebacteria. *Nature* **318**, 233–5.

Gast, P. W. 1968. Trace element fractionation and the origin of tholeiitic and alkaline magma types. *Geochimica et Cosmochimica Acta* **32**, 1057–86.

Gélinas, L., J. Lajoie and C. Brooks 1977. The origin and significance of Archaean ultramafic volcaniclastics from Spinifex Ridge, Lamotte Township, Quebec. Geological Association of Canada, Special Publication 16, 8–20.

George, D. G., L. T. Hunt, L. L. Yeh and W. C. Barker 1985. New perspectives on bacterial ferredoxin evolution. *Journal of Molecular Evolution* **22**, 20–31.

Gerlach, T. M. and E. J. Groeber 1985. Volatile budget of Kilauea volcano. *Nature* **313**, 273–4.

Gilbert, W. 1986. The RNA world. *Nature*, **319**, 618.

Glassley, W. E., D. Bridgwater and J. Konnerup-Madsen 1984. Nitrogen in fluids effecting retrogression of granulite facies gneisses: a debateable mantle connection. *Earth and Planetary Science Letters* **70**, 417–25.

Glikson, A. Y. 1979. Early Precambrian tonalite–trondhjemite sialic nuclei. *Earth Science Reviews* **15**, 1–73.

Glikson, A. Y. and B. M. Jahn 1985. REE and LIL elements, Eastern Kaapvaal Shield, South Africa: evidence of crustal evolution by 3-stage melting. In *Evolution of Archaean supracrustal sequences*, L. D. Ayres, P. C. Thurston, K. D. Card and W. Weber (eds.) 303–24. Geological Association of Canada, Special Paper, 28.

Goldstein, S. L., R. K. O'Nions and P. J. Hamilton 1984. A Sm–Nd isotopic study of atmospheric dusts and particulates from major river systems. *Earth and Planetary Science Letters* **70**, 221–36.

REFERENCES

Goodwin, A. M. 1979. Archaean volcanic studies in the Timmins–Kirkland Lake–Noranda region of Ontario and Quebec. *Geological Survey of Canada Bulletin* **278**.

Goodwin, A. M. 1981. Archaean plates and greenstone belts. In *Precambrian plate tectonics*, A. Kroner (ed.). 105–36. Amsterdam: Elsevier.

Goodwin, A. M., H. G. Thode, C.-L. Chou and S. N. Karkhansis 1985. Chemostratigraphy and origin of the late Archaean siderite–pyrite-rich Helen Iron Formation, Michipicoten belt, Canada. *Canadian Journal of Earth Sciences* **22**, 72–84.

Green, A. H. and A. J. Naldrett 1981. The Langmuir volcanic peridotite-associated nickel deposits: Canadian equivalents of the Western Australian occurrences. *Economic Geology* **76**, 1503–23.

Green, D. H. 1975. Genesis of Archaean peridotitic magmas and constraints on Archaean geothermal gradients and tectonics. *Geology* **3**, 15–18.

Green, D. H., I. A. Nicholls, M. J. Viljoen and R. P. Viljoen 1975. Experimental demonstration of the existence of peridotite liquids in earliest Archaean magmatism. *Geology* **3**, 11–14.

Gresham, J. J. and G. D. Loftus-Hills 1981. The geology of the Kambalda nickel field, Western Australia. *Economic Geology* **76**, 1373–416.

Groves, D. I. and W. D. Batt 1984. Spatial and temporal variations of Archaean metallogenic associations in terms of evolution of granitoid–greenstone terrains with particular emphasis on the Western Australian Shield. In *Archaean geochemistry*, A. Kroner, G. N. Hansen and A. M. Goodwin (eds.), 73–98. Berlin: Springer.

Groves, D. I., D. R. Hudson, R. J. Marston and J. R. Ross (eds.) 1981. Special issue on nickel deposits and their host rocks in Western Australia. *Economic Geology* **76**, 1289–783.

Groves, D. I., G. N. Phillips, S. E. Ho and S. M. Houston 1985. The nature, genesis and regional controls of gold mineralisation in Archaean greenstone belts of the Western Australia shield: a brief review. *Transactions of the Geological Society of South Africa* **88**, 135–48.

Groves, D. I., E. A. Korkiakoski, N. J. McNaughton, C. M. Lesher and A. Cowden 1986. Thermal erosion by komatiites at Kambalda, Western Australia and the genesis of nickel ores. *Nature* **319**, 136–9.

Groves, D. I., G. N. Phillips, S. E. Ho, C. A. Henderson, M. E. Clark and G. M. Woud 1984. Controls on distribution of Archaean hydrothermal gold deposits in Western Australia. In *Gold '82*, R. P. Foster, (ed.), 689–712. Geological Society of Zimbabwe, Special Publication 1. Rotterdam: Balkema.

Gupta, R., J. M. Lanter and C. R. Woese 1983. Sequence of the 16S ribosomal RNA from halobacterium volcanii, an archaebacterium. *Science* **221**, 656–9.

Haggerty, S. E. 1986. Diamond genesis in a multiple constrained model. *Nature* **320**, 34–8.

Hall, D. H. and W. C. Brisbin 1982. Overview of regional geophysical studies in Manitoba and northwestern Ontario. *Canadian Journal of Earth Sciences* **19**, 2049–59.

Hallbauer, D. K. 1975. The plant origin of the Witwatersrand 'carbon'. *Minerals, Science and Engineering* **7**, 111–31.

Hallbauer, D. K., H. M Jahns and H. A. Beltmann 1977. Morphological and anatomical observations on some Precambrian plants from the Witwatersrand, South Africa. *Geologische Rundschau* **66**, 477–91.

Hallberg, J. A. and A. Y. Glikson 1981. Archaean granite–greenstone terrains of Western Australia. In *Precambrian of the Southern Hemisphere*, D. R. Hunter (ed.), 33–104. Amsterdam: Elsevier.

Hambrey, M. and W. B. Harland 1981. *Earth's pre-Pleistocene glacial record*. Cambridge: Cambridge University Press.

Hamilton, P. J. 1977. Sr isotope and trace element studies of the Great Dyke and Bushveld mafic phase and their relation to early Proterozoic magma genesis in southern Africa. *Journal of Petrology* **18**, 24–52.

Hamilton, P. J., R. K. O'Nions and N. M. Evensen 1977. Sm–Nd dating of Archaean basic and ultrabasic volcanics. *Earth and Planetary Science Letters* **36**, 263–8.

Hamilton, P. J., R. K. O'Nions, D. Bridgwater and A. Nutman 1983. Sm–Nd studies of Archaean metasediments and metavolcanics from West Greenland and their implications for the Earth's early history. *Earth and Planetary Science Letters* **62**, 263–72.

Hamilton, P. J., N. M. Evensen, R. K. O'Nions, A. Y. Glikson and A. H. Hickman 1981. Sm–Nd dating of the North Star basalt, Warrawona Group, Pilbara Block, Western Australia. In *Archaean Geology*, J. E. Glover and D. I. Groves (eds.), 187–192. Special Publication 7, Geological Society of Australia.

Hamilton, P. J., N. M. Evensen, R. K. O'Nions, H. S. Smith and A. J. Erlank 1979. Nd–Sm dating of Onverwacht volcanics, South Africa. *Nature* **279**, 298–300.

Hamilton, P. J., R. K. O'Nions, N. M. Evensen, D. Bridgwater and J. H. Allaart 1978. Sm–Nd isotopic investigations of the Isua supracrustals, and implications for mantle evolution. *Nature* **272**, 41–3.

Hanes, J. A., York, D. and C. M. Hall 1985. An $^{40}Ar/^{39}Ar$ geochronological and electron microprobe investigation of an Archaean pyroxenite and its bearing on ancient atmospheric conditions. *Canadian Journal of Earth Sciences* **22**, 947–58.

Hansen, E. C., R. C. Newton and A. S. Janardhan 1984. Pressures, temperatures and metamorphic fluids across an unbroken amphibolite facies to granulite facies transition in Southern Karnataka, India. In *Archaean geochemistry* A. Kröner, G. N. Hansen and A. M. Goodwin (eds.), 161–81. Berlin: Springer.

Hargreaves, R. B. 1986. Faster spreading or greater ridge length in the Archaean? *Geology* **14**, 750–52.

Harley, S. L. 1985. Garnet–orthopyroxene bearing granulites from Enderby Land, Antarctica: metamorphic pressure–temperature–time evolution of the Archaean Napier complex. *Journal of Petrology* **26**, 819–56.

Harris, N. B. W. 1985. Metamorphism and evolution of the central zone, Limpopo mobile belt. *Geological Society of London Newsletter* **14**, 40.

Harris, N. B. W. and T. J. B. Holland 1984. The significance of cordierite–hypersthene assemblages from the Beitbridge region of the Central Limpopo belt: evidence for rapid decompression in the Archaean. *American Mineralogist* **69**, 1036–49.

Harris, N. B. W., R. W. Holt and S. A. Drury 1982. Geobarometry, geothermometry and late Archaean geotherms from the granulite facies terrain of South India. *Journal of Geology* **90**, 509–27.

Harrison, N. M. 1968. A reassessment of the stratigraphy of the Precambrian basement complex around Que Que, Gwelo District, Rhodesia. Geological Society of South Africa Annexure to Vol. LXXI, *Symposium on the Rhodesian Basement Complex*, ed. D. J. L. Visser, 113–24.

Harrison, N. M. 1970. The geology of the country around Que Que, Rhodesia. *Geological Survey Bulletin* **67**.

Hart, M. H. 1979. The evolution of the atmosphere of the earth. *Icarus* **33**, 23–39.

Hart, R. J., L. O. Nicolaysen and N. H. Gale 1981. Radioelement concentrations in the deep profile through Precambrian basement of the Vredefort structure. *Journal of Geophysical Research* **86**, 10639–52.

Hart, R. J., H. J. Welke and L. O. Nicolaysen 1981. Geochronology of the deep profile through Archaean basement at Vredefort, with implications for early crustal evolution. *Journal of Geophysical Research* **86**, 10663–80.

Hartle, R. E. and H. A. Taylor 1983. Identification of deuterium ions in the ionosphere of Venus. *Geophysical Research Letters* **10**, 965–8.

Hasegawa, M., Y. Iida, T. Yano, F. Takaiwa and M. Iwabuchi 1985. Phylogenetic relationships among eukaryotic kingdoms inferred from ribosomal RNA sequences. *Journal of Molecular Evolution* **22**, 32–38.

Hawkesworth, C. J. and M. J. Bickle 1976. Rhodesian Rb–Sr geochronology from 3.6–2.0 b.a., a brief review. *20th Annual Report of the Research Institute of African Geology*, (ed). M. P. Howard, University of Leeds, 22–7.

Hawkesworth, C. J. and R. K. O'Nions 1977. The petrogenesis of some Archaean volcanic rocks from Southern Africa. *Journal of Petrology* **18**, 487–519.

Hawkesworth, C. J., S. Moorbath, R. K. O'Nions and J. F. Wilson 1975. Age relationship between greenstone belts and granites in the Rhodesian Archaean craton. *Earth and Planetary Science Letters* **25**, 251–62.

Hawkesworth, C. J., M. J. Bickle, A. R. Gledhill, J. F. Wilson and J. L. Orpen 1979. A 2.9 b.y. event in the Rhodesian Archaean. *Earth and Planetary Science Letters* **43**, 285–7.

Hayes, J. M. 1983. Geochemical evidence bearing on the origin of aerobiosis: a speculative hypothesis. In *Earth's earliest biosphere*, J. W. Schopf (ed.), 290–301. Princeton, NJ: Princeton University Press.

Hayes, J. M., I. R. Kaplan and K. W. Wedeking 1983. Precambrian organic geochemistry, preservation of the record. In *Earth's earliest biosphere*, J. W. Schopf (ed.), 93–104. Princeton, NJ: Princeton University Press.

Hazen, R. M. 1976. Effects of temperature and pressure on the crystal structure of forsterite. *American Mineralogist* **61**, 1280–93.

Hazen, R. M. 1977. Effects of temperature and pressure on the crystal structure of ferromagnesian olivine. *American Mineralogist* **62**, 286–95.

Hegner, E., A. Kröner and A. W. Hofmann 1984. Age and isotope geochemistry of the Archaean Pongola and Ushushwana suites in Swaziland, southern Africa: a case for crustal contamination of mantle-derived magma. *Earth and Planetary Science Letters* **70**, 267–79.

Heinrichs, T. 1984. The Umsoli chert, turbidite testament for a major phreatoplinian event at the Onverwacht/Fig Tree transition (Swaziland Supergroup, Archaean, South Africa). *Precambrian Research* **24**, 237–84.

Helmstaedt, H., W. A. Padgham and J. A. Brophy 1986. Multiple dikes in Lower Kam Group, Yellowknife greenstone belt: evidence for Archaean sea-floor spreading? *Geology* **14**, 562–66.

Henderson, J. B. 1975a. *Sedimentological studies of the Yellowknife Supergroup in the Slave Structural Province*. Geological Survey of Canada, Paper 75–1, A, 325–9.

Henderson, J. B. 1975b. Archaean stromatolites in the nothern Slave Province, Northwest Territories, Canada. *Canadian Journal of Earth Sciences* **12**, 1619–30.

Henderson, J. B. 1981. Archaean Basin evolution in the Slave Province, Canada. In *Precambrian plate tectonics*, A. Kroner (ed.), 213–35. Amsterdam: Elsevier.

Henderson-Sellers, A. 1983. *The origin and evolution of planetary atmospheres*. Bristol: Adam Hilger.

Henderson-Sellers, A. and J. G. Cogley 1982. The Earth's early hydrosphere. *Nature* **298**, 832–5.

Henderson-Sellers, A. and A. W. Schwartz 1980. Chemical evolution and ammonia in the early Earth atmosphere. *Nature* **287**, 526.

Herzberg, C. T. 1983. Solidus and liquidus temperatures and mineralogies for anhydrous garnet–lherzolite to 15 GPa. *Physics of Earth and Planetary Interiors* **32**, 193–202.

Herzberg, C. T. 1984. Chemical stratification in the silicate Earth. *Earth and Planetary Science Letters* **67**, 249–60.

Herzberg, C. T. 1985. Does olivine float in magmas at high pressures? *EOS* **66**, 404.

Herzberg, C. T. and M. J. O'Hara 1985. Origin of mantle peridotite and komatiite by partial melting. *Geophysical Research Letters* **12**, 541–4.

Hess, H. H. 1938. A primary peridotite magma. *American Journal of Science*, Series 5, **35**, 321–44.

Hess, H. H. 1960. *Stillwater igneous complex, Montana: a quantitative mineralogical study.* Geological Society of America, Memoir 80.

Hess, H. H. 1962. History of ocean basins. In *Petrological studies: a volume in honor of A. F. Buddington*, A. E. J. Engel, H. L. James and B. F. Leonard (eds), 599–620. Geological Society of America.

Hickman, A. H. 1981. Crustal evolution of the Pilbara block, Western Australia in *Archaean geology*, J. E. Glover and D. I. Groves (eds.), 57–70. Geological Society of Australia, Special Publication 7.

Hickman, A. H. 1984. Archaean diapirism in the Pilbara block, Western Australia. In *Precambrian tectonics illustrated*, A. Kröner and R. Greiling (eds), 113–27. Stuttgart: E. Schweizerbart'sche Verlagsbuchhandlung.

Hickman, A. H. and S. L. Lipple 1978. *Explanatory notes on the Marble Bar geological sheet.* Geological Survey of Western Australia, Sheet SF50-8, Perth.

Hickman, M. H. 1976. Geochronological investigations in the Limpopo belt and part of the adjacent Rhodesian craton. In *Annual Report*, M. P. Coward, ed., **20**, 30. Research Institute of African Geology, University of Leeds.

Hickman, M. H. 1978. Isotopic evidence for crustal reworking in the Rhodesian Archaean craton, southern Africa, *Geology* **6**, 214–16.

Hinton, R. W. and J. V. P. Long 1979. High resolution ion-microprobe measurement of lead isotopes: variations within single zircons from Lac Seul, Northwestern Ontario. *Earth and Planetary Science Letters* **45**, 309–25.

Ho, S. E., D. I. Groves and G. N. Phillips, 1985. Fluid inclusions as indicators of the nature and source of ore fluids and ore depositional conditions for Archaean gold deposits of the Yilgarn block, Western Australia. *Transactions of the Geological Society of South Africa* **88**, 149–58.

Hodder, R. W. and W. Petruk (eds.) 1982. *Geology of Canadian gold deposits*. Geology Division, Canadian Institute of Mining and Metallurgy, Special Volume 24.

Hodgsen, C. J. and P. J. MacGeehan 1982. Geological characteristics of gold deposits in the Super Province of the Canadian Shield. In *Geology of Canadian gold deposits*, R. W. Hodder and W. Petruk (eds.), 211–32. Canadian Institute of Mining and Metallurgy, Special Volume 24.

Hoffman, P. F. 1986. A simple tectonic model for crustal accretion in the Slave Province: a 2.7–2.5-Ga 'granite–greenstone' terrain, N.W. Canada. Abstracts, *Workshop on the tectonic evolution of Greenstone belts*, Lunar and Planetary Institute, Houston, Supplement, 33.

Hoffman, S. E., M. Wilson and D. S. Stakes 1986. An inferred oxygen isotope profile of Archaean Oceanic Crust, Onverwacht Group, South Africa. *Nature*, **321**, 55–8.

Hofmann, H. J., P. C. Thurston and H. Wallace 1985. Archaean stromatolites from Uchi greenstone belt, northeastern Ontario. In *Evolution of Archaean supracrustal sequences*, L. D. Ayres, P. C. Thurston, K. D. Card and W. Weber (eds.), 125–32. Geological Association of Canada, Special Paper 28.

Hofmeister, A. M. 1983. Effect of a hadean terrestrial magma ocean on crust and mantle evolution. *Journal of Geophysical Research* **88**, 4963–83.

Holm, N. G. 1985. New evidence for a tubular structure of β-iron (III) oxide hydroxide-akaganéite. *Origins of Life* **15**, 131–9.

Holm, N. G., M. J. Dowler, T. Wadsten and G. Arrhenius 1983. β-FeOOH.Cl$_2$ (akaganéite) and Fe$_{1-x}$0 (wustite) in hot brine from the Atlantis II Deep (Red Sea) and the uptake of amino acids by synthetic β-FeOOH.Cl$_2$. *Geochimica et Cosmochimica Acta* **47**, 1465–70.

Holmes, A. 1913. *The age of the earth*. London: Harper and Brothers.

REFERENCES

Holmes, A. 1946. An estimate of the age of the earth. *Nature* **157**, 680–4.

Horrocks, P. C. 1980. Ancient Archaean supracrustal rocks from the Limpopo mobile belt. *Nature* **286**, 596–9.

Hostetler, C. J. 1981. A possible common origin for the rare gases on Venus, Earth and Mars. *Proceedings of the 12th Lunar and Planetary Science Conference*, 1387–93.

Houtermans F. G. 1946. Die isotopenhaufigkeiten in naturlichen blei und das alter des Urans. *Naturwissenschaften* **33**, 185–6, 219.

Huebner, M., T. K. Kyser and E. G. Nisbet 1986. Stable isotope geochemistry of high grade metapelites from the central zone of the Limpopo belt. *American Mineralogist*, **71**, 1343–53.

Hunter, D. R. 1970. The ancient gneiss complex in Swaziland. *Transactions of the Geological Society of South Africa* **73**, 107–50.

Hunter, D. R. (ed.) 1981. *Precambrian of the Southern Hemisphere*. Amsterdam: Elsevier.

Huppert, H. E. and R. S. J. Sparks 1981. The fluid dynamics of a basaltic magma chamber replenished by an influx of hot dense ultrabasic magma. *Contributions to Mineralogy and Petrology* **75**, 279–89.

Huppert, H. E. and R. S. J. Sparks 1985a. Komatiites I: Eruption and flow. *Journal of Petrology* **26**, 694–725.

Huppert, H. E. and R. S. J. Sparks 1985b. Cooling and contamination of mafic and ultramafic magmas during ascent through continental crust. *Earth and Planetary Science Letters* **74**, 371–86.

Huppert, H. E., R. S. J. Sparks, J. S. Turner and N. T. Arndt 1984. Emplacement and cooling of komatiitic lavas. *Nature* **304**, 19–22.

Hurley, P. M. 1968. Absolute abundance and distribution of Rb, K and Sr in the Earth. *Geochimica et Cosmochimica Acta* **32**, 273–84

Hurley, P. M. and J. R. Rand 1969. Pre-drift continental nuclei. *Science* **164**, 1229–42.

Hurley, P. M., H. Hughes, G. Faure, H. W. Fairbairn and W. H. Pinson 1962. Radiogenic [87]Sr model of continental formation. *Journal of Geophysical Research* **67**, 5315–34.

Hutchinson, R. W. 1982. Syn-depositional hydrothermal processes and Precambrian sulphide deposits. In *Precambrian sulphide deposits*, R. W. Hutchinson, C. D. Spence and J. M. Franklin (eds.), 196–255. Geological Association of Canada, Special Paper 25.

Irvine, T. N., D. W. Keith and S. G. Todd 1983. The J-M platinum–palladium reef of the Stillwater Complex, Montana: II. Origin by double-diffusive convective magma mixing and implications for the Bushveld Complex. *Economic Geology* **78**, 1287–334.

Ito, E., D. M. Harris and A. T. Anderson 1983. Alteration of oceanic crust and geologic cycling of chlorine and water. *Geochimica et Cosmochimica Acta* **47**, 1613–24.

Jackson, E. D. 1961. *Primary textures and mineral associations in the ultramafic zone of the Stillwater Complex, Montana*. US Geological Survey Professional Paper 358.

Jackson, M. P. A. 1984. Archaean structural styles in the Ancient Gneiss Complex of Swaziland, Southern Africa. In *Precambrian tectonics illustrated*, A. Kroner and R. Greiling (eds.), 1–18. Stuttgart: Schweizerbart.

Jacob, F. 1983. Molecular tinkering in evolution. In *Evolution from molecules to men*, D. S. Bendall (ed.), 131–44. Cambridge: Cambridge University Press.

Jacobsen, S. B. and G. J. Wasserburg 1979. The mean age of mantle and crustal reservoirs. *Journal of Geophysical Research* **84**, 7411–28.

Jacobsen, S. B. and G. J. Wasserburg 1980. Sm–Nd isotopic evolution of chondrites. *Earth and Planetary Science Letters* **50**, 139–55.

Jacobsen, S. E., J. E. Quick and G. J. Wasserburg 1984. A Nd and Sr isotopic study of the Trinity peridotite: implications for mantle evolution. *Earth and Planetary Science Letters* **68**, 361–78.

376

REFERENCES

Janardhan, A. S., R. C. Newton and E. C. Hansen, 1982. The transformation of amphibolite facies gneiss to charnockite in southern Karnataka and northern Tamil Nadu, India. *Contributions to Mineralogy and Petrology* **79**, 130–49.

Javoy, M., F. Pineau and C. J. Allègre 1982. Carbon geodynamic cycle. *Nature* **300**, 171–3.

Javoy, M., F. Pineau and C. J. Allègre 1983. Reply to J. C. G. Walker. *Nature* **303**, 730–1.

Jeffreys, A. J. 1982. Evolution of globin genes. In *Genome evolution*, G. A. Dover and R. B. Flavell (eds.), 157–76. Systematics Association, Special Volume 20. London: Academic Press.

Jeffreys, A. J., S. Harris, P. A. Barrie, D. Wood, A. Blanchetot and S. M. Adams 1983. Evolution of gene families: globin genes. In *Evolution from molecules to men*, D. S. Bendall (ed.), 175–96. Cambridge: Cambridge University Press.

Jensen, L. S. 1980. Gold mineralisation in the Kirkland Lake – Larder Lake areas. In *Genesis of Archaean volcanic hosted gold deposits*, E. G. Pye and R. G. Roberts (eds). 29–46. Ontario Geological Survey, Miscellaneous Paper 97.

Jolliffe, A. W. 1955. Geology and iron ores of Steep Rock Lake. *Economic Geology* **50**, 373–98.

Jolly, W. T. 1982. Progressive metamorphism of komatiites and related Archaean lavas of the Abitibi area, Canada. In *Komatiites*, N. T. Arndt and E. G. Nisbet (eds.), 247–66. London: Allen & Unwin.

Jones, W. R., J. W. Peoples and A. L. Howland 1960. Igneous and tectonic structures of the Stillwater Complex, Montana. *US Geological Survey Bulletin*, 1071–4.

Kaine, B. P., R. Gupta and C. R. Woese 1983. Putative introns in tRNA genes of prokaryotes. *Proceedings of the US National Academy of Sciences* **80**, 3309–12.

Kalkowsky, E. 1908. Oolith and stromatolith in norddeutschen Buntsandstein. *Zeitschrift Deutsche Geologische Gesellschaft* **60**, 68–125.

Karvinen, W. O. 1982. Geology and evolution of gold deposits, Timmins area, Ontario. In *Geology of Canadian gold deposits*, R. W. Hodder and W. Petruk (eds.), 101–12. Canadian Institute of Mining and Metallurgy, Special Volume 24.

Kasting, J. F., J. B. Pollack and T. P. Ackerman 1984. Response of Earth's atmosphere to increases in solar flux and implications for loss of water from Venus. *Icarus* **57**, 335–55.

Kaula, W. M. 1984. Tectonic contrasts between Venus and Earth. *Geophysical Research Letters* **11**, 35–7.

Keays, R. R. 1982. Palladium and iridium in komatiites and associated rocks: application to petrogenetic problems. In *Komatiites*, N. T. Arndt and E. G. Nisbet (eds.), 435–58. London: Allen & Unwin.

Keays, R. R. 1984. Archaean gold deposits and their source rocks: the upper mantle connection. In *Gold '82*, R. P. Foster (ed.), 17–52. Geological Society of Zimbabwe, Special Publication 1. Rotterdam: Balkema.

Keep, F. E. 1929. The geology of the Shabani mineral belt, Belingwe District. *Southern Rhodesia Geological Survey Bulletin* **12**.

Kerrich, R. and W. S. Fyfe 1981. The gold-carbonate association: source of CO_2 and CO_2-fixation reactions in Archaean lode deposits. *Chemical Geology* **33**, 265–94.

Kerrich, R. and R. W. Hodder 1982. Archaean lode gold and base metal deposits: chemical evidence for metal fractionation into independent hydrothermal reservoirs. In *Geology of Canadian gold deposits*, R. W. Hodder and W. Petruk (eds.), 144–60. Canadian Institute of mining and metallurgy, Special Volume 24.

Kerrich, R. and G. P. Watson 1984. The Macassa mine Archaean lode gold deposit, Kirkland Lake, Ontario: geology, patterns of alteration and hydrothermal regimes. *Economic Geology* **79**, 1104–30.

Kimura, M. 1979. The neutral theory of molecular evolution. *Scientific American* **241**, 98–126.

377

Kimura, M. 1981a. Was globin evolution very rapid in its early stages? A dubious case against the rate-constancy hypothesis. *Journal of Molecular Evolution* **17**, 110–13.

Kimura, M. 1981b. Estimation of evolutionary distances between homologous nucleotide sequences. *Proceedings of the National Academy of Sciences, USA*, **78**, 454–8.

Knechtel, M. M. 1959. Stratigraphy of the Little Rocky Mountains and encircling foothills, Montana. *US Geological Survey Bulletin* **1072-N**, 723–52.

Knoll, A. H. and E. S. Barghoorn 1977. Archaean microfossils showing cell division from the Swaziland System of South Africa. *Science* **198**, 396–8.

Knuckey, M. J., C. D. A. Comba and G. Riverin 1982. Structure, metal zoning and alteration at the Millenbach deposit, Noranda, Quebec. In *Precambrian sulphide deposits*, R. W. Hutchinson, C. D. Spence and J. M. Franklin (eds.), 255–96. Geological Association of Canada, Special Paper 25.

Koeppel, V. H. and R. Saager 1974. Lead isotopic evidence on the detrital origin of Witwatersrand pyrites and its bearing on the provenance of the Witwatersrand gold. *Economic Geology* **69**, 318–31.

Korstgård, J. and I. Ermanovics 1985. Tectonic evolution of the Archaean Hopedale block and the adjacent Makkovik Subprovince, Labrador, Newfoundland. In *Evolution of Archaean supracrustal sequences*, L. D. Ayres, P. C. Thurston, K. D. Card and W. Weber (eds.), 223–38. Geological Association of Canada, Special Paper 28.

Kramers, J. D. 1979. Lead, uranium, strontium, potassium and rubidium in inclusion-bearing and mantle-derived xenoliths from Southern Africa. *Earth and Planetary Science Letters* **42**, 58–70.

Krapez, B. 1984. Sedimentation in a small, fault-bounded basin: the Lalla Rookh sandstone, East Pilbara block. In *Archaean and Proterozoic basins of the Pilbara, Western Australia*, J. R. Muhling, D. I. Groves and T. S. Blake, (eds.), 89–110. University of Western Australia, Geology Department and University Extension, Publication 9.

Kristmansdottir, H. 1982. Alteration in the IRDP drillhole compared with other drill holes in Iceland. *Journal of Geophysical Research* **87**, 6525–31.

Krogh, T. E. 1973. A low contamination method for hydrothermal decomposition of zircon and extraction of U and Pb for isotopic age determinations. *Geochimica et Cosmochimica Acta* **37**, 485–94.

Krogh, T. E. and G. L. Davis 1973. The effect of regional metamorphism on U–Pb systems in zircon and a comparison with Rb–Sr systems in the same whole rock and its constituent minerals. *Carnegie Institute of Washington Yearbook* **72**, 601–10.

Krogh, T. E., N. B. W. Harris and G. L. Davis 1976. Archaean rocks from the eastern Lac Seul region of the English River Gneiss belt, northwestern Ontario, part 2: geochronology. *Canadian Journal of Earth Sciences* **13**, 1212–15.

Kröner, A. 1981 (ed.), *Precambrian plate tectonics*. Amsterdam: Elsevier.

Kröner, A. 1984. Evolution, growth and stabilization of the Precambrian lithosphere. In *Structure and evolution of the continental lithosphere*, H. N. Pollack and J. R. Murthy (eds.), 69–106. Physics and Chemistry of the Earth, vol. 15. Oxford: Pergamon Press.

Lake, J. A. 1986. An alternative to archaebacterial dogma. *Nature* **319**, 626.

Lake, J. A., E. Henderson, M. Oakes and M. W. Clark 1984. Eocytes: a new ribosome structure indicates a kingdom with a close relationship to eucaryotes. *Proceedings of the National Academy of Sciences, USA, Biological Sciences* **81**, 3786–90.

Lamb, S. H. 1984. Structures on the eastern margin of the Archaean Barberton Greenstone belt, northwest Swaziland. In *Precambrian tectonics illustrated*, A. Kröner and R. Greiling (eds.), 19–39. Stuttgart: Schweizerbart.

Langan, R. T. and N. H. Sleep 1982. A kinematic thermal history of the earth's mantle. *Journal of Geophysical Research* **87**, 9225–35.

Langford, F. F. 1955. *Geology of the Geco mine in the Manitouwadge area, District of Thunder Bay, Ontario*, MA thesis, Queen's University, Kingston, Ontario.

Laubscher, D. H. 1963. *The origin and occurrence of chrysotile asbestos and associated rocks in the Shabani and Mashaba areas*. PhD thesis, University of the Witwatersrand, Johannesburg.

Lewis, J. S. and R. G. Prinn 1984. *Planets and their atmospheres*. Orlando Florida: Academic Press.

Light, M. P. R. 1982. The Limpopo mobile belt: a result of continental collision. *Tectonics* 1, 325–42.

Lilly, P. A. 1981. Shock metamorphism in the Vredefort collar: evidence for internal shock sources. *Journal of Geophysical Research* 86, 10689–700.

Lindgren, W. 1928. *Mineral deposits*, 3rd edn., New York: McGraw Hill.

Lopez-Martinez, M., D. York, C. M. Hall and J. A. Hanes 1984. Oldest reliable $^{40}Ar/^{39}Ar$ ages for terrestrial rocks: Barberton Mountain Komatiites. *Nature* 304, 352–4.

Lovelock, J. E. 1979. *Gaia: A new look at life on Earth*. Oxford: Oxford University Press.

Lovelock, J. E. and L. Margulis 1974. Homeostatic tendencies of the Earth's atmosphere. *Origins of Life* 5, 93–103.

Lovelock, J. E. and L. Margulis 1984. Gaia and geognosy: towards a science of the biosphere. In M. B. Rambler, *Global ecology: towards a science of the biosphere*, Jones and Bartlett.

Lowe, D. R. 1980. Stromatolites 3400 Myr-old from the Archaean of Western Australia. *Nature* 284, 441–3.

Lowe, D. R. 1982. Sedimentological comparison of sedimentary units within the principal volcanic sequences of Archaean greenstone belts in South Africa, Australia and Canada. In *IAS Abstracts*, 11th International Congress in Sedimentology, Hamilton, Ontario, Canada, International Association of Sedimentologists, 1.

Lowe, D. R. 1983. Restricted shallow-water sedimentation of early Archaean stromatolitic and evaporitic strata of the Strelley Pool chert, Pilbara block, Western Australia. *Precambrian Research* 19, 239–83.

Lowe, D. R. 1985. Sedimentary environment as a control on the formation and preservation of Archaean volcanogenic massive sulphide deposits. In *Evolution of Archaean supracrustal sequences*, L. D. Ayres, P. C. Thurston, K. D. Card and W. Weber (eds.), 193–201. Geological Association of Canada, Special Paper 28.

Lowe, D. R. and G. R. Byerly 1986. Sedimentological and stratigraphical evolution of the southern part of the Barberton greenstone belt: a case of changing provenance and stability. Abstracts, *Workshop on the tectonic evolution of Greenstone Belts*, Lunar and Planetary Institute, Houston 72–4.

Lowe, D. R. and L. P. Knauth 1977. Sedimentology of the Onverwacht Group (3.4 billion years), Transvaal, South Africa, and its bearing on the characteristics and evolution of the early Earth. *Journal of Geology* 85, 699–723.

Ludden, J., C. Hubert and C. Gariépy 1986. The tectonic evolution of the Abitibi belt, Canada. *Geological Magazine* 123, 153–66.

Lugmair, G. W. 1974. Sm–Nd ages: a new dating method. *Meteoritics* 9, 369.

Lugmair, G. W., N. B. Scheinin and K. Marti 1975. Sm–Nd age and history of Apollo 17 basalt 75075: evidence for early differentiation of the lunar exterior. *Proceedings of the 6th Lunar Science Conference*, 1419–29.

Lyell, Sir C. 1872. *Principles of geology*, 11th edn. London: John Murray. See. Vol. 1. p. 75.

Maas, R., M. T. McCulloch, I. H. Campbell and P. R. Coad 1986. Sm–Nd and Rb–Sr dating of an Archaean massive sulphide deposit: Kidd Creek, Ontario. *Geology* 14, 585–8.

Macgregor, A. M. 1928. The geology of the country around Lonely Mine, Bubi District. *Southern Rhodesia Geological Survey Bulletin* 11.

Macgregor, A. M. 1947. An outline of the geological history of Southern Rhodesia. *Southern Rhodesia Geological Survey Bulletin* **38**.

Macgregor, A. M. 1951. Some milestones in the Precambrian of Southern Rhodesia. *Transactions of the Geological Society of South Africa* **54**, xxvii–lxxi.

Macgregor, B. I. and N. W. Bliss 1968. The Barton farm magnesite deposit, Gatooma, Rhodesia. In *Symposium on the Rhodesian Basement Complex*, D. J. L. Visser (ed.), 159–74. Annexure to vol. 71, *Transactions of the Geological Society of South Africa*.

Maiden, K. J. 1984. Metamorphic features of stratiform gold ores in the Barberton greenstone belt, eastern Transvaal. In *Gold '82*, R. P. Foster (ed.), 325–38. Geological Society of Zimbabwe, Special Publication 1. Rotterdam: Balkema.

Maitland, A. G. 1906. Third report on the geological features and mineral resources of the Pilbara Goldfield. *Western Australia Geological Survey bulletin*, No. 23.

Maitland, A. G. 1908. The geological features and mineral resources of the Pilbara goldfield. *Western Australia Geological Survey Bulletin* **40**.

Margulis, L. 1979. Symbiosis and evolution. In *Life: origin and evolution*, C. E. Folsome (ed.), 101–10. New York: W. H. Freeman. (Reprinted from *Scientific American* August 1971).

Margulis, L. and J. E. Lovelock 1981. Atmospheres and Evolution. In *Life in the universe*, J. Billingham (ed.), 79–101. Cambridge, Mass: MIT Press.

Margulis, L. and J. Stolz 1983. Microbial systematics and a Gaian view of the sediments. In *Biomineralization and biological metal accumulation*, P. Westbrook and E. W. de Jong (eds.), 27–53. D. Riedel, Dordrecht, Holland.

Margulis, L., B. D. D. Grosovsky, J. F. Stolz, E. J. Gong-Collins, S. Lenk, D. Read and A. Lopez-Cortes 1983. Distinctive microbial structures and the pre-Phanerozoic fossil record. *Precambrian Research* **20**, 443–77.

Marston, R. J., D. I. Groves, D. R. Hudson and J. R. Ross 1981. Nickel sulfide deposits in Western Australia: a review. *Economic Geology* **76**, 1330–63.

Martin, A. 1978. The geology of the Belingwe-Shabani schist belt. *Rhodesia Geological Survey Bulletin* **83**.

Martin, A., E. G. Nisbet and M. J. Bickle 1980. Archaean stromatolites of the Belingwe greenstone belt, Zimbabwe (Rhodesia). *Precambrian Research* **13**, 337–62.

Martin, H. J. 1964. The Bikita tinfield. *Southern Rhodesia Geological Survey Bulletin* **58**, 114–32.

Mason, T. R. and V. von Brunn 1977. 3-Gyr old stromatolites from South Africa. *Nature* **266**, 47–9.

Matsui, T. and Y. Abe 1986. Impact-induced atmosphere and oceans on Earth and Venus, *Nature*, **322**, 526–8.

Matthews, P. E. and R. H. Scharrer 1968. A graded unconformity at the base of the early Precambrian Pongola system. *Transactions of the Geological Society of South Africa* **71**, 257–72.

Mattioli, G. S. and B. J. Wood 1986. Upper mantle oxygen fugacity recorded by spinel lherzolites. *Nature* **322**, 626–8.

McConchie, D. 1984. A depositional environment for the Hamersley Group: palaeogeography and geochemistry. In *Archaean and Proterozoic basins of the Pilbara, Western Australia*, J. R. Muhling, D. I. Groves and T. S. Blake (eds.), 144–90. University of Western Australia, Geology Department and University Extension, Publication 9.

McKenzie, A. S. and D. P. McKenzie 1983. Isomerization and aromatization of hydrocarbons in sedimentary basins formed by extension. *Geological Magazine* **120**, 417–70.

McKenzie, D. P. and F. M. Richter 1981. Parameterized thermal convection in a layered region and the thermal history of the Earth. *Journal of Geophysical Research* **86**, 11667–80.

McKenzie, D. P. and N. O. Weiss 1975. Speculations on the thermal and tectonic history of the earth. *Geophysical Journal of the Royal Astronomical Society* **42**, 131–74.

380

McKenzie, D. P. and N. Weiss 1980. *The thermal history of the Earth.* Geological Association of Canada, Special Paper 20, 575–90.

McKenzie, D. P., E. G. Nisbet and J. G. Sclater 1980. Sedimentary basin development in the Archaean. *Earth and Planetary Science Letters* 48, 35–41.

McLennan, S. M. and S. R. Taylor 1980. Th and U in sedimentary rocks: crustal evolution and sedimentary recycling. *Nature* 285, 621–4.

McLennan, S. M. and S. R. Taylor 1982. Geochemical constraints on the growth of the continental crust. *Journal of Geology* 90, 347–61.

Melton, C. E. and A. A. Giardini 1980. The isotopic abundance of argon included in an Arkansas diamond and its possible significance. *Geophysical Research Letters* 7, 461–4.

Mennell, F. P. and A. Frost 1926. Notes on the occurrence of platinum in the Great Dyke, with special reference to Belingwe and Selukwe. *Proceedings of the Rhodesia Scientific Association* 25, 2–8.

Miall, A. D 1978. Lithofacies types and vertical profiles models in braided river deposits: a summary. In *Fluvial sedimentology*, A. D. Miall (ed.), 597–604. Canadian Society of Petroleum Geologists, Memoir 5.

Michard-Vitrac, A., J. Lancelot, C. J. Allègre and S. Moorbath 1977. U–Pb ages on single zircons from the early Precambrian rocks of West Greenland and the Minnesota river valley. *Earth and Planetary Science Letters* 35, 449–53.

Miller, R. G. and R. K. O'Nions 1985. Source of Precambrian chemical and clastic sediments *Nature* 314, 325–30.

Minter, W. E. L. 1978. A sedimentological synthesis of placer gold, uranium and pyrite concentrations in Proterozoic Witwatersrand sediments. In *Fluvial sedimentology*, A. D. Miall (ed.), 801–29. Canadian Society of Petroleum Geologists, Memoir 5.

Moorbath, S. M. 1977. Ages, isotopes and evolution of Precambrian continental crust. *Chemical Geology* 20, 151–87.

Moorbath, S. 1983. The most ancient rocks. *Nature* 304, 585–6.

Moorbath, S. and P. N. Taylor 1981. Isotopic evidence for continental growth in the Precambrian. In *Precambrian plate tectonics*, A. Kröner (ed.), 491–526. Amsterdam: Elsevier.

Moorbath, S., J. F. Wilson and P. Cotterill 1976. Early Archaean age for the Sebakwian group at Selukwe, Rhodesia. *Nature* 264, 536–8.

Moore, R. O. and J. J. Gurney 1986. Pyroxene solid solution in garnets included in diamond. *Nature* 319, 553–5.

Morgan, P. 1985. Crustal radiogenic heat production and the selective survival of ancient continental crust. *Proceedings of the 15th Lunar and Planetary Science Conference, Journal of Geophysical Research* 90, C561–570.

Morris, R. C. 1980. A textural and mineralogical study of the relationship of iron ore to banded iron-formation in the Hamersley Iron Province of Western Australia. *Economic Geology* 75, 184–209.

Morris, R. C. 1983. Supergene alteration of banded iron formation. In *Iron formation: facts and problems*, A. F. Trendall and R. C. Morris (eds.), 513–34. Amsterdam: Elsevier.

Mossman, D. J. and B. Dexter Dyer 1985. The geochemistry of Witwatersrand-type gold deposits and the possible influence of ancient prokaryotic communities on gold dissolution and precipitation. *Precambrian Research* 30, 303–20.

Moubray, R. J., E. L. Brand, P. K. Hofmeyr and M. Potter 1979. The Hunters Road nickel prospect. In *A symposium on mineral deposits and the transportation and deposition of metals*, C. R. Anhauesser, R. P. Foster and T. Stratton (eds.), 109–16. Geological Society of South Africa (Rhodesian Branch), Special Publication 5.

Muenow, D. W., D. G. Graham, N. W. K. Liu and J. R. Delaney 1979. The abundance of volatiles in Hawaiian tholeiitic submarine basalts. *Earth and Planetary Science Letters* 42, 71–6.

Muir, M. D. 1978. Occurrence and potential uses of Archaean microfossils and organic matter. In *Archaean cherty metasediments: their sedimentology, micropalaeontology, biogeochemistry and significance to mineralization*, J. E. Glover and D. I. Groves (eds.), 11–21. University of Western Australia, Geology Department and Extension Service, Publication 2.

Muir, M. D. and P. R. Grant, 1976. Micropalaeontological evidence from the Onverwacht Group, South Africa. In *The early history of the Earth*, B. F. Windley (ed.), 595–609. London: Wiley Interscience.

Muir, T. L. 1982. Geology of the Hemlo area, district of Thunder Bay. *Ontario Geological Survey Report* 217.

Muir, T. L. 1983. Geology of the Hemlo–Heron Bay area. In *The geology of gold in Ontario*, A. C. Colvine, (ed.), 230–9. Ontario Survey Miscellaneous Paper 110.

Murray, P. A. and S. H. Zinder 1984. Nitrogen fixation by a methanogenic archaebacterium. *Nature* 312, 284–6.

Myers, J. S. 1984. Archaean tectonics of the Fiskenaesset region of southwest Greenland. In *Precambrian tectonics illustrated*, A. Kröner and R. Greiling (eds.), 95–112. Stuttgart: Schweizerbart.

Myers, J. S. and K. P. Watkins 1985. Origin of granite-greenstone patterns, Yilgarn Block, Western Australia. *Geology* 13, 778–80.

Naqvi, S. M. 1986. Geochemical characters and tectonic evolution of the Chitradurga schist belt: an Archaean suture(?) of the Dharwar Craton, India. Abstracts, *Workshop on the tectonic evolution of Greenstone belts*, Lunar and Planetary Science Institute, Houston, 84–85.

Nagy, B., M. H. Engel, J. E. Zumberge, M. Ogino and S. Y. Cheng 1981. Amino acids and hydrocarbons 3800-Myr old in the Isua Rocks, southwestern Greenland. *Nature* 289, 53–6.

Naldrett, A. J. (ed.), 1979. Nickel sulfide and platinum-group-element deposits. *The Canadian Mineralogist* 17, 141–514.

Naldrett, A. J. and I. H. Campbell 1982. Physical and chemical constraints on genetic models for komatiite-related Ni-sulphide deposits. In *Komatiites*, N. T. Arndt and E. G. Nisbet (eds.), 421–34. London: Allen & Unwin.

Naldrett, A. J. and L. J. Cabri 1976. Ultramafic and related mafic rocks: their classification and genesis with special reference to the concentration of nickel sulphides and platinum group elements. *Economic Geology* 71, 1131–58.

Naldrett, A. J. and A. R. Turner 1977. The geology and petrogenesis of a greenstone belt and related nickel sulphide mineralization at Yakabindie, Western Australia. *Precambrian Research* 5, 43–103.

Nash, O. 1940. The lama. In *The face is familiar*. New York: Little, Brown & Co.

Nesbitt, R. W. and S. S. Sun 1980. Geochemical features of some Archaean and post-Archaean high-magnesian and low-magnesian tholeiites. *Philosophical Transactions of the Royal Society, London* Series A, 297, 229–42.

Nesbitt, R. W., S. S. Sun and A. C. Purvis 1979. Komatiites: geochemistry and genesis. *Canadian Mineralogist* 17, 165–86.

Newman, Cardinal J. H. 1880. *Apologia pro vita sua*. London: Longmans, Green, Reader & Dyer.

Newton, R. C., J. V. Smith and B. F. Windley 1980. Carbonic metamorphism, granulites and crustal growth. *Nature* 288, 45–50.

Nickel, K. G. and D. H. Green 1985. Empirical geothermobarometry for garnet peridotites and implications for the nature of the lithosphere, kimberlites and diamonds. *Earth and Planetary Science Letters* 73, 158–70.

Nicolaysen, L. O., R. J. Hart and N. H. Gale 1981. The Vredefort radioelement profile extended to supracrustal strata at Carltonville, with implications for continental heat flow. *Journal of Geophysical Research* **86**, 10653–61.

Nisbet, E. G. 1980. Archaean stromatolites and the search for the earliest life. *Nature* **294**, 395–6.

Nisbet, E. G. 1982a. Definition of 'Archaean' – comment and a proposal on the recommendations of the international subcommission on Precambrian stratigraphy. *Precambrian Research* **19**, 111–18.

Nisbet, E. G. 1982b. The tectonic setting and petrogenesis of komatiites. In *Komatiites*, N. T. Arndt and E. G. Nisbet (eds.), 501–26. London: Allen & Unwin.

Nisbet, E. G. 1984a. Gold in the upper greenstones of the Belingwe greenstone belt: a model. In *Gold '82*: R. P. Foster (ed.), 583–94. Geological Society of Zimbabwe, Special Publication 1. Rotterdam: Balkema.

Nisbet, E. G. 1984b. Modelling mantle temperatures in the Archaean. *Nature* **309**, 110.

Nisbet, E. G. 1984c. Turbulence in petrology – the behaviour of komatiites. *Nature* **309**, 14–15.

Nisbet, E. G. 1984d. The continental and oceanic crust and lithosphere in the Archean: isostatic, thermal and tectonic models. *Canadian Journal of Earth Sciences* **21**, 1426–41.

Nisbet, E. G. 1985a. Putting the squeeze on rocks. *Nature* **315**, 541.

Nisbet, E. G. 1985b. The geological setting of the earliest life forms. *Journal of Molecular Evolution* **21**, 289–98.

Nisbet, E. G. 1986a. Archaean mantle models. *Nature* **320**, 306–7.

Nisbet, E. G. 1986b. RNA and hydrothermal systems. *Nature* **321**.

Nisbet, E. G. and G. A. Chinner 1981. Controls on the eruption of mafic and ultramafic lavas, Ruth Well Ni–Cu prospect, West Pilbara. *Economic Geology* **76**, 1729–35.

Nisbet, E. G. and C. M. R. Fowler 1982. The thermal background to metamorphism – I: Simple one-dimensional models. *Geoscience Canada* **9**, 161–4.

Nisbet, E. G. and C. M. R. Fowler 1983. Model for Archaean plate tectonics. *Geology* **11**, 376–9.

Nisbet, E. G. and C. T. Pillinger 1981. In the beginning. *Nature* **289**, 11–12.

Nisbet E. G. and D. Walker 1982. Komatiites and the structure of the Archaean mantle. *Earth and Planetary Science Letters* **60**, 105–13.

Nisbet, E. G. and D. Walker 1983. Reply to A. Y. Glikson. *Earth and Planetary Science Letters* **66**, 329–30.

Nisbet, E. G., M. J. Bickle and A. Martin 1977. The mafic and ultramafic lavas of the Belingwe greenstone belt, Rhodesia. *Journal of Petrology* **18**, 521–66.

Nisbet, E. G., J. F. Wilson and M. J. Bickle 1981. The evolution of the Rhodesian craton and adjacent Archaean terrain. In *Precambrian plate tectonics*, A. Kröner (ed.), 161–83. Amsterdam: Elsevier.

Nisbet, E. G., M. J. Bickle, A. Martin and J. L. Orpen 1983. Controls on the formation of the upper greenstones, Belingwe belt, Zimbabwe. *Archaean Crustal Study Project* University of Saskatchewan and of Zimbabwe, 163–96.

Nockolds, S. R., R. W. O'B, Knox and G. A. Chinner 1978. *Petrology for students.* Cambridge: Cambridge University Press.

Nutman, A. P. 1984. Early Archaean crustal evolution of the Isukasia area, southern West Greenland. In *Precambrian tectonics illustrated*. A. Kröner and R. Greiling (eds.), 79–94. Stuttgart: Schweizerbart.

Nutman, A. P., J. H. Allaart, D. Bridgwater, M. Rosing and E. Dimroth 1984. Stratigraphic and geochemical evidence for the depositional environment of the Early Archaean Isua supracrustal belt, southern West Greenland. *Precambrian Research* **25**, 365–96.

Obar, R. and J. Green 1985. Molecular archeology of the mitochondrial genome. *Journal of Molecular Evolution* **22**, 243–51.

Odom, D. G., N. Lahav and S. Chang 1979. Prebiotic nucleotide oligomerization in a fluctuating environment: effects of kaolinite and cyanamide. *Journal of Molecular Evolution* **12**, 259–64.

Odom, D. G., M. Rao, J. G. Lawless and J. Oró 1979. Association of nucleotides with homoionic clays. *Journal of Molecular Evolution* **12**, 365–7.

O'Hara, M. J. 1965. Are ocean floor basalts primary magma? *Nature* **220**, 683–6.

O'Hara, M. J. 1977. Geochemical evolution during fractional recrystallization of a periodically refilled magma chamber. *Nature* **266**, 503–7.

O'Hara, M. J. and C. T. Herzberg 1985. Origin of mantle peridotite and komatiite by partial melting. *Geophysical Research Letters* **12**, 541–4.

O'Hara, M. J. and G. Yarwood 1978. High-pressure–temperature point on an Archaean geotherm, implied magma genesis by crustal anatexis and consequences for garnet–pyroxene thermometry and barometry. *Philosophical Transactions of the Royal Society of London* Series A, **288**, 441–56.

O'Hara, M. J., M. J. Saunders and E. L. P. Mercy 1975. Garnet–peridotite, primary ultrabasic magma and eclogite: interpretation of upper mantle processes in kimberlites. *Physics and Chemistry of the Earth* **9**, 571–604.

Ohtani, E. 1984. Generation of komatiite magma and gravitational differentiation in the deep upper mantle. *Earth and Planetary Science Letters* **67**, 261–72.

Ohtani, E. 1985. The primordial terrestrial magma ocean and its implication for stratification of the mantle. *Physics of Earth and Planetary Interiors* **38**, 70–80.

Ojakangas, R. W. 1985. Review of Archaean clastic sedimentation, Canadian Shield: major felsic volcanic contributions to turbidite and alluvial fan-fluvial facies associations. In *Evolution of Archaean supracrustal sequences*. L. D. Ayres, P. C. Thurston, K. D. Card and W. Weber (eds.), 23–48. Geological Association of Canada, Special Paper 28.

Oldham, J. W. 1968. A short note on recent geological mapping of the Shabani area. In *Symposium on the Rhodesian Basement Complex*, D. J. L. Visser (ed.), 189–94. Transactions of the Geological Society of South Africa **71**, Annexure.

O'Nions, R. K. and E. R. Oxburgh 1983. Heat and helium in the Earth. *Nature* **306**, 429–31.

O'Nions, R. K., N. M. Evensen and P. J. Hamilton 1979. Geochemical modelling of mantle differentiation and crustal growth. *Journal of Geophysical Research* **84**, 6091–102.

O'Nions, R. K., P. J. Hamilton and P. J. Hooker 1983. A Nd isotope investigation of sediments related to crustal development in the British Isles. *Earth and Planetary Science Letters* **63**, 229–40.

Orpen, J. L. 1978. *The geology of the southwestern part of the Belingwe greenstone belt and adjacent country – the Belingwe Peak area*. PhD thesis, University of Zimbabwe.

Orpen, J. L. and J. F. Wilson 1981. Stromatolites of 3500 Myr and a greenstone–granite unconformity in the Zimbabwean Archaean. *Nature* **291**, 218–20.

Owen, T., R. D. Cess and V. Ramanathan 1979. Enhanced CO_2 greenhouse to compensate for reduced solar luminosity on early Earth. *Nature* **277**, 640–1.

Ozima, M. and F. A. Podosek 1984. *Noble gas geochemistry*. Cambridge: Cambridge University Press.

Ozima, M., F. A. Podosek and G. Igarashi 1985. Terrestrial xenon isotope constraints on the early history of the Earth. *Nature* **315**, 471–4.

Padgham, W. A. 1985. Observations and speculations on supracrustal succession in the Slave Structural Province. In *Evolution of Archaean supracrustal sequences*, L. D. Ayres, P. C. Thurston, K. D. Card and W. Weber (eds.), 133–52. Geological Association of Canada, Special Paper 28.

REFERENCES

Page, N. J. 1977. *Stillwater Complex, Montana: rock succession, metamorphism and structure of the complex and adjacent rocks.* US Geological Survey Professional Paper 999.

Panella, G. 1976. Geophysical inferences from stromatolite lamination. In *Stromatolites*, M. R. Walter (ed.), 673–85. Amsterdam: Elsevier.

Patchett, P. J. and C. Chauvel 1984. The mean life of continents is currently not constrained by Nd and Hf isotopes. *Geophysical Research Letters* **11**, 151–3.

Patchett, P. J., W. M. White, H. Feldmann, S. Kielinczuk and A. W. Hofmann 1984. Hafnium/rare earth element fractionation in the sedimentary system and crustal recycling into the Earth's mantle. *Earth and Planetary Science Letters* **69**, 365–75.

Patterson, G. C. 1984. Field trip guidebook to the Hemlo area. Ontario Geological Survey Miscellaneous Paper 118.

Pearton, T. N. 1982. Gold and antimony mineralization in altered komatiites of the Munchism greenstone belt, South Africa. In *Komatiites*, N. T. Arndt and E. G. Nisbet (eds.), 459–75. London: Allen & Unwin.

Pearton, T. N. 1984. The role of carbonate alteration in Archaean gold mineralization. In *Gold '82*, R. P. Foster (ed.), 687. Geological Society of Zimbabwe, Special Publication 1.

Percival, J. A. and K. D. Card 1983. Archaean crust as revealed in the Kapuskasing uplift, Superior Province, Canada. *Geology* **11**, 323–6.

Percival, J. A. and K. D. Card 1985. Structure and evolution of Archaean crust in Central Superior Province, Canada. In *Evolution of Archaean supracrustal sequences*, L. D. Ayres, P. C. Thurston, K. D. Card and W. Weber, (eds.), 179–92. Geological Association of Canada, Special Paper 28.

Percival, J. A., K. D. Card, R. P. Sage, L. S. Jensen and L. E. Luhta 1983. The Archaean crust in the Wawa–Chaplean–Timmins region. In *Workshop on cross-section of Archaean crust*, L. D. Ashwal and K. D. Card (eds.), 99–169, L.P.I. Technical Report 83-03, Lunar and Planetary Institute, Houston.

Peterman, Z. E. 1979. Strontium isotope geochemistry of late Archaean to late Cretaceous tonalites and trondhjemites. In *Trondhjemites, dacites and related rocks*, F. Barker (ed.), 133–47. Amsterdam: Elsevier.

Phillips, D. E., M. J. E. Sternberg and F. J. Sutton 1983. Intimations of evolution from the three-dimensional structures of proteins. In *Evolution from molecules to men*, D. S. Bendall (ed.), 145–74. Cambridge: Cambridge University Press.

Phillips, R. J. and M. C. Malin 1983. The interior of Venus and tectonic implications. In *Venus*. D. M. Hunten, L. Colin, T. M. Donahue and V. I. Moroz (eds.), 159–214. Tucson: University of Arizona Press.

Phillips, R. J., W. M. Kaula, G. E. McGill and M. C. Malin 1981. Tectonics and evolution of Venus. *Science* **212**, 879–87.

Pidgeon, R. T. 1978. 3450 my-old volcanics in the Archaean layered greenstone succession of the Pilbara block, Western Australia. *Earth and Planetary Science Letters* **37**, 421–8.

Podmore, F. 1970. The shape of the Great Dyke of Rhodesia as revealed by gravity surveying. *Special Publication of the Geological Society of South Africa* **1**, 610–20.

Podmore, F. 1982. Progress report: the first Bouguer anomaly map of Zimbabwe. *Transactions of the Geological Society of South Africa* **85**, 127–33.

Porter, D. J. and K. G. MacKay 1981. The nickel sulphide mineralisation and metamorphic setting of the Forrestania area, Western Australia. *Economic Geology* **76**, 1524–49.

Postgate, J. R. 1984. New kingdom for nitrogen fixation. *Nature* **312**, 194.

Pretorius, D. A. 1975. The depositional environment of the Witwatersrand gold fields: a chronological review of speculations and observations. *Minerals, Science and Engineering* **7**, 18–47.

Pyke, D. R., A. J. Naldrett and O. R. Eckstrand 1973. Archaean ultramafic flows in Munro Township, Ontario. *Geological Society of America bulletin* **84**, 955–78.

385

Ramsay, J. G. 1965. Structural investigations in the Barberton Mountain Land, Eastern Transvaal. *Transactions of the Geological Society of South Africa* **66**, 353–401.

Rankama, K. 1970. Proterozoic, Archaean and other weeds in the Precambrian rock garden. *Geological Society of Finland Bulletin* **42**, 211–22.

Rao, M., D. G. Odom and J. Oró 1980. Clays in prebiological chemistry. *Journal of Molecular Evolution* **15**, 317–31.

Reymer, A. and G. Schubert 1984. Phanerozoic addition rates to the continental crust and crustal growth. *Tectonics* **3**, 63–78.

Richards, J. R. and J. G. Blockley 1984. The base of the Fortescue Group, Western Australia: further galena lead isotope evidence on its age. *Australian Journal of Earth Sciences* **31**, 257–68.

Richardson, S. H., A. J. Erlank and S. R. Hart 1985. Kimberlite-borne garnet peridotite xenoliths from old enriched subcontinental lithosphere. *Earth and Planetary Science Letters* **75**, 116–28.

Richardson, S. H., J. J. Gurney, A. J. Erlank and J. W. Harris 1984. Origin of diamonds in old enriched mantle. *Nature* **310**, 198–202.

Richter, F. M. 1984. Regionalised models for the thermal evolution of the Earth. *Earth and Planetary Science Letters* **68**, 471–84.

Richter, F. M. 1985. Models for the Archaean thermal regime. *Earth and Planetary Science Letters* **73**, 350–60.

Richter, F. M. and D. P. McKenzie 1978. Simple plate models of mantle convection. *Zeitschrift für Geophysik* **44**, 441–71.

Rigden, S. M., T. J. Ahrens and E. M. Stolper 1984. Densities of liquid silicates of high pressures. *Science* **226**, 1071–4.

Robertson, I. D. M. 1973. The geology of the country around Mount Towla, Gwanda District. *Rhodesia Geological Survey Bulletin* **68**.

Robertson, I. D. M. and M. C. du Toit 1981. The Limpopo Belt. In *Precambrian of the Southern Hemisphere*, D. R. Hunter (ed.), 641–71. Amsterdam: Elsevier.

Roddick, J. C. 1984. Emplacement and metamorphism of Archaean mafic volcanics at Kambalda, Western Australia – geochemical and isotopic constraints. *Geochimica et Cosmochimica Acta* **48**, 1305–18.

Rogers, N. and C. Hawkesworth 1984. New date for diamonds. *Nature* **310**, 187–8.

Rossbacher, L. A. and S. Judson 1981. Ground ice on Mars: inventory, distribution and resulting landforms. *Icarus* **45**, 39–59.

Rutherford, E. 1907. Some cosmical aspects of radioactivity. *Journal of the Royal Astronomical Society of Canada* **1**, 145–65.

Rutherford, E. 1929. Origin of actinium and the age of the Earth. *Nature* **123**, 313–4.

Rutherford, E. and F. Soddy 1903. Radioactive change. *Philosophical Magazine* **6**, v., 576–91.

Rutland, R. W. R. 1981. Structural framework of the Australian Precambrian, *Precambrian of the Southern Hemisphere*, D. R. Hunter (ed.), 1–32. Amsterdam: Elsevier.

Saager, R. and M. Meyer 1984. Gold distribution in Archaean granitoids and supracrustal rocks from Southern Africa: a comparison. In *Gold '82*, R. P. Foster (ed.), 53–70. Geological Society of Zimbabwe, Special Publication 1. Rotterdam: Balkema.

Saager, R., M. Meyer and R. Muff 1982. Gold distribution in supracrustal rocks from Archaean greenstone belts of southern Africa and from Palaeozoic ultramafic complexes of the European Alps: metallogenetic and geochemical implications. *Economic Geology* **77**, 1–24.

Salop, L. J. 1982. *Geological evolution of the Earth during the Precambrian*. Berlin: Springer.

Sandiford, M. 1985. The metamorphic evolution of granulites at Fyfe Hills; implications for

Archaean crustal thickness in Enderby Land, Antarctica. *Journal of Metamorphic Geology* **3**, 155–78.

Sarda, P., T. Staudacher and C. J. Allègre 1985. $^{40}Ar/^{36}Ar$ in MORB glasses: constraints on atmosphere and mantle evolution. *Earth and Planetary Science Letters* **72**, 357–75.

Scharer, U. and C. J. Allègre 1985. Determination of the age of the Australian continent by single grain zircon analysis of Mt. Narryer metaquartzite. *Nature* **315**, 52–5.

Schidlowski, M. 1979. Antiquity and evolutionary status of bacterial sulphate reduction: sulphur isotope evidence. *Origins of Life* **9**, 299–311.

Schidlowski, M. 1980a. Antiquity of photosynthesis: possible constraints from Archaean carbon isotope record. In *Biogeochemistry of ancient and modern environments*. P. A. Trudinger, M. R. Walter and B. J. Ralph (eds.), 47–54. Australian Academy of Science.

Schidlowski, M. 1980b. The atmosphere. In *The Handbook for Environmental Chemistry*, O. Hutzinger (ed.), volume 1, Part A, 1–16.

Schidlowski, M. 1984. Biological modulation of the terrestrial carbon cycle: isotope clues to early organic evolution. *Advances in Space Research* **4**, 183–93.

Schidlowski, M., J. M. Hayes and I. R. Kaplan 1983. Isotopic inferences of ancient biochemistries: carbon, sulfur, hydrogen and nitrogen. In *Earth's earliest biosphere*. J. W. Schopf (ed.), 149–86. Princeton, NJ: Princeton University Press.

Schiotte, L., D. Bridgwater, A. P. Nutman and A. B. Ryan 1985. Chemical and isotopic effects of late Archaean high-grade metamorphism and granite injection on early Archaean gneisses, Saglek–Hebron, northern Labrador. *Journal of the Geological Society of London*, in press.

Schopf, J. W. (ed.) 1983. *Earth's earliest biosphere*. Princeton, NJ: Princeton University Press.

Schopf, J. W. and E. S. Barghoorn 1967. Alga-like fossils from the Early Precambrian of South Africa. *Science* **156**, 508–12.

Schopf, J. W. and M. R. Walter 1983. Archaean microfossils: new evidence of ancient microbes. In Earth's earliest biosphere, J. W. Schopf (ed.), 214–39. Princeton NJ: Princeton University Press.

Schreyer, W. and K. Abraham 1979. Symplectic cordierite–orthopyroxene–garnet assemblages as products of contact metamorphism of pre-existing basement granulites in the Vredefort structure, South Africa, and their relations to pseudotachylite. *Contributions to Mineralogy and Petrology* **68**, 53–62.

Schrödinger, E. 1944. *What is life?* Cambridge: Cambridge University Press.

Schubert, G. and A. P. S. Reymer 1985. Continental volume and freeboard through geological time. *Nature* **316**, 336–9.

Schulze, D. J. 1986. Calcium anomalies in the mantle and a subducted metaserpentine origin for diamonds. *Nature* **319**, 483–5.

Schwartz, A. W. and A. Henderson-Sellers 1984. Glaciers, volcanic islands and the origin of life. *Precambrian Research* **22**, 167–74.

Schwartz, R. M. and M. O. Dayhoff 1978. Origins of procaryotes, eukaryotes, mitochondria and chloroplasts. *Science* **199**, 395–403.

Schwerdtner, W. M. 1984. Archaean gneiss domes in the Wabigoon subprovince of the Canadian Shield, northwestern Ontario. In *Precambrian tectonics illustrated*, A. Kröner and R. Greiling (eds.), 129–34. Stuttgart: Schweizerbart.

Schwerdtner, W. M., J. Morgan and G. M. Stott 1985. Contacts between greenstone belts and gneiss complexes within the Wabigoon Subprovince, northeastern Ontario. In *Evolution of Archaean supracrustal sequences*, L. D. Ayres, P. C. Thurston, K. D. Card and W. Weber (eds.), 117–24. Geological Association of Canada, Special Paper 28.

Schwerdtner, W. M., D. Stone, K. Osadetz, J. Morgan and G. M. Stott 1979. Granitoid complexes and the Archaean tectonic record in the southern part of northwestern Ontario. *Canadian Journal of Earth Sciences* **16**, 1965–77.

Sclater, J. G., C. Jaupart and D. Galson 1980. The heat flow through oceanic and continental crust and the heat loss of the earth. *Reviews of Geophysics and Space Physics* **18**, 269–311.

Sclater, J. G., B. Parsons and C. Jaupart 1981. Oceans and continents: similarities and differences in the mechanisms of heat loss. *Journal of Geophysical Research* **86**, 11535–52.

Scott, D. R. and D. J. Stevenson 1985. Magma solitary waves. *Terra Cognita* **5**, 212–3.

Sedgwick, A. and Sir R. I. Murchison 1835. *On the Silurian and Cambrian systems, exhibiting the order in which the older sedimentary strata succeed each other in England and Wales.* Report, British Association (Dublin), 11, 59–61.

Seward, T. M. 1984. The transport and deposition of gold in hydrothermal systems. In *Gold '82*, R. P. Foster (ed.), 165–84. Geological Society of Zimbabwe, Special Publication 1. Rotterdam: Balkema.

Sheraton, J. W., L. A. Offe, R. J. Tingey and D. J. Ellis 1980. Enderby Land, Antarctica – an unusual Precambrian high grade metamorphic terrain. *Journal of the Geological Society of Australia* **27**, 1–18.

Shklanka, R. 1972. *Geology of the Steep Rock Lake area, district of Rainy River.* Ontario Department of Mines and Northern Affairs, Geology Report 93.

Simmons, B. D. and geological staff 1973. Geology of the Millenbach massive sulphide deposit, Noranda, Quebec. *Canadian Institute of Mining and Metallurgy Bulletin*, 67–78.

Simpson, C. 1981. Occurrence and orientation of shatter cones in Pretoria Group quartzites in the collar of the Vredefort 'Dome': impact origin precluded. *Journal of Geophysical Research* **86**, 10701–6.

Sims, P. K. 1980. Subdivision of the Proterozoic and Archean eons: recommendations and suggestions by the International Subcommission on Precambrian Stratigraphy. *Precambrian Research* **13**, 379–80.

Sklarew, D. A. and B. Nagy 1979. 2,5-Dimethylfuran from 2.7×10^9 year old Rupemba–Belingwe stromatolite: potential evidence from remnants of carbohydrates. *Proceedings of the US National Academy of Sciences* **76**, 10–14.

Slawson, W. F. 1976. Vredefort core: a cross-section of the upper crust? *Geochimica Cosmochimica Acta* **40**, 117–21.

Sleep, N. H. 1979. Thermal history and degassing of the earth: some simple calculations. *Journal of Geology* **87**, 671–86.

Sleeper, H. L. and L. E. Orgel 1979. The catalysis of nucleotide polymerization by compounds of divalent lead. *Journal of Molecular Evolution* **12**, 357–64.

Smith, H. S. and A. J. Erlank 1982. Geochemistry and petrogenesis of komatiites from the Barberton greenstone belt, South Africa. In *Komatiites*, N. T. Arndt and E. G. Nisbet (eds.), 347–98. London: Allen & Unwin.

Snowden, P. A. 1984. Non-diapiric batholiths in the north of the Zimbabwe Shield. In *Precambrian tectonics illustrated*, A. Kröner and R. Greilung (eds.), 135–46. Stuttgart: Schweizerbart.

Snowden, P. A. and M. J. Bickle 1976. The Chinamora batholith: diapiric intrusion or interference fold. *Journal of the Geological Society of London* **132**, 131–7.

Spence, C. D. and A. F. de Rosen-Spence 1975. The place of sulfide mineralization in the volcanic sequence at Noranda, Quebec. *Economic Geology* **70**, 90–101.

Spohn, T. and G. Schubert 1982. Modes of mantle convection and the removal of heat from the earth's interior. *Journal of Geophysical Research* **87**, 4682–96.

Spooner, E. T. C. and W. S. Fyfe 1973. Sub-sea floor metamorphism, heat and mass transfer. *Contributions to Mineralogy and Petrology* **42**, 287–304.

Squyres, S. W. 1984. The history of water on Mars. *Annual Review of Earth and Planetary Sciences* **12**, 83–106.

Srikantappa, C., M. Raith and D. Ackermand 1985. High-grade regional metamorphism of ultramafic and mafic rocks from the Archaean Sargur terrane, Karnataka, South India. *Precambrian research* **30**, 189–219.

Stagman, J. G. 1978. An outline of the geology of Rhodesia. *Rhodesia Geological Survey Bulletin 80*.

Stakes, D. S., J. W. Shervais and C. A. Hopson 1984. The volcanic–tectonic cycle of the FAMOUS and AMAR valleys, Mid-Atlantic Ridge (36°47′N): evidence from basalt glass and the phenocryst compositional variations for a steady-state magma chamber beneath the valley mid-sections, AMAR 3. *Journal of Geophysical Research* **89**, 6995–7028.

Stanistreet, I. G., M. J. de Wit and R. E. P. Fripp 1981. Do graded accretionary spheroids in the Barberton greenstone belt indicate Archaean deep water environment? *Nature* **293**, 280–4.

Stanistreet, I. G., M. J. de Wit and I. Paris 1982. Cherts of the Barberton greenstone belt and their palaeoenvironmental and palaeotectonic significance. In *IAS Abstracts*, 11th International Congress on Sedimentology, Hamilton, Ontario, International Association of Sedimentologists, 1.

Steiger, R. H. and E. Jaeger 1977. Subcommission on geochemistry: convention on the use of decay constants in geo- and cosmochronology. *Earth and Planetary Science Letters* **36**, 359–62.

Stevenson, D. J., T. Spohn and G. Schubert 1983. Magmatism and thermal evolution of the terrestrial planets. *Icarus* **47**, 466–89.

Stockwell, C. H. 1961. Structural provinces, orogenies and time classification of rocks of the Canadian Shield, In *Geological Survey of Canada Paper* **61–17**, 108–118.

Stockwell, C. H. 1973. *Revised Precambrian timescale for the Canadian Shield*. Geological Survey of Canada, Paper 72–52.

Stockwell, C. H. 1982. *Proposals for time classifications and correlation of Precambrian rocks and events in Canada and adjacent areas of the Canadian Shield. Part 1: a time classification of Precambrian rocks and events*. Geological Survey of Canada Paper 80–19.

Stolper, E., D. Walker, B. H. Hager and J. F. Hays 1981. Melt segregation from partially molten source regions: the importance of melt density and source region size. *Journal of Geophysical Research* **86**, 6261–71.

Stowe, C. W. 1968. The geology of the country south and west of Selukwe. *Rhodesia Geological Survey Bulletin 80*.

Stowe, C. W. 1984. The early Archaean Selukwe Nappe, Zimbabwe. In *Precambrian tectonics illustrated*, A. Kröner and R. Greiling (eds.), 41–56. Stuttgart: Schweizerbart.

Strother, P. K. and E. S. Barghoorn 1980. Microspheres from the Swartzkoppie Formation, a review. In *The origins of life and evolution*, H. O. Halvorsen and K. E. van Holde, (eds.), 1–19. New York: Alan R. Liss.

Stuart, G. W., T. Zengheni and R. A. Clark 1986. Crustal structure of the Limpopo mobile belt, Zimbabwe. *Geophysical Journal of the Royal Astronomical Society* **85**, 261.

Sun, S. S. 1984. Geochemical characteristics of Archaean ultramafic and mafic volcanic rocks: Implications for mantle composition and evolution. In *Archaean geochemistry*, A. Kröner, G. N. Hanson and A. M. Goodwin (eds.), 25–46. Berlin: Springer.

Sun, S. S. and R. W. Nesbitt 1977. Chemical heterogeneity of the Archaean mantle, composition of the Earth and mantle evolution. *Earth and Planetary Science Letters* **35**, 429–48.

Sun, S. S., R. W. Nesbitt and A. Y. Sharaskin 1979. Geochemical characteristics of mid-ocean ridge basalts. *Earth and Planetary Science Letters* **44**, 119–38.

Takahashi, E. and C. M. Scarfe 1985. Melting of peridotite to 14 GPa and the genesis of komatiite. *Nature* **315**, 566–8.

Tankard, A. J., M. P. A. Jackson, K. A. Eriksson, D. K. Hobday, D. R. Hunter and W. E. L. Minter 1982. *Crustal evolution of Southern Africa.* New York: Springer.

Taylor, S. R. and S. M. McLennan 1981. The composition and evolution of the continental crust: rare earth element evidence from sedimentary rocks. *Philosophical Transactions of the Royal Society, London,* Series A **301**, 381–99.

Taylor, S. R. and S. M. McLennan 1985. *The continental crust: its composition and evolution.* Oxford: Blackwell.

Todd, S. G., D. W. Keith, D. J. Schissel, L. L. Leroy, E. L. Mann and T. N. Irvine 1982. The J-M platinum–palladium reef of the Stillwater Complex, Montana: I. stratigraphy and petrology. *Economic Geology* **77**, 1454–80.

Towe, K. M. 1983. Precambrian atmospheric oxygen and banded iron formations: a delayed ocean model. *Precambrian Research* **20**, 161–70.

Trendall, A. F. 1983. The Hamersley basin. In *Iron formation: facts and problems,* A. F. Trendall and R. C. Morris (eds.), 69–130. Amsterdam: Elsevier.

Trevor-Roper, H. 1985. Seas of unreason. *Nature* **313**, 407–8.

Turcotte, D. L. 1980. On the thermal evolution of the Earth. *Earth and Planetary Science Letters* **48**, 58.

Turner, J. S., Huppert, H. E. and R. S. J. Sparks 1985. Komatiites II: experimental and theoretical investigations of post-emplacement cooling and crystallisation, *Journal of Petrology,* in press.

Ujike, O. 1985. Geochemistry of Archaean alkalic volcanic rocks from the Crystal Lake area, east of Kirkland Lake, Ontario, Canada. *Earth and Planetary Science Letters* **73**, 333–44.

Usselman, T. M., D. S. Hodge, A. J. Naldrett and I. H. Campbell 1979. Physical constraints on the characteristics of nickel-sulfide ores in ultramafic lavas. *Canadian Mineralogist* **17**, 361–72.

Vail, J. R. 1968. Orogenic deformation and the Archaean craton of Rhodesia. In Symposium on the Rhodesian Basement Complex, D. J. L. Visser (ed.), 47–52. *Transactions of the Geological Society of South Africa* **71**, Annexure.

van Niekerk, C. B. and A. J. Burger 1978. A new age for the Ventersdorp acidic lavas. *Transactions of the Geological Society of South Africa* **81**, 155.

van Zijl, J. S. V. 1977. Electrical studies of the deep crust in various tectonic provinces of Southern Africa. In *The Earth's crust,* J. G. Heacock (ed.), 470–500. American Geophysical Union, Monograph.

Veizer, J. and S. L. Jansen 1979. Basement and sedimentary recycling and continental evolution. *Journal of Geology* **87**, 341–70.

Veizer, J. and S. L. Jansen 1985. Basement and sedimentary recycling – 2: time dimension to global tectonics. *Journal of Geology* **93**, 625–43.

Veizer, J., W. Compston, J. Hoefs and M. Nielson 1982. Mantle buffering of the early oceans *Naturwissenschaft* **69**, 173–80.

Viljoen, M. J. 1984. Archaean gold mineralisation and komatiites in southern Africa. In *Gold '82,* R. P. Foster (ed.), 595–628. Geological Society of Zimbabwe, Special Publication 1. Rotterdam: Balkema.

Viljoen, M. J. and A. Bernasconi 1979. The geochemistry, regional setting and genesis of the Shangani–Damba Nickel deposits, Rhodesia. In *A symposium on mineral deposits and the transportation of deposition of metals,* C. R. Anhaeusser, R. P. Foster and T. Stratten (eds.), 67–98. Special Publication 5, Geological Society of South Africa.

Viljoen, M. J. and R. P. Viljoen 1969a. An introduction to the geology of the Barberton granite-greenstone terrain. In *The upper mantle project*, 9–28. Special Publication **2**, Geological Society of South Africa (and associated papers).

Viljoen, M. J. and R. P. Viljoen 1969b. Evidence for the existence of a mobile extrusive peridotite magma from the Komati Formation of the Onverwacht Group. In *The upper mantle project*, 87–112. Geological Society of South Africa Special Publication **2**. See also nine other papers by the same authors in this volume.

Viljoen, R. P., R. Saager and M. J. Viljoen 1970. Some thoughts on the origin and processes responsible for the concentration of gold in the early Precambrian of Southern Africa. *Mineralium Deposita* **5**, 164–80.

Viljoen, M. J., R. P. Viljoen and T. N. Pearton 1982. The nature and distribution of Archaean komatiite volcanics in South Africa. In *Komatiites*, N. T. Arndt and E. G. Nisbet (eds), 53–80. London: Allen & Unwin.

Villanueva, E., K. R. Luehrsen, J. Gibson, N. Delihas and G. E. Fox 1985. Phylogenetic origins of the plant Mitochondrion based on a comparative analysis of 5S Ribosomal RNA sequences. *Journal of Molecular Evolution* **22**, 46–52.

von Brunn, V. and D. K. Hobday 1976. Early Precambrian tidal sedimentation in the Pongola Supergroup of South Africa. *Journal of Sedimentary Petrology* **46**, 670–9.

von Damm, K. L., J. M. Edmond, B. Grant, C. I. Measures, B. Walden and R. F. Weiss 1985. Chemistry of submarine hydrothermal solutions at $21°N$, East Pacific Rise. *Geochimica et Cosmochimica Acta* **49**, 2197–220.

von Neumann, J. 1966. *Theory of self-reproducing automata* (posthumously edited by A. W. Burks). Urbana: University of Illinois Press.

Walker, D. 1983. Lunar and terrestrial crust formation. *Journal of Geophysical Research, Proceedings of the Fourteenth Lunar and Planetary Science Conference* **1**, B17–26.

Walker, D. 1986. Melting equilibria in multicomponent systems and liquidus/solidus covergence in mantle peridotite. *Contributions to Mineralogy and Petrology*, **92**, 303–7.

Walker, D. and C. T. Herzberg 1985. Implications of possible liquidus–solidus convergence in mantle peridotite at high pressures *EOS* **66**, 403–4.

Walker, J. C. G. 1983a. Possible limits on the composition of the Archaean ocean. *Nature* **302**, 518–20.

Walker, J. C. G. 1983b. Carbon geodynamic cycle. *Nature* **303**, 730–1.

Walker, J. C. G. and P. Brimblecombe 1985. Iron and sulfur in the pre-biological ocean. *Precambrian Research* **28**, 205–22.

Walker, J. C. G., P. B. Hays and J. F. Kasting 1981. A negative feedback mechanism for the long-term stabilization of the Earth's surface temperature. *Journal of Geophysical Research* **86**, 9776–82.

Walker, R. G. 1978. A critical appraisal of Archaean basin–craton complexes. *Canadian Journal of Earth Sciences* **15**, 1213–18.

Walker, R. R. and G. W. Mannard 1974. Geology of the Kidd Creek Mine – a progress report. *Canadian Institute of Mining and Metallurgy Bulletin*, 41–56.

Walker, R. R., A. Matulich, A. C. Amos, J. J. Watkins and G. W. Mannard 1975. The geology of the Kidd Creek Mine. *Economic Geology* **70**, 80–9.

Walter, M. R. 1983. Archaean stromatolites: evidence of the Earth's earliest benthos. In *Earth's earliest biosphere*, J. W. Schopf (ed.), 187–213. Princeton: Princeton University Press.

Walter, M. R., R. Buick and J. S. R. Dunlop 1980. Stromatolites 3,400–3,500 Myr old from the North Pole area, Western Australia. *Nature* **284**, 443–5.

Watkeys, M. K. 1979. *Explanation of the geological map of the country west of Beitbridge*. Rhodesia Geological Survey Short Report No. 45.

Watkeys, M. K. 1983. Brief explanatory notes on the provisional geological map of the

Limpopo belt and environs. *Special Publication of the Geological Society of South Africa* **8**, 5–8.

Watson, A. J. and J. E. Lovelock 1983. Biological homeostatis of the global environment: the parable of the 'daisy' world. *Tellus* **35B**, 284–9.

Watson, A. J., T. M. Donahue and W. R. Kuhn 1984. Temperatures in a runaway greenhouse on the evolving Venus. *Earth and Planetary Science Letters* **68**, 1–6.

Weaver, B. L. and J. Tarney 1979. Thermal aspects of komatiite generation and greenstone belt models. *Nature* **279**, 689–92.

Weaver, B. L. and J. Tarney 1984. Major and trace element composition of the continental lithosphere. In *Structure and evolution of the continental lithosphere*, H. N. Pollack and V. R. Murthy (eds.), 39–68. Physics and Chemistry of the Earth, vol. 15. Oxford: Pergamon Press.

Welhan, J. A. and H. Craig 1983. Methane, hydrogen and helium in hydrothermal fluids at 21°N on the East Pacific Rise. In *Hydrothermal processes at seafloor spreading centers*, P. A. Rona, K. Bostrom, L. Lanbier and K. J. Smith, Jr. (eds.), 391–407. NATO Advanced Research Institute. New York: Plenum Press.

Welke, H. and L. O. Nicolaysen 1981. A new interpretive procedure for whole rock U–Pb systems applied to the Vredefort crustal profile. *Journal of Geophysical Research* **86**, 10681–8.

Wells, P. R. A. 1979. Chemical and thermal evolution of Archaean sialic crust, Southern West Greenland. *Journal of Petrology* **20**, 187–226.

Wells, P. R. A. 1980. Thermal models for the magmatic accretion and subsequent metamorphism of continental crust. *Earth and Planetary Science Letters* **46**, 253–65.

Wernicke, B. 1985. Uniform-sense normal simple shear of the continental lithosphere. *Canadian Journal of Earth Sciences* **22**, 108–25.

Westheimer, F. H. 1986. Polyribonucleic acids as enzymes. *Nature* **319**, 534–6.

White, W. M. nd J. Patchett 1984. Hf–Nd–Sr isotopes and incompatible element abundancies in island arcs: implications for magma origins and crust-mantle evolution. *Earth and Planetary Science Letters* **67**, 167–85.

Whitehouse, M. J. and S. Moorbath 1986. Pb–Pb systematics of Lewisian gneisses – implications for crustal differentiation. *Nature* **319**, 488–9.

Wigley, T. M. L. and P. Brimblecombe 1981. Carbon dioxide, ammonia and the origin of life. *Nature* **291**, 213–5.

Wiles, J. W. 1957. Gold deposits and mines. *Southern Rhodesia Geological Survey Bulletin* **44**, part II.

Wilks, M. E. and E. G. Nisbet 1985. Archaean stromatolites from the Steep Rock Group, N. W. Ontario, Canada. *Canadian Journal of Earth Sciences* **22**, 792–9.

Williams, D. A. C. 1979. The association of some nickel sulfide deposits with komatiitic volcanism in Rhodesia. *Canadian Mineralogist* **17**, 337–50.

Williams, D. A. C. and R. G. Furnell 1979. Reassessment of part of the Barberton type area, South Africa. *Precambrian Research* **9**, 325–47.

Williams, N. 1986. Exploring for magmatic origins. *Nature* **321**, 812.

Wilson, A. H. 1977. *The petrology and structure of the Hartley Complex of the Great 'Dyke', Rhodesia.* PhD thesis, University of Rhodesia.

Wilson, A. H. 1982. The geology of the Great Dyke, Zimbabwe: the Ultramafic Rocks. *Journal of Petrology* **23**, 240–92.

Wilson, A. H. and J. F. Wilson 1981. The Great 'Dyke'. In *Precambrian of the Southern Hemisphere*, D. R. Hunter (ed.), 572–8. Amsterdam: Elsevier.

Wilson, J. F. 1968a. The Mashaba igneous complex and its subsequent deformation. In *Symposium on the Rhodesian Basement complex*, D. J. L. Visser (ed.), 175–88. Geological Society of South Africa Annexure to Vol. LXXI.

Wilson, J. F. 1968b. The geology of the country around Mashaba. *Geological Survey of Rhodesia Bulletin* **62**.

Wilson, J. F. 1973. The Rhodesian Archaean craton – an essay in cratonic evolution. *Philosophical Transactions of the Royal Society, London*, Series A, **273**, 389–411.

Wilson, J. F. 1964. *The geology of the country around Fort Victoria*. Geological Survey of Southern Rhodesia Bulletin No. 58.

Wilson, J. F. 1979. A preliminary reappraisal of the Rhodesian basement complex. *Geological Society of South Africa, Special Publication* **5**, 1–23.

Wilson, J. F. 1981. The Mashaba igneous complex. In *Precambrian of the Southern Hemisphere*, D. R. Hunter (ed.), 570–2. Amsterdam: Elsevier.

Wilson, J. F. 1981. The granitic–gneiss greenstone shield, B. Zimbabwe. In *Precambrian of the Southern Hemisphere*, D. R. Hunter (ed.), 454–99. Amsterdam: Elsevier.

Wilson, J. F. and N. M. Harrison 1973. Recent K–Ar age determinations on some Rhodesian granites. *Geological Society of South Africa Special Publication* **3**, 69–78.

Wilson, J. F., M. J. Bickle, C. J. Hawkesworth, A. Martin, E. G. Nisbet and J. L. Orpen 1978. Granite–greenstone terrains of the Rhodesian Archaean craton. *Nature* **271**, 23–7.

Windley, B. F. 1984. *The evolving continents*, 2nd edn. Chichester: Wiley.

Windley, B. F. and S. M. Naqvi (eds.), 1977. *Archaean geochemistry*. Amsterdam: Elsevier.

Wise, D. H. 1974. Continental margins, freeboard and the volumes of continents and oceans through time. In *The geology of the continental margins*, C. A. Burke and C. L. Drake (eds.), 45–58. Berlin: Springer.

Woese, C. R. 1981. Archaebacteria. *Scientific American* **244**(6), 98–125.

Woese, C. R. 1983. The primary lines of descent and the universal ancestor. In *Evolution from molecules to men*, D. S. Bendall, (ed.), 209–34. Cambridge: Cambridge University Press.

Worst, B. G. 1960. The Great Dyke of Southern Rhodesia. *Southern Rhodesia Geological Survey Bulletin* **47**.

Worst, B. G. 1962. The geology of the Buhwa Iron ore deposits and adjoining country, Belingwe district. *Southern Rhodesia Geological Survey Bulletin* **53**.

Wright, P. A., J. M. Thomas, A. K. Cheetham and A. K. Nowak 1985. Localizing active sites in zeolite catalysts: neutron powder profile analysis and computer simulation of deuteropyridine bound to gallozeolite-L. *Nature* **318**, 611–4.

Wyllie, P. J. 1981a. Experimental petrology of subduction, andesites and batholiths. *Transactions of the Geological Society of South Africa* **84**, 281–91.

Wyllie, P. J. 1981b. Experimental and thermal constraints on the deep-seated parentage of some granitoid magmas in subduction zones. In *Migmatites, melting and metamorphism*, M. P. Atherton and C. D. Gribble (eds.), 3–51. Shiva Geology.

Yorath, C. J. and R. D. Hyndman 1983. Subsidence and thermal history of the Queen Charlotte Basin. *Canadian Journal of Earth Sciences* **20**, 135–59.

York, D. 1984. Cooling histories from ^{40}Ar/^{39}Ar age spectra. *Annual Review of Earth and Planetary Sciences* **12**, 383–409.

Zaug, A. J. and T. R. Cech 1986. The intervening sequence RNA of Tetrahymena is an enzyme. *Science* **231**, 470–75.

Zindler, A. 1982. Nd and Sr isotopic studies of Komatiites and related rocks. In *Komatiites*, N. T. Arndt and E. G. Nisbet (eds.), 399–420. London: Allen & Unwin.

Zuckerkandl, E. and L. Pauling 1965. Molecules as documents of evolutionary history. *Journal of Theoretical Biology* **8**, 357–66.

Zumberge, J. E., A. C. Sigleo and B. Nagy 1978. Molecular and elemental analysis of the carbonaceous matter in the gold and uranium bearing Vaal Reef carbon seams, Witwatersrand Sequence. *Minerals, Science and Engineering* **10**, 223–46.

Author index

Numbers in *italics* refer to text figures.

Subject index

Numbers in *italics* refer to text figures

Abitibi belt 73, 202, *6.26*
accuracy 12
adiabat 314
aftband 268
age 14
age of Earth 28
age–depth curve 150
Agincourt 132
aktualismus 8, *1.2*
Alexo 29, 241, *2.6*
alkaline suite 206–7, *6.4*
alluvial fan–fluvial facies 151
Ancient Gneiss Complex, Barberton 184
andesites 198–206
Archaean-continental thickness 146–9, 178, 182, 190, 195
Archaean-definition 3, 4, 9, 10
Archaean-seawater 128–30
archaebacteria 137, 138, 141, 142, 143
Argon–argon method 16–17
asbestos, blue 304
asbestos, white 298
atmosphere, mean age 329
atmospheric CO_2 334–5

Baicalia 119
banded ironstones 11, 53, 62, 74, 91, 138, 165–6, 252, 280, 300, *4.20*, *5.5–7*, *5.10*
Barberton Mountain Land 17, 23, 60, 62, 92, 104, 107, 108, 124, 125, 149, 162, 164, 225, 229, 239, 241, 257, 261, *2.2*, *3.17–18*, *4.4–8*, *6.26*
basins 71
Beitbridge 151, 181
Belingwe 101, 149, 164, 229, 234, 239, 245, *3.13*, *3.23*, *3.34–40*, *4.10–15*, *6.26*, *8.17*
Belingwean, Supergroup 53, 90
Bend Formation 91
Bikita Tinfield 305
Blake River Group 274, *6.2*
blocking temperature 14, *2.1*
blueschist 190
Broadlands system 251

Brockman Iron Formation 302
Brooklands Formation 91, *3.15*
Buchwa 300–2, *3.9*
Bulawayan 53, 92
Bulawayo 16
Bushveld Complex 290

calc-alkaline series 199–206, *6.3*, *8.10*
carbonates 9, 48, 68
catastrophism 7, *1.2*
Central Rand Group 154, 268, *7.8*
charnockite 83
Cheshire Formation 92, 113, 128, 132, *3.39*, *4.11*, *4.20*
Chibi batholith 95, *3.9*
Chilimanzi suite 57
Chimamora batholith 79
Chitradurga belt 170
chloroplast 139
CHUR 22, 34, 172, 175, *2.7*, *2.10*, *2.11*, *5.16*
CH_4 342, 350, 351
CMAS 238, *6.20*
coffee 7
concordia 25, *2.5*
Conophyton 119
continental growth 246–8, *6.27*
continental thickness *5.24*
convection in mantle 307–13
core formation 31
corundum 304
cover succession 45
CO_2 163, 193, *8.14*
craton, definition 36, 48
crust mean age *5.15*
crustal residence 171–7, *5.15*
cyanobacteria 130, 131, 132, 133

daisy planet 338, *8.14*, *8.15*
Dales Gorge Member 303
Darwinism 341
Darwin's pond 342
date 14
degassing 328–9
delta notation 127

399